WHAT'S HAPPENING TO
PUBLIC HIGHER EDUCATION?

WHAT'S HAPPENING TO PUBLIC HIGHER EDUCATION?

The Shifting Financial Burden

Edited by
Ronald G. Ehrenberg

The Johns Hopkins University Press
Baltimore

© 2006 Ronald G. Ehrenberg
Printed in the United States of America on acid-free paper

First published in 2006 by Greenwood Press

Johns Hopkins Paperbacks edition published 2007
9 8 7 6 5 4 3 2 1

The Johns Hopkins University Press
2715 North Charles Street
Baltimore, Maryland 21218-4363
www.press.jhu.edu

ISBN 13: 978-0-8018-8713-0
ISBN 10: 0-8018-8713-5

Library of Congress Control Number: 2007925427

A catalog record for this book is available from the British Library.

What's Happening to Public Higher Education? by Ronald G. Ehrenberg
(ACE/Praeger series in Higher Education) was originally published in hard
cover by Praeger, an imprint of Greenwood Publishing Group, Inc., Westport,
CT. Paperback edition by arrangement with Greenwood Publishing Group, Inc.
All rights reserved.

To my wife Randy, who makes everything worthwhile.

CONTENTS

PREFACE

I have been on the faculty at Cornell University since 1975. Cornell is unique among private institutions of higher education in the United States because 4 of the 10 colleges on its Ithaca campus—the Colleges of Agriculture and Life Sciences, Human Ecology, Veterinary Medicine, and the School of Industrial and Labor Relations—are operated by Cornell under a contract with New York State. These four units receive appropriations from New York State through the State University of New York (SUNY) budget. Thus, they have been subject to the same state funding pressures described in *What's Happening to Public Higher Education?* that our nation's public institutions have faced during the last 30 years.

These units have the freedom to set their own tuition levels that many other public universities have not had in the past, but their tuition increases have not always been large enough to compensate for the funding cutbacks that SUNY imposed on them. Thus these colleges' financial positions have deteriorated relative to the colleges that are in the private part of Cornell. A term as a Cornell vice president in the mid-1990s and my years on the faculty have allowed me to observe first hand the funding differences that have arisen between public and private higher education in the United States and the effects of these differences on the institutions, their faculty, and their students.

Since 1998, financial support for the Cornell Higher Education Research Institute (CHERI), which I direct, has been generously provided by the Andrew W. Mellon Foundation, the Atlantic Philanthropies (USA) Inc., and the TIAA-CREF Institute. CHERI has provided me with the freedom to work on higher education research topics that I consider socially important.

It should be no surprise to the reader that my students and I have devoted much time to studying issues facing public higher education in the United States. CHERI hosts an annual research conferences and our spring 2005 conference was devoted to analyzing public higher education at the turn of the twenty-first century. *What's Happening to Public Higher Education?* evolved from that conference.

The revised versions of the conference papers that appear in this volume, as well as my introductory remarks, benefited greatly from the discussions that took place at the conference. The other authors and I are deeply indebted to the formal discussants at the conference: Jane Wellman (Institute for Higher Education Policy), Charlotte Kuh (National Research Council), Pat Callan (National Center for Public Policy and Higher Education), Jeffrey Groen (U.S. Bureau of Labor Statistics), James Monk (University of Richmond), and Hank Dullea (Cornell University). Their remarks materially improved our work, and they forced us to think about issues that we had ignored. I owe a special debt of gratitude to Darrlyn O' Connell, my executive assistant at CHERI, who was responsible for all of the arrangements for the conference and who prepared the final manuscript for this volume.

An earlier version of John Wiley's paper appeared in the November 2003 issue of *Madison* magazine. An earlier version of Liang Zhang and my paper appeared in the *Journal of Human Resources* 40 (Summer 2005): 647–659. I am grateful to *Madison* magazine and the University of Wisconsin Press for their permission to publish the revised versions of these two papers in *What's Happening to Public Higher Education?*

INTRODUCTION

Ronald G. Ehrenberg

A t the start of the twenty-first century, public higher education appears to be in a state of crisis. The share of state funding going to higher education has declined by more than one-third during the last 30 years. Reductions in tax rates in many states led to structural deficits in state government budgets that made it difficult for the states to find the funds to support the more than 50 percent increase in public higher education enrollments that has taken place since 1974. Several recessions during the period, including the economic downturn that started at the turn of the century, led many states to periodically cut their real state appropriations per student at public higher education institutions. As a result, between 1974 and 2004, state appropriations to public higher education institutions grew at an average annual rate that exceeded the rate of increase in consumer prices by only about 0.6 percent a year.

The rate of increase in consumer prices is widely believed to understate the rate of inflation that colleges and universities face because the bundle of goods and services that colleges and universities buy is different from the bundle of goods and services that consumer purchase. The average annual rate of growth of one widely used index of the prices faced by higher education, the Higher Education Price Index (HEPI), exceeds the average annual rate of growth in the consumer price index by about 0.4 percent a year during the period.[1] Hence, real state appropriations per student at public higher education institutions were essentially the same at the start and the end of the period.

As I discussed in my book, *Tuition Rising: Why College Costs So Much* (Harvard University Press, 2002), selective private higher education institutions have increased their tuition levels, on average, by 2 to 3.5 percent a year above the rate of inflation for longer than anyone can remember, and private tuition increases of this magnitude took place during the last 30 years as well. Although public higher education institutions have, on average, raised their tuition levels by roughly the same rate as the privates did since the mid-1970s, tuition levels at the publics started at a much lower base; and, as a result, the sum of their tuition level and state appropriations per student increased by much less than tuition levels did at the privates. Thus the resource base of public higher education has fallen relative to the resource base of private higher education.

Research conducted by researchers at the Cornell Higher Education Research Institute (CHERI) and others during the last 5 years has described some of the situations that have resulted from these changes. Average faculty salaries at public doctoral institutions have declined relative to average faculty salaries at private doctoral institutions, which undoubtedly make it more difficult for the publics to attract high-quality faculty.[2] Lower average salaries also make it more difficult to retain existing faculty, and we have shown that turnover rates of associate professors are higher at public doctoral-level institutions that at privates.[3] Student faculty ratios have increased at public universities at the same time as they decreased at private universities.[4] Finding resources to provide funds for the growing cost of start-up packages also is more difficult for the publics, as start-up cost packages for scientists and engineers are typically lower at public than at private universities. The public universities also tend to fund a greater portion of their start-up packages by keeping faculty lines vacant, which has implications for the quality of undergraduate education.[5] So, too, does the practice of increasingly substituting non-tenure–track, full-time faculty and part-time faculty for full-time faculty in an effort to meet student course demand during a period of contracting resources. Indeed, data from one large public system, the State University of New York (SUNY) system, indicate that during the decade of the 1990s, the percentage of undergraduate credit hours taught by tenure and tenure-track faculty fell by more than 22 percentage points at the four university centers.[6] Increasing tuition levels at four-year public institutions have led two-year colleges to increasingly become the entry point for access to public higher education for many students.[7]

Put simply, public higher educational institutions, where about 80 percent of all college students and 65 percent of all four-year college students are educated, appear to be in serious trouble. Limitations on their state funding may both restrict access to public higher education and reduce its quality in the future. Given the competitive pressures that our nation faces in a increasingly knowledge-driven world and the importance of higher education as a vehicle for social mobility, the United States needs to have a strong public higher education system.

Given these concerns, CHERI brought together a number of prominent higher education researchers, senior university and system administrators, and higher education policy analysts in May 2005 for a conference, "Assessing Public Higher Education at the Start of the 21st Century." The chapters in this volume are revisions of the conference papers, plus two new policy pieces that are authored by two distinguished university leaders, John Wiley, Chancellor of the University of

Wisconsin-Madison, and F. King Alexander, President of California State University, Long Beach.

The first four chapters in *What's Happening to Public Higher Education?* set the stage by providing the reader with background data on national trends, an analysis of the forces that have led to these trends, and empirical studies of the effects on students of some of the changes that I noted previously. These chapters are somewhat more technical than those contained in the rest of the volume; I summarize some of their major findings here so that readers who are less interested in technical details can briefly scan these chapters and then move on to the next section.

Michael Rizzo addresses three major changes in state funding of education that occurred during the last quarter of the twentieth century: the decline in education's share of the state budget, the decline in higher education's share of state educational funding, and the decline in the share of higher education funding that goes to public higher education institutions (as opposed to directly to students in the form of grant aid). The last is a direct result of the growth in state funded merit scholarship programs, which followed the establishment of the HOPE Scholarship program in Georgia in 1993; today 13 states have state merit scholarship programs.

Thomas Kane and Peter Orszag have previously pointed out the role that growing Medicaid expenditures have played in crowding out state higher educational expenditures.[8] Rizzo's analyses suggest a number of other important factors that help to explain the three changes that he has observed. First, tuition increases at public higher education institutions, which often are induced by state funding cutbacks, in turn appear to lead to subsequent state funding cutbacks. Second, the burden of court-ordered mandates to expand state funding of public elementary and secondary education, which have occurred in a number of states, have been borne at least partially by public higher education, in terms of cutbacks in, or reductions in the growth of, state appropriations for public higher education. Finally, as the difference in the racial composition of the adult population and the college age population in a state widens, a greater share of the state resources for higher education are directed to students in the form of merit scholarships, rather than as appropriations to public higher education institutions.

During the discussion that followed the presentation of Rizzo's paper at the conference, a number of participants stressed that an additional contributing factor is that states have realized they are "leaving money on the table" if they pursue a high-state appropriation, low-tuition strategy (a point that F. King Alexander emphasizes in his concluding essay). In many states, increases in tuition will be associated with the generation of more federal Pell grant revenues for the state; students from lower income families will have the tuition increase fully covered by an increase in their Pell grants. Hence raising tuition (and cutting state appropriations or the rate of growth of state appropriations) is a way of shifting the cost of public higher education in a state from state taxpayers to the nation's taxpayers as a whole. Participants bemoaned the fact that federal financial aid policies encourage states to cut back on state appropriations to public higher education rather than to expand appropriations. In contrast, increases in state Medicaid expenditures result in increases in matching federal dollars and this provides an incentive for states to expand their Medicaid funding.

The next two chapters focus on the growing use of full-time and part-time, non-tenure–track faculty in public higher education. In an earlier paper, Liang Zhang and I documented the growth that has occurred in both of these types of "contingent" faculty in public higher education. For example, between 1989 and 2001, the ratio of part-time faculty to total full-time faculty rose from .269 to .377 at a set of public higher education institutions.[9] Moreover, as might be expected, we also showed that much of the substitution of contingent for tenure-track faculty arose from the cost savings in terms of the lower salaries, and for part-timers often lower benefits, which such substitution permits the institution.

Of great concern, however, is the impact that the growing use of contingent faculty has on undergraduate students at public higher education institutions. If contingent faculty do not adversely impact on undergraduate students, pleas by university administrators and faculty that the quality of their institutions is being reduced are likely to fall on deaf ears in state capitols. On the other hand, if the increasing use of contingent faculty can be shown to adversely impact on undergraduate students, governors and legislatures may think twice before making further cuts to public higher education.

The chapter by Zhang and me analyzes institutional-level panel data from the *College Board* and other sources to ascertain whether, as an institution increases its usage of part-time or full-time, non-tenure–track faculty, its undergraduate students' graduation rates fall, other factors held constant. We find that the increased usage of either type of contingent faculty is associated with a decline in graduation rates at four-year institutions, with the largest impact being felt at the public masters' level institutions.

In their chapter, Eric Bettinger and Bridget Terry Long use a unique individual record dataset for all students enrolled in public higher education in the state of Ohio. These data allow them to analyze how the proportion of classes that students take in their first semester at college that are taught by adjuncts influences the students' probabilities of persisting at the institution into their second year. They find that students with "adjunct-heavy" course schedules are less likely to persist into their second year. Taken together, these two chapters suggest that public higher education institutions need worry about how the expansion of their usage of contingent faculty influences undergraduate students.[10]

The final chapter in this section, by Gary Blose, John Porter, and Edward Kokkelenberg, addresses directly the impact of expenditure-per-student levels on graduation rates of students at public four-year colleges and universities. The authors stress that focusing on unadjusted expenditure per student data tells one little about the resources actually devoted to educating students at an institution, because the mix of students across majors varies across institutions and the cost of educating students varies widely across majors at an institution. Although national data on the cost of educating students by major do not exist, the State

University of New York (SUNY) system uses a unique dataset to compute the relative costs of educating students by major and then use these relative cost data, along with data on the distribution of majors at each institution, to estimate an "adjusted expenditure per student" measure for each institution.

Blose, Porter, and Kokkelenberg find, holding other factors expected to influence graduation rates constant, that public higher education institutions with larger adjusted expenditure per students tend to have higher graduation rates. This effect is most pronounced for four-year graduation rates; the relationship between expenditures per student and graduation rates gets progressively smaller as they move to consider five-year and then six-year graduation rates. Hence, their message is that there is "no such thing as a free lunch"; reducing expenditures per students in public higher education does tend to lead to a slowdown in students' progress to degrees.[11]

The 10 chapters in the next section of *What's Happening to Public Higher Education?* focus on individual states; the authors were asked to describe how public higher education has evolved over the last quarter century in their states and how these changes have affected the public higher education institutions, as well as students and potential students at the institutions. The states chosen all have large public higher education systems and are representative of all sections of the nation; they include (with the authors names in parentheses) California (Gerald Kissler and Ellen Switkes), Georgia (Christopher Cornwell and David Mustard), Illinois (F. King Alexander and Daniel Layzell), Michigan (Stephen DesJardins, Allison Bell, and Iria Puyosa), North Carolina (Betsy Brown and Robert Clark), Pennsylvania (Donald Heller), Texas (Lisa Dickson), Virginia (Sarah Turner), Washington (William Zumeta), and Wisconsin (David Olien).

The authors of these chapters were given considerable latitude about the content of their chapters. Some focus on the flagship research university in the state; others discuss what has happened to public higher education statewide. All trace the changes in state appropriations and tuition levels that have occurred. Many address the changes in faculty salaries that occurred and the changing mix of faculty between tenured and tenure-track and contingent faculty. A number focus on the impact of funding changes on graduate education, on the way in which financial aid policies have changed at the state and institutional levels, and how the latter, in turn, has influenced from where in the distribution of family incomes students are being drawn. Finally, some discuss new innovative polices being undertaken in a state to try to restore the health of its public universities and/or to guarantee access to qualified students from all socioeconomic and racial/ethnic backgrounds.

All the states have been hit by funding cuts during the recent recession and most have suffered long-run declines in state appropriations per student, largely because enrollment growth has outstripped the state's ability, or willingness, to provide appropriations increases. Many of the flagship campuses have moved along the path of raising resident undergraduate tuition to try to offset cuts in per capita state appropriations. The tuition increases typically only offset part of the reductions in state appropriations, and the increases often generate political pressure to limit the authority of the public universities to raise tuition (which may occur soon in Illinois) or to roll back previous tuition increases (which occurred in recent years in both California and Virginia). A number of state institutions have aggressively increased tuition for out-of-state undergraduates to try to generate revenues, but only a few have been able to increase their out-of-state student enrollment shares, and the University of Wisconsin at Madison has found that when out-of-state tuition increases too much, enrollment of out-of-state students declines. Some reported efforts to make professional graduate programs self-sustaining by substantially raising tuition levels for those programs.

Many report concerns that their faculty members' salaries are falling relative to their private sector competitors, which is making recruitment and retention of faculty more difficult. Most report substantial increases in the usage of lecturers and teaching assistants, which, as the chapters by Ehrenberg and Zhang, and Bettinger and Long show, may adversely affect undergraduate students, if other factors are held constant. Other factors, however, are not always held constant, and several state institutions report efforts to improve student persistence and graduation rates that have been successful; these efforts have had both academic and financial payoffs to the universities.

A number of institutions report institutional strategies to enhance their accessibility to students from lower-income families and other under represented groups. Examples of public flagships that have undertaken such efforts are the University of North Carolina Chapel Hill with its "Carolina Covenant" and the University of Virginia with its "Access UVA" programs; both programs guarantee that students who have incomes less than twice the federal poverty level can attend the institutions without incurring any debt. Both programs include comprehensive efforts by the universities to recruit more students from low-income families and, in the case of Virginia, a promise to report to the state each year on the socioeconomic distribution of its student body.[12] Similarly, the University of Texas "Longhorn Opportunity Scholarship" program provides scholarships to students from high schools whose students were historically underrepresented in the University of Texas student body, as well as coordinated focused mentoring opportunities designed to provide substantial assistance to the students in their first year of enrollment.[13]

Whether other campuses within these states or flagship campuses in other states can develop resource streams to support these types of efforts, to maintain/expand socioeconomic and racial ethnic diversity of their student bodies, is an open question. Indeed, other chapters report that increasing tuition levels, coupled with limitations on institutional and state funds for need-based financial aid, have been associated with a reduction in the share of students from lower-income families in their flagship campuses' undergraduate student bodies.

Discussions about the impact of privatization of public higher education tend to focus on the implications for undergraduate students and whether higher undergraduate tuition levels would discourage some students from attending, or completing college. Often lost in the discussion is how cutbacks in state support will affect graduate education, research, and public service/extension activities at public universities.[14] The chapters that discuss California and Wisconsin stress the negative effects that cutbacks in state support have had on graduate education; enrollments in graduate programs in Wisconsin are lower today then they were in 1993. Graduate enrollments have expanded in the University of North Carolina system, but as the out-of-state tuition levels increase rapidly at the university, so too does the cost of tuition waivers for graduate teaching and research assistants from out of states. As these costs are borne by departmental budgets (teaching assistants) and external faculty research grants (research assistants), the combination of cutbacks in state support and increased tuition levels inevitably must lead either to a reduction in the numbers of teaching and research assistants employed at the university or a shift toward enrolling a greater share of graduate students from residents of the state; the latter may lead to a reduction in the average quality of graduate students attending the university. Either will lead to a reduction in the ability of the university to mount its undergraduate teaching and its research programs.

A long and growing body of literature suggests that our nation's level of economic growth is related to the investments that we make in research and development and that graduate students have major input into the research process.[15] Hence any reduction in the quantity and quality of research conducted by our nation's public universities will have serious repercussions for our society's future economic well-being.

Public higher education institutions, especially the land grants, have an obligation to serve the population of the entire state, not just the students attending the institutions. Through agricultural, consumer, and industrial extension services, these institutions have been major transmitters of knowledge to American farmers, consumers, workers, and industry. Cutbacks in state funding for public higher education have led to cutbacks in state appropriations for the land grant activities of public higher education and, as the costs of these activities cannot be shifted onto the backs of undergraduate students in the form of still higher tuitions, cutbacks have forced the units pursuing these activities to become more entrepreneurial. They can use the profits generated from groups that can afford to pay for services (e.g., large corporations) to subsidize the provision of services to underserved populations, services that previously were financed by the state. With increasing pressures to generate their own revenues, however, it is natural for extension services to spend a greater share of their time on commercial activities and less on serving the public at large.

More generally, public higher education benefits many more of a state's citizens than just those attending the state's public higher education institutions or receiving services from extension activities of these institutions. Research indicates that there is a social return to higher education that includes increased income for noncollege graduates, increased state tax revenues, increased intergenerational mobility, and lower welfare costs.[16] If cutbacks in state funding and increases in public tuitions reduce the fraction of American high school students going on to and completing college, we will all be worse off.

The final section of *What's Happening to Public Higher Education?* consists of two chapters written by leaders of a major public research university and a public comprehensive university. John Wiley, Chancellor of the University of Wisconsin-Madison, argues that it is unlikely that we will see any public universities go private. He notes that support for the core mission of educating students at public higher education institutions comes from state appropriations, tuition revenues, endowment income, and annual giving. He argues that reductions in state appropriations cannot be offset by continually increasing tuitions to levels charged at private institutions, because the latter's high tuition levels are misleading; a large percentage of tuitions at private institutions are returned to students in the form of "tuition discounts." If public universities aggressively move toward a high tuition strategy, such as the Miami University of Ohio has already done, they will find that the need for tuition discounts (in the form of either merit or need-based aid) to help them "craft the classes" that they want will substantially reduce the net tuition revenue they will obtain from the higher tuition levels.[17]

Wiley argues that to improve, or at least maintain, the quality of public higher education in the face of reduced state appropriations, will require large increases in endowment income and annual giving at the public institutions. However, he presents calculations that show that the magnitudes of the increases in endowments that would be required are much too large to be feasible. Hence he fears that privatization of public higher education, moving to a low-state appropriation, high-tuition policy, will inevitably lead to declines in both the quality of public higher education and access for students from lower-income families. He believes that either would have adverse consequences for the nation. He concludes that we need a serious public policy discussion that describes the public, as well as private, benefits of having a highly educated workforce, and the need to maintain the quality of public higher education, and then leads to some decisions about how the costs of public higher education should be apportioned between the recipients of higher education (who receive the private benefits) and the public at large (who receive the public benefits).

F. King Alexander, the President of California State University, Long Beach, views what is transpiring in public higher education through the lenses of both a president of a public comprehensive and a higher education finance scholar. After discussing the important commonalities and main themes that he finds in the chapters in the first two sections of *What's Happening to Public Higher Education?* he argues for the need for a new federal debate on higher education that would focus on the crisis in American public higher education and the increasing lack of consistent policies by state governments to address the growing societal and economic demands for more universal access.

Alexander notes that the last significant debate regarding the role of the federal government in higher education took place during the 1960s and early 1970s. This debate led to the development of policies to address access for lower income students that largely benefited private colleges and universities. He argues, however, that the new debate must address the crisis facing public higher educa- tion institutions and the states that are already making high tax efforts to support their public higher education institutions. He contends that the great diversity of American higher education is under threat because of the privatization of public higher education institutions and the increasing abdication of responsibilities for higher education by many state governments. He concludes by advocating for a number of new federal policies that would be designed to create incentives and disincentives that would encourage states to maintain or increase tax support for their public institutions and discourage the continued shift of the costs of public higher education toward students and their families.

Fifteen years ago, Henry Rosovsky wrote that "fully two-thirds to three-quarters of the best universities in the world are located in the United States."[18] Many of these institutions are flagship public campuses. Taken together, the papers pre- sented at the conference do not provide an optimistic view of how these campuses and other public institutions in their states have fared over the last 30 years or of their likely futures. The twin goals of increasing, or at least maintaining, both the quality of public higher education institutions and their accessibility to students from all family income levels will be difficult to achieve in the years ahead. Policy- makers and the broader public need to seriously consider the points made in the chapters by Wiley and Alexander.

NOTES

1. *2005 HEPI* (Wilton, Conn.: Commonfund Institute, 2005), table A.

2. Ronald G. Ehrenberg, "Studying Ourselves: The Academic Labor Market." *Journal of Labor Economics* 21 (April 2003): 267–87.

3. Matthew Nagowski, "Associate Professor Turnover at American Colleges and Uni- versities" *American Economist* (in press).

4. Thomas J. Kane and Peter R. Orszag, "Funding Restrictions at Public Universities: Effects and Policy Implications" (Washington, D.C.: Brookings Institution Working Paper, September 2003).

5. Ronald G. Ehrenberg, Michael J. Rizzo, and Scott S. Condie, "Start Up Costs in American Research Universities," *CHERI* Working Paper No. 33 (March 2003), available at www.ilr.cornell.edu/cheri.

6. Ronald G. Ehrenberg and Daniel B. Klaff," Changes in Faculty Composition within the State University of New York System: 1985–2001", *CHERI* Working Paper No. 38 (August 2003).

7. Ronald G. Ehrenberg and Christopher S. Smith, "Analyzing the Success of Student Transitions from 2-Year to 4-Year Institutions Within a State." *Economics of Education Review* 23 (February 2004): 11–28.

8. Thomas J. Kane and Peter R. Orszag, "Higher Education Spending: The Role of Medicaid and the Business Cycle," *Brookings Institution Policy Brief No. 124* (Washington, D.C.: Brookings Institution, September 2003).

9. Ronald G. Ehrenberg and Liang Zhang, "The Changing Nature of Faculty Employ- ment" in *Recruitment, Retention and Retirement in Higher Education: Building and Managing*

the Faculty of the Future, eds. Robert Clark and Jennifer Ma. (Northampton Mass.: Edward Elgin Publishing, 2005).

10. The United University Professions (UUP), the union representing faculty at the State University of New York, successfully argued in the debate over funding for public higher education in New York State during the winter of 2005 that increased usage of part-time faculty at SUNY, was responsible for students being unable to find the classes they needed to graduate because part-time faculty teaching is often concentrated during certain times of the day (late afternoons and evenings).

11. As one might expect, they also find that institutions whose students have higher entrance test scores have higher graduation rates. They point out that, with limited resources, the goals of expanding access to public higher education and raising graduation rates may be in conflict.

12. See www.unc.edu./carolinacovenant and www.virginia.edu/accessuva for details of these programs.

13. See www.utexas.edu/student/connexus/scholars

14. These issues are discussed more fully in Ronald G. Ehrenberg, "The Perfect Storm and the Privatization of Public Higher Education," *Change* 38 (January/February 2006): 46–53.

15. Many of these studies are summarized in Ronald G. Ehrenberg, "Graduate Education, Innovation and Federal Responsibility," *Communicator* 38 (July 2005): 1–5.

16. Michael J. Rizzo, "The Public Interest in Higher Education" in *Education and Economic Development* (Cleveland Ohio: Federal Reserve Bank of Cleveland, May 2005).

17. They may also find, as Miami University of Ohio did in the summer of 2005, that the governor and legislature may not always allow them to raise in-state tuition as much as they had hoped.

18. Henry Rosovsky, *The University: An Owners Manual* (New York: W. W. Norton and Co., 1990), 29.

PART I

Setting the Stage

CHAPTER 1

State Preferences for Higher Education Spending: A Panel Data Analysis, 1977–2001

Michael J. Rizzo

F ew observers would disagree that America's stellar economic, scientific, political, and cultural standing is largely a result of the proliferation of its system of education throughout the states since the nation's founding. Further, it is not a coincidence that America's permanent place among the global powers occurred only after public funds from our various legislative entities began spilling into a growing higher education system, changing it from a largely private domain of the elite aristocracy to a tool for the lower and middle class public to achieve the "American Dream" as well.[1] Despite this fact and despite the large literature espousing the many benefits of investing in education, public higher education seems to be increasingly falling out of favor with both voters and governments alike.

The goal of this chapter is to explain why public higher education *institutions* find themselves in the precarious budget situations they are in today. Among my findings are that changes in observable state characteristics can explain little of the observed decrease in higher education budget shares. Generally speaking, public higher education spending has been crowded out by increasing demands for state support of K12 education as a result of court-mandated equalization programs, but more important because of the great deal of discretion legislatures have over higher education spending. That institutional efforts to raise private money and to increase tuition rates have been met with sharp cuts in budget shares, coupled with projected future enrollment pressures and the political popularity of non-need–based aid program expansion, casts a pall on the ability of our public institutions to maintain accessibility and quality much longer.

It should be emphasized that public universities are accustomed to their state funding being at the mercy of economic cycles. In bad budget times, higher education typically bears a disproportionate burden of state funding cuts, with the full expectation that it will be compensated during a recovery. This is not surprising given that higher education is the single largest discretionary item in state budgets. Higher education is also an attractive target for the legislative ax because of its ability to draw revenue from a variety of sources, most prominently tuition—a feature unique to this state budget item. That higher education funding *levels* fluctuate so much is well known and is not the focus of this chapter. Rather, I emphasize that, in *relative* terms, higher education funding has not fluctuated with the business cycle. Public higher education has faced a continuous precipitous drop in state governmental priority for nearly three decades.

In real terms, the level of state funding for public higher education doubled from $30 billion in 1974 to nearly $60 billion in 2000. As a result of the growth in public enrollments, however, the bottom line in Figure 1.1 shows that per student funding increased in real terms by less than 1 percent per year (25.9 percent overall). Real current educational and general expenditures per student (less dollars spent on sponsored research) in public higher education, shown in the top line of Figure 1.1, grew by more than 3 percent per year (130 percent overall).[2] As a result, although state appropriations in 1974 were generous enough to cover 78 percent of the cost of schooling, in 2000 this support has fallen to just 43 percent.[3] That public universities and colleges are turning to tuition to more than make up for lost state appropriations has raised the ire of both taxpayers and politicians.

What is less well known is that public education has undergone a sea change in public priorities during this time period. While most laypeople, administrators, and even statehouse representatives focus on the dollar values of the state

Figure 1.1
Growth in state appropriations versus current educational and general expenditures (net of sponsored research) per full-time equivalent student at all public universities, 1973–1974 to 2000-01AY

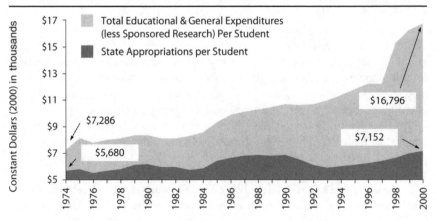

appropriations, little attention is paid to how higher education fares in relation to other budget items within each state. It is to this *relative* funding that I now turn.

As Figure 1.2 indicates, between the fiscal year (ending) 1972 to 2001, the average (across states) share of total state general fund expenditures on education (EDSHARE) fell from a high of 39.9 percent in 1972 to a low of 35.0 percent in 1993, with a slight recovery to 36.1 percent over the remainder of the decade.[4] The decrease has not been monotonic, but there is a clear downward trend; the cyclical behavior appears to revolve around this trend, and the slight recovery in the late 1990s does not return shares anywhere near their pre-1990s levels.

The decline in relative state support for education has occurred throughout the distribution of states—in those that have traditionally devoted a large share of resources to public education (North Carolina's share has fallen from 51 to 41 percent) and those that have not (Massachusetts's share has fallen from 30 to 22 percent). In fact, only 11 states have seen increases over this period, with an average increase of about 4 percent.

There is nothing particularly sacred about education's share of the budget, and the many factors thought to be responsible for its decline are well known. Medicaid expenditures have skyrocketed as a result of large increases in caseloads (it is a means-tested entitlement program), escalating prescription drug costs, and lagging support from the federal government. An aging and growing population is putting further stress on health care expenditures and other state services. Corrections expenditures have been growing because of more vigilant prosecution, mandatory sentencing laws, and the resulting expansion of prison capacity. Whether education's falling out of favor represents demographic changes alone

Figure 1.2
Average share of state general expenditures on education: 1971–1972 to 2000–2001

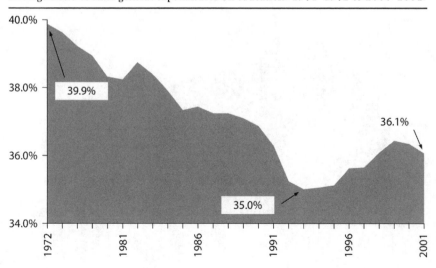

or a shift of funding priority is unclear and is analyzed in the empirical section of the chapter.

Figure 1.3 describes how the average share of state educational budgets allocated to public higher education (HESHARE) has changed in the United States between FY72 and FY01. After a sharp increase in the early 1970s, higher education's share has fallen steadily.[5] Since 1977, the average share of education budgets allocated to higher education across states fell more than 6 percentage points from 22.6 percent to 16.4 percent after peaking at 23.5 percent in 1982 (a 27 percent drop). The most precipitous declines occurred during the recessions of the early 1980s and 1990s, but the lush budget environment in the 1990s was insufficient to halt the bleeding.

This decline occurred in the vast majority of states. States such as Oregon, Wisconsin, and California that initially expended well over 25 percent of their education budget on higher education have all cut their higher education share by more than 40 percent (12 percentage points), and states such as Vermont, Massachusetts, New Hampshire, and Delaware that initially expended less than 19 percent of their education budget on higher education have also cut their shares by more than 35 percent (6 percentage points). Even those states where advances were made (only four states increased their share overall during the period) have seen much of it weathered away by the end of the period. In fact, only one state has seen its higher education share increase since 1990 (New Mexico).

A further strain being placed on public higher education institutions is revealed in Figure 1.4. Fueled by the popularity of merit-based aid programs in the 1990s,

Figure 1.3
Average share of state education expenditures on higher education: 1971–1972 to 2000–2001

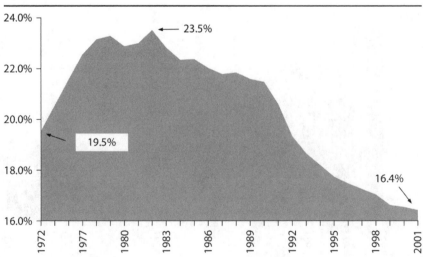

the share of higher education funding going directly to institutions (INSHARE) declined over the period, from 97.2 percent in 1977 to 93.5 percent in 2002, with most of the decline occurring after the implementation of Georgia's HOPE scholarship program in 1993.[6] Student aid dollars ultimately make their way back to the institution that an aid recipient attends, but this aid travels with the student and cannot be depended on to support institutional operations.

States that were initially less generous to institutions have continued to increase their support for students. For example, New York, Vermont, Illinois, and Pennsylvania all decreased their shares to institutions from 83 to 90 percent to less than 77 to 85 percent. On the other hand, many states were changing their funding strategies and moving aggressively to expand student aid programs from nearly nonexistent in 1977 to substantial in 2002. Among these states are Georgia, Louisiana, Florida, South Carolina, New Mexico, and Arkansas, which averaged an 11 percentage point drop in the share allocated to institutions over the entire period and 8 percentage point since 1993 alone.

Although the dollar magnitude of the "loss" is far smaller than that represented in Figures 1.2 and 1.3, this trend should be worrisome nonetheless. Proponents of direct student aid programs champion its cause for two primary reasons: student access and to ensure an accrual of economic benefits within a state. Recent empirical evidence, however, suggests that the ability of student aid programs to achieve these two goals is very limited. With regard to student access, policymakers have long feared that more generous student aid packages would encourage institutions to capture these additional revenues through higher tuition and other fees, thereby

Figure 1.4
Average share of state higher education expenditures to institutions: 1976–1977 to 2001–2002

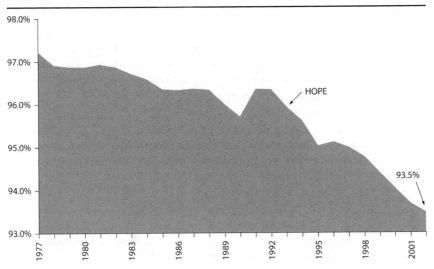

negating the impact of the aid programs. Bridget Long (2004) and Michael Rizzo and Ronald Ehrenberg (2004) provide evidence that supports this view.

With regard to economic development, there is a belief that increasing the generosity of direct student aid awards (and merit programs in particular) would both increase the propensity for students to attend colleges in their home states and increase the propensity for these talented students to remain in state after graduating.[7] A number of studies have found that generous student aid programs result in more talented students remaining in state to attend college, but Jeffrey Groen (2004) found that although students who attend college within a state are more likely to remain in the state, the magnitude is much too small to justify using economic development as a rationale for merit-based student aid programs.

The combined effect of the trends depicted in Figures 1.2 through 1.4 indicates that if public higher education institutions had been able to simply maintain their budget shares at 1977 levels, in an average state, institutions would have garnered an additional $605 million per year. To appreciate the magnitude of this sum, consider that it represents fully 50 percent of the *total* public higher education budget in an average state ($1.2 billion). Had states been able to retain these dollars, the $3,781 per full time equivalent student it represents would have been sufficient to cover an additional 23 percent of institutional expenditures or 114 percent of in-state undergraduate tuition at an average public four year institution in 2001. These declines have occurred steadily and almost unnoticeably for more than 20 years; however, institutional responses to this funding withdrawal have enjoyed no such anonymity.[8]

DATA

The analysis in this chapter involves a broad panel dataset that was assembled from more than 30 different sources between 1977 and 2001.[9] Table 1.1 reports summary statistics for six categories of variables used in the analysis. The income and budget measures and the demographic characteristics are derived largely from U.S. Census sources, and the enrollment pressure, competing interests, political, and higher education specific characteristics are derived from less prominent sources. The table presents data for two representative years (1977 and 2001) to highlight how each of the explanatory variables has changed over time. All year references represent fiscal years ending on June 30 of the corresponding year, and all dollar values used in the analysis herein represent constant 1998 dollars.

Table 1.2 displays the level of general fund budget expenditures, education budget expenditures, and higher education budget expenditures for four representative states and the national average and is useful for assessing the magnitude of the impacts of regression estimates presented in the next section. These data indicate that even very small percentage changes in budget shares translate into very large dollar amounts. For instance, a 1 percent increase in the HESHARE in an average state would result in an additional $75 million for higher education nationwide, and as much as a quarter-billion additional dollars in New York.

Table 1.1
Summary Statistics for Baseline and Selected Variables and Years

	1977			2001		
	Mean	Min	Max	Mean	Min	Max
Income and Budget Measures:						
Median Household Income (1980 earliest)	33,457	24,321	51,100	40,402	28,445	52,744
75–25 Income Ratio (1980 earliest)	3.1	2.7	3.7	3.3	2.8	4.0
Per Capita Federal Transfers	557	302	1,587	992	533	1,869
Demographics:						
Median Age	28.4	23.8	33.5	35.5	27.1	38.9
Share of Population 5–17	25.6	22.0	29.4	20.3	17.6	25.2
Share of Population 18–24	14.4	12.3	17.5	10.5	8.5	15.7
Share of Population >65	11.4	2.7	17.9	13.4	6.2	18.7
Percent Nonwhite (1981 earliest)	16.9	1.4	67.0	20.5	3.1	75.7
Share 5–17 Population Nonwhite	20.4	0.6	70.7	25.8	4.3	83.8
Share 18–24 Population Nonwhite	20.0	2.5	63.4	25.3	4.8	75.2
Share >25 Population Nonwhite	15.7	1.2	68.9	21.2	2.2	63.0
Share >65 Population Nonwhite	11.6	0.4	72.0	11.6	1.0	77.2
Share Pop 25 and Older w/ HS Degree	65.5	50.0	81.5	85.4	78.2	91.7
Share Pop 25 and Older w/ College Degree	15.3	8.3	22.7	25.2	14.8	36.2
In-Migration % (All) (1980, 1990, 2000)	13.0	5.6	32.1	12.0	6.4	27.5

(Continued)

Table 1.1
(Continued)

	1977 Mean	1977 Min	1977 Max	2001 Mean	2001 Min	2001 Max
Out-Migration % (All Ages)	10.9	6.3	29.6	9.6	5.7	20.0
In-Migration % (College Age)	21.1	8.4	45.3	21.5	10.3	39.3
Out-Migration % (College Age)	10.8	6.2	29.8	9.5	4.8	20.7
Enrollment Pressure						
Share HE Enroll Privates (1999 latest)	21.0	0.0	56.7	23.9	5.0	61.5
Share K12 Enroll Privates (1981 earliest)	9.4	1.6	19.0	9.2	2.4	16.7
Share HE Enroll 2-Years (1999 latest)	22.5	0.0	53.0	27.3	3.6	56.0
Enrollment Rate (1999 latest)	53.5	6.9	140.0	58.4	30.1	101.2
FTE HE Enrollment (2000 latest)	161,464	9,082	10,74,346	214,367	16,290	1,329,270
K12 Enrollment (2000 latest)	871,775	89,295	4,313,926	934,034	91,757	6,050,609
Capacity	1.23	0.80	2.08	0.82	0.33	2.14
SAT (1980 earliest)	945	784	1,062	1,069	974	1,196
Competing Interests & Economic Conditions:						
Crime Rate (per 100,000)–(1998 latest)	4,968	2,391	8,461	4,714	2,469	7,272
Health (Share >65 × Health CPI) (2000 latest)	6.0	1.4	9.5	32.7	14.9	45.8
Unemployment Rate	7.0	3.3	10.4	3.9	2.2	6.6

Unemp. Rate Nonwhites (1978 earliest)	12.3	0.0	22.2	7.3	16.7
#States with Court K12 Reform	2			24	
GSP Share Finance, Ins, Real Est, Svc (1978 earliest)	25.4	18.4	46.6	37.9	56.1
Share GF Revs-Corp Income Tax	6.1	0.0	13.7	4.0	12.4
Share GF Revs-Indiv Income Tax	18.3	0.0	41.9	23.9	47.1
Share GF Revs-Lotteries	0.4	0.0	3.1	1.8	8.0
Share GF Revs-Sales Taxes	35.4	4.8	62.4	29.9	66.7
Political Factors:					
#States with Democrat Governor	37			17	
Assembly Seats per Senate Seats	3.02	1.67	16.67	2.95	16.46
Assembly Seats per 100,000 Population	5.9	0.0	47.3	4.6	32.0
Senate Seats per 100,000 Population	2.1	0.0	7.9	1.6	7.3
Voting Participation Rate	52.0	22.4	69.5	51.4	67.4
Higher Education Factors:					
Endowment per Student (1996 latest)	1,562	58	11,432	2,850	21,997
Giving per Student	526	0	2,047	2,824	7,282
Ph.D. degrees / BA degrees	3.12	1.18	6.78	3.14	5.57

(Continued)

Table 1.1
(Continued)

	Mean	1977 Min	Max	Mean	2001 Min	Max
Proportion HH w/Inc. Below Pell Max	64.4	43.0	76.8	56.7	42.0	71.0
Research Expenditures per Capita	36	8	203	82	29	174
Share Ph.D. awarded in Science and Eng.	61.3	33.0	100.0	67.4	35.1	96.3
Avg Instate Tuition at 4-Years (1999 latest)	1,637	829	2,968	3,225	1,960	6,894

Note: All dollar values are constant.

Table 1.2
Representative Budget Measures in $Millions for FY2001

	General Fund	Education (share)	Higher Education (share)
National Average	20,867	7,491	1,231
		35.9%	16.4%
Iowa	11,199	4,397	871
		39.3%	19.8%
New York	89,237	23,569	3,353
		26.4%	14.2%
North Carolina	28,860	11,960	2,452
		41.4%	20.5%
Texas	58,183	24,805	4,087
		42.6%	16.5%

EMPIRICAL MODEL AND RESULTS

To explain the budget share outcomes described previously, I move to a multi-variate analysis. I estimate three equations using panel data, with the state-year as my unit of analysis, in which the share of the public general fund budget allocated to education (in state i and year t), the share of the education budget allocated to higher education (in state i and year t), and the share of the higher education budget allocated to institutions (in state i and year t) are specified to be functions of the total available resources at the legislature's disposal, demographic character-istics, enrollment pressures, economic conditions, competing budgetary interests (including private alternatives), political factors, state institutional characteris-tics, and random error terms. The error terms, u_{it}, are decomposed into a fixed time component, a fixed cross-sectional component, and a random component varying over time and across observations. Models are then estimated assuming several possible treatments of the random components and cross-sectional com-ponents of the error terms.[10] For each of the three outcome measures I propose the following model:

$$Outcome_{it} = \sum_{k=1}^{K} B_k \chi_{itk} + c_i + \gamma_t + \varepsilon_{it}$$

These three equations can be viewed as approximating political economic equilibrium conditions from an underlying structural demand and supply model. Empirical estimates should therefore be carefully interpreted. For example, it might be difficult to assess whether my results in the EDSHARE equation arise from differences in legislative demand for educational spending, or differences in the technology of supplying educational services to states with different demographic characteristics. It might seem reasonable to exclude the ethnic share of the population from the education production function, which suggests that the demographic effects associated with these variables are likely to result from demand side factors alone. Interpretation of the effect of fluctuations in the school-age population is more difficult, for example, because economies of scale in education could make it possible to deliver the same education to a larger cohort with a less than proportional expansion in education spending.[11]

The parameters of interest, β_k, answer the question, "holding all other factors constant, what is the expected change in the budget share within a state if some observable factor increases by one unit?" The inclusion of state effects (c_i) and year effects (γ_i) allow me to take full advantage of the panel nature of the data and understand why budget shares *change within a state* over time. Inclusion of state effects controls for unobservable state-specific factors that are constant over time. These factors might include climate, presence of national parks, high levels of average wages, historical factors, etc., each presumed to vary across states, but to have a constant impact over time within states. If the state effects were excluded from these regressions, the answer may be misleading if the excluded state effects were correlated with explanatory variables in the model. For example, states with no parkland will have more resources available to devote to higher education. If the level of out-migration is negatively correlated with the number of state parks, however, then the estimated effect of out-migration on the HESHARE would not only pick up the investment decision that states face, but also the impact of a state park system on higher education budgets.

Year effects are included in the models to control for unobserved, time-specific factors that are constant across all states. These factors include changes in federal laws, federal court decisions, international conflicts and trade patterns, changes in the value of the Pell grant, changes in technology and the education production function, etc.—each presumed to change over time, but to impact all states in the same way. Inclusion of time effects also removes the impacts of systematic changes in the explanatory variables so that the results presented below reflect within-state responses to idiosyncratic shocks alone. For example, when systematic changes in enrollment pressures are controlled for, one might expect to observe smaller changes in budget shares when there are idiosyncratic shocks to enrollment pressure, as a result of competitive tax pressures, institutional capacity, and other factors unique to a given state.[12]

Baseline Estimates

I estimate equation 1 via ordinary least squares (OLS) for each of the three outcome measures I am interested in. Table 1.3 presents OLS regression estimates for the EDSHARE and HESHARE equations; Table 1.4 presents OLS estimates for the INSHARE equation. The dependent variables are each defined in percentage

Table 1.3
Ordinary Least Squares Baseline Regressions for Education's Share of General Fund Budgets and Public Higher: Education's Share of the Education Budget Within Estimates

	EDSHARE (I)		HESHARE (II)	
Median Income in $1,000 (INC)	−1.27	*	0.61	*
	(0.28)	—	(0.23)	—
Squared Income (INC2)	0.011	*	−0.004	*
	(0.002)	—	(0.002)	—
75–25 Income Ratio (INEQU)	−5.13	*	4.12	*
	(1.81)	—	(1.52)	—
Share of Population >65 Years Old (ELDERLY)	−0.41	*	0.22	**
	(0.18)	—	(0.13)	*
Share of Population Aged 5–24 (SCHOOLAGE)	0.62	*	—	—
	(0.12)	—	—	—
Share Pop. 18–24 / Share Pop. 5–17 (COLRATIO)	—	—	0.13	*
	—	—	(0.04)	—
Nonwhite schoolage / Nonwhite non-schoolage (SCHOOLRACERATIO)	1.42	—	—	—
	(1.10)	—	—	—
Nonwhite college pop / Nonwhite K12 pop (COLK12RACE)	—	—	−0.15	—
	—	—	(0.14)	—
(Nonwhite college pop / Nonwhite K12 pop) *Share Adult Population Nonwhite (RACEINTERACT)	—	—	0.04	*
	—	—	(0.01)	—
In-Migration (share population in state today that did not reside here 5 years ago) (INMIG)	0.02	*	−0.02	—
	(0.05)	—	(0.03)	—
Out-Migration (share of population in state 5 years ago that does not reside here today) (OUTMIG)	0.06	—	−0.13	*
	(0.06)	—	(0.06)	—
Federal Transfers per Capita ($1,000) (FEDTRAN)	−0.56	—	—	—
	(0.36)	—	—	—

(Continued)

Table 1.3
(Continued)

	EDSHARE (I)		HESHARE (II)	
Unemployment Rate (UNEMP)	−0.05	—	−0.22	*
	(0.06)	—	(0.05)	—
Health Costs (HEALTH)	−0.02	—	—	—
	(0.06)	—	—	—
Crime Rate (CRIME)	0.03	—	—	—
	(0.12)	—	—	—
Court Reform State (COURT)	1.18	*	−1.19	*
	(0.30)	—	(0.25)	—
Within R^2	0.319	—	0.663	—
Observations	1250	—	1250	—

* **Bold 95% significance,** ** *italics* = 90%.

Notes: All regressions include year effects and dummy variables correcting for missing values that equal 1 when the relevant explanatory variable is missing and 0 otherwise. All also include interactions between income level and distribution and EDSHARE and INSHARE include relative price measures, none of which are statistically relevant and measures controlling for private enrollment pressures. In-migration and out-migration for EDSHARE equation are rates for entire population. For HESHARE and INSHARE, rates are calculated for college-age population alone. The missing values of the explanatory variables take a value of 0 when the missing dummy equals 1. All within R2 represent proportion of within variation in outcome explained by changes in explanatory variables exclusive of the state effects. Standard errors in (parentheses).

point terms, so that an estimated coefficient of 2.5, for instance, indicates that an increase in an independent variable of 1 unit results in an increase in the relevant share by 2.5 percentage points.[13] All of the results discussed next are *ceteris paribus*, holding all other factors constant.[14]

Results in column (i) of Table 1.3 suggest that changes in the distribution of income and age composition within a state are responsible for changes in the EDSHARE depicted in Table 1.2. Each $1,000 increase in real household income (INC) results in a 1.3 percentage point loss in education's share of the overall budget. This relationship is nonlinear, however, and reaches a minimum at $58,000 just beyond the distribution of income observed in 2001 (Maryland = $53,000). Results also suggest that the increasing inequality of income (INEQU) has resulted in a decline in preferences for public education. Together, these estimates suggest that changes in the distribution of income have accounted for more than 100 percent of the observed changes in the EDSHARE since 1977.[15]

Table 1.4
Ordinary Least Squares Regressions for Institutional Share of Public Higher
Education Budgets—Within Estimates

	Baseline (I)		(II)	
Median Income, in $1,000 (INC)	0.23	—	0.27	—
	(0.16)	—	(0.17)	—
Squared Income (INC2)	−0.001	—	−0.002	—
	(0.001)	—	(0.001)	—
75–25 Income Ratio (INEQU)	1.59	—	1.67	—
	(1.09)	—	(1.07)	—
Share of Population >65 Years Old (ELDERLY)	0.38	*	0.38	*
	(0.10)	—	(0.10)	—
Share of Population Aged 18-24 (COLLEGE)	0.275	*	0.374	*
	(0.116)	—	(0.076)	—
Nonwhite college / Nonwhite non-college (COLRACERATIO)	−0.009	*	−0.005	—
	(0.003)	—	(0.007)	—
In-Migration (share population in state today that did not reside here 5 years ago) (INMIG)	0.01	—	0.02	—
	(0.02)	—	(0.02)	—
Out-Migration (share of population in state 5 years ago that does not reside here today) (OUTMIG)	−0.09	**	−0.11	*
	(0.05)	—	(0.05)	—
Unemployment Rate (UNEMP)	0.03	—	0.02	—
	(0.04)	—	(0.04)	—
Share College Enroll Privates (COLPRV)	0.019	—	0.033	*
	(0.012)	—	(0.012)	—
Share College Enroll Two-Years (TWOYEAR)	−0.006	—	−0.005	—
	(0.012)	—	(0.012)	—
Proportion Below Pell (PELL)	−0.06	*	−0.07	—
	(0.03)	—	0.03	*
PELL × COLLEGE (PELLPOP)	(0.0037)	**	0.0039	**
	(0.0022)	—	(0.0022)	—
Regional Nonresident Tuition ($1,000) (REGTUIT)	−0.21	*	−0.14	—
	(0.09)	—	(0.09)	—
PhD Degrees Awarded per BA	−0.15	—	−0.14	—
	(0.12)	—	(0.11)	—
Degrees Awarded (PHDBA) SAT (100 points) (SAT)	0.29	**	0.31	**
	(0.18)	—	(0.17)	—

Table 1.4
(Continued)

	Baseline (I)		(II)	
Merit Aid State (MERIT)	−2.86	*	−6.89	*
	(0.27)		(3.49)	—
MERIT × INC	—	—	0.06	—
	—	—	(0.09)	—
MERIT × COLRACERATIO	—	—	0.12	*
	—	—	(0.03)	—
INC × COLRACERATIO	—	—	−0.0001	—
	—	—	(0.0002)	
	—	—		*
MERIT × INC × COLRACERATIO	—	—	−0.0029	—
	—	—	(0.0009)	—
Within R²	0.390	—	0.411	—
Observations	1250	—	1250	—

*__Bold 95% significance__, ** *italics* = 90%.

Notes: All regressions include year effects and dummy variables correcting for missing values that equal 1 when the relevant explanatory variable is missing and 0 otherwise. All also include interactions between income level and distribution and EDSHARE and INSHARE include relative price measures, none of which are statistically relevant. In-migration and out-migration for EDSHARE equation are rates for entire population. For HESHARE and INSHARE, rates are calculated for college-age population alone. The missing values of the explanatory variables take a value of 0 when the missing dummy equals 1. All within R2 represent proportion of within variation in outcome explained by changes in explanatory variables exclusive of the state effects. Standard errors in (parentheses).

The changing age composition within a state produced expected changes in the EDSHARE. Changes in the fraction of the population that is school age (SCHOOLAGE) were positively correlated with the EDSHARE, and an increase in the share of the population that is elderly (ELDERLY) caused a fall in the EDSHARE. Prior research by Poterba (1997), Case et al. (1993), and Borge and Rattso (1995) all find a negative correlation between student cohort size and per pupil education funding levels. Although there is a strong positive effect of student cohort size on budget shares, one cannot infer how expenditures per student will fare. Although the point estimate on the elderly share does not appear large, it implies that by the year 2025, when the elderly share is expected to increase by an average of 5 percentage points, that education will lose an additional 2 percentage points in state budgetary priority, representing nearly a half-billion dollars in an "average" state (2001 dollars).[16]

An important finding is that in state-years after a court rules that a state's K12 education finance system is unconstitutional (COURT), the share of the general fund budget allocated to education increases by 1.2 percentage points. This result is consistent with the finding of Murray et al. (1998) finding that court reforms in 16 states led to an average increase in per capita K12 spending of 23 percent.

Turning to the HESHARE results in column (ii), I find that in addition to the factors that affect EDSHARES in column (i), changes in demographic heterogeneity, migration patterns, and economic conditions help explain why public higher education has been crowded out by K12 education. Changes in the income distribution have worked in HESHARE's favor, but the effects are offset by the losses suffered through education's declining priority in the overall budget process. Increases in household income of $1,000 (INC) result in increases in HESHARE by 0.6 points throughout the entire range of observed income (the maximum is reached at $79,000).[17] Estimates also suggest that an increase of income inequality within a state (INEQU) results in a larger share of the available education dollars being allocated to higher education. This result, although positive for higher education, may not be in the best interests of society at large. Previous research by Hansen and Weisbrod (1969a), Windham (1972), and UNESCO (2003) suggest that the economic middle and upper classes have been able to shift income toward them in the political process using the higher education finance system, and that in places where inequality is severe, investments in higher education will exacerbate the existing income differentials.[18]

Age demographic shifts have also worked in favor of higher education. Although states are favorably responsive to changes in the relative size of the college-age cohort to the K12-age cohort (COLRATIO), there is also modest evidence that aging populations (ELDERLY) look more favorable on higher education than K12 education. This result may reflect a lower perceived relative tax price for higher education by the elderly or a more immediate public benefit perceived to be available through financing university research.[19]

Taken together, income distribution and age demographic shifts indicate that higher education's share of the education budget should have risen by nearly 5 percentage points since 1977. Since the HESHARE declined by approximately 6 points, other factors must account for an 11 percentage point decline.

Two estimates, out-migration and unemployment, help predict why higher education may face difficulties in the future, but they are not able to explain the observed changes in the past. Although the estimated coefficient on the out-migration of the college-aged population (OUTMIG) suggests that increases in out-migration led states to devote fewer resources to higher education, during this time the average level of out-migration across states has remained fairly constant.[20] Similarly, I find that as the unemployment rate (UNEMP) increases by 1 percent, states respond by cutting the HESHARE by .22 points; however, the average unemployment rate over this time period fell by 2.5 percent.

The estimates in column (ii) suggest a trend that demographic heterogeneity can have an important effect on education spending. I have included two variables in this equation to capture these impacts. First, I include a variable for the ratio of the college-aged population that is nonwhite relative to the K12-age population that is nonwhite (COLK12RACE). To see whether the impact of this heterogeneity varies according to the racial makeup of the non-school–age population in the state, I also interact it with the share of the population ages 25 and older that is nonwhite (RACEINTERACT). Although not statistically significant, an interesting result is that as the college-age population becomes more nonwhite relative to the K12 population, states devote more resources to the population that is "whiter"; however, the impact of this heterogeneity becomes statistically significant and larger when the non-school–age adult population is more homogeneous.[21]

K12 court reforms have had a large impact on the HESHARE. The estimates suggest that as a state moves to more centralized methods of K12 financing (COURT), the average impact over time has been to decrease the share of the education budget allocated to public higher education by 1.2 points. In an average state in 2001, this represents $90 million more that public higher education would have been allocated in the absence of the reform program. This result somewhat contradicts the work of Murray et al. (1998). Although they conclude that the increased expenditures on K12 education did not come at the expense of any other budget item, their study ended in 1994. Taken together with the EDSHARE result, I find that public higher education spending has been partially crowded out by the increased K12 expenditures resulting from the K12 court reforms.[22]

The estimated effects of the independent variables on INSHARES in the left-hand column (i) of Table 1.4 can be described briefly. The relationship between demographic changes and the share of higher education budgets appropriated directly to institutions is strong. Increases in the share of the population that is college age (COLLAGE) result in higher INSHARES, so that the subsidy is received by a larger pool of people than would otherwise be the case. However, the size of the college-age cohort fell markedly between 1972 and the early 1990s, resulting in a 1-point loss in the INSHARE. Aging populations tend to support institutions rather than students as well. The Pell grant variables yield interesting results. As more households become eligible for federal Pell grant awards (PELL), it appears that states respond by reducing the share of aid awarded to institutions, and that this effect is larger when the share of the population that is college age (PELLPOP) is larger, although the overall magnitude is minimal. Because more students would be eligible to receive Pell grants (and federal subsidized and unsubsidized loans) when tuition rates are higher, there is a perverse incentive built into the federal financial aid system that encourages states to behave strategically.

As with the HESHARE, ethnic heterogeneity across age cohorts has an important impact on the INSHARE, with the share going to institutions falling when the college-age population becomes more nonwhite relative to the adult non-college–age population (COLRACERATIO).[23] Whether this decline is due to an effort to direct merit aid away from nonwhites or because nonwhites have a larger demand for state need-based aid cannot be immediately discerned from this result.

Looking to the bottom panel of the table, the estimates suggest that movement to a merit aid program (MERIT) reduces the INSHARE by nearly 3 percentage points. Also, as the nonresident tuition rates at public four-year institutions in the geographic region (REGTUIT) increase, states are increasingly turning to student aid rather than institutional appropriations, explaining approximately 1 percentage point in the INSHARE drop. Again, the reasons for doing so are unclear. It may be the case that higher regional tuitions permit instate publics to charge higher tuitions as well, reducing the pressure on direct state support, or reduce the demand for own residents leaving the state. It may also be the case that higher regional tuition signals an improvement in school quality, and in an effort to compete with these institutions, the state induces its resident students to stay by providing them with larger student aid packages.

Column (ii) presents regression estimates that try to explain the motivation for the increasing popularity of state student merit aid programs. Taking liberty with nomenclature and variable interpretation, I accomplish this by including four additional variables to the specification in column (i): second order interaction terms between the merit aid variable (MERIT) and the median income level (INC); MERIT and the relative nonwhite college age population (COLRACERATIO); INC and COLRACERATIO; and finally, a fully interacted variable of MERIT × COLRACERATIO × INC.[24] This fully interacted model is akin to a natural experiment approach that answers the question, "Do merit aid states that have heavily nonwhite college populations favor broad based institutional aid or more targeted student based aid?" The results are disheartening. Although the impacts of the variables in the baseline specification are largely unchanged by the inclusion of the interacted variables, the first-order impact of moving to merit aid programs grows dramatically to nearly 7 percentage points. The variable of interest, MERIT × COLRACERATIO × INC, which can be viewed as a continuous analog to a "difference-in-difference-in-differences" estimator, yields a statistically significant negative result. Considered liberally, this implies that although merit aid states with large nonwhite college-age populations favor institutional support, these states only do so when income is low. When income is high in these states, student aid is preferred, with the somber implication that the increasing popularity of merit aid programs has not been altruistically motivated. Targeted, non-means–tested programs seem to be used to redistribute income to middle- and upper-income families and to avoid providing broad-based support to economically disadvantaged members of the populace.

Extensions—Incremental Budgeting

It has been suggested that states make funding decisions on an incremental basis, with previous budget levels taken as given when determining current budget allocations.[25] Consider the HESHARE equation as an example. The interpretation is that for any level of budgeted funds for education, the legislators first make expenditures for the minimum level of services required to be provided by K12 and higher education. Then with the remaining budgeted funds, they choose the optimal *increments* to these budget levels, which depends only on the increments to the minimum

Table 1.5
Dynamic Panel Estimation on Baseline Regressions: Incremental Estimates Using
Dynamic Panel GMM Estimator

	EDSHARE (2)		HESHARE (4)		INSHARE (6)	
1-Period Lagged Outcome (LAG)	0.73	*	0.56	*	0.53	*
	(0.03)		(0.03)		(0.03)	

*Bold 95% significance, ** *italics* = 90%.

expenditures, not on the absolute levels. Table 1.5 presents the parameter estimates
(θ) from reestimating the baseline equations using the Arellano-Bond dynamic
panel estimation technique when lagged dependent variables are included in the
specification.[26] State budgeting would be strictly incremental if the estimated effects
of the lagged dependent variables were each equal to one. If the coefficients equal
zero, then the entire budget is determined "from scratch" each budget cycle. Therefore values of θ between 0 and 1 provide for the possibility that expenditures within
any budget category can be cut to some extent during that budget cycle.

It is not surprising that the estimates in Table 1.5 indicate that budget shares
are determined only in part by an incremental process. Looking to the EDSHARE
results, the coefficient on the lagged variable (LAG) indicates that in each period,
73 percent of the EDSHARE budget is preserved, with the remaining 27 percent left
to legislative discretion. As one might expect, it appears that legislatures exercise
more discretion the more narrowly defined the budget share is. Fifty-six percent of
the HESHARE is determined by the level of HESHARE one period earlier, whereas
just over half the INSHARE decision is based on the prior year's allocation.

Extensions—Augmented Specifications[27]

I reestimate each baseline specification by adding groups of variables that capture political and voting characteristics, the sources of state general fund revenues,
the composition of gross state product by industry, higher education specific variables, and other demographic characteristics. Inclusion of any single group of
variables had virtually no impact on the original baseline estimates.

Augmented EDSHARE regressions yield few notable results. The only important political variable is that as the state government moves from multiparty
control to single party control, the education budget share increases.[28] Without
exception, results indicate that as the importance of all industry sectors increases
relative to that of the sectors aside from Finance, Real Estate, Insurance and Services, education budgets expand; however, all of these sectors have seen dramatic
decreases in their contributions to state economies since 1977. Results indicate
that the changing industrial composition has contributed to a 1.6 percentage
point decline in the EDSHARE.[29]

Augmented HESHARE regressions indicate that political and higher education-specific factors are important. Uniparty governments prefer to fund K12 education, and this result does not depend on the specific party that is in control. The composition of political interests within state legislatures, represented by the number of assembly seats per senate seats, produces an interesting (albeit of small magnitude) result. The estimate indicates that as local representation becomes more prevalent in statehouses relative to representation of larger geographic areas, higher education does more poorly.[30] States spend larger shares on higher education when larger shares of doctoral degrees are awarded in science and technology fields. Legislatures are also more supportive of higher education when a larger share of students attend two-year colleges, presumably as a result of the low cost of these colleges and because their accessibility allows for the subsidy to be received by a larger pool of residents. This may also reflect political factors, however, as community colleges are more numerous and reside in more political districts than their four-year counterparts.

A dramatic and concerning result from these regressions is a negative and significant coefficient estimate on real private giving per student at public research universities within a state. As state funding continues to lag, public universities have increasingly looked to private donations to supplement their revenue streams. Some observers, however, have worried that states would view these revenues as replacements for future state appropriations and allow institutional appropriations to lag in the future. Their fears are well founded. Despite the seemingly small point estimate (each additional $1,000 per student raised resulting in a 0.36 point loss in the HESHARE), the magnitude of this crowding out cannot be ignored, especially in the most recent decade. For example, public research universities in Maine have increased their annual private giving per student by $5,800 since 1990. The coefficient estimate indicates that their HESHARE should have dropped by 2.1 points as a result, which explains nearly all of Maine's 2.3 point decline over this period. In fact, for each of the five states that have seen their public universities increase per-student giving by over $3,000, the average fall in HESHARES has been 6.4 points; the five states that have not increased private fundraising efforts since 1990 have seen their shares fall by only 3.9 points.[31] This result also casts doubt on the ability of public universities to generate rainy-day funds or to stockpile appropriations in lush times (as their private counterparts can do), because of a fear that future appropriations would be smaller in response.

Turning to the INSHARE results, the augmented estimates indicate that political factors are contributing to the decline in institutions' share of higher education budgets. The estimates indicate that as voter participation rates increase, and as a state moves from a Republican governor to a Democrat governor, student aid increases in attractiveness relative to institutional appropriations, though the magnitude of these effects is small.

Although there is a strong negative relationship between the share of doctoral degrees awarded in the sciences and institutional aid shares, this may simply reflect the impacts of targeted student aid programs many years earlier. As with the

HESHARE results, institutional efforts to raise private funds seem to be met with retaliatory action by the states. Every $1,000 increase in real private giving per student results in 0.23 points of the higher education budget leaving institutional coffers and going into the hands of the students.

Extensions—Subsamples of Data[32]

Table 1.6 depicts how the three budget share measures have changed from 1977 to 2001 in different subsamples of the states. Although none of the reported changes within each category are statistically different from one another at the 95 percent level, several glaring patterns stand out. It appears that nonreform states (K12 court mandates), non-Northeast states, low population density states, and states governed by a single political party have cut their EDSHARES the most, whereas two-year budget cycle states, court reform states, limited governor power states, politically competitive states, and multiparty states have cut their HESHARES the most. Finally, it appears that students have benefited over institutions in single-year budget cycle states, in states where governors have substantial appropriative power, in dense states, and in states controlled by multiple political parties.

When the baseline models are reestimated on these different subsamples of data, five broad observations are worth highlighting. First, from estimating each equation separately for the years 1977–1982, 1983–1992, and 1993–2001, it is apparent that changes in economic factors are increasing in importance on EDSHARES and HESHARES over time. The most concerning individual result was that, whereas a 1 percentage point increase in the unemployment rate between 1977 and 1982 resulted in a decline in HESHARES by 0.1 points, today a similar increase results in nearly a half-point decline in the HESHARE.[33]

Second, states with funding formulas respond more dramatically to changes in enrollment pressures than do nonformula states, as expected. Further, few variables are significant in the HESHARE equation estimated on the formula states, indicating that funding formula states may do a better job at insulating higher education from the budget ax than nonformula states.

Third, changes in competing interests (health and crime spending) and federal transfers have a substantial impact on EDSHARES depending on the subsample of states one looks within. For example, in states where governors have power to reduce appropriations without legislative approval, and in states that operate on a two-year budget cycle, increases in federal grants per capita result in sizable decreases in the education budget share. Further, the increasing cost of health care has crowded out education in states that operate on a single-year budget cycle, in states with multi-party governments, in states where governors have significant power, and especially in high-density states.

Fourth, the impacts of racial heterogeneity on the HESHARE and INSHARE equations have been increasing over time. With respect to the HESHARE, increasing ethnic heterogeneity across age groups have led to the largest

Table 1.6
Percentage Point Changes in Outcomes by State Institutional Characteristics

Institutional Characteristic		ΔEDSHARE	ΔHESHARE	ΔINSHARE
Autonomy of Higher Education Institutions*	Yes (25 states)	-3.28	-5.77	-3.58
	No (25 states)	-3.85	-6.51	-3.51
Budget Cycle Length	2-Years (23 states)	-3.03	-7.27	-2.81
	1-Year (27 states)	-4.01	-5.17	-4.17
Court Reform State in 2001	Yes (24 states)	-2.42	-7.15	-3.02
	No (26 states)	-4.91	-5.22	-4.03
Funding Formula	Yes (29 states)	-4.23	-5.71	-3.78
	No (21 states)	-2.63	-6.74	-3.22
Governor Can Reduce Appropriations w/out Approval	Yes (37 states)	-3.66	-5.6	-4.26
	No (13 states)	-3.27	-7.68	-1.52
New England / North East	Yes (9 states)	-2.04	-5.69	-4.45
	No (41 states)	-3.89	-6.24	-3.35

(*Continued*)

Table 1.6
(Continued)

Institutional Characteristic		ΔEDSHARE	ΔHESHARE	ΔINSHARE
Political Competition**	Competitive (25 states)	−3.29	−6.77	−3.44
	Noncompet. (25 States)	−3.84	−5.51	−3.65
Population Density	Dense (25 states)	−2.96	−6.02	−4.77
	Less Dense (25 states)	−4.17	−6.26	−2.32
Uniparty Government	Yes (43% of state-years)	−5.25	−5.44	−2.62
	No (57% of state-years)	−2.10	−6.40	−3.92

Notes: Represent 1977–2001.

No raw changes are statistically different across categories at 95 percent.

Uniparty states not constant over time, so changes are for inconsistent.

* Lowry.

** Holbrook and Van Dunk.

declines in states that exercise more control over their public institutions, in nonformula states, and in those where governors have significant power over appropriations cuts. Further, in the INSHARE equation, increasing ethnic heterogeneity has caused institutional shares to decline in states with annual budget reviews, in less densely populated states and in those with a high degree of political competition.

Fifth, although column (ii) of Table 1.3 indicates that an aging state population looks favorably on higher education, it turns out that this result is driven by the impact the aging population had in the 1970s. Regression estimates indicate that in the 1990s, as the share of the population that is over 65 increased by 1 percentage point, the HESHARE fell by 0.56 points. This effect is statistically different than the effect in the 1970s with more than 99 percent confidence. Further, the impact (favorable) of aging in the HESHARE and INSHARE equations is driven by states outside of the Northeast. There is also evidence that the impact of an aging population has larger effects when political competition is greatest.

Extensions—Tuition

Tuition rates at public higher education institutions are determined by the level of state support (Lowry 2001, Rizzo and Ehrenberg 2004) and are often implicitly set by the legislatures or governors in a state. In just one of many examples, the state of Massachusetts and the University of Massachusetts agreed to keep tuition low in the 1990s in return for strong support from the state, but are now considering changing this policy.[34] In any case, just as federal legislators are loathe to increase the maximum value of the Pell grant because of concerns about the Bennett hypothesis, state legislators may respond to increasing tuition rates by cutting future appropriations, giving rise to a cycle of further tuition increases and budget cuts.[35] Higher tuition rates may also cause future appropriations to be cut simply because they generate distaste for higher education. As tuition rates are also likely a function of a long history of state appropriations as well, it would be difficult to estimate its impact on current budget shares.

I reestimated the HESHARE regression including a one-period lag of the enrollment weighted average tuition at four-year public institutions in a state as an explanatory variable.[36] Coefficient estimates on the one-period lagged tuition suggest that when tuition increases by $1,000 one year before this budget cycle, legislatures respond by cutting the HESHARE by 3.4 points. Although the estimates of the other explanatory variables in the model are unaffected by this change, I also tested a specification in which the one-period lag of tuition is instrumented for by lagged values of variables that are expected to have an impact on tuition, but that might not be expected to directly impact HESHARES one year later.[37] The results are striking and indicate that when lagged tuition increases by $1,000 within a state, HESHARES are slashed by 6.3 points, with no resulting changes in the other estimated parameters.

Although these results should be viewed with caution, they are very sugges-
tive.[38] Real average public tuition rates at four-year institutions have grown by
approximately $1,500 since 1972. The coefficient estimate here indicates that
HESHARES fell by almost 9.5 percentage points as a result of increasing tuition
rates, thereby explaining a majority of the missing 11 percentage point decline
already described.

CONCLUSION

Although no universally accepted structural (theoretical) model of political
economic equilibrium exists, empirical specifications describing preferences for
public spending on public education yield valuable insights into why public higher
education is facing an alarming fiscal crisis. The empirical evidence in this chapter
suggests that all of the observed 4 percentage point decline in education's share
of state general fund budgets has been attributable to changes in the income
distribution within states. Although measures of competing interest groups seem
not to have crowded out education spending, their effects are confounded by their
having differential impacts in different subsamples of states.

Although collectively, observable within-state changes are unable to explain
the 6 percentage point decline in the share of the education budget allocated to
public higher education since 1977, there is substantial evidence that the discretionary nature of higher education spending and its ability to independently raise
revenues have caused its decline. Dynamic panel estimates indicate that states do
not practice strictly incremental budgeting and exercise considerable discretion
over the determination of the higher education–K12 funding allocation. Further,
estimates on a sample split by three different time periods indicate that the sensitivity of higher education budget shares to declining labor market conditions has
increased over time. Attempts by public institutions to respond to lagging state
appropriations by increasing tuition or private fundraising efforts have been met
with substantial chagrin by state legislatures and calls into question exactly what
institutions are expected to do in the face of budget difficulties as they rapidly
spiral toward the private equilibrium.

The 3.9 percentage point decline in the share of higher education budgets
allocated to public institutions, as opposed to students, can be fully explained by
changes in the relative size of the college-age cohort, increases in nonresident
tuition rates in the geographic region, and a movement to merit aid programs in
10 states during the past decade. Investigation of the merit aid result reveals that
the increasing popularity of non-means–tested aid has not been altruistically
motivated. These targeted programs are used to redistribute income to well-off
families and to avoid providing broad-based institutional support that would
benefit economically disadvantaged members of the populace. A hypothesis
advanced by current president of California State University, Long Beach; F.
King Alexander (2001), that federal aid programs provide perverse incentives
for higher education funding in that low tax effort states are rewarded with more

federal aid than high tax effort states, is supported by these results as well. As more households in a state become eligible to receive a federal Pell grant, states respond by moving aid away from institutions and toward students. In fact, these perverse incentives may account for some of the unexplained decline in the HESHARE described previously. The more support a state provides for its public institutions, and hence the lower the tuition rates, the less federal aid its students will be eligible to receive. This is consistent with the result in Rizzo and Ehrenberg (2004), that increases in federal Pell grant generosity and state need-based grant aid awards result in increases in in-state tuition levels at flag-ship public universities.

Several additional results deserve attention. Similar to other studies, I found that court-mandated K12 equalization schemes have resulted in substantial increases in K12 spending within states. Unlike these studies, however, I found that nearly one-third of the total spending increase has come at the expense of public higher education, representing $280 per full-time public college student in an average-size state. Also, ethnic heterogeneity across age cohorts results in state funding being allocated to the schooling cohorts that look most similar to the non-school–age population in a state.

The apparent race to the bottom in state funding for public higher education has serious implications for academic quality at our public colleges and universities, as well as for the productivity and security of our nation in the future. No institution is immune from the resource squeeze. The University of Michigan is being forced to make tradeoffs just like Wichita State University and Tompkins-Cortland Community College. The decisions each face are different (e.g., Michigan might decide between increasing the size of its introductory classes or hiring more part-time faculty; Wichita State might decide between keeping faculty salaries constant while accommodating increased enrollments or increasing faculty salaries but turn-ing deserving students away), but the causes are the same. In nearly all 50 states, the share of state tax dollars ultimately finding its way to public higher education institutions has fallen by well over 25 percent in the last 30 years, and schools and states are rapidly spiraling toward the private high-tuition equilibrium.

With the Higher Education Act up for reauthorization in 2006, much attention will be paid to the high sticker prices of colleges and universities or the unpleasant outcomes of institutional decisions forced by the aforementioned tradeoffs.[39] What will largely be ignored are the questions of how we got here and who ultimately bears the burden of the withdrawal of state funding. Like a fish tank that leaks a drop of water per week, the problem will go largely unnoticed until after several years someone complains that their fish are near death because there's so little room to swim. There's only so many roofs that higher education institutions can delay maintaining; they cannot continue to seek temporary financial equilibrium by marginalizing the future.[40]

A continued decline in state support for public institutions will result in innu-merable negative consequences for the students who attend, or hope to attend, them in the future. Among the consequences are continued tuition increases,[41] movement away from full-time tenure-track faculty toward part-time faculty and graduate student instructors, increases in student-faculty ratios, an erosion of liberal arts and humanities programs in favor of more practical and professional programs, increases in time to degree and dropout rates, a decline in public service expenditures, an increase in loan burden on students attending college, a limitation of program offerings, and a multitude of additional factors. Further, future budget cutbacks are likely to have a disproportionate negative impact on community colleges, which rely on a larger share of their operating budget from state sources and where a larger share of minority and first-time college attendees are enrolled. These changes may not be dramatic in any single year, but over time, the resource gap and faculty quality gap between the public and private institutions will be so large as to render a private education and a public education two entirely different products.[42]

A recent issue of the *Chronicle of Higher Education* asked a variety of higher education experts how they would deal with the tuition crisis facing our institutions, particularly public institutions.[43] Although this discussion is laudable, one can't help but feel uneasy with the topic's implicit acceptance that policies of broad state support and low tuition are historical relics. There are steps that states and institutions can take, however, to ensure that this does not happen. It would be comforting to see comparative rates of return analyses on different state spending items to justify why higher education is falling out of favor, although those statistics are notoriously difficult to calculate. Among the other steps are an increased participation in tuition reciprocity programs and cross-institutional cooperation.[44] Institutions can attempt to secure multiyear budget appropriations from legislatures to stop the destructive pattern of mid-year budget cuts. State tax codes can be revised and our public institutions can do a better job of marketing the "local public good" aspect of their product. Although programs such as funding formulas may be popular ways to secure financing for institutions, the determination of the formulas themselves are subject to political debate and may also result in a suboptimal distribution of student types within institutions as a result of institutional attempts to take advantage of these formulas.

Funding for education is a (less than) zero sum game played out in statehouses across the nation. States decide how much to spend on education, then decide how much to allocate to each sector, and for years have acted as if K12 funding is more sacred than higher educational institutional spending. For instance, each state maintains a "rainy day fund" that is supposed to smooth the effects of budget shocks. In 2001, New York met the needs for a 5 percent K12 budget increase and maintained the current levels of its student aid program (Tuition Assistance Program) out of this fund, but none of it was tapped for SUNY and CUNY institutional needs. In the 2003–2004 fiscal year, 24 of 44 states surveyed by the State Higher Education Executive Officers indicated that they expected to receive decreases in the level of state spending for public higher education, and in the 18 states that expected increases, in real per student terms funding is expected to remain flat. Demographic changes and the higher profile of K12 education also do not bode well for public higher education's future. A dramatic shift in public and legislative priority is required to ensure that future generations of students have access to public higher education that is of comparable quality to what is available today. An even larger commitment will be required to make this endeavor affordable and to keep our public institutions from falling further behind their private counterparts.

NOTES

1. Goldin and Katz (1999) present an excellent analysis of the shaping of American public higher education during the time that it is commonly believed that America took its place on the world stage, 1890–1940.

2. The sharp increase in reported expenditures may be due to differences in accounting and institutional reporting beginning with the 1997 academic year. Data before this year are reported in a different source than later data. Even if in the unlikely event that actual expenditure levels were flat since 1997, however, overall growth for the period would have been approximately 70 percent.

3. A large body of literature has been devoted to this phenomenon. I will not examine the reasons for expenditure growth in any detail in this chapter. This growth may be a reflection of improvements in quality, but it is also likely a result from the increasingly fierce competitive environment institutions are operating in. For a detailed discussion on this matter, see Ehrenberg (2000).

4. I analyze expenditures made from state general fund budgets because this is the fund where legislatures and governors have the most appropriative discretion. This is the predominant fund for financing a state's operations. Revenues coming into the general fund derive from a variety of broad-based state taxes. The trends that I present later look similar if one were to analyze total state expenditures as well.

5. Allow me to begin the discussion of the "fall" with 1977. The rise in the early 1970s can be attributed to a number of factors. Chief among them are states preparing for the children of the baby boomers attending college and leaving the K12 sector, accommodation of the enrollment surges as a result of the Vietnam War draft deferments, and a residual effect of the space and arms race that culminated in the moon landing in 1969.

6. By the end of FY2001, 13 states had instituted merit-based aid programs similar to Georgia's HOPE program (Krueger 2001). These states are Alaska, Arkansas, Florida, Georgia, Kentucky, Louisiana, Maryland, Michigan, Mississippi, Nevada, New Mexico, South Carolina, and West Virginia. Some states have had small merit programs for more than 30 years, which were targeted to specific ethnic groups or students with specific skills, but the popularity of broad-based programs and their growth did not begin until Georgia's HOPE program exploded on the scene in 1993. The concurrent growth in need-based aid awards may signal that a paradigmatic shift away from broad-based in-kind aid policies is underway.

7. It is believed that areas with a more highly educated workforce have higher wage levels than other areas—and with more highly educated people earning more and therefore paying higher taxes (Moretti 2004). It is also believed that more highly talented students

are most likely to attend colleges outside of the home state and do not return on graduating (Hoxby 1997).

8. It must be emphasized that the national averages presented in Figures 1.2 through 1.4 are not driven by one particular state or group of states. Appendix Figure 1.1 combines the information in these figures to present, for each state, the share of general fund expenditures directly allocated to public higher education institutions from 1977–2001. The steady declines are remarkably similar across all states. Even in states where there had been some recovery during the mid-1990s (California, Louisiana, Florida, Massachusetts), the budget shares never returned anywhere near their initial levels, and they began to fall again as the economy declined in 2001. The decline in higher education's share of state public education budgets represents more than 16 percent of the cost of educating a FTE student. In fact, the amount this loss represents would have been enough to cover 83 percent of the cost of instate tuition at a public four-year institution in 2001!

9. A complete description of the data can be found in Rizzo (2004).

10. Baseline models assume that the random errors are uncorrelated across each equation and uncorrelated over time. Models are then estimating controlling for auto-correlated error terms and/or with the error terms correlated across equations. Models are also estimated assuming that that error variances are both independent of, and dependent on, the explanatory variables in the model. See Rizzo (2004).

11. As the "amount" of higher education services captured by voters is not observable, but expenditures are, it may be necessary to model the production side of the market for public higher education services; however, it would be extremely difficult to formulate a model of institutional supply. State higher education is not likely to be produced efficiently (meaning that individual schools deliver services at minimum cost). Measuring higher education outputs is also notoriously difficult. Quality is an important output, but how can one effectively measure it? If a state focused on measured tangible outputs, universities might focus on minimizing quality and maximizing some tangible output, but this is at odds standard models of prestige maximization. So, what I do here should be viewed as a partial equilibrium analysis.

12. For example, impacts of K12 enrollment changes on HESHARE changes would be net of any national trends in K12 enrollments. It is agreed that rising K12 enrollments were a key factor in the growth of state and local spending in the late 1950s and 1960s, as well as in the 1990s. Allowing for year effects removes such systematic changes in the size of the school-age population from affecting the results in this analysis.

13. Models were also estimated using a variety of definitions for most of the independent variables and produced qualitatively similar results. For example, in models where the age distribution is entered continuously, I find that the EDSHARE decreases as the median age of the state increases, ceteris paribus.

14. Although some state-level variables do not exhibit great variation year over year, during t he entire 30-year period of the sample there is considerable variation. Regression results using three-year moving averages or five-year intervals of data are qualitatively similar to the results reported later. Further, a cursory analysis of the outcome data indicates that the largest changes have occurred for the HESHARES. If one were to rank the states according to the budget share measures, one would observe that the rank order correlation on each outcome is not constant over time for the HESHARE, and is much more constant for the EDSHARE and INSHARE. For example, the correlation of state rankings on EDSHARE between 1977 and 2001 is 0.67; the correlation of state rankings on HESHARE is 0.36,

indicating that changes at the macro-economic level are not solely responsible for changes in the HESHARE, but rather state specific factors are important.

15. Real income increased by approximately $6,000 over the entire period; the ratio of income of the 75th percentile to the 25th percentile increased by 0.2 points since 1977.

16. http://www.census.gov/population/projections/nation/summary/np-t3-f.pdf. This may also partially be picking up the impacts of the increasing Medicaid burden within states, as older adults make up a large fraction of beneficiaries.

17. To highlight, an increase in median income in an average state of $1,000 would result in higher education reaping 17 percent of the education budget as opposed to 16.4 percent. However, each $1,000 increase in median income also results in a decline in the EDSHARE to 34.9 percent from 36.1 percent in 2001. Therefore higher education's share of the overall budget remains roughly constant at 5.9 percent.

18. However, Lee, Ram, and Smith (1999), Cardak (1999), Hight and Pollock (1973), and Biggs and Dutta (1999) present evidence that the system of higher education finance can also be useful to redistribute income toward the economically less advantaged.

19. A majority of the wealthy older adults is concentrated in home equity, from which property taxes are assessed to finance local schools. Further, as income levels are smaller, they pay fewer (or no) income taxes and are often granted discounts on state sales taxes that might be used to finance higher education appropriations.

20. However, wages and other factor prices may fall when out-migration increases, so lower higher education expenditures may not necessarily indicate that lower levels of service are being provided in the face of out-migration patterns.

21. In other words (ignoring the fact that I am estimating changes for a moment), higher education funding decreases more in states with more heterogeneous racial compositions across different school-age cohorts. The more white the non-school–age population, the more precipitous this decline will be. Only a couple of researchers have looked into this variable. Poterba (1997) found that different racial mix affects funding for K12 education at the state level, but Ladd and Murray (2001) did not find evidence at the local level.

22. The total loss is near $60 million according to 2001 figures for the average state. In the absence of the reforms, higher education in an average state received 16.4 percent of the education budget, which received 36.1 percent of the overall budget, or about 5.9 percent of the overall budget. After the reform, higher education receives only 15.2 percent of the education budget, which received 37.2 percent of the overall budget, or about 5.6 percent. The general fund budget in an average state in 2001 was approximately $20 billion.

23. In results not reported in Table 3.2, it appears as though the effect of the racial heterogeneity is felt most acutely by states whose populations are aging fastest. When an interaction between the share of the population 65 years and older with the ethnic heterogeneity variable is included in this model, the first-order impact of the ethnic heterogeneity disappears, but I find that support for institutions by older adults falls as the college-age population becomes more nonwhite.

24. For the sake of brevity, I do not present the estimates from intermediate regressions that introduced the second-order interactions independently. In each of these regressions, the second-order interactions were each statistically significant and of the expected sign. MERIT × COLRACERATIO yielded positive and statistically significant results, indicating that states that move to merit aid tend to favor student aid less when the college-age population is increasingly nonwhite and providing support for the notion that the rising importance of merit aid programs has been largely a political scheme to attract middle and upper class white votes and dollars. MERIT × INC yields statistically

significant negative results, which can be interpreted as when income increases in the merit aid states, support for student aid is more dramatic than when income increases in the nonmerit aid states. INC × COLRACERATIO yields a statistically significant negative result, indicating that when income increases in states with relatively more nonwhite college-age population, broad-based institutional support falls more than when a state is less nonwhite in its college-age population.

25. It has also been put forth that budgetary decisions may move away from incremental budgeting in scarce times because of the increased competition for resources when resources are limited. In these cases, other practices may be adopted. ("The Profession of Budgeting." *Public Budgeting and Finance* v10, n2 (Summer 1990): 102–06 Standard No: ISSN: 0275–1100.)

26. To be consistent with the estimates in Tables 1.3 and 1.4, I want to preserve my "fixed effects assumption" that the unobserved state-specific effects are correlated with the observed explanatory variables. Until recently, dynamic panel estimation techniques were unable to accommodate this assumption. They required an explicit specification of the distribution of ci, and also required that its conditional expectation (on X) to be zero. Instrumental variables generalized methods of moments techniques have now been developed that take first differences and use lagged differences or lagged levels of the dependent variables as instruments for the endogenous lagged dependent variable. See Greene (2000, pp. 582–584) and Wooldridge (2002, pp. 412 and 493–495) for more detailed discussions. Complete results and discussion can be found in Rizzo (2004). Baseline results are largely unaffected by this specification change.

27. See Rizzo 2004 for complete results.

28. This result is invariant to the specific party that is in control (Rizzo 2004).

29. The share of gross state product generated from FIRE grew by 13 points between 1978 and 2001. The magnitude of the estimate could be retrieved from a regression including only the share of GSP from FIRE, and omitting all other GSP variables. I do not include this variable in the baseline results because of its high correlation with the median income variable and the share of schooling that occurs in the private sector. Therefore it is difficult to assess what this variable represents.

30. Although one might expect this variable to vary only in cross section, only 13 states did not change the number of assembly seats between 1977 and 2001, and only 10 experienced no changes in the number of assemblypersons per senator. Aside from capturing the impacts of self-interested assemblypersons, this variable may also reflect demographic factors, as changes in legislative representation and even in district lines are a function of changing population sizes and ethnic heterogeneity.

31. I plan to examine this issue in greater detail in the future. There is an obvious concern about timing and/or endogeneity. With regard to timing, I estimated equations using a 1 period lag of giving and find even stronger results—with the coefficient rising to –0.420 (0.104). I plan to reestimate this equation with an instrument for giving. See Ehrenberg and C. Smith (2003) for a description of the factors that should be included.

32. Complete write-up and additional results in Rizzo 2004.

33. It is also worth noting that the positive impact of SAT on INSHARES in Table 1.4 is due to the positive effect this variable had on institutions in the 1970s. There is a statistically significant and sizable negative effect in the most recent decade, indicating that as high school student quality increases, states are increasingly turning to student aid programs, likely in an attempt to keep these students from leaving the state.

34. Jeffrey Selingo, *Chronicle of Higher Education* (2001). Under Governor Romney's plan, the state's flagship public campus, the University of Massachusetts at Amherst, would be spun off "to become a premier research university." Making it independent from the system, the governor said, would allow the institution to increase tuition rates to be more in line with other public flagships so that it could "more successfully recruit out-of-state students and compete for top research faculty and grants."

35. The Bennett hypothesis was advanced by former Secretary of Education William Bennett and suggested that increases in federal student grant aid would be quickly captured by colleges and universities through rapid increases in tuition.

36. Durbin-Wu-Hausman tests indicate that *in changes* the one-period lead, the current period level, and one period lag are all endogenous in the HESHARE equation. Tests also indicate that the two-period lead and two-period lag are not endogenous. The test is executed by regressing the suspected endogenous variable on all other exogenous variables and computing the residuals from this regression. The test for endogeneity is simply a t-test on the coefficient of this residual when it is included in the original outcome equation along with the suspected endogenous variable.

37. These variables include combinations of enrollments, share of enrollments in two-year programs, share of enrollments in graduate programs, regional nonresident tuition rates, average faculty salaries (or a proxy for this), share of enrollments in private higher education, share of doctoral degrees awarded in sciences, research dollars per faculty in the state, and some specifications with regard to further lags of tuition.

38. For instance, some schools will increase tuition in a year in anticipation of *future* appropriations cuts, making it difficult to disentangle the impacts of tuition and state support on each other.

39. The HEA was originally set to expire on December 31, 2005, but President George W. Bush extended the Act to last until March 31, 2006. The reauthorization bill will be debated and amended in the intervening period.

40. See Rizzo (2004) for detailed analysis of policy implications and recommendations for future research.

41. Although high tuition, high need-based aid strategies are actually quite progressive, the sticker shock created by the high sticker prices, especially at two-year colleges, may scare those away who are at the margin of college attendance. The College Board estimates that the largest public high school class on record will graduate in 2008, and that a majority of these students will come from minority populations and those who would be the first generation to attend college; so the sticker shock is of considerable concern.

42. As Brewer, Eide, and Ehrenberg (1999) have shown, there is already a distinct advantage to attending an elite private college.

43. *Chronicle of Higher Education*, September 19, 2003 (Volume 50, Issue 4).

44. See www.ilr.cornell.edu/CHERI and click on "surveys" for a description of these reciprocity programs.

CHAPTER 2

Do Tenured and Tenure-Track Faculty Matter?

Ronald G. Ehrenberg and Liang Zhang

During the last two decades, there has been a significant growth in the share of faculty members in American colleges and universities who are employed in part-time or full-time non-tenure–track positions (Anderson 2002; Baldwin and Chronister 2001; Conley, Leslie, and Zimbler 2002; Ehrenberg 2004; Ehrenberg and Zhang 2004). This substitution of *contingent* faculty for tenure and tenure-track faculty is at least partially due to the growing financial pressures faced by public and private higher education institutions, coupled with the lower cost of non-tenure–track faculty members (Ehrenberg and Zhang 2004).

Much attention has been directed to the impact of this growing substitution on the job markets for new PhDs and the attractiveness of doctoral study to American college graduates.[1] The growing use of contingent faculty, coupled with the lower salaries and benefits that they receive, has also led to a growing movement to have contingent faculty covered by collective bargaining agreements.[2] Somewhat surprisingly, however, few studies have addressed whether the increased substitution of part-time and full-time non-tenure–track faculty for tenure-track faculty, on balance, has adverse affects on undergraduate students, such as less learning, longer times-to-degree, lower graduation rates, or lower propensities of students to go on to postgraduate study.[3] Analyses of such issues are essential if public institutions want to make the case to legislatures and governors and private institutions want to make the case to their trustees that improved funding that would permit increased usage of full-time tenure and tenure-track faculty members would enhance student outcomes. Absent such evidence, growing financial pressures faced by institutions will likely lead to a continuation of the increasing use of contingent faculty members.

Ours is the first study to address whether increased usage of part-time and full-time non-tenure–track faculty adversely influences the graduation rates of students enrolled in four- and two-year American colleges and universities. We use panel data for a large sample of institutions over 15 years to analyze these questions. The data come from *The College Entrance Examination Board's Annual Survey of College Standard Research Compilation* data file (henceforth *College Board data*), the *IPEDS Faculty Salary Survey*, and other Department of Education sources. After the first section briefly describes the data and the changes in graduation rates and faculty shares that occurred during the sample period, the second section presents our analytical framework and our empirical results findings for graduation rates from four-year institutions. The final section briefly discusses some extensions of our analyses and our findings for two-year colleges and is followed by concluding comments.

THE DATA

Each year the *College Board data* contains information on the characteristics of entering students at each institution, the characteristics of the institution, and the graduation rate of a cohort of undergraduate students who entered the institution at an earlier date. Our econometric analyses use data from the 1986–1987 through the 2000–2001 academic years.[4]

The *College Board data* provides us with information on the size of each entering class, the proportion of underrepresented minority students in the class, the proportion of out-of-state students in the class, the average age of entering first-year students, the 25th and 75th percentile SAT math and verbal scores of first-year students, and total enrollment at the institution. These data also permit us to compute information on the percentage of faculty at each institution that is part-time. Information on the percentage of full-time faculty at each institution that are tenured or on tenure tracks is available each year from the *IPEDS Faculty Salary Survey*. Data on the number of undergraduate students who receive Pell grants and the average Pell grant per recipient at each institution each year are obtained from the office that administers the federal Pell Grant Program within the U.S. Department of Education.

The *College Board data* provides information on graduation rates for full-time first-year students who entered each institution at an earlier date. The 1986–1987 and 1987–1988 *College Board data* contained information on the four-year graduation rate for students who entered college four years earlier. The 1988–1989 to 1997–1998 data contained information on the five-year graduation rates for students who entered college five years before each of these surveys. Finally, from 1998–1999 forward, the *College Board data* reports information on the six-year graduation rates for students who entered college six years before each survey date.

Table 2.1 presents information on how graduation rates, the percentages of faculty that are full-time, and the percentages of full-time faculty that have tenure or are on tenure tracks changed during the sample period.[5] Although average graduation rates increase when the period over which the rates are measured increase first from four to five and then from five to six years, the five-year graduation rate clearly trended downward during the 1988 to 1997 period.[6] The percentage of faculty that are full-time at these institutions also declined during the period by about five percentage points, and the percentage of full-time faculty that are tenured or on tenure-tracks declined by about 2.5 percentage points during the nine years that data are available for this variable.[7]

Table 2.1
BA Graduation Rate, Percentage of Full-Time Faculty, and Percentage of Full-Time Faculty on Tenured and Tenure-Track Lines

Year	BA Graduation Rate	Percentages of Faculty that are Full-Time	Percentages of Full-Time Faculty on Tenured or Tenure-Track Lines
1986 (4)	46.51	73.45	—
1987 (4)	45.01	72.88	—
1988 (5)	55.86	72.61	—
1989 (5)	54.50	72.11	87.62
1990 (5)	52.88	71.26	86.72
1991 (5)	51.49	71.69	86.94
1992 (5)	50.57	72.37	86.70
1993 (5)	50.27	72.10	86.57
1994 (5)	49.91	71.60	86.25
1995 (5)	49.59	70.87	86.34
1996 (5)	49.72	70.26	85.90
1997 (5)	48.60	70.21	85.21
1998 (6)	53.09	70.14	—
1999 (6)	52.66	69.46	—
2000 (6)	53.21	68.17	—

(x) graduation rate is the x year graduation rate for full-time first-year students who first enrolled at the institution x years earlier.

In estimating the impacts of the share of part-time faculty and the share of full-time faculty that are not on tenure tracks on graduation rates, it is important to "match up" the share variables with the correct entering cohort variables. We assume that the relevant share variables are those during the first four years that an individual is enrolled in college. So, for example, the six-year graduation rates reported in the 2000–2001 *College Board data* are for students who first enrolled as freshman in the fall of 1994. Hence we compute the relevant part-time faculty and non-tenure–track faculty shares that this cohort of students experienced by averaging the values that their institutions reported in the 1994, 1995, 1996, and 1997 *College Board data* files. Similarly, the relevant entering characteristics of these students (test scores, out-of-state status, racial/ethnic status, and age at entry) come from the 1994 *College Board data* file for this group. Because of the need to "match up" data from various surveys, institutional graduation rate data used in our econometric analyses come from the 1991–1992 to 2000–2001 *College Board data*, and earlier data are used only to provide explanatory variables.

ECONOMETRIC RESULTS

Our analytical approach is to use our panel data to estimate models in which the five-year (or six-year) graduation rate of full-time students who entered institution i in year t (G_{it}) is specified to be a function of characteristics of the students and of the institution (X_{it}), the percentage of faculty that are part-time at the institution averaged over the first four years that the students were enrolled at the institution (P_{it}), the percentage of full-time faculty that are employed in tenure-track positions at the institution averaged over the first four years that the students were enrolled at the institution (F_{it}), institutional fixed effects (n_i), year fixed effects (u_t), and a random error term (e_{it}),

$$G_{it} = a_0 + a_1 X_{it} + a_2 P_{it} + a_3 F_{it} + n_i + u_t + e_{it}, \tag{2.1}$$

where the a_k are the parameters to be estimated.

The characteristics of the students included in the model are the average proportion of undergraduate students receiving Pell grants at the institution during the first four years after the students enrolled and the average Pell grant per recipient (to control for the fraction of students from lower income families at the institution), the share of underrepresented minority students in the entering class, the share of in-state students in the entering class, the average age of entering students, and the averages of the 25th and 75th percentile mathematics and verbal SAT scores of the entering class. Institutional level characteristics included in the model are the average number of faculty at the institution during the four years after the freshman enroll at the institution and the full-time equivalent number of freshman at the institution. The graduation rate variable represents a five-year graduation rate for most of the sample years, but a six-year graduation rate for the last few years. This difference is controlled for in the estimation by the inclusion of the year dichotomous variables, which also capture the effect of other time-specific omitted variables.[8]

Table 2.2 reports our estimates of this model for our sample as a whole and for subsamples of public, private, doctoral, masters, and liberal arts institutions. Turning first to the control variables, entering freshman students with higher mathematics SAT scores (and in some specification higher verbal SAT scores) have higher graduation rates, other factors being held constant. Increases in the share of undergraduate students receiving Pell grants are associated, other factors being held constant, with lower graduation rates; and in some specifications, the higher the average Pell grant received by recipients (which suggests either lower family income and in some cases higher tuition levels), the lower the graduation rate. Both of these findings suggest that graduation rates of lower income students are lower than those of other students.[9] Neither the proportion of underrepresented minority students, the proportion of in-state students, nor the average age of entering freshman is related to the institution's graduation rate. Finally, increases in the total number of faculty at the institution, holding constant the number of full-time equivalent (FTE) freshman are associated with higher graduation rates.

Quite strikingly, our estimates suggest that, other factors held constant, increases in either the percentage of faculty that are part-time or the percentage of full-time faculty that are not on tenure tracks, is associated with a reduction in graduation rates. The magnitudes of these relationships are larger at public colleges and universities than at private academic institutions. Other factors held constant, a 10 percent increase in the percentage of faculty that is part-time at a public academic institution is associated with a 2.65 percent reduction in the institution's graduation rate. Similarly, a 10 percent increase in the percentage of full-time faculty that are not on tenure-track lines at a public college or university is associated with a 2.22 percent reduction in the institution's graduation rate. Moreover, the estimates in the last three columns of the table suggest that the magnitude of these effects is greatest at master's level institutions.

Table 2.3 provides estimates of the coefficients of the percentage of part-time faculty and percentage of full-time faculty employed in non-tenure–track positions obtained from specifications that allow the effects of all variables to vary within both public and private higher education by institution type. The magnitudes of these effects are largest at the public masters' level institutions. Other factors held constant, a 10 percent increase in the percentage of part-time faculty is associated with a reduction in the graduation rate of 3 percent, whereas an increase in the proportion of full-time faculty not on tenure-track lines is associated with a reduction in the graduation rate of 4.4 percent at these institutions.[10] For each institutional type, increased usage of these types of faculty has a larger

Table 2.2
Panel Data Estimates of Graduation Rate Equations* (t statistics)

	All	Public	Private	Doctoral	Master	Liberal Arts
Percentage of part-time faculty	-0.1397 (-7.73)	-0.2651 (-7.40)	-0.0711 (-3.34)	-0.0937 (-2.56)	-0.1829 (-5.53)	-0.0868 (-2.51)
Percentage of full-time faculty that are not on tenure-track lines	-0.0895 (-4.76)	-0.2228 (-3.91)	-0.0778 (-4.24)	-0.1134 (-2.38)	-0.1154 (-3.62)	-0.0387 (-1.43)
Average Pell grant per recipient	-0.0063 (-3.37)	-0.0018 (-0.48)	-0.0005 (-0.24)	-0.0123 (-2.82)	-0.0008 (-0.25)	0.0035 (1.18)
Proportion of Pell grant recipients	-0.0833 (-3.86)	-0.3057 (-4.19)	-0.1025 (-4.90)	-0.2104 (-2.81)	-0.0013 (-0.04)	-0.1218 (-3.93)
Number of faculty	0.0021 (3.25)	0.0054 (5.55)	0.0033 (3.29)	0.0017 (1.95)	0.0001 (0.03)	0.0604 (4.98)
Full-time equivalent enrollment of entering freshmen	0.012 (0.91)	0.0241 (1.43)	-0.0321 (-0.86)	0.0241 (1.49)	-0.0617 (-1.69)	0.1381 (1.26)
Proportion of minority students	-0.0224 (-0.85)	0.1039 (1.90)	-0.0247 (-0.91)	0.0521 (0.84)	-0.0279 (-0.71)	-0.0907 (-1.75)
Proportion of in-state students	-0.0077 (-0.52)	-0.0001 (0.00)	-0.0182 (-1.04)	0.0325 (0.96)	-0.0059 (-0.26)	0.0184 (0.66)
Average age of entering freshmen	0.3206 (1.87)	0.1541 (0.50)	0.0184 (0.09)	0.7114 (1.72)	0.4199 (1.58)	-0.256 (-0.99)

Average of 25th and 75th percentile math SAT scores of entering students	0.0372 (5.70)	0.0414 (3.03)	0.0431 (6.00)	0.0339 (2.40)	0.0335 (3.07)	0.0368 (3.50)
Average of 25th and 75th percentile verbal SAT scores of entering students	0.0191 (2.84)	0.0163 (1.13)	0.0145 (1.98)	0.032 (2.18)	0.0051 (0.47)	0.0125 (1.19)
# observation (# institution)	4966(734)	1305(207)	3661(527)	1052(152)	1716(261)	2198(321)
R-squared	0.9271	0.9194	0.9039	0.9468	0.9104	0.9151

* Also included in the models are institution and year dichotomous variables.

Table 2.3
Estimated Coefficients of Faculty Type Variables from Subsample Models* (t statistics)

	Public Institutions			Private Institutions		
	Doctoral	Master	Liberal Arts	Doctoral	Master	Liberal Arts
Percentage of part-time faculty	−0.1234 (−2.05)	−0.3032 (−5.34)	−0.5747 (−3.24)	−0.0554 (−1.49)	−0.145 (−3.40)	−0.0775 (−2.13)
Percentage of full-time faculty not on tenure-track lines	−0.1555 (−0.99)	−0.4358 (−4.63)	−0.043 (−0.54)	−0.0959 (−2.81)	−0.077 (−2.32)	−0.0191 (−0.63)
#observations (# institutions)	522(87)	514(91)	152(27)	425(64)	1026(165)	1827(292)

* Also included in each model are all of the control variables, and the year and institution dichotomous variables included in the models underlying table 2.

effect on students at public higher education institutions than on students at private higher education institutions.

EMPIRICAL EXTENSIONS

Several extensions of our analyses warrant brief discussion. First, one might hypothesize that increased reliance on part-time or full-time non-tenure–track faculty might have a differential impact on students from different places in the SAT distribution of American college students. In particular, it may be that students scoring low would be hurt the most by increased reliance on these types of faculty. However, when we tested whether this was true, by allowing the coefficients of these variables to vary with the SAT scores of entering students at the institution (dividing the institutions into three categories), we found no evidence of differential impacts by average SAT scores.

Second, one might be concerned that the increased usage of part-time and full-time non-tenure–track faculty at an academic institution is symptomatic of an institution that is undergoing financial stresses and that other things are happening simultaneously at the institution, such as reductions in course offerings. Hence, it may be these other things that are causing the reduction in graduation rates that we observe, not the changing nature of the faculty employed at the institution. However, when we reestimated our models, including general educational expenditures per FTE student as an additional explanatory variable, the estimated effects of changes in the faculty variables were similar to those that we reported in Tables 2.2 and 2.3.

Third, the data that institutions report to the *College Board* are not audited for accuracy by any outside group, and this leads to concerns about data accuracy. In particular, we found a number of cases in which the exact same values for the number of part-time faculty and the number of full-time faculty at an institution were submitted by an institution to the *College Board* for a number of consecutive years. Although this may reflect the relatively slow pace at which things change in academia or a constant faculty size at some small institutions, it also may reflect measurement or reporting errors. However, when we reestimated our models, leaving out institution/year observations in which the value of either of these variables was identical to the value reported by the institution in the previous year, on balance we obtained similar point estimates of these coefficients.[11]

Fourth, the *College Board data* also contain information for many institutions on the fraction of entering freshman that complete their first-year and the fraction of entering freshman that return for the second year. This permits us to estimate models similar to those presented in Table 2.2, save that the dependent variable becomes either the first-year completion rate or the return-for-second-year rate, and the faculty type variables and other variables now refer only to the students' freshman year. When we estimated such models, however, we found fewer statistically significant "faculty type" effects, and those that were significant were of much smaller magnitude than the comparable coefficients in the graduation rate equations. For example, we found evidence that increasing the percentage of part-time faculty by 10 percentage points would decrease the first-year completion rate by only 0.5 percentage points at public colleges and universities and would have no impact on the percentage of freshman students who returned for their second year, whereas increasing the percentage of full-time faculty that were not on tenure tracks by 10 percentage points had no impact on either outcome at public academic institutions.

Fifth, the *College Board data* contain information for some two-year colleges on three-year graduation rates and the percentage of entering freshman that return to the institutions for their second year of study. Tenure-track status data are not available for these institutions, but we found no evidence that increasing the percentage of part-time faculty members at two-year colleges adversely influences either of these outcomes.

Finally, one of the reasons often given for academic institutions, especially research universities, expanding their usage of part-time and full-time non-tenure–track faculty is that their tenured and tenure-track faculty are spending more time on research and less time teaching. So the costs to undergraduate students of the increased usage of more contingency faculty may be offset by a greater volume of research being produced by the regular faculty at the institution.

To test this proposition, we analyzed panel data generated between 1989 and 1999 and regressed the logarithm of an institution's externally funded real (in 1999 dollars) research and development expenditures per full-time tenured and tenure-track faculty member on the percentage of its full-time faculty that were not in tenure-track positions in the year, the percentage of its faculty that were part-time in the year, and institutional and year dichotomous variables. We found that an increase in the share of full-time faculty that were not on tenure-track lines has a small positive effect on the volume of external research and development expenditures per full-time tenured and tenure-track faculty member at the institution, with the effect being the largest at the doctoral institutions. So the use of more full-time non-tenure–track faculty is associated with increased external research volume for the full-time tenured and tenure-track faculty. These models also indicated that increases in the percentage of part-time faculty members at these institutions had no effect on the external research volume per full-time tenured and tenure-track faculty member at the institution.

CONCLUDING REMARKS

Ours is the first study using panel data on institutions that has provided evidence that the growing use of part-time and full-time non-tenure–track faculty adversely affects undergraduate students enrolled at four-year colleges and universities by reducing their five- and six-year graduation rates. For any given size, increase in the shares of either part-time or full-time non-tenure–track faculty, the magnitudes of these negative effects appear to be larger at public institutions than they are at private institutions and appear to be largest at the public masters' level (comprehensive institutions). When other factors are held constant, a 10 percent increase in the number of part-time faculty at a public masters' level institution is associated with about a 3 percent reduction in the graduation rate at the institution and a 10 percent increase in the number of full-time faculty that are not on tenure-track lines is associated with about a 4.4 percent reduction in the graduation rate at the institution.

We must caution that a study using institutional level data, such as ours, cannot conclusively prove that the decline in the graduation rates that we estimate occurs when, say, the proportion of part-time faculty increases results from increased drop-out rates for the students who actually study with part-time faculty. We may be capturing a much more complicated institutional relationship, and more research addressing this topic using individual level data would clearly be valuable.

In addition, the costs of reduced graduation rates must be balanced against the cost savings that accrue to the institutions from substituting less costly for more costly faculty members. For example, the average salary of full-time lecturers (most of whom are not on tenure tracks) at public master's institutions was $43,129, whereas the average cost of assistant professors (most of whom are on tenure tracks) at public master's institutions was $49,725 in 2003–2004.[12] Thus for every assistant professor who is replaced by a lecturer, an institution would save, on average, $6,596, or 13.2 percent. This calculation ignores that many assistant professors "mature" into more expensive associate and full professors and that lecturers often teach larger classes and more classes per semester than tenured and tenure-track faculty. Furthermore, to say that an institution's five- or six-year graduation rate is reduced when it employs more part-time or full-time non-tenure–track faculty does not tell us whether the reduction implies that the students never graduate from college or implies that their graduation is delayed one or more years. The evidence we report briefly on first-year drop-out rates suggest that the answer is probably a combination of both outcomes.

Cost savings from substituting part-time faculty, who often receive much less generous benefit packages as well as lower salaries, is likely to be much larger. However, Bettinger and Long (2004) have reported that having a part-time faculty member as an instructor, on average, leads to a decreased likelihood that a student will take subsequent classes in a subject, which surely is an additional cost to students. The impact of both types of substitution on a whole range of issues including faculty governance, student advising, and curriculum development and the evolution of the curriculum must all be addressed in a more complete cost/benefit analysis of these changes.

APPENDIX

Appendix Table 2.1
BA Graduation Rate, Percentage of Full-time Faculty, and Percentage
of Tenured and Tenure-track Faculty, Consistent Sample

Year	BA Graduation Rate	Percentages of Full-time Faculty	Percentages of Full-Time Faculty on Tenured and Tenured Track Lines
1986 (4)	53.41	73.21	—
1987 (4)	52.94	72.95	—
1988 (5)	61.39	72.44	—
1989 (5)	59.63	71.83	87.63
1990 (5)	59.32	71.02	87.33
1991 (5)	59.70	71.08	87.76
1992 (5)	60.25	71.72	87.58
1993 (5)	60.47	71.45	87.57
1994 (5)	60.83	71.04	87.25
1995 (5)	60.65	70.45	87.17
1996 (5)	61.35	70.01	86.66
1997 (5)	60.83	69.72	85.89
1998 (6)	62.71	69.31	—
1999 (6)	63.08	68.83	—
2000 (6)	63.04	66.99	—
# obs.	122	1022	1159

NOTES

1. Ehrenberg and Rizzo (2004).
2. See Smallwood (2003), for example.
3. Bolge (1995) used data from a single community college and found no evidence that students learn less in remedial mathematics classes when they are taught by part-time rather than tenure-track full-time faculty. Harrington and Schibik (2001) studied a single Midwestern comprehensive institution and found that the greater the proportion of part-time faculty members that students have during their first semester in college, the lower the probability that they return for their second semester. Bettinger and Long (2004) used a unique dataset of individual student-record data for Ohio public four-year

institutions to analyze the impact of a student's having an adjunct or graduate assistant instructor, as compared to a full-time faculty member (regardless of the faculty member's tenure-track status) on the probability that the student takes a subsequent class in the subject. After controlling for the process by which students are assigned to or select into classes with different types of instructors, they found that, on average, having a part-time faculty member or a graduate assistant instructor reduces the likelihood that students will take subsequent classes. However, the effects are small and differ by subject matter: although such instructors reduce the likelihood of taking subsequent classes in the humanities, they increase the likelihood in some of the technical and professional fields.

4. More recent *College Board* data are available, but our analyses end with 2000–2001 because of the lack of availability of more recent data from other sources that we needed for our analyses.

5. These numbers are averages each year for the institutions reporting a variable in that year. Sample sizes differ across the variables in each year because the variables come from three different sources. Appendix Table 2.1 presents the same information for smaller sets of institutions that reported data for each variable in all years and the results for these samples are quite similar.

6. Remember these are the graduation rates for the classes that entered between fall 1983 and fall 1992.

7. Changes in these variables varied across institutional types in our sample during the nine-year period. The average five-year graduation rate fell by 8.1 percent at public institutions, but only by 3.6 percent at private institutions and by 9.7 percent at masters institutions, but by smaller amounts at doctoral and bachelors institutions. Similarly, the average percentage of faculty that are full-time fell by 1.8 percent at public institutions, but by 3.6 percent at the private universities, and these changes were largest at the masters and bachelors institutions. Finally, the percentage of full-time faculty that were tenured or on tenure-tracks fell by about 1 percent at public institutions, but by 5.2 percent at private institutions, and these changes were the largest at the bachelor level institutions.

8. We are implicitly assuming here that the difference between the five- and six-year graduation rates at an institution do not vary across institutions.

9. As Stinebrickner and Stinebrickner (2003) have shown, lower graduation rates for students from lower-income families reflect factors other than the direct financial cost of attending college.

10. The larger part-time faculty coefficient for public liberal arts colleges is based on only 27 institutions.

11. At the suggestion of the referees, we conducted several other sensitivity analyses. The impact of SAT scores on graduation rates may depend more on the 25th percentile level than it does on the 75th percentile of a school's SAT distribution. So we reestimated the model in column 1 of Table 2.2, entering these two percentile levels separately. As expected, changes in the former did have larger effects on graduation rates than changes in the latter; however, this change in specification did not change our estimates of the effects of changes in faculty "types" on graduation rates. Another change was to restrict the sample to years for which we had five-year graduation rate data; when the model in column 1 of Table 2.2 was reestimated using this smaller sample, the coefficients of our faculty-type variables remained statistically significant, but declined slightly in magnitude. Finally, a referee was concerned that if the faculty-type variables at an institution always changed

in the same direction, we may be confounding the effects of changes in faculty type with changes in other omitted variables that are moving in a trend. To test for this possibility, we restricted our sample to institutions in which the faculty-type variables both increased and decreased during the period (remember that we are using four-year averages for these variables) and again reestimated the model. When we did this, we obtained faculty-type coefficients that were similar to those reported in column 1.

12. Ehrenberg (2004), survey report Table 2.4.

CHAPTER 3

The Increasing Use of Adjunct Instructors at Public Institutions: Are We Hurting Students?

Eric P. Bettinger and Bridget Terry Long

djuncts, defined as part-time instructors, are becoming an increasing proportion of college faculties. From 1987 to 1999, the percentage of courses taught by adjuncts at four-year colleges increased by 30 percent. The trends were especially pronounced at public institutions, with public research universities experiencing a 50 percent increase and public doctoral universities increasing the use of adjunct instructors by 80 percent during the period (NCES 1997, 2001). Although some of these increases have been made to accommodate the growing number of students enrolling in higher education, college administrators at some institutions have preferred hiring adjuncts over traditional faculty members. Between 1993 and 1998, 40 percent of universities eliminated full-time faculty positions in favor of adjuncts (NCES 2001).

The trend in adjunct usage is driven by many factors. In our previous work (Bettinger and Long 2004, 2005), we documented many of these factors. For example, adjuncts are as much as 80 percent less expensive than full-time faculty (CUPA-HR 2001). This cost savings is even greater considering that adjuncts often do not receive employment benefits (NCES 2001). Also, mandatory retirement was eliminated in 1994; hence, the cost of granting tenure has increased (Ehrenberg 2002). This may have led universities to employ fewer tenure-track

The names are listed alphabetically, and the researchers share authorship equally. The authors thank the Ohio Board of Regents for their support. Rod Chu, Darrell Glenn, Robert Sheehan, and Andy Lechler provided invaluable help with the data. Erin Riley and Suzan Akin provided excellent research assistance. All opinions and mistakes are our own.

faculty members as non-tenured, temporary labor, adjunct instructors afford colleges cost savings and greater flexibility.

The increased use of adjuncts has been especially marked at public institutions, and cost is likely to have been an important driver. Public colleges and universities have experienced significant uncertainty in state appropriations and support in recent years as other government demands and economic trends have reduced the amount given to postsecondary institutions (Rizzo, 2004). Therefore these institutions have been especially motivated to find ways to cut instructional costs, and the increasing use of adjunct instructors may reflect this.

The increased use of adjuncts is not without critics. The National Institute of Education (1984) claimed that adjuncts cannot provide the same quality of education because many adjuncts do not have doctoral degrees or other terminal degrees. Furthermore, the Modern Language Association (MLA) has claimed that the increased usage of part-time faculty has led to a deterioration in university quality (MLA 2002). Several studies document the growing trend in adjunct teaching (Burgan, Weisbuch, and Lowry 1999; Balch 1999) and their employment conditions (Gappa 2000, NCES 2001), but education researchers have just begun to produce research relating the use of adjuncts to student outcomes.

Research has been slow to develop in this field primarily because of a lack of data linking students and their collegiate outcomes to instructors and their characteristics. National datasets such as Baccalaureate and Beyond and the National Education Longitudinal Study of 1988 document students' experiences and outcomes. Other datasets such as the National Study of Postsecondary Faculty document characteristics of universities' faculties. Without a way to link students and their instructors, researchers have had to focus on either case studies on particular institutions (e.g., Norris 1991) or comparisons of institution-level outcomes and institution-specific experiences with adjuncts (e.g., Ehrenberg and Zhang 2004). In recent years, however, state higher educational systems in Ohio, Florida, and elsewhere have begun to make system-wide data available to researchers. These data provide rich detail on students' experiences with adjuncts at the institutional level, as well as in specific classes and departments. We use administrative data from Ohio's four-year colleges in this chapter. Ohio's data include college transcripts on students' course-taking behavior and performance, as well as the characteristics of the corresponding faculty member responsible for each course. In addition, the Ohio Board of Regents (OBR) provides information on each student's background, high school performance and academic interests, and college entrance examination scores.

In research to date, evidence suggests that adjuncts may have both positive and negative effects. For example, recent work by Ronald Ehrenberg and Liang Zhang (which is part of this conference) shows that universities with a greater reliance on adjuncts tend to have higher dropout rates. Bettinger and Long (2005) report that even among students with similar schedules, dropout rates increase as students take more courses from adjuncts. Meanwhile in other work (Bettinger and Long 2004), we find that students taking their introductory courses from adjuncts are more likely to take subsequent courses in the same subject compared with students who had full-time faculty members. This is especially true in professional disciplines such as engineering and education, suggesting that adjuncts may help foster student interest in some subjects.

Of course, analyzing the impact of adjunct instructors is not straightforward. Understanding their effects is much more difficult than just comparing the outcomes of students with and without adjuncts. As we show later, students who take courses from adjuncts differ systematically from students who do not have them, and so students may be actively trying to avoid or be assigned an adjunct instructor. For example, students in classes with adjuncts tend to have lower ACT scores and are less likely to denote interest in the subject as a potential major. This is true even within courses that offer multiple sections with different types of instructors. Also, certain departments rely more heavily on adjuncts, and as students choose their schedules, some students may be more likely to have an adjunct instructor because of interests in a particular department. There may be other unobservable characteristics that determine who takes adjuncts and who does not, and if these characteristics are also related to educational outcomes (such as student ability), then simple comparisons will be biased.

To overcome this possibility, we use an instrumental variable strategy. A good instrument should be correlated with the endogenous variable of interest—taking courses from adjuncts. It should also be uncorrelated with the student outcome of interest, which in this chapter is student persistence from the first to second year of school. Our specific instrument relies on variation in the department composition of faculties. As we observe in our data, when professors retire, take a leave of absence, or make some other commitment, teaching loads are affected. Consequently, from year to year, there is variation in the number of full-time faculty who are available to teach courses. This variation is likely exogenous to student outcomes, but as we show later, these movements in faculty are correlated with adjunct usage. When departments face unexpected fluctuations in faculty numbers, they often fill these temporary vacancies with adjuncts.

Similar to our other work (Bettinger and Long 2005), our basic results suggest that students who have more adjunct instructors during their first semester are less likely to persist into their second year. We also review the evidence from our earlier work, which suggested that adjuncts can be effective instructors in many disciplines. Students who take courses, particularly in professional fields, take more subsequent courses in the same department. Therefore, although the use of adjuncts leads to lower overall student persistence, adjunct instructors also encourage subsequent enrollments in a subject. Our results are consistent with the conclusions of Ehrenberg and Zhang: adjuncts may teach effectively in many fields, but they do not appear to help integrate first-year students into the university.

The next section reviews the literature relating student outcomes to teacher characteristics and previous research on the growing use of adjuncts. Then, we present a theoretical framework and discuss the data and empirical strategies. The last section summarizes and discusses the conclusions of the study.

LITERATURE REVIEW

Although little is known about how faculty characteristics affect student out-comes in higher education, the relationship between student outcomes and teacher quality has been a perennial theme in the K12 literature. There is a large litera-ture that traces how teacher experience, education, college performance, gender, and other characteristics correlate with student outcomes (e.g., Rockoff 2004, Ehrenberg and Brewer 1994, Hanushek 1986). The studies find, for example, that teacher quality positively affects students as does experience, completion of higher degrees (although not always estimated to have a positive effect), and teacher licensure. Researchers have also characterized how changes in educational policies affect teacher supply. For example, Hoxby (2002) measured what types of teacher characteristics districts value when they face strong competitive pressures. Figlio and Rueben (2001) used the test scores of education majors to gauge how tax limits affect the quality of new teachers. Each study is motivated by the assumption that the supply of different types of teachers affects student outcomes.

In terms of higher education, few studies explore the link between student outcomes and faculty characteristics. Many studies, however, track the increased reliance of colleges and universities on adjunct instructors. Several studies docu-ment the growing use of adjuncts. Foremost, David Leslie provides a wealth of information on this trend in a series of articles. In *The Growing Use of Part-Time Faculty* (1998a), Leslie used the 1993 National Survey of Postsecondary Faculty to quantify the increase. He found that 42 percent of teaching faculty members at that time were part-time. Moreover, there is a great deal of variation by institution type and discipline. Research universities were least likely to employ them; public, two-year faculties were 60 percent part-time. Other work provides further evi-dence of the growing use of adjuncts. Burgan, Weisbuch, and Lowry (1999) found an increase in the use of instructors on term contracts when analyzing a survey of non-tenure–track faculty. Similarly, Balch (1999) claimed that the increased use of part-time faculty is a trend that will continue to persist.

Other studies discuss trends at particular institutions. For example, Jackson (1999) documented the growth of temporary and part-time appointments at Maryland's public colleges from 1981 to 1998. Researchers have also examined the institutional impact of adjuncts at their particular institutions. For instance, Haeger (1998) discussed the problems and solutions associated with adjunct instructors at Towson University.

Although higher education researchers have been hampered by a lack of data in determining the impact of adjuncts on student outcomes, several have specu-lated about their likely effects. Leslie (1998b) noted that adjuncts could affect education quality because fewer have doctoral degrees. In addition to affecting instruction, Pisani and Stott (1998) argued that the use of adjuncts erodes the quality of student advising, and others suggest that part-time faculty affect the dis-tribution of other departmental tasks such as committee work. The MLA (2002), the National Institute of Education (1984), and the Education Commission of the

States (Palmer 1998) have all issued reports or policy statements that link the growing use of part-time professors and declines in educational quality. On the other hand, Leslie and Gappa (1995) argued that part-time faculty could help broaden academic programs by introducing real-world experiences into the classroom. Others have documented the employment conditions and dissatisfaction of adjuncts (Gappa 2000, Fulton 2000). Given the fact that many have expressed feelings of being treated as second-class citizens, Leslie and Gappa (1995) questioned how their treatment affects the quality of education that adjuncts are able to supply.

Three studies use new datasets to explore the impact of adjuncts. Ehrenberg and Ziang (2004) examined the effects of adjuncts on student dropout rates using institutional-level data from a national sample of four-year colleges. In their analysis, they related information on the proportion of incoming freshmen who persist into their second year to data on what proportion of classes are taught by adjuncts at each college. They found a negative relationship between persistence and adjunct usage—heavy reliance on adjuncts is correlated with higher dropout rates. One concern with this study that highlights the difficulty in estimating the effects of adjuncts is that schools with a higher proportion of adjuncts may also be more likely to have students on the margin of dropping out, and this could bias the results. For example, in the data we examined, students at nonselective institutions typically have poorer academic performance in high school and are more likely to have adjunct instructors than students at selective institutions. However, the results draw attention to the effects of adjuncts on student outcomes and provide some hint of the empirical difficulties inherent in estimating the impact of adjuncts.

In other work, we estimated the effects of adjuncts on student engagement in specific subjects and on persistence (Bettinger and Long 2004, 2005). Similar to the methodology used in this chapter, we used exogenous variation in the faculty available to teach in a given semester. This variation leads students to be more or less likely to take a particular course from an adjunct professor, depending on the semester that the student enrolls in the course. We link these initial enrollments to subsequent course-taking behavior, major choice, and persistence. Our findings suggest that adjuncts are effective in many fields in motivating students to take subsequent classes in the same subject. This is especially true in professional fields where adjuncts often have prior professional work experience, which they can share with students. Similarly we found that adjuncts can positively affect the likelihood that students major in a particular subject. Similar to this chapter, however, we found that adjuncts negatively affect student persistence into the second year.

Our prior work also looks at the effectiveness of graduate student instructors. We found that these instructors are often not as proficient as either full-time faculty or adjunct professors in encouraging students to enroll in subsequent courses. Other researchers have also looked at these issues at particular institutions. For example, Borjas (2000) analyzed the impact of foreign teaching assistants on economics students' performances at Harvard, and Norris (1991) also examined the effect of non-native English-speaking teaching assistants on students at the University of Wisconsin. These studies focus on small samples at selective institutions, but the results are similar to those found using our sample of the diverse set of public four-year colleges in Ohio.

THEORETICAL FRAMEWORK

In this section, we sketch two economic models to characterize the importance of knowing the effects of adjuncts on students. We also suggest reasons why students who take classes with adjuncts may differ systematically from other students.

The Demand for Adjuncts: Course-Taking Behavior

One way to model the effects of adjuncts is to look at how students choose courses. Presumably, students choose the course, schedule, and faculty member that maximizes utility (current leisure/work and future educational returns), and they can either have an adjunct or tenure-track instructor. The two types of instructors may differ in several possible ways. First, teaching ability and quality may differ by type of instructor. On the one hand, adjunct teachers are not as involved in research, so to the extent that research influences teaching quality, full-time faculty may be better teachers. On the other hand, adjuncts do not have research or service requirements and can therefore specialize in teaching.

Adjunct and full-time professors may also differ in their general knowledge. Because adjuncts are typically temporary, adjuncts often do not have the same stock of information about the university as full-time professors. For example, adjunct professors may not be as effective as full-time faculty in advising students or in arranging research opportunities that may prepare students for graduate-level education and integrate them into their undergraduate studies. In the extreme case, if adjunct faculty do not help to integrate students into the college as a whole, then one might expect students taking many courses with adjuncts to be disaffected and to withdraw. Moreover, adjuncts often have temporary contracts and may not be able to develop multiyear relationships with students. In some disciplines, however, adjuncts may provide more effective and practical knowledge to students. For example, students may prefer to take a class in management from the retired ex-CEO of a Fortune 500 company than a new, 26-year-old assistant professor.

The types of instructor students have for a given subject may also influence their choices. For example, students may choose their courses (and majors) based on their comparative advantage in a given subject (i.e., students choose to take classes and/or major in subjects in which they have a strong foundation of knowledge). If a student takes a course from a particular type of instructor and gains additional knowledge in a subject, then that could change the subject in which the student has a comparative advantage. This could be particularly important because of general education requirements that force students to take classes in multiple subjects. Exposure to different kinds of instructors in those required courses could change a student's comparative advantage to an unexpected subject. Likewise, if early exposure to a potential major results in little information being acquired, the student might change to another field. This might especially be the case if knowledge in one course affects students' success in subsequent courses. These patterns of encouraging new majors or losing intended majors could have serious implications for departmental enrollments and, at many places, institutional funding.

Finally, students' beliefs of the relative effectiveness of full-time versus adjunct instructors could impact their course selection. Regardless of the truth, beliefs about the relative quality of the different types of instructors along the dimensions described previously could prompt students to sort across classes and sections in nonrandom ways. If the students who exercise instructor choice based on beliefs differ from other students, the match of instructors to students will suffer from selection. To the degree that the student characteristics are also related to educational outcomes, comparisons of students with and without adjunct instructors will be biased. Our results highlight that students of higher ability appear to avoid adjunct instructors.

The Supply of Adjuncts and Specialization within Departments

We could also model the interaction between students and adjuncts from the supply-side. Assume universities and departments attempt to maximize student outcomes, faculty research, and other outputs while minimizing costs. In this model, the key tradeoff for university administrators is whether the benefits of adjuncts outweigh their costs. To highlight some of the issues, we assume momentarily that the university only produces teaching. In this case, the cost savings of adjuncts should be directly compared to the consequences of having them teach. If part-time and full-time faculty are perfect substitutes in terms of educational quality, then part-time faculty (i.e., adjuncts) can help reduce or maintain smaller class sizes without any loss of quality. If part-time and full-time faculty are imperfect substitutes, however, then the university suffers a cost. These costs may be the loss of prestige associated with a reduction in quality, an increase in student dropouts, and decreases in student enrollments or the number of student majors in a given department.

We can make similar comparisons in terms of student advising. If part-time faculty are not as effective advisors as full-time faculty, then an increased reliance on adjuncts may impose costs on the university. There may also be administrative costs to managing a faculty with more adjuncts. For instance, positions with adjunct instructors tend to suffer from frequent turnover. As a result, administrators have to continually locate, hire, and manage a changing workforce. Departments may be able to minimize costs by employing full-time faculty instead of adjuncts in places where the marginal cost of an adjunct is higher (e.g., attracting top students in honors sections of a course). Being able to quantify these costs can help administrators fully weigh the costs and benefits.

Once we include research products from a university, the cost-benefit analysis changes. If part-time and full-time faculty are complements, then part-time faculty might facilitate greater specialization and increased research productivity among the full-time faculty. Because departments enjoy a cost savings with adjunct faculty, they have surplus that can be reallocated to full-time faculty. This surplus could take the form of teaching buyouts, research funds, or other items that enhance research productivity. The result could be increased research productivity. As before, there may be substantial heterogeneity among departments in the optimal mix of part-time and full-time faculty.

Although most of the decisions on hiring adjuncts typically take place at the department or school level, the use of adjuncts also poses some interesting principal-agent problems within the hierarchy of the university. For example, university administrators (the principals) care about maximizing research and teaching productivity. These administrators may see adjunct teachers as a means to free up full-time faculty to do research while providing a dedicated teaching workforce.[1] Department chairs may also care about these objectives, but an additional concern is enrollment in their field. Enrollment patterns generally influence the allocation of funds across departments, and if adjuncts negatively affect student enrollment in a subject, then they could also influence resource allocation. As such, universities where the flow of resources does not track enrollments may encourage the hiring of adjuncts more than other universities. Moreover, beyond a threshold, adjuncts may reduce the research climate if they replace full-time faculty and are less engaged in discussions of academic research. The optimal use of adjuncts by department chairs, hence, depends on the net "cost" of adjuncts to the area. This framework suggests that knowing the effects of adjuncts on enrollment is important in assessing the costs of adjuncts.

EMPIRICAL STRATEGY AND ISSUES

The Data

This chapter focuses on full-time, traditional-age, first-time freshmen who entered public, four-year colleges in Ohio in fall 1998 or fall 1999. The data are provided by the respective institutions to the OBR and include information on student demographics, enrollment, credit hours completed, and grade point averages. Furthermore, OBR has linked the student records to ACT and SAT records. Most Ohio students take the ACT examination, and the ACT records include the highest test score of the student and the most recent responses to the ACT survey, which includes important student-reported information on high school preparation, performance, and academic interests.

The most important sources of information for this project are the students' transcripts, which detail every course in which a student enrolls.[2] From these data, we know the following information for each section of each course: topic covered, how many hours the course was worth, a faculty identifier for the faculty member chiefly responsible for the course, and whether the student passed or failed the course. We use the faculty identifier to link courses to the faculty members responsible for the course. For each faculty member, we observe whether the faculty is full-time or part-time, tenure or non-tenure–track, highest degree completed, age, race, gender, title, and to a limited extent salary. Following the national literature on adjunct teaching, we refer to adjuncts as part-time faculty.

One limitation of this data is that we do not observe how many years a particular faculty member has been affiliated with a particular university (although we can measure this from 1998 to 2003). We also cannot track movements of faculty to other universities or their professional activities at a particular university (including concurrent appointments at other universities). Another limitation is that the data include only students attending Ohio public universities. Students from Ohio who attend universities in other states, and students who attend private schools in Ohio are excluded from the sample.[3] Also, students who transfer from Ohio public institutions to institutions located in other states are indistinguishable in the data from students who drop out of college. This potential bias, however, should be very small, as the percentage of students who likely transferred to private institutions or those outside of the state make up a small fraction of the total number of observed dropouts. Furthermore, these data do a much better job at tracking students than previous work.

Table 3.1 shows characteristics of students in our sample. The first two columns show data for all full-time students who entered one of the 13 main university

Table 3.1
Full-time, Traditional-Age Students at Four-Year, Public Colleges in Ohio

	All Students	Students at Selective Four-years	Student at Nonselective Four-years
Female	.5471	.5513	.5413
White	.8508	.8701	.8235
Black	.0815	.0600	.1118
ACT Score (36 max)	22.41	23.24	21.25
	(4.22)	(4.03)	(4.22)
Observations	43,177	25,312	17,865

Notes: Standard deviations are shown in the parentheses. Sample is restricted to first-time, full-time freshmen who are of traditional age (18 to 20 years old) and entered a public, four-year college in Ohio during fall 1998 or fall 1999. Students must also have taken the ACT. Selective institutions are defined as "competitive" institutions by Barron's Educational Guides (1997) and include Bowling Green State University, Miami University, The Ohio State University, Ohio University, and Youngstown State University.

campuses in 1998 or 1999 for the first time. We restrict ourselves to traditional age students (i.e., students entering as freshmen between 18 and 20 years old). The first column shows characteristics of all Ohio students; the subsequent columns describe characteristics of students at the five selective colleges in Ohio and the other eight open admission four-year colleges, respectively.[4]

About 6 percent of students at selective colleges are African American, and 11.1 percent of students at nonselective colleges are African American. The average ACT score for students is about 23 (out of 36) at selective colleges and about 21 at nonselective colleges. Women make up about 55 percent of the student bodies at selective samples and 54 percent of the student body at nonselective colleges.

Table 3.2 shows the distribution of adjunct usage across universities in Ohio. To maintain the anonymity of institutions (as part of our agreement with the Ohio Board of Regents), we mask the names of the institutions. The average first-year student takes between 18 and 42 percent of courses during their first semester from adjuncts. There are five campuses where students take at least 30 percent of courses in their first semester from adjuncts. There is much more variation in students' exposures to graduate students. The average first-year student takes

Table 3.2
Percent of Enrollments with Adjunct and Graduate Students
Instructors during the First Semester of College

	Enrollments with Adjuncts in First Semester	Enrollments with Grad Students in First Semester
A	32.15	11.38
B	26.93	7.44
C	39.89	2.70
D	33.93	30.70
E	18.53	17.43
F	22.73	24.48
G	24.00	20.46
H	42.76	5.97
I	23.71	11.49
J	39.64	1.36
K	17.98	40.80

Notes: Rows identify four-year campuses in Ohio. The average is over all courses taken by any first-time freshmen in the fall semester of their first year. The sample includes students whose initial enrollment was in fall 1998 or fall 1999.

between 1 and 40 percent of courses during their first semester from graduate students.

Although there is much variation across campuses, students' experiences within campuses also exhibit much heterogeneity. Depending on their schedules, students may have substantially different experiences with adjuncts. We demonstrate this in Table 3.3 by showing how adjunct usage varies across departments in Ohio. The

Table 3.3
Use of Adjunct and Graduate Student Instructors by Institution and Subject

	Percent of Instructors That Are Adjuncts (part-time)		Percent of Instructors That Are Graduate Students	
	Selective Campuses	Nonselective Campuses	Selective Campuses	Nonselective Campuses
All Departments	16.81	21.76	19.92	3.44
Computer Science	41.37	50.65	20.71	1.62
Business	23.20	17.97	3.99	1.20
Education	20.09	36.38	32.22	5.63
Foreign Languages	17.97	26.09	26.93	4.73
Humanities	17.26	20.57	28.64	4.91
English	20.61	17.19	28.53	7.59
History	19.70	14.21	28.09	4.48
Journalism and Communication	17.24	19.47	8.93	0.69
Mathematics and Statistics	17.02	17.71	16.50	4.31
Engineering	15.68	5.314	4.25	0.43
Social Sciences	14.58	24.02	22.75	3.00
Economics	16.06	25.14	13.37	1.67
Political Science	5.92	10.63	22.09	2.54
Sociology	7.47	13.19	27.55	6.05
Sciences	8.10	8.58	8.83	3.93
Biological Sciences	5.67	6.55	10.26	3.97
Physical Sciences	13.15	3.67	11.57	2.94

Notes: Restricted to active faculty teaching between 1998 and 2003 at the undergraduate level. Selective institutions are defined as having competitive, nonopen admissions (Bowling Green State University, University of Cincinnati, Kent State University, Miami University, The Ohio State University, and Ohio University). The subgroups shown under the departments are not a complete list.

sample here includes all instructors teaching between 1998 and 2003. Column 1 shows the distribution within selective colleges; column 2 shows the distribution at nonselective colleges. Columns 3 and 4 show reliance on graduate students. As the table illustrates, there are differences both across departments and across selective and nonselective campuses. Generally, nonselective colleges rely more heavily on adjuncts. Also, there is substantial adjunct representation in computer science, business, and education. In these professional fields, adjuncts tend to have work experience. The biological and physical sciences, political science, and sociology departments employ fewer adjunct instructors. Hence, a student majoring in these fields will be less likely to encounter adjuncts. Professional fields such as business also have heavier reliance on adjuncts than other classes.

Empirical Strategies

We focus on the student as the level of observation. By doing so, we can measure the effect on outcomes such as persistence. The key dependent variable is the percentage of courses that students take from adjunct faculty during their first semester. We can relate this to outcomes such as dropout rates and likelihood of transferring to other schools. We will estimate equation 3.1 in these models:

$$y_i = \alpha + \beta Adjunct_i + \gamma X_i + C_j + P_{ij} + \varepsilon_i \qquad (3.1)$$

where $Adjunct_i$ is defined above and X_i includes controls for student i's background, high school performance, and academic interests before college. Also, we control for differences by institution, we include fixed effects for the campus of attendance denoted by Cj. The P_{ij} is a series of "portfolio" effects. These portfolio effects are a series of dummy variables that control for the unique mix of classes that a student takes. We motivate their inclusion and discuss them in greater depth later.

Student Selection Issues

As we show in Tables 3.2 and 3.3, there is substantial heterogeneity across institutions and across departments. There is also substantial heterogeneity in adjunct usage both within universities and within departments at specific universities. In fact, the distribution of students across courses taught by adjuncts and full-time faculty members may not be random at all. This may be due to a combination of supply and demand issues. For example, if adjuncts are more likely to teach in particular departments or during evenings or weekends, then certain types of students will be more likely to have them in courses (e.g., students with particular interests/abilities or who are more likely to take evening courses). Also, students may choose courses based on the type of instructor. As discussed previously, students might prefer full-time professors if they perceive that they produce greater knowledge or provide better advising than adjunct faculty, and the preferences for particular types of instructors may be stronger within a student's major. If students who take adjunct professors are systematically different from other students, then raw comparisons of students with adjuncts to students without adjuncts may be biased. Hence, OLS estimates of equation 3.1 may be biased.

Table 3.4 demonstrates the relationship between adjunct usage and student characteristics. The dependent variable is the proportion of credits taken from adjuncts during a student's first semester (either fall 1998 or fall 1999). We regress this against students' ACT scores, race, gender, state of residence, age, and campus fixed effects. As the coefficient on ACT demonstrates in the first column, students with higher ACT scores take a smaller proportion of their classes from adjuncts. The relationship is statistically significant over a 95 percent confidence

Table 3.4
Determinants of the Proportion of Classes from Adjuncts in First Semester

	(1)	(2)	(3) IV-First Stage
Act Composite	−0.004**	−0.003**	−.003***
	(0.00020)	(0.0002)	(.0002)
Black	−0.001	−0.003	−.003
	(0.004)	(0.004)	(.004)
Male	−0.0003	−0.003*	−.004**
	(0.001)	(0.002)	(.001)
In-state	0.010	0.011	.014
	(0.020)	(0.019)	(.018)
Age	0.001	0.002	.003**
	(0.001)	(0.002)	(.001)
Average Deviation from Steady-State Level of :			
Assistant Professors			−.220***
			(.0154)
Associate Professors			−.077***
			(.017)
Full Professors			−.179***
			(.011)
Portfolio Effects	No	Yes	Yes
Observations	40977	40977	40977
R-squared	0.491	0.591	0.440

Robust standard errors are in parentheses. Regressions also include controls for campus fixed effects.
* significant at 10%; ** significant at 5%; *** significant at 1%.

interval. In the case of race, gender, state of residence, and age, we do not find any statistically significant relationships.

In the second column of Table 3.4, we estimate the same regression except that we include "portfolio" effects. The portfolio effects are a series of dummy variables representing every possible schedule that students may have taken in their first semester. For example, one portfolio may include English, math, biology, and economics. Another portfolio may include English, physics, math, and a foreign language. By including portfolio effects, we are comparing students across campuses and years who took a similar selection of courses. As the coefficient on ACT score shows, even among students with similar schedules, students with higher ACT scores are less likely to take adjuncts during their first semester. In this second regression, it also appears that men take fewer courses from adjuncts, although this relationship is only marginally significant.

There are a number of reasons why ACT and the likelihood of having adjuncts may be negatively related. Some universities allow students with high ACT scores to register for classes sooner than other students. If these students prefer to take full-time faculty or are more likely to choose a known commodity (e.g., Professor Smith) over an unknown commodity (e.g., the generic term *staff* listed in the course catalogue), then one would expect a negative relationship between adjuncts and ACT scores. Similarly, if departments assign adjuncts to classes at times of the day that are less likely to attract top students (e.g., night classes), then we would expect a negative relationship between adjuncts and ACT scores. Regardless of the reason, however, the relationship between adjuncts and ACT scores is problematic to simple comparisons of students taking adjuncts and not taking adjuncts.

In our previous work, we found similar results when analyzing data at the student-subject level. Within departments, students with lower ACT scores are more likely to take adjuncts. Even among students who took the same course as their introduction to a given department, students with lower ACT scores are more likely to take adjuncts. Moreover, we found that students who expressed interest in a given subject are less likely to take courses from adjuncts.

So, how should one proceed econometrically? First, there is an open concern over whether the observed selection on ACT scores fully captures adjunct-taking behavior. If so, then controlling for ACT scores should rectify the selection problem. One might also question whether the observed selection on ACT scores is economically significant and not only statistically significant. Because of our large sample sizes throughout the chapter, we will often find statistically significant results that are precisely estimated. In the student level regressions, the marginal effect of a one point increase in the ACT score corresponds to a 0.3 percent decrease in the percentage of their instructors who are adjunct professors. These effects are extremely small, suggesting that selection, if caused by observable ACT scores, may be quantitatively small.

The more problematic case, however, is the case where selection is based on unobservable characteristics. Underlying the observable effect of ACT scores may be a more problematic unobservable characteristic (e.g., the desire to attend graduate school). We can control for the portion of this unobservable characteristic that ACT scores explain, but we cannot be sure that we fully control for the omitted variable bias resulting from this unobservable characteristic. Because this unobservable characteristic would likely affect student outcomes, it will bias simple OLS comparisons of adjunct takers and nontakers.

Instrumental Variables

Because OLS may be biased because of the relationship between unobservable characteristics that may affect both student success and student sorting, we rely on instrumental variables (IV) to estimate out the effect of adjuncts on student outcomes. For IV to work, we must find an instrument that is correlated with adjunct-taking behavior but uncorrelated with any unobserved selection process. One such instrument is the deviation from the steady-state number of tenured and tenure-track faculty. In our data, we observed five fiscal years of department level faculty data. Across semesters and years, the proportion of faculty that are assistant professors, associate professors, or full professors varies. This variation comes from a number of sources such as promotions, retirements, leaves of absence, and unexpected outcomes in the hiring process.

To capture this variation, we estimate the deviation from the steady-state department levels of assistant, associate, and full professors for every department. We use the three different levels of faculty because there are some differences in teaching loads across faculty ranks. Variation in these proportions is correlated with the likelihood that a department relies on adjuncts to teach a course in a given term but likely uncorrelated with student outcomes. In student-subject level regressions, we can directly compare these department-level deviations to the likelihood that a student took a course from a particular type of professor in a particular department in a given semester. When we run the student-level regressions, we combine the variations from the individual departments by creating a student-level weighted average of the variations where the weights are the semester hours of the courses the students took during their first semesters.

In the student-level regressions, this still may be problematic because of the composition of students' schedules. If a student takes courses from a series of departments where the probability (given our instrument) of taking an adjunct is high, then our instrument will reflect the fact that this student had a heavy adjunct schedule; however, the instrument will also reflect potential effects from taking a schedule with this combination of classes. It may be that students with this type of schedule are predisposed to withdraw regardless of the type of instructors in the courses. Hence, from a causal perspective, it is unclear whether the use of adjuncts or the combinations of classes from particular departments influenced students' dropout behaviors. Similar to Bettinger and Long (2005), we can fix the problem caused by aggregating our instrument by including controls for the specific schedules of the students. Earlier we mentioned "portfolio effects." The "portfolio effects" control for the different schedules. Hence, when we include these portfolio effects, we are comparing outcomes among students with the same schedule. In terms of our instrumental variables strategy, we are parsing out the effect of schedule design from our aggregated instrument. The variation that is then left in our instrument is coming from variation across campuses and years rather than across different schedules.

The first-stage results are shown in column 3 of Table 3.4. The coefficient on the deviation from steady-state number of assistant professors is −.220. It is highly significant. The interpretation of the results suggests that if across all of the departments in which a student is taking classes, there is on average a 1 percent increase in the number of assistant professors relative to the steady-state number of assistant professors, then the student will have about 22 percent fewer adjuncts in their first semester. As a numerical example, suppose that a student takes five three-credit courses from five different departments. If each of those departments is above their steady-state level of assistant professors by about 1 percent, they will employ fewer adjuncts. Of the five courses, students will take about one fewer course from an adjunct than they might have otherwise because of the surplus of assistant professors in each of the departments. Similarly, deviations from steady-state in associate and full professors will lead to students being more likely to have adjunct instructors.

EMPIRICAL RESULTS

We present our basic results in Table 3.5. The first two columns show OLS estimates of the effects of adjuncts on dropout rates. These columns show no effect of adjuncts on dropout rates. The point estimate is small and the confidence intervals are tight. Even when we control for students schedules in column 2, we find little evidence that adjuncts affect dropout rates; however, these OLS estimates are likely biased. As we showed in Table 3.4, students with higher ACT scores are more likely to have adjuncts. Although we control for ACT scores in these regressions, there may be unobservable characteristics related to taking an adjunct that are missing from the equation. For example, suppose that students search for the "easiest" professor. Finding an "easy" professor may enhance a student's grades and consequently reduce the likelihood of dropping out. If adjuncts are "easier" graders (as found in Moore and Trahan 1998) than full faculty, then students who are more concerned with finding "easy" professors will be more likely to take adjuncts. If this is the case, then OLS should be biased downward.

In columns 3 and 4, we show IV estimates of the effects of adjuncts on dropout rates. In contrast to the first columns, the IV results suggest that as students take more adjuncts in their first semester, their likelihood of dropping out also increases. The magnitude of the coefficient in column 3 is large, implying that a 1 percentage point increase in the level of adjuncts corresponds to a 1 percentage point increase in dropout rates. These results strongly suggest that adjuncts negatively affect student engagement at the university; however, they may be difficult

Table 3.5
Ordinary Least Squares and Instrumental Variables Estimates of Effects on Dropout
Rates

	(1)	(2)	(3)	(4)
	OLS		IV	
Proportion of Classes from	0.004	0.007	1.15**	0.601**
Adjunct in First Semester	(0.012)	(0.014)	(0.348)	(0.253)
ACT Score	−0.008**	−0.007**	−0.003*	−0.005**
	(0.0004)	(0.001)	(0.002)	(0.001)
Proportion of Classes from			0.366**	0.432**
Grad Student in First			(0.118)	(0.195)
Semester				
Class Schedule Portfolio	No	Yes	No	Yes
Effects				
Observations	40977	40977	40977	40977

Robust standard errors are in parentheses. Regressions also include controls for race, gender, state of
residence, age, and campus fixed effects.
* significant at 10%; ** significant at 5%.

to interpret because they do not control for student course selection. Column 4
shows results that correct for course selection by including portfolio effects. The
coefficient on the percentage of courses from adjuncts is positive as before but
much smaller in magnitude. A 1 percentage point change in the percentage of
courses taught by adjuncts corresponds to a 0.6 percent change in the likelihood
of dropping out.

Table 3.5 also includes a control for the proportion of graduate students that
students have during their first semester. We treat this as endogenous as well and
instrument for it like we do for the proportion of adjuncts. Similar to the effect of
adjuncts, we find that as the proportion of courses a student takes from graduate
student increases, so too does the likelihood that this student drops out.

The interpretation of these results is straightforward and unambiguous. In the
first semester of students' academic careers, it matters what types of professors
they meet on campus. If they take large proportions of classes from adjuncts and
graduate students (after controlling for selection bias), they are more likely to drop
out of the institution. This likely validates claims that adjuncts are ill-prepared to
help integrate new students into a specific college. It also may give some empirical
justification for mentoring programs or other programs designed to help first-year
students interact directly with full-time faculty in their initial semester at school,
as these programs may lessen the negative impact of adjuncts by helping to integrate students with full-time faculty members.

CONCLUSION

Estimating the effects of adjuncts on student outcomes is an important yet difficult task. Given the recent trends toward increased use of adjunct instructors, knowing their impact on student outcomes is a first-order priority. This chapter takes an important step in identifying the effects. The central contribution is twofold. First, this chapter demonstrates how simple comparisons of students who take adjuncts to students who do not are somewhat misleading. Students with high ACT scores systematically avoid adjuncts. If similar sorting takes place along unobservable characteristics, simple comparisons will be biased. Moreover, students in some departments (e.g., humanities) and at some schools (e.g., non-selective colleges) are more likely to take adjunct instructors. Simple comparisons may not control for differences in students' schedules, which may be correlated with both the prevalence of having an adjunct and persistence.

As a second contribution, we present an instrumental variables approach to control for these selection issues. We exploit variation in faculty composition to identify shifts in the likelihood that students take adjuncts. If the proportion of faculty members with a given rank drops relative to the steady-state, then students are more likely to take adjuncts. This creates exogenous variation that we can then use to identify the effects of adjuncts on dropout rates. Our results suggest that adjuncts adversely affect student dropout rates. Even when we compare students with similar schedules, we find the same results. The results, when coupled with those in our previous work, suggest mixed results for adjuncts.

On the one hand, taking an "adjunct-heavy" course schedule negatively affects students. In their first semester, taking courses from full-time faculty members appears to be important for retention. This may provide some empirical evidence to support the shifts in some colleges to staff first-semester classes with full-time faculty. Reducing the quantity of time that students must rely on adjunct instructors while increasing interactions with full-time faculty may facilitate student engagement at the institution. On the other hand, such a solution is expensive. Adjuncts are inexpensive relative to full-time faculty. Moreover, in many fields, adjuncts are effective teachers who can motivate students to continue studying in a given discipline. For example, in other work we find adjunct instructors to have positive impacts on students in fields closely tied to specific professions. This may suggest that the impact of adjunct instructors could differ during various times in a student's academic career. Future research may shed additional light on the costs and benefits of using adjunct instructors.

NOTES

1. University administrators may be concerned that increased use of adjuncts may affect their competitiveness with similar institutions, but these concerns are likely ameliorated by the fact that public universities in Ohio have similarly increased their reliance on adjuncts over the last decade.

2. For schools on quarters rather than semesters, Ohio Board of Regents converts the hours to semester hours.

3. Miami University and The Ohio State University are the top-ranked public universities in Ohio. Miami University is the only university to be referred to as "highly selective" by the *Barron's Guide to College* (Barron's 1997). In the 2002 version of *U.S. News & World Reports'* college rankings, Miami ranks in the second tier (53rd-131st) of national universities with doctoral programs. Other high-ranking institutions in Ohio (e.g., Oberlin) are private colleges.

4. We define selective institutions as the "competitive" institutions defined by *Barron's Educational Guides* (Barron's 1997). These include Bowling Green State University, Miami University, The Ohio State University, Ohio University, and Youngstown State University.

CHAPTER

The Effect of Institutional Funding Cuts on Baccalaureate Graduation Rates in Public Higher Education

Gary L. Blose, John D. Porter, and Edward C. Kokkelenberg

INTRODUCTION

Funding cutbacks in public higher education are common and have been exacerbated by increasing enrollments and inflation. Graduation rates have garnered recent interest as public institutions have heard calls from state legislators and school administrators to show evidence of increased efficiency in rapid throughput at the college or university[1] and to penalize or curtail the enrollments of "perpetual students." This recent attention appears to be the result of concerns with costs to the state and may not reflect concerns about the education of the student.[2]

The relationship between funding and an institution's graduation rates is complex and may vary over the broad range of institutional types, missions, and disciplines in higher education. This present study considers public higher education from the cost point of view and uses data at the institutional level.[3]

This chapter develops and tests a heuristic model of a different and more correct allocation of costs to the various missions or multiple products of higher education and finds that the effect of reduced state funding, when properly measured, is associated with reduced graduation rates. There is no free lunch.

THE ISSUES AND GRADUATION RATES

Prospective students and parents have long recognized graduation rates as a tangible and comprehensive measure of institutional quality. Ivy League universities and the best liberal arts colleges have six-year graduation rates in excess of

90 percent and the best public institutions are not far behind[4]; however, the average five-year baccalaureate graduation rate of all public colleges and universities is just 41.2 percent (ACT Institutional file 2005). Although high graduation rates have been viewed as a marker for institutional excellence, the higher education community recognizes that graduation rates also reflect admission standards, the academic strength of the enrolled students, and the resources institutions devote to instruction, to remediation, and to retention. Many possible explanations for individual student or institutional graduation rate differentials have been studied, and it has been found that student experiential variables, student ability, other precollege variables, and institutional variables are all important.[5]

Presidents and trustees of public institutions maintain that comparing the graduation rates of their schools to those of the of Ivy League is unfair, not just because they, as a public institution, may enroll students of lower academic caliber, but more important because their institutions do not receive the resources necessary to achieve the higher graduation rates. The effect of institutional funding on graduation rates thus needs to be studied to ascertain whether the assertion of the presidents and trustees is true, or if the call from state legislators for increased throughput is feasible.

In the following discussion, the assumption is that the institution's efforts devoted to increasing graduation rates and retention can be summarized by expenditures per student. This cost will include all instructional materials, faculty, support staff, student services, student counseling, athletics, libraries, computing, student health services, etc.

Society has decided that higher education should not be limited to those with extraordinary talent or wealth, but open to all and that creates a problem for those who hope to use the graduation and retention rates as measures of institutional performance. This is especially true in the public sector where colleges and universities are expected to provide educational opportunities to a broad spectrum of the state's population. Meeting the state's demand for higher education requires a variety of college types to accommodate the range of academic ability and personal/family resources of those wanting access to the system. It is quite probable that widening academic access, if done by higher education in total, will result in lower graduation rates for most time periods unless steps are taken to help the ill-prepared remediate, acclimate, and benefit from higher education. All of these efforts require added resources.

Therefore, understanding the relationship between resource availability and an institution's graduation rates will be most useful in determining the effect, if any, of state cutbacks on students.

INSTITUTIONAL FUNDING LEVELS AND INSTRUCTION

Much of the literature on graduation rates and retention is descriptive and/or discusses the relationship among various student and institutional characteristics and graduation rates. The direct effect of funding levels differentiated by academic fields of study and by institutional mission, however, has not been assessed. Baseline studies by Tinto (1975 and 1993), Bean (1980), Pascarella and Terenzini (1991), and Astin (1992) omit the role of resources, other than student financial assistance. Kuh's (2002) research into student engagement finds that most, if not all, of the educational engagement factors studied have significant financial implications for the institution.

More recently, Ryan (2004) explored the relationship between institutional funding levels and graduation rates using a methodology similar to the one used herein. Ryan found a significant and positive relationship between institutional funding for instruction and academic support, but not student services. His study, although helpful, is of limited value because the institutions were a mix of public and private and excluded masters and doctoral-granting colleges and universities. The missions of public and private institutions differ, as do their governance and funding structures. By combining public and private institutions, Ryan may have confounded the results of his investigation. Further, any exploration of the effect of funding on graduation rates should include masters and doctoral institutions, because such institutions consume the majority of the available resources devoted to public higher education. Ryan excluded these institutions because of the diversity of their missions and complexity of untangling their funding and costs. This chapter provides a more general perspective.

Little can be discerned without considering differences in institutional mission, when comparing differences in levels of funding, as the priority given to the three academic missions (undergraduate, graduate, or first professional), as well the emphasis on research and public service, varies widely in public higher education.[6] Further, within each mission, colleges and universities produce education and research in a myriad of academic disciplines, and each requires different inputs and bears different costs and, indeed, often engages different technologies. Thus, treating a college or a university as a single product firm is akin to treating General Electric as a single product firm: both require much more detail to understand and model the cost functions and the production functions, and to derive policy precepts.

Hence, the initial approach to this issue is to derive a mission-weighted measure of the program costs per full-time student equivalent. Institutions do not publish costs allocations in sufficient detail, however, nor does any national data source capture this detail by institution. Thus some adjustment for mission differences must be made when comparing the costs or funding levels of institutions.

Second, even within a mission, institutions differ in enrollment at the various undergraduate levels. For example, the number and percentage of freshman and other class levels vary among institutions resulting in different instructional costs. The IPEDS Fall Enrollment Survey and other national data sources collect only the number of full- and part-time headcounts of undergraduate, graduate, and first-professional students, but some adjustment to the estimated full-time equivalent student (FTES) demand on institutional resources must be made.

Third, instructional costs are also idiosyncratic to the academic discipline, as well as the student's academic level. For example, the same level of FTES in undergraduate engineering and business would not generate the same cost burden as history or psychology. When comparing funding levels among institutions, some adjustment for the mix of academic disciplines taught by those institutions must be made. The IPEDS surveys do not collect either discipline-based instructional costs or enrollment by academic program, and even if a "normalized" cost for each discipline were known, there is the problem that the distribution of FTES load by discipline within each institution is unknown. Hence, when comparing funding levels among institutions, some accommodation must be made for the differing FTES mix by the academic programs offered by the institution and for the unknown enrollment distribution.

SUNY COST ALLOCATION MODEL AND METHODOLOGY

Information maintained by The State University of New York (SUNY) was used to approximate the necessary costs and output variables and to address these issues.[7] SUNY is interested in assessing the relative level of resource support for its academic programs against the funding levels of other public colleges and universities. To accomplish this goal, SUNY calculates a "normalized" cost per FTES for baccalaureate granting institutions. For almost 30 years, most of SUNY's four-year colleges and universities have participated in a course and section cost allocation system. This system joins such information with financial and spatial information in arriving at a cost per credit hour for lower division, upper division, master's and doctoral level courses. SUNY uses this information in a budget allocation model that allocates resource support for the courses taught by the institution. In the mid-1990s, SUNY estimated the academic program cost of programs offered by the 28 SUNY colleges and universities participating in the course data collection system and linked actual course costs, which were derived from faculty salary and departmental support costs, to the courses taken by students during a given semester.

These costs, when aggregated by students within an academic program, yield an average program cost of all SUNY students enrolled in a particular academic program. SUNY's costs are not the exact costs of other institutions, but this study requires only that the relative academic program costs hold across institutions.

The application of the SUNY allocation model to other public institutions requires the following assumptions: (1) the relative cost differentials among SUNY academic programs are reasonable proxies for the cost differentials that exist throughout U.S. public higher education, (2) the IPEDS Completions Survey distribution of degrees granted by academic program is a reasonable proxy for an institution's enrollment by discipline and student level, and (3) an estimate of an institution's undergraduate FTES load is the number of full-time undergraduate students plus one-third of the number of part-time undergraduate students.

The final methodological step is to compute an undergraduate expenditure level per FTES student. This is accomplished by dividing the adjusted FTES by the discipline-adjusted costs. Then, the FTES workload estimates by academic discipline are inflated or deflated based on the indexed program costs using SUNY cost data. The result is a normalized FTES workload level that adjusts for the difference in funding required by the disciplines offered by the institution. Further details of the method of adjustment are available from the authors on request.

MODELING FOUR-, FIVE-, AND SIX-YEAR GRADUATION RATES[8]

College rankers often include graduation rates (e.g., *U.S. News & World Report*) along with generic institutional data to develop their rankings. These data are obtained from a college's response to the IPEDS surveys or other national surveys such as the College Board Annual Survey of Colleges.

The typical analysis often employs a multiple regression model using graduation rate as the dependent variable and a set of institutional characteristics as the independent variables. The result is used to calculate a predicted graduation rate for each college that is adjusted for any institutional characteristic included in the model. If the actual college graduation rate exceeds the predicted value, the college is assumed to be doing a good job at graduating students by the college ranking services.

The present analysis builds on this concept but adds a cost component and limits the study to public institutions. The hypothesis is that higher undergraduate expenditure levels should result in more output or higher graduation rates after adjusting for other institutional dimensions related to student retention and graduation.

The dependent variables considered are four-, five-, and six-year graduation rates for baccalaureate students (G4), (G5), and (G6). Explanatory variables are percent male (M), percent full-time (F), average SAT score squared (SAT2),[9] out-of-state tuition differential over in-state tuition (OSTD), and total undergraduate expenditures per undergraduate FTES, adjusted and with mandatory financial transfers (AE). The validity of the AE is verified by comparing the results to a model with total undergraduate expenditures per FTES unadjusted (E). Presumably, if the estimations proposed herein have merit, the inclusion of AE will have better statistical significance and contribute to a better explanation of the relationship between funding and graduation rates than will a model using E, the traditional measure of funding. The AE model used here is given as:

$$G_{i,j} = \alpha + \beta_1 M_i + \beta_2 F_i + \beta_3 SAT2_i + \beta_4 OSTD_i + \beta_5 AE_i + u_{i,j}$$

The model using E is exactly the same except for the use of E rather than AE. The other variables are as defined previously, and they, together with a stochastic error term with the usual assumed properties, u, make up the model. The subscript, i, denotes the institution and $j = 4, 5, 6$.

REGRESSION RESULTS

After the adjusted expenditure variable was constructed, the data were examined for problems and logical inconsistencies, and this resulted in the elimination of about 30 institutions from the dataset.[10] A number of inclusive models
were tested, some with cross or interactive terms and also with polynomials in
explanatory variables, all in the spirit of Hendry seeking a parsimonious model.[11]
The final simple model, including AE as the measure of funding, is reported in
Table 4.1 using data from 416 institutions for the entering cohort of students in
the fall of 1997. The overall fit of all of the models developed is well represented
by the results reported in Table 4.1.[12] Here the adjusted R squares are between
0.673 and 0.733.

The chief variable of interest, adjusted expenditures per FTES, AE, is
statistically significant; and the adjusted R-square rose for each of the graduation
rates for all models tested when compared to the unadjusted expenditures.[13] AE
shows a consistent positive relationship to graduation rates regardless of time to
degree, but the effect of funding diminishes with the length of time to degree. The
coefficient declines from 0.933 to 0.641 and thence to 0.404 for four-, five- and
six-year graduation rates, respectively. Thus higher levels of funding are associated with earlier graduation. If this result holds on further study, spending more

Table 4.1
Ordinary Least Squares Estimates of Coefficients (t-statistics in parentheses)

Variable/Statistic	Symbol	Units	In 4 years	In 5 years	In 6 years
Intercept	alpha		−47.272 (−14.37)	−51.891 (−14.52)	−42.259 (−12.30)
Avg. SAT Squared	SAT	100 pts	0.00405 (17.64)	0.00471 (18.85)	0.00447 (18.62)
Male (%)	M	decimal	−37.707 (−6.31)	−21.07 (−3.25)	−12.60 (−2.02)
Full-Time (%)	F	decimal	37.706 (11.76)	50.003 (14.34)	45.503 (13.58)
Out-of-State Tuition	OSTD	000 $	0.329 (2.01)	0.710 (3.99)	0.867 (5.07)
Adjusted Expenditures	AE	000 $	0.933 (5.78)	0.641 (3.65)	0.404 (2.39)
Adj. R squared			0.673	0.733	0.733
Number of Obs			416	416	416

Office of Institutional Research and Analysis, The State University of New York.

money up front might reduce a college's overall expenditures per granted degree, as a higher percentage of students would graduate in four years.

Table 4.1 shows other results consistent with initial expectations and the literature.[14] Average SAT score is a good proxy for initial ability and hence a good predictor of college success.[15] The percentage of undergraduate students who are males is negatively related to graduation rates,[16] and the percentage of undergraduates enrolled for full-time study is positively related to graduation rates.[17] A higher nonresident tuition differential above resident tuition is also a significant predictor and this may be interpreted as a measure of academic excellence.[18]

Another way to look at these results is to quantify the responses to changes in the values of several of the explanatory variables. An increase of $1,000 in the per student expenditures will yield a 1.09 percentage point increase in four-year graduation rates, about a 5 percent increase in the four-year rates. On the other hand, a rise of 10 points in the SAT scores is calculated to result in a 0.79 percentage point increase in the four-year graduation rate, or about three-fourths of what $1,000 would do. Thus, a 10-point rise in SAT scores is equivalent in its effect on graduation rates to an increase of $722 in adjusted total undergraduate expenditures per full-time-equivalent undergraduate student (AE). Another way of looking at this outcome is that if an institution planned to move from the average four-year graduation rate for the data of 21.2 percent to the upper quartile of 27.5 percent, it would take an increase of about 80 points in the average SAT score of the entering students, or added expenditures of almost $5,800 per student.

These results emphasize that expenditures, properly measured and adjusted, as well as SAT scores or admission standards are strongly related to graduation rates. The reader is cautioned that these examples and values are extremes, and the model may not be valid for such significant shifts in graduation rates. These results are also limited, as the data are from a single cross section and not longitudinal or panel, and several variables adjudged important in the literature have not been included. The latter fact may result in omitted variable bias, which means that the estimated coefficients, and thus the effects of changes in test scores or funding may be biased.

POLICY ISSUES

Properly measured, expenditures per student are important to graduation rates. State governments that ignore this fact and call for higher graduation rates and do not increase funding (but rather cut funding) will not have success.

There appears to be a tradeoff between access and graduation rates. As long as public institutions continue their mission of open access, they may have to devote more resources to the educational mission if the current levels of graduation rates are to improve. If the four-year graduation rates slide further, then the age-adjusted level of human capital in a state's workforce will decline; and the direct costs to parents, students, and states will increase. The opportunity costs to society and its elements will also increase as a result of delayed entry into the workforce, deferred income tax revenues, and possible trade-offs between construction capital to expand capacity versus instructional expenditures.

States and administrators may have a perverse incentive to rethink programmatic and service emphasis to increase graduations rates at lower costs by ignoring the market's demands and society's needs for graduates in disciplines that tend to be expensive. This may occur in states where funding is linked to graduation rates without recognition of discipline-based cost differentials. Alternatively, administrators may pursue a strategy to increase graduation rates by lowering programmatic standards. In the short run, higher graduation rates would be judged well by society, but the costs of producing an unprepared workforce may be reflected in the market's assessment of the institution's reputation in the long run.

The current pricing model in public higher education may not be tenable. If there is a relationship between graduation rates and the costs of producing graduates in one discipline versus another, charging a single tuition rate for undergraduate education may not be financially supportable in the long run.

Finally, this research confirms that the national data are deficient in this regard. The establishment of a regular data collection of program-based financial and enrollment data from institutions of higher education would facilitate both further study and the reconciling of decision makers' desires to their actual accomplishments.

FUTURE RESEARCH

Further research into the issues of the influence of resource availability on graduation rates and time to degree is warranted to determine whether the findings hold when applied more broadly. Extensions of this study could improve the data, model specification, and methodology used to adjust expenditures.

This study uses cross-sectional data from one entering cohort and one year's expenditures, but education (and subsequent graduation) is a process covering many years. Graduation is measured at four-, five-, and six-year intervals, but the resources required to achieve the outcome span multiple periods. The present study considers the graduation rates of the cohort of first-time, full-time undergraduate students entering in the fall of 1997, and resources expended in academic 2000–2001. A more thorough study would consider resources expended over multiple years, as well as graduation rates from multiple cohorts. Such a treatment would reflect the dynamic nature of the phenomenon of interest.[19]

The cohort of students used in calculating graduation rates encompasses less than half the total number of students served during the period that the cohort is in attendance for many public colleges and universities. The costs of serving transfer students and others should be addressed. What are the costs and benefits to the individual, the state, society and industry from supporting a system where the majority of the students transfer, change major, pursue multiple majors, or delay graduation? And most important, how do state budget cuts affect these students?

The methodology used by the authors adopts an arbitrary allocation of indirect costs for academic support, student services, institutional support, and mandatory transfers to the primary missions of instruction, research, and public service. Although the allocation method used is recognized in higher education, the findings would be strengthened by considering program and function expenditures independently in the model. It may be that such expenditures affect graduation rates in ways that the present model fails to illuminate; for example, the relationship between instructional expenditures and student services and graduation rates may not be the same.[20]

The effect of SUNY's program costs on the study, used in estimating the amount of resources expended on undergraduate education, needs review. A further comparison of the allocation template with other states' experience would test the validity of the method of adjusting undergraduate expenditures. The problem is that academic program cost data for public higher education is nonexistent. There may be ways to use data sources, such as the Delaware Instructional Cost Study (Middaugh, 2001), to overcome this limitation, as many states have performed discipline-based cost studies in recent years.

Several other issues require further research including the addition of the post-doctoral mission as an output, the exploration of the value of early expenditures to ensure the reenrollment of freshmen, and the inclusion of temporal factors that other researchers have found meritorious.

Although the model presented is both simple and principally linear, it may be too simple, as there is some indication of nonlinearity. Hence the testing of the sensitivity of the results to model specification, as well as the exploration of other student outcome and institutional performance measures, appears to be useful.

APPENDIX: VARIABLES

The names of the public institutions included in this study are available from the authors on request.

Four, Five and Six Year Graduation Rates for Baccalaureate Students (G4), (G5), (G6)

Four-, five-, and six-year graduation rates for the cohort of first-time full-time baccalaureate degree-seeking students entering the college in fall 1997. (Source: IPEDS AY 2003 Graduation Rate Survey.)

Total Undergraduate Expenditures per Undergraduate FTES (E)

As described previously, IPEDS financial statistics and enrollment by program and academic program costs allow the decomposition of institutional expenditure by student level. The dollars are included on a per FTES (student) basis to adjust the expenditures for institutional size. (Source: IPEDS FY 2000–01 Financial Statistics Survey, IPEDS Fall 2000 Fall Enrollment Survey and IPEDS AY 2000–01 Completions Survey.)

Percent Male (M)

Prior research has shown that males tend to graduate at lower rates than females; they also take longer to graduate. This may contribute to the observed differences in institutional graduation rates in higher education. (Source: College Board Annual Survey of Colleges.)

Percent Full-time (F)

Institutions of higher education serve many different populations. Nontraditional populations tend to exhibit patterns of behavior that lead to higher attrition rates and longer time to degree. It is possible that the greater the representation of full-time students in an institution's undergraduate class, the higher the four-, five, and six-year graduation rates. (Source: College Board Annual Survey of Colleges.)

Average SAT Score (SAT)

College entrance examinations are the strongest single predictor of academic success in higher education; such academically prepared students have higher retention and graduation rates. (Source: College Board Annual Survey of Colleges.)

Out-of-State Tuition (OST)

All public colleges and universities charge nonresident students a higher tuition rate. The willingness of nonresidents to pay the higher rate may indicate a higher commitment to earn a degree. It also may reflect perceived quality. (Source: College Board Annual Survey of Colleges.)

NOTES

1. Graduation rates have long been of concern. See for example McNeely (1937), Spady (1971), and Bean (1980). The time-to-graduate rate ranged from 28.2 percent for open public institutions to 74 percent for highly selective ones in 2003 according to ACT (2005). There is now a journal, *The Journal of Academic Retention*, devoted to research on retention and time taken to graduate.

2. The time students spend in exploring different majors and taking elective courses may better prepare them to be lifelong learners and citizens. From this perspective, time-to-degree and graduation rates are not the only measures of the educational output; but the intelligence, the existence of a breadth of knowledge, understanding, and personal

satisfaction of the citizenry, as well as their contribution to the commonweal, are. These outcomes are not tested in this chapter.

3. See Verry and Davies (1976) for a thorough discussion of the economics of the university's costs and outputs.

4. The top public four-year rate is 80 percent for The College of William and Mary, and the top 10 public schools had a four-year average graduation rate of 66 percent. The six-year numbers are 90 and 84 percent, respectively.

5. A good introduction to modern research on this issue together with a good bibliography is given in DesJardins, Kim, and Rzonca (2002–2003). See also Braxton and Hirschy (forthcoming), Berger and Lyons (forthcoming), and Porter (2003–2004). Many of the issues are identified in Habley and McClanahan (2005). Adelman (1999) is also useful.

6. Universities are increasingly training postdoctoral students-researchers, but that mission's output is deemed small in this study.

7. A model based on such information measures the world through a SUNY lens, but the size of SUNY (more than 414,000 students) and diversity of the institutions within the system (64 colleges and universities—associate, baccalaureate, masters, doctoral, and first-professional institutions—research, comprehensive, and specialized institutions) suggest that SUNY relative program costs may be applicable to other public institutions.

8. The idea of a traditional four-year degree program is not universal. Many engineering and architectural programs and some other programs such as three-two programs take five years to complete, and several schools have experimented with three-year programs. These details are ignored here.

9. The SAT score level proved not to be statistically significant for these data, but the square of the SAT score was significant and these results are reported.

10. This was done by constructing Box plots and distributions for each variable and examining the outliers. The next step was to consider the correlation matrix for multicollinearity and relationships among the remaining data. Approximately 25 institutions were removed for partial data and logical inconsistencies. An additional three institutions were removed because these institutions were identified by the Hat matrix test as being from a different data-generating process. These were The Citadel, North Carolina Central University, and Virginia Military Institute.

11. See Hendry, Leamer, and Poirier (1990).

12. A number of other explanatory variables and a quadratic functional form were investigated but are not reported here. The simple results presented are derived as Hendry, Leamer, and Poirier (1990) suggest. The adjusted R squared was used to select among the models.

13. When the model was run with unadjusted undergraduate expenditures per student, E, the variable was not statistically significant except in a bivariate model and for a subset of the data. This supports the authors' contention that adjusting for institutional mission, student levels, and discipline mix is important.

14. See for example Tinto (1993).

15. SAT scores were entered as a quadratic, but the linear term was rejected as not statistically significant. The results in Table 4.1 are for regressions that include only SAT squared.

16. Compare this to studies of gender-differentiated performance in college such as Ballard and Johnson (2005), which shows women expect to do less well than men in specific courses, and Kokkelenberg, Dillon, and Christy (2006) who find women do better in college.

17. All of the students used in calculating the four-, five-, and six-year graduation rates initially enrolled at the college as full-time students. The variable, % full-time, denotes a general, first-year demographic characteristic of the undergraduate student body.

18. Initially, the model included the out-of-state tuition as an explanatory variable and as a proxy for academic excellence, which is not specifically included elsewhere in the model. For example, an alumni network or a reputation in certain disciplines would not be in the funding variable (AE). The model reported in Table 4.1 used the differential between out-of -state tuition and resident tuition for this proxy. Rizzo and Ehrenberg (2004) reported on a major study on resident-nonresident tuition and discuss why differentials might exist. Among other things they found evidence that public institutions use nonresident enrollments to serve nonfinancial interests, and "that higher-quality public universities charge higher tuition to both in-state and out-of state students"(White, 2004).

19. It also makes sense if data at the institutional level can be expanded to have a student level component that may lead to a reconciliation of the two types of studies now in vogue. Additional precollege variables beyond SAT scores, perhaps AP credits and prior collegiate experience, need to be considered.

20. See Ryan (2004).

PART II

Individual State Experiences

CHAPTER

The Effects of a Changing Financial Context on the University of California

Gerald R. Kissler and Ellen Switkes

LARGE TRENDS IN CALIFORNIA

At the beginning of the twenty-first century, California's fiscal problems are consistent with the trends identified by Ray Sheppach (2003), the Executive Director of the National Governor's Association. Despite a relatively mild recession, California has experienced a fiscal crisis caused by two structural factors: an eroding tax base and an explosion in health care costs.

Also consistent with national trends, the percentage of the state budget going to higher education, including the University of California, has been declining over the last four decades, and the current fiscal crisis has led to more budget cuts and tuition and fee increases over the last four years. As we argue in the next two sections, the changing nature of the economy and the demographics of the state have increased the importance of higher education, but state appropriations to the University of California have declined.

More Important for California's Economy and Quality of Life

Economic Trends

The last two economic downturns have had a disproportionate effect on California's economy. With the downturn in the aerospace industry, Californians suffered more than those in most states during the long and deep recession of the early 1990s. There was some recovery during the Internet boom period of the late 1990s, but California was also hit particularly hard when the Internet bubble burst in the spring of 2000. Policymakers in California realize the need to stimulate job creation to reduce unemployment rates, but restoring California's comparative

Figure 5.1
U.S. average earnings and unemployment rates by level of education

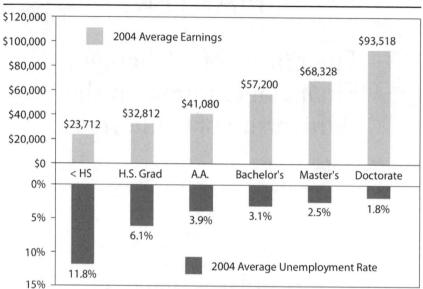

advantage in a global, knowledge-based economy means not just more jobs, but more well-paying jobs.

With the shift to a knowledge-based economy, more of a product's value is added before and after manufacturing by professionals and managers who typically have advanced levels of education and skills. As a result, employers are willing to pay an "education premium" for these workers. As the national data in Figure 5.1 show, incomes are higher and unemployment rates are lower on average for those with more education. Even though the sample size does not permit the Bureau of Labor Statistics to produce these data by state, it is reasonable to assume that these relationships hold in California as well. The only way to raise average income in California, therefore, is to move the workforce to the more advanced levels of education on the right side of Figure 5.1, because we cannot compete on the basis of low-skilled jobs with those in other countries who are willing to work for one-tenth of U.S. wages.

The University of California (UC) has always been important to the economy and the quality of life of the state's citizens, but it is even more important today with the shift to a knowledge-based economy. As a result, there is increasing interest from business and government leaders in technology transfer and the production of what Peter Drucker (1959) called "knowledge workers." These professionals and managers are not only the lifeblood of knowledge-based industries, but also the ones who add the most value to products and services in all industries.

The Bureau of Labor Statistics aggregates hundreds of occupations into 11 major categories. As Figure 5.2 shows, the fastest growing occupational categories

Figure 5.2
Percent increase in California jobs by occupational category

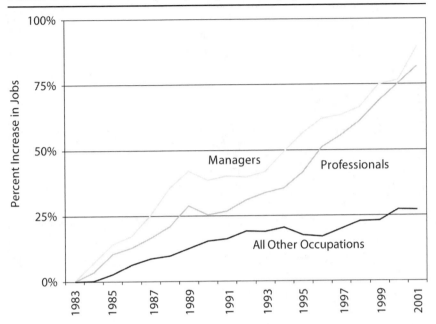

in California are professional and managerial jobs. In the early 1980s, one-fourth of all jobs in the state were in these two categories. Today they represent one-third of California's jobs. Most of these jobs require at least a baccalaureate degree, and many require a master's or doctoral degree; but California's four-year colleges and universities have not been meeting the needs. A study conducted by the Public Policy Institute of California (Betts 2000) estimates that only half the college graduates hired in California, filling new positions and replacing those who leave, were educated in this state.

Demographic Trends

California is a large and rapidly growing state, and more of its citizens will want and need a university education for those professional and managerial jobs. The state's population grew from 24 million in 1980 to 37 million in 2005. State demographers estimate continued growth to 44 million in 2020 and 52 million by 2040. These are impressive growth figures, but the shift in the ethnic composition of the population is even more dramatic. During that 60-year period, Hispanics will increase from 19 percent of the total population to 50 percent, Asians will increase from 5 percent to 13 percent, and non-Hispanic Caucasians will decline from 67 percent to 26 percent. The percentage of African Americans will remain the same (8% and 7%, respectively, see Figure 5.3)

Figure 5.3
Change in the ethnic composition of California's population between 1980 and 2040

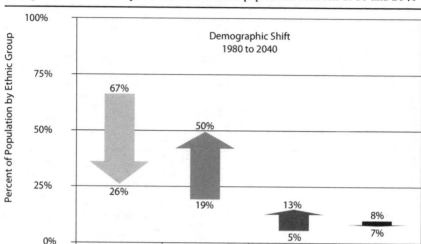

Demographers have forecast sharp growth in the number of high school graduates during the current decade. Called Tidal Wave II, this bulge moving through the public schools reflects not only the echo of the baby boom but also high birthrates and immigration levels in California. Figure 5.4 shows two forecasts for the number of high school graduates in California. The 1998 series was available when the University's long-range enrollment plan was developed in 1999. The most recent projection reflects even greater growth with a plateau, not a dip, after 2008.

Policymakers expect the University to provide a pathway to upward social mobility for California's new citizens and UCs actual enrollments have grown even faster than those envisioned in the University's 1999 enrollment plan because the demographers underestimated the actual growth in high school graduates and because a larger percentage of those who meet the University's eligibility requirements are applying for admission to the UC campuses. As a result, the University is hiring faculty and constructing new facilities, including a new campus, as fast as possible.

The UC Board of Regents, however, has expressed concern about maintaining quality during this period of unprecedented growth, and that was *before* the economic recession and the onset of California's current fiscal crisis. Therefore the Regents have been monitoring a series of qualitative benchmarks and early warning indicators during this period of rapid growth (University of California 2002, 2003).

Figure 5.4
Two forecasts of California high school graduates

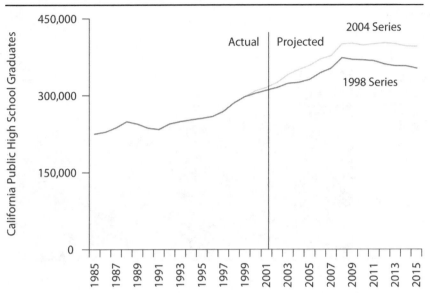

Less Taxpayer Support for Higher Education

When looking at levels of taxpayer support for higher education, it is important to separate the short-term effects of the business cycle from long-term trends. As shown in Figure 5.5, higher education's lower priority is not simply the effect of California's current fiscal crisis. The decline in the University of California's share of State General Fund expenditures from 7 percent to 3.5 percent has occurred over the last 35 years. During this period taxes have been cut and other spending priorities, such as prisons, health care, and social service programs, have consumed a larger share of state spending. For example, the sharpest drop occurred in 1978—the year voters approved Proposition 13, which lowered property taxes and required the state to backfill the lost school revenue with State General Funds.

The economic recessions at the beginning of the 1980s, 1990s, and the current decade resulted in declining state revenue and less support for higher education. In fact, testimony before the Assembly Higher Education Committee in October 2003, indicated that higher education typically is cut more than average during economic downturns, and receives above average increases during better periods but does not catch up to past levels. Politicians justify this pattern because colleges and universities, unlike many other state programs, have an alternate revenue source (i.e., tuition and fees).

During each of the last three economic downturns in the early 1980s, 1990s, and the current decade, the state appropriation to the University of California and

Figure 5.5
University of California's declining share of the state general fund budget

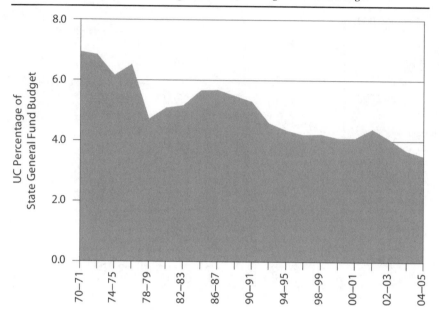

Figure 5.6
University of California funding lags during recessions and catches up when the economy rebounds

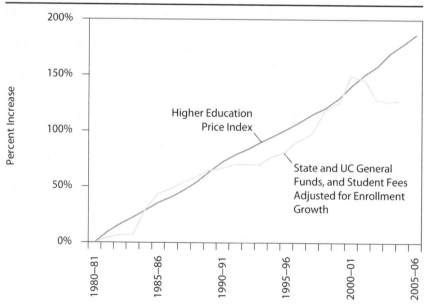

other core financial support fell behind (Figure 5.6). The solid line in Figure 5.6 is the Higher Education Price Index, which reflects increasing prices for college and university spending, analogous to the Consumer Price Index for consumer spending. The dashed line in the graph is the amount of core financial support (state appropriation, tuition and fee revenues, and other UC General Funds) per student.

In the early 1980s, after Proposition 13 had passed, state funding did not keep pace with the high rates of inflation at that time and salaries fell behind the market. In the mid-1980s, Governor Deukmejian made a conscious effort to provide catch-up funding for public higher education, but there were more budget cuts during the long and deep recession of the early 1990s. Once again tuition and fees were raised to offset a portion of the cut (approximately one-fourth). During the economic boom period of the late 1990s, Governor Davis provided catch-up funding and blocked student fee increases, but there have been severe budget cuts and sharp fee increases again over the last four years.

Californians have been proud of the state's "no tuition" policy, even though what the University of California calls student fees are now as high as tuition at other leading public universities. The boom and bust nature of student fee increases in California tracks the business cycle (Figure 5.7). During periods of economic growth, governors and legislators have provided increased state funds to the University so that fees would not have to be increased. In contrast, student

Figure 5.7
UC undergraduate fees in current and constant dollars

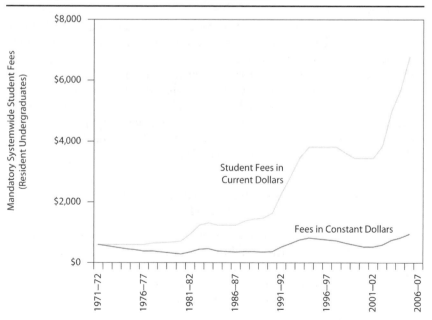

fees have been increased sharply to offset partially budget cuts during economic downturns. Over the long term, however, student fee are approximately where they would have been if the 1971–1972 level had been adjusted annually for the growth in California's per capita personal income.

SHORT-TERM EFFECTS OF CALIFORNIA'S FISCAL CRISIS
What Caused the Current Fiscal Crisis?

California's recession early in the current decade was relatively mild and short lived. Why then, was the state thrown into a fiscal crisis? Even though the state was hard hit by the energy crisis, it did not cause the fiscal crisis because it sold bonds to create the cash to purchase long-term energy contracts at lower rates. Because ratepayers will be paying back these bonds for many, many years, this action by the governor and the legislature, in effect, took the energy crisis off the State General Fund books. Rather than the energy crisis, California's fiscal crisis was caused by an overcommitment on a permanent basis of temporary tax revenue from the Internet bubble.

During the late 1990s, high-tech companies offered stock options to attract scientists, engineers, programmers, managers, and executives. While the Internet bubble was rising, many employees made more from their stock options than their salaries, and investors experienced extraordinary gains on their investments in these companies. Because capital gains and stock options are taxed as ordinary income in California, the State General Fund experienced extraordinary growth.

Capital gains and stock options revenue was only 6 percent of the State General Fund in 1995 but had grown to 25 percent at the peak in 2000. Unfortunately, too much of this temporary revenue increase was spent for continuing programs and services. When the Internet bubble burst, capital gains and stock options revenue declined precipitously. Between 2000 and 2002, the State General Fund lost $12.4 billion in revenue from this source. This sudden drop in State General Fund revenue could not have happened at a worse time for higher education, which was trying to expand at unprecedented rates to accommodate the increase in high school graduates, commonly called Tidal Wave II.

How Did the Crisis Affect the University of California's Budget?

Even before California's current fiscal crisis, many of the UC regents expressed concern about the University's ability to maintain quality during this period of rapid growth. That concern grew to alarm between 2001 and 2004, as each governor's budget contained more cuts and as the governor imposed mid-year cuts to help the state adjust to lower revenue estimates.

Figure 5.8
Actual state funding for University of California in comparison to a normal workload
budget under an agreement with the governor

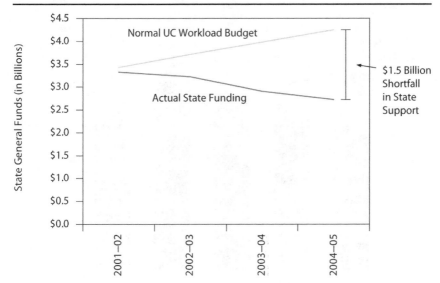

Over a four-year period the state appropriation to the University of California
fell by 15 percent while enrollment *grew* by 19 percent. Instead of rising from $3.3
billion to $4.2 billion to pay for enrollment growth and adjust for inflation, the
UC state appropriation fell to $2.7 billion (cf., Figure 5.8). In spite of the sharp
student fee increases shown in Figure 5.7, less than one-third of the $1.5 billion
shortfall shown in Figure 5.8 was offset by tuition and fee increases.

Figure 5.9 helps to make sense of these large numbers by comparing what it
costs to educate a student today with the cost in 1985, before the long, deep recession in the early 1990s and the current fiscal crisis. All the numbers in Figure 5.9
are expressed in 2004–2005 dollars.

In 1985–1986, it cost approximately $9,000 to educate a UC student. After
adjusting for inflation, that number would be approximately twice as large in
2004–2005. In the mid-1980s, more than 80 percent of the money came from the
state appropriation, which is the solid portion at the bottom of each bar. Over the
last 20 years, the state dollars per student have declined from $15,100 to $9,120.
As a result, the state is now funding less than 60 percent of the cost of instruction.
Student fees have increased substantially to offset some, but not all, of the loss of
state dollars. As a result, the University of California is spending $2,650 less now
than it was in 1985–1986 to educate a student. Rising prices are *not* due to UC
costs spiraling out of control. Students are paying more today solely because the
state subsidy has declined.

Figure 5.9
The $2,650 funding gap in resources available to educate a University of California student

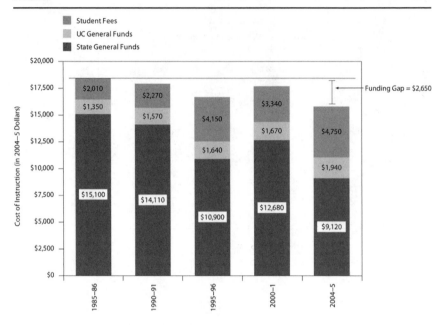

As UC President Dynes (2005) said, the shortfall of $1.5 billion in State funding

> has affected the quality of a UC education because the University has less money to spend on each student. The $2,650 funding gap means larger classes, less time with faculty outside the classroom, fewer library resources, and more obsolete equipment. It also means that students are paying a larger share of the cost of their education and getting less for it.

How Did UC Adjust to the Budget Cuts?

The UC Board of Regents and the President tried to minimize the effect of the budget cuts on the educational program by cutting administration, state-supported research, and public service programs first. They also raised student fees and out-of-state tuition to offset most of the direct impact on the educational program. As California's fiscal crisis entered its third and fourth years, however, this strategy collapsed, and all parts of the budget were eventually affected. Consequently, faculty and staff salaries fell behind the market, academic support

Figure 5.10
Library resource sharing among U.C. campuses

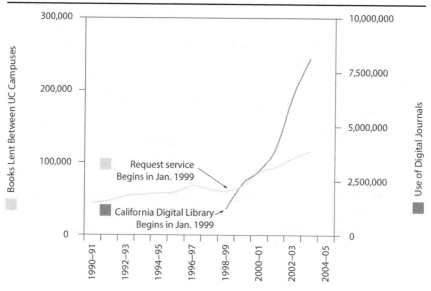

budgets suffered, facilities budgets were not adjusted for higher energy costs, the deferred maintenance backlog grew, graduate student support levels did not match those of peer institutions, etc.

Over the last four years, the University has looked for greater efficiencies to make more effective use of its limited state funding. For example, academic support budget cuts have affected its libraries, but the University took advantage of being a multi-campus system and used technology to improve access to its library collections. The California Digital Library allows students and faculty from every campus to request articles from more than 7,000 journals available to UC scholars online. These articles are delivered electronically to the desktop, rather than by trucks driving between campuses.

As shown in Figure 5.10, interlibrary book loans have increased from 44,000 to 116,000; however, the electronic delivery of research journal articles to the desktop has skyrocketed from 1.2 million to 8.1 million. The cost-effective California Digital Library has been a great success, but there is an important lesson to be learned from this project: the University is now reaping the benefits of investments in technology made in better times. The campuses have identified some other cost-saving measures in academic support functions that cannot be implemented because the University does not have the resources to make the necessary up-front investments.

The University has also taken steps to streamline and reduce costs in its business operations:

- Strategic Procurement Initiative: This initiative leverages the enormous buying power of a multi-campus system to lower costs from vendors. In addition to better prices, this initiative will allow the University to buy goods and services more efficiently and to monitor prices more closely.
- Information Technology Procurement: The University has greatly expanded its coordination of computer hardware and software procurement, which will save our departments significant dollars each year.
- Debt Restructuring: The University took advantage of historically low interest rates to refinance more than $1.1 billion in outstanding bonds for capital projects. This initiative will provide substantial savings in debt service over the next 32 years.

In short, the University of California has taken a number of steps to streamline its administrative processes and leverage the power of a multi-campus system. Nevertheless, there is simply no way to compensate for the cumulative effects of cuts shown in Figures 5.8 and 5.9, even with the sharp student fee increases shown in Figure 5.7.

HOW DID THE RECENT BUDGET CUTS AND FEE INCREASES AFFECT UC'S EDUCATIONAL PROGRAM?

State taxpayer support for higher education declined over the last three decades, and tuition increases at public colleges and universities have offset only a fraction of those cuts (Kane and Orszag 2004, Rizzo 2004). In contrast, private funding and tuition have increased steadily at private universities during this period. As a result, the gap in available resources between public and private universities has grown (Ehrenberg 2004). Some (cf., Ehrenberg 2000; 2004) have concluded that:

- Faculty recruitment and retention at public universities have been affected by low faculty salaries, which are well behind those of private institutions.
- Public universities have substituted non-tenure–track faculty for ladder rank positions to save money, which has consequences for the quality of the educational experience.
- Budget cuts at public universities have led to higher student/faculty ratios and larger class sizes, which affect the quality of undergraduate education.
- The growing gap in support for graduate students and academic support services, such as libraries, reduces the quality of the educational experience at public universities and affects their ability to recruit the best graduate students.
- Less state subsidy and higher prices could be prohibitive for low-income students and will squeeze middle-class families.

As demonstrated in the first two sections of this chapter, the long-term national trend toward a declining percentage of the state budget going to higher education is also true of California, as is the short-term budget cutting at the beginning of the current decade. Indeed, the devastating impact of the collapse of the Internet bubble has arguably been harder on California's technology-heavy economy than other states. Had the state's loss of tax revenue resulted in proportionate cuts to higher education, the impact on California's colleges and universities would have been catastrophic, changing in fundamental ways the very nature of the institutions.

The catastrophe was avoided, however, by borrowing billions to cover non-energy–related operating budget shortfalls and shifting much of the financial impact to future generations. Although not catastrophic, the University of California has nevertheless experienced large budget cuts. In the remainder of this section, we examine whether the effects of these fiscal forces on the University of California are consistent with the national trends for public universities.

Has Faculty Recruitment and Retention Been Affected by Lagging Salaries?

UC Must Hire 7,000 Faculty Between 1998 and 2010

Faculty demographics reflect a combination of retirements and separations, as well as new hires. The period of rapid expansion of student enrollment to accommodate Tidal Wave II has also been a period of increased retirement of UC faculty.

Figure 5.11 shows the age profile of UC faculty. The 1990 profile was made before the University offered an early retirement incentive program to eligible

Figure 5.11
Age distribution of University of California faculty at three points in time

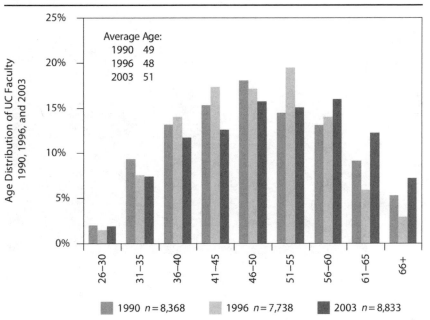

Average Age:
1990 49
1996 48
2003 51

1990 n=8,368   1996 n=7,738   2003 n=8,833

faculty and staff (Switkes 2001). That program, offered between 1991 and 1994, resulted in the retirement of 2,000 tenured faculty and caused the dip in faculty numbers and the drop in the average age reflected in the 1996 data in Figure 5.11. The solid bars reflect more recent data on the age distribution of the faculty. The larger percentage of faculty over age 55 portends an increasing wave of retirements and the need for even more faculty recruiting.

Since 2000, UC campuses have been recruiting faculty for both growth and replacements as fast as they can. The long-range enrollment plan assumed growth of 60,000 students over a 12-year period (1998 to 2010) and called for hiring 7,000 new faculty (an average of 585 per year). Figure 5.12 illustrates the model developed to estimate faculty hiring on the general campuses and the health sciences. Not shown are the unprecedented 586 hires in 2003–2004, a University of California record.

Figure 5.12
University of California faculty recruitment and retention plan

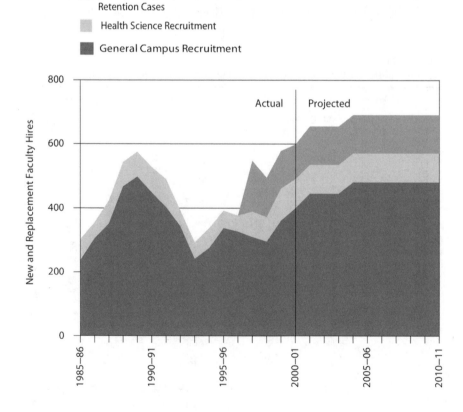

UC Faculty Salaries Are Below Market

Faculty salaries have fallen 10 percent below market during California's fiscal crisis (Figure 5.13). The growing lag in faculty and staff salaries is one of the areas of greatest concern as a result of years of underfunding of the University's budget. No funds were provided for salary increases for 2003–2004 or 2004–2005, although those faculty who were eligible for merit increases[1] did receive them because the University made additional internal budget cuts.

There Has Not Yet Been a Significant Impact on Recruitment and Retention

Had the drop in UC faculty salaries relative to its peer institutions had an effect on retention, one would have expected to see an increase in separations. With the exception of the increasing number of retirements noted previously, however, the annual rates of separation for both assistant professors and tenured faculty continue to be very modest (varying between 1.0 and 1.3 percent over the last 4 years). The University's efforts to block faculty raids from competing universities, however, have not been without cost. Matching outside offers of faculty being recruited by other institutions is expensive and causes unwelcome inequities in salaries among colleagues.

Figure 5.13
Average faculty salaries for the University of California in relation to those of peer universities

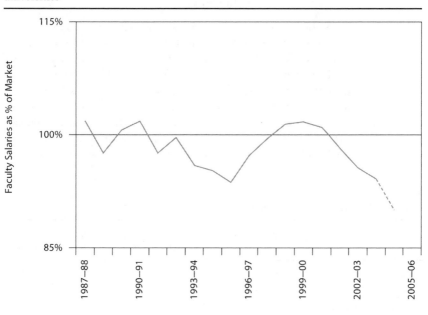

The faculty recruitment and start-up costs for new faculty are very high, and the University's recruiting difficulties are compounded by the high cost of housing in California. However, UC campuses have continued to hire large numbers of new faculty, including a record number in 2003–2004. The University of California continues to recruit excellent faculty for a number of reasons; among them is the fact that the University offers an excellent benefits and superior retirement package. This could change, however, because Governor Schwarzenegger has proposed major changes in public retirement programs, including the one offered by the University of California. If approved by the legislature or by the voters through the initiative process in the form proposed by the Governor, these changes would seriously damage faculty recruitment and retention at the University of California.

Has The University of California Relied on Part-time Faculty to Cut Costs?

To test this hypothesis, payroll records for general campus faculty (excluding the health sciences) were analyzed for several years. As shown in Table 5.1, the percentage of regular faculty has remained steady for more than 20 years. The University of California has *not* reacted to the budget cuts by hiring a larger percentage of lecturers, instructors, and other temporary faculty.

Have the Budget Cuts and Fee Increases Affected the Education Experience?

In the mid-1960s, the University's budgeted student/faculty ratio was 14.5 to 1. In the early 1970s, it increased to 17.6 to 1, where it stayed for nearly 20 years. During the budget cuts of the early 1990s, it rose to 18.7 to 1. As a result, the University's student/faculty ratio is higher than the average of the four public comparison universities and much higher than those of the four private comparison schools.

During California's recent fiscal crisis governors twice proposed further increases in the student/faculty ratio and made associated cuts in the University's budget totaling $70 million. The University of California has constitutional autonomy, however, and the board of regents chose not to implement those increases in the

Table 5.1
The Mix of General Campus Faculty in the University of California

	1981 (%)	1985 (%)	1990 (%)	1995 (%)	2000 (%)	2004 (%)
Regular Professorial Faculty	79	79	81	80	78	80
Lecturers, Instructors and Other Temporary Faculty	21	21	19	20	22	20

student/faculty ratio. Instead, the president was directed to cut campus budgets on a temporary basis and develop a multiyear plan to restore the $70 million.

In addition, campuses have made it a high priority to provide students with the classes they need to graduate. Campuses made a commitment to add 1,000 lower division classes and instituted a program of freshman seminars to address concerns about large, impersonal classes. In addition, increased use of summer session and increased participation of regular faculty in summer session teaching have made it easier for undergraduates to complete their programs of study on time. The success of these and other efforts can be seen in persistence and graduation rates (Figure 5.14).

Ninety-two percent of the entering freshman class returns to enroll in the second year. The five-year graduation rate for entering freshman has increased slightly from 69 to 73 percent over the last 10 years. It is important to note, however, that students are taking fewer quarters to complete their degrees and the four-year graduation rate has increased more than the five-year rate. In a perverse way, higher fees seem to have encouraged students to complete their studies more rapidly.

Have Budget Cuts Affected the Ability to Recruit the Best Graduate Students?

Before the onset of California's fiscal crisis, there was concern about the university's ability to recruit the best graduate students. Therefore the president appointed a

Figure 5.14
Persistence and graduation rates of students who enter the University of California as freshmen

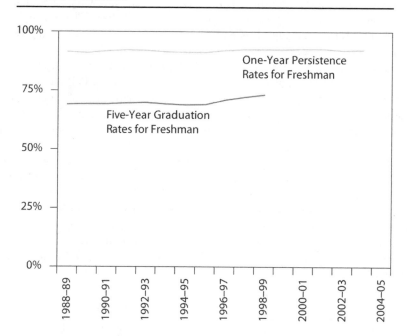

Commission on the Growth and Support of Graduate Students to study the problem and develop recommendations. The Commission (2001) found the most serious problem to be in doctoral fellowships. Those applicants who were offered a fellowship by a UC campus but chose to attend another university typically received an offer from the competing institution that was a net $2,000 higher than the UC offer after accounting for differences in the cost of living in different regions.

In response, the University of California took a number of steps to close the gap. Over the next four years, however, the fees for graduate academic students almost doubled ($3,609 in 2001–2002 to $6,897 in 2005–2006), and there was widespread concern that UC offers were falling further behind. However, a follow-up study found that the fellowship offers accepted by those choosing to attend another university were still approximately $2,000 higher than the offer from a UC campus, apparently because those competing institutions were also facing budget problems.

Have Tuition Increases Affected the Enrollment or Academic Performance of Undergraduates from Low-income Families?

In accordance with the Master Plan for Higher Education, the University of California sets its eligibility requirements to serve the top one-eighth of California high school graduates. Enrolling these students is predicated on students and their families being able to afford a University of California education. Affordability is a function of the cost of attendance and the availability of financial aid.

The University of California's financial aid programs are designed to make UC financially accessible to all students through a combination of part-time work during the academic year and work during the summer; borrowing; parental contribution in accordance with their ability to pay; and then federal, state, and UC grants and scholarships. Students from low-income families are eligible for Pell grants. In each of the past few years, UC campuses have received national acclaim for enrolling large numbers of Pell recipients. Despite the sharp increases in undergraduate fees, almost one in three UC students is a Pell recipient. As shown in Figure 5.15, UC figures are much higher than those of other leading research universities because the university distributes an unusually large amount of institutional aid and because its eligibility pool has a large percentage of applicants from low-income families.

Enrolling low-income students does not necessarily mean that they will be able to stay in school and graduate. A recent presentation to the UC Board of Regents by Provost M.R.C. Greenwood (March 2005) addressed this concern. She demonstrated that first-year persistence rates for low-income students (for families with incomes of less than $40,000) were the same as those for middle- and high-income students. Low-income students took a little longer to graduate, but graduation rates after six years were similar to those for students from middle-income families.

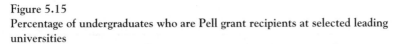

Figure 5.15
Percentage of undergraduates who are Pell grant recipients at selected leading universities

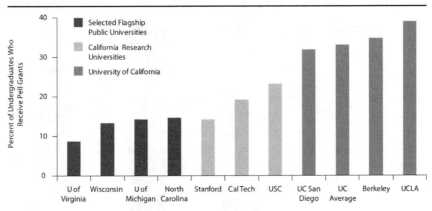

The University of California's enviable record in enrolling and graduating low-income students despite large student fee increases is attributable, in large part, to the availability of financial aid. Scholarships and grants, excluding loans, increased from $730 million in 2001–2002 to more than $1 billion in 2004–2005. On the national scene this would be considered a "moderate tuition/high aid" policy. The state legislature has increased the amount of financial aid available through the Student Aid Commission and the University of California has increased its commitment of internal funds. Current regental policy returns 25 percent of the increase in undergraduate student fees in the form of financial aid. These additional dollars have been targeted so that low-income undergraduate students have not been affected by the fee increases.

As a result, most low-income students are able to enroll and complete their degrees without accumulating large amounts of debt. Figure 5.16 shows the percentage of students who graduated in 2003-2004 with no debt, manageable debt, and high debt at four income levels. In this chart, high debt is defined as debt requiring more than 9 percent of the average student's starting salary. As can be seen in Figure 5.16, many graduating seniors chose not to borrow at all, even 26 percent of the low-income students.

Very few UC students graduated with high debt. Even among low-income students, only 4 percent graduated with high debt. In addition, repayment plans are available to help them manage their debt, including extended payment plans, graduated plans, and income-contingent plans. In short, the impact of tuition and fee increases on low-income families has been minimized by sharp increases in financial aid. Access has been maintained for low-income students under the University of California's "moderate tuition/high aid" policy, but California's fiscal crisis has stretched middle-income families.

Figure 5.16
Debt carried at graduation by University of California undergraduates by income level

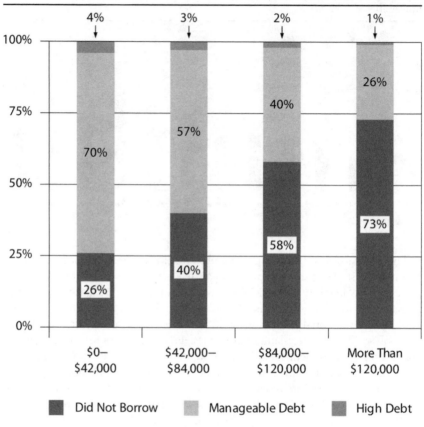

CONCLUSION

In the section of this chapter on "Less Taxpayer Support for Higher Education," we said that it was important to separate the short-term budgetary effects of a bursting Internet bubble from long-term trends in the funding of public higher education. The state of California has followed the long-term, national trend of governors and legislators giving a lower priority to higher education. For example, the percentage of the State General Fund Budget appropriated to the University of California declined from 7 percent in 1970 to 3.5 percent in 2004–2005. Correspondingly, the State General Fund appropriation to the university as a percentage of total revenue declined from 41 to 19 percent over that same period.

The short-term pattern in most states of budget cuts to higher education during the recent economic downturn has also occurred in this state. California's loss of capital gains and stock options revenue was one of the worst in the nation, and the resulting fiscal crisis led to reductions in state appropriations to the university of 15 percent over the last four years, while enrollment was growing by 19 percent.

The University of California took several actions to minimize the impact of these reductions in state funding. Despite sharp increases, student tuition and fee increases offset less than one-third of the total cut. Those additional tuition and fee revenues, however, were targeted and offset much of the impact on instructional programs, but there were large cuts in other areas. Steps were taken to streamline administrative processes to make better use of limited state funds. Also, the university used technology and leveraged the power of a multi-campus system to soften the effects on academic support budgets. Nevertheless, the quality of the educational program has been affected, and salaries for both faculty and staff are well below market.

To determine the effectiveness of the University of California's strategies, we tested several hypotheses about the impact of budget cuts on public universities. We found that UC faculty salaries had fallen behind those of the privates, but the gap had not substantially affected recruitment and retention. Unlike the pattern at many other public institutions, the university has not substituted more non-tenure–track faculty for ladder rank positions to save money. Even though governors in California had cut budgets and proposed to increase the student/faculty ratio twice, the university chose to protect the quality of the educational program by cutting budgets in other areas temporarily and establishing a long-term plan to restore the former budgeted student/faculty ratio.

In terms of students, we found that the tuition and fee increases at the University of California had a larger impact on graduate than undergraduate students. Graduate student support, particularly fellowships for doctoral students, is behind market and the Academic Senate has made this a high priority. The impact of the tuition and fee increases on low-income undergraduate students, however, has been minimized by substantial increases in financial aid.

In short, the University of California seems to have avoided in the short run some of the more serious effects on the academic program of the loss of state funds. A new compact with Governor Schwarzenegger ends four years of budget cutting and provides a floor for future budget increases. But, what about the future? The compact is not a guarantee of future funding but rather a good-faith effort by the governor to fund it and a good-faith effort on the part of the university to meet the accountability elements. Agreements like this one have been broken in the past during economic downturns, and it could happen again.

Of course, this state faces a long list of other competing needs. Like the governors in other states, Governor Schwarzenegger is struggling with budget priorities, such as below-average school funding and rising health care costs. And future governors will be faced with a huge bill for health care and other social services when the baby boomers retire.

On the other hand, California's economy, which is currently the sixth largest in the world, is well positioned for competitiveness in the twenty-first century with R&D-intensive industry clusters, such as information technology and software in the Silicon Valley, aerospace in Los Angeles, and pharmaceuticals in San Diego. As the Chairman of the Federal Reserve Board, Alan Greenspan told then Governor Gray Davis (2001) a few years ago, California's economy will go through its ups and downs but over the long term this state will do relatively well because it has more research universities than any other.

The 10 campuses of the University of California are critical pieces of the fabric of higher education, which has been so important to the state's economy and quality of life. A decline in the quality of educational programs and research enterprises would not be in the public interest and must not be allowed to happen.

NOTE

1. University of California faculty have a regular pre- and post-tenure review process that provides a detailed merit review every two to four years depending on rank. This review continues throughout all faculty members' careers and consists of an examination of their accomplishments in teaching, research, and service by their department colleagues and the dean. On most UC campuses, the file is then evaluated by a campus-wide faculty committee, with final approval by the provost. Advancement is not automatic (cf., Switkes 1999).

CHAPTER 6

Assessing Public Higher Education in Georgia at the Start of the Twenty-first Century

Christopher Cornwell and David B. Mustard

This chapter examines public higher education in Georgia and compares it with its counterparts in other states. First, we develop a context for understanding Georgia's track record by comparing the state's recent changes in demographic, economic, employment, and education with those of the rest of the nation. These comparisons show that Georgia has experienced rapid population and economic growth over the last 15 years. Therefore it is not surprising to find that employment and enrollment in higher education grew substantially faster in Georgia than it did in the rest of the nation. Second, we briefly describe the institutional landscape of Georgia's higher education sector. We explain the governing mechanisms and how the public institutions are categorized, and it highlights distinctive institutions like the state's historically black colleges and universities (HBCUs). Third, we assess the inputs (e.g., appropriations, tuition and financial aid policy, and faculty) and outputs (e.g., enrollment, retention, and graduation) of the state's higher education system. Overall, there have been significant gains in Georgia compared to other states during the 1990s. However, since the 2001 recession, Georgia's measures have dropped precipitously relative to the performance in other states. Finally, we offer some concluding remarks.

GEORGIA IN CONTEXT

Before we assess public higher education in Georgia, it is important to place the state's higher-education sector in an appropriate context. At a minimum, this requires taking account of the state's population and economy, both in terms of

Table 6.1
Population Demographics
Georgia versus United States, 1990–2003

Characteristic	Georgia			U.S.		
	1990	2003	%Δ	1990	2003	%Δ
Total (millions)	6.478	8.685	34.1	248.791	290.810	16.9
% White	71.0	67.5	−4.9	80.3	80.5	0.2
% Black	30.0	28.8	−4.0	12.1	12.8	5.8
% Hispanic	1.7	6.2	264.7	9.0	13.7	52.2
% 18–24	11.1	10.2	−8.1	10.5	9.9	−5.7
Public High-School Graduates (thousands)	56.6	67.1	18.6	2,320.3	2,684.9	15.7
% High School Graduate	70.9	85.1	20.0	75.2	84.6	12.5
% with BA	19.3	25.0	29.5	20.3	27.2	34.0

Source: Bureau of Economic Analysis and Statistical Abstract of the United States.

current levels and recent growth rates. Table 6.1 compares Georgia with the entire United States in terms of population demographics that are related to higher education trends. Georgia is the ninth most populous state, with approximately 8.7 million people. Its population has grown 34.1 percent since 1990, which is more than twice that of the nation as a whole and 65 percent greater than that of the other southeastern states. Like the rest of the United States, the racial composition of Georgia's population has changed in the last 15 years, largely because of the influx of Hispanics. Since 1990, Georgia's Hispanic population share increased more than threefold, from 1.7 to 6.2 percent. With the rise in Hispanics, its white and black population shares have declined slightly since 1990. Still, Georgia has the fourth largest black population and the fourth highest black population share at 29 percent. In contrast, the overall U.S. population is only 12.8 percent black.

As the U.S. population grows older, the college-going cohort is shrinking in relative terms, both in Georgia and the nation. Nevertheless, the number of public high school graduates rose 18.6 percent in Georgia between 1990 and 2003, which is 3 percentage points greater than the national increase. Similarly, the percentage of Georgia's population with a high school diploma jumped 20 percent during this period, compared with only a 12.5 percent increase in the rest of the United States. By 2003, Georgia overtook the nation in terms of the size of its high school graduate population share. The state also made considerable strides in the stock of bachelor's degrees, but its population

Table 6.2
Income and Employment
Georgia versus United States, 1990–2003

Variable	Georgia			U.S.		
	1990	2003	%Δ	1990	2003	%Δ
GSP, GDP (in 1996 dollars)	164.8	273.9	66.2	6,630.7	9,335.4	40.8
Median Household Income (in 2000 dollars)	36,218	42,508	17.4	39,119	42,873	9.6
Per Capita Personal Income (in 2000 dollars)	21,868	27,953	27.8	24,196	30,033	24.1
Percent Below Poverty Level	15.8	12.1	−23.4	13.5	11.7	−13.3
Total Employment (in millions)	3.2	4.4	37.5	123.3	146.5	18.8
Employment in Higher Education (in thousands)	32.2	49.5	53.7	1,539.7	1,825.0	18.5

Source: Statistical Abstract of the United States.

share with a bachelor degree still lags behind that of the United States, 25 to 27.2 percent.

Next we compare Georgia and the United States in terms of some fundamental economic measures. Table 6.2 provides output, income, and employment data for Georgia and the United States in 1990 and 2003. As with population growth over the last 15 years, Georgia outpaced the United States in all three economic measures. Georgia's gross state product rose 66.1 percent, which is almost 50 percent greater than the increase in gross domestic product over the period. The state's median household income jumped 17.4 percent, which almost doubled the national increase. At $42,508, median household income in Georgia is now only about $350 less than the U.S. median. Commensurate with its gains in output and income, the share of Georgia's population living in poverty fell 23.4 percent to put its current poverty rate on par with the rest of the United States. Between 1990 and 2003, total employment in Georgia grew 37.5 percent, twice as fast as the U.S. employment rate and three percent more than the state's population. A disproportionate share of employment growth occurred in higher education, which increased 53.7 percent, from 32,200 to 49,500. By comparison, the employment growth rate in higher education for the entire United States increased only 18.4 percent, or only one-third that of Georgia.

In sum, Georgia was one of the fastest growing states over the last 15 years, both in terms of population and income. As a result of this growth, its population shares of high school and college graduates and its poverty rate converged to the national averages. Against this backdrop, Georgia's higher education sector expanded dramatically, albeit with disparate impacts across the distributions of institution and student quality.

GEORGIA'S HIGHER EDUCATION INSTITUTIONAL LANDSCAPE

Georgia supports 68 public postsecondary institutions: 21 four-year colleges and universities, 13 degree-granting two-year colleges, and 34 technical schools that specialize in certificate and diploma programs. The 34 degree-granting two-year and four-year institutions make up the University System of Georgia (USG) and are governed by an 18-member board of regents (BOR). The regents are appointed by the governor, one from each of the state's 13 congressional districts and 5 at-large representatives. The BOR elects a chancellor who serves as the chief administrative officer of the USG. Georgia's technical schools are administered through the state's Department of Technical and Adult Education (DTAE) and are accountable to a state board that is constituted similarly to the BOR.

Georgia further classifies its 21 four-year institutions as research universities,[1] regional universities,[2] state universities,[3] or state colleges.[4] The two flagship campuses are the University of Georgia (UGA) and Georgia Institute of Technology (GA Tech). (See the map of Georgia's degree-granting colleges and universities by classification.) In 1996, the "state university" classification was extended to many former state colleges that had expanded their missions. The key distinctions moving from the first to last institution class are the emphases on research, the scope of degree offerings, the scale of operation, and the sphere of influence.

Table 6.3, which summarizes headcount enrollment levels and changes since 1995, gives some perspective on the "market shares" of each USG institution class. Total enrollment in USG schools rose 21.4 percent over the last 10 years, which is slightly greater than the percentage increase in high school graduates. State and two-year colleges experienced the greatest percentage gains (46.2 and 38.4, respectively), increasing their shares of USG enrollment. The state and two-year college gains came primarily at the expense of the research and regional universities, whose enrollment shares (32 and 10.5 percent) dropped slightly since 1995. Overall, USG class enrollment shares remained relatively stable. From a broader perspective that includes the DTAE schools, this stability is somewhat misleading. From 1995 to 2003 (the latest year data are available), the DTAE share of all postsecondary enrollment rose from 33.4 to 61.2 percent as the number of students enrolled in technical schools more than doubled from 69,057 to 153,444. This period is marked by the introduction and expansion of Georgia's HOPE (Helping Outstanding Pupils Educationally) program, but the bulk of the enrollment increases for both USG and DTAE schools occurred after 2000, when

Map 6.1 Map of Georgia's Colleges and Universities

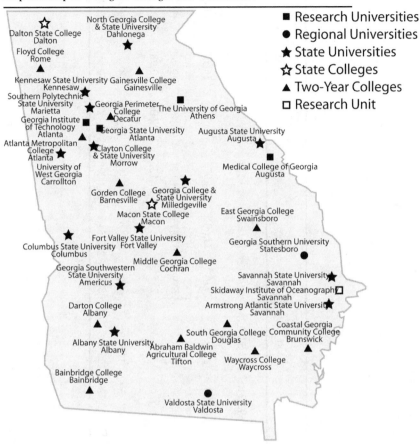

Source: University System of Georgia.

the state and national economies entered a recession. One apparent outcome of the economic downturn was a substitution away from relatively more expensive private and out-of-state colleges to in-state public institutions.

Given Georgia's relatively large African American population, an important subset of the "state university" class is its three public HBCUs: Albany State University, Fort Valley State University, and Savannah State University. Combined with the state's five private HBCUs (Clark Atlanta University, Morehouse College, Morris Brown College, Paine College and Spelman College), they account for a significant fraction of its four-year college enrollment and more than 45 percent of all blacks attending college in Georgia.

Georgia has 31 private four-year schools, five of which are for-profit institutions such as the DeVry Institute of Technology. Only one, Emory University, is highly

Table 6.3
Headcount Enrollment
University System of Georgia, 1995–2004

Institution Class	1995	1996	1997	1998	1999	2000	2001	2002	2003	2004	Percent Change
Research Universities	69,983	68,298	69,410	69,171	70,805	72,098	76,012	79,337	81,095	80,063	14.4
Regional Universities	23,742	24,111	23,744	23,290	23,205	22,976	23,601	24,975	26,251	26,500	11.6
State Universities	66,812	66,671	66,834	64,530	65,180	65,659	67,575	73,141	78,488	79,967	19.7
State Colleges	6,832	6,643	6,656	6,526	6,793	7,255	8,132	9,126	9,604	9,985	46.2
Two-Year Colleges	39,115	38,609	38,745	36,585	37,823	37,890	42,226	46,519	51,582	54,144	38.4
USG Total	206,484	204,332	205,389	200,102	203,806	205,878	217,546	233,098	247,020	250,659	21.4

Source: University System of Georgia.

selective with a market that extends beyond the region. The vast majority are small liberal arts colleges with costs of attendance far less than Emory and more on par with the out-of-state charges at public four-year institutions.

ASSESSING THE INPUTS

In this section, we review the recent changes in Georgia's state appropriations for higher education, tuition, financial aid, and faculty composition, pay, and employment. However, no assessment of the state's higher education system—inputs or outputs—can ignore the effects of its lottery-financed HOPE financial aid program, which was introduced in 1993. Cornwell, Leidner, and Mustard (2005) document that HOPE's impact extends well beyond Georgia, as nearly 30 state-sponsored merit programs have started since 1993, about 15 of which closely follow the Georgia model. Therefore, we first provide an overview of the HOPE program.

Georgia's HOPE Program

Through its HOPE program, Georgia distributes two types of financial aid: a merit-based scholarship and a non-merit–based grant. To qualify for the scholarship, students must graduate from a Georgia high school with a "B" average. The scholarship pays all tuition and fees and $300 of book expenses to students attending degree-granting public institutions. For the 2005–2006 academic year, the value of the award is about $4,600 at the state's flagship institutions.[5] HOPE scholars attending private, degree-granting institutions receive a fixed payment of $3,000. Once in college, students must maintain a "B" average with a minimum number of credits to retain the award. Because it has no merit requirements, the HOPE Grant is an entitlement; however, it applies only to nondegree programs at two-year and technical schools. The grant covers tuition and mandatory fees, and students receive it for coursework required for a certificate or diploma.

Table 6.4 disaggregates program disbursements by the number of awards and dollars of aid from 1993 to 2002.[6] Degree-granting institutions accounted for 55 percent of all awards and 78 percent of total aid during this period, with four-year colleges and universities representing 44 and 60 percent of these totals, respectively. Thus, program resources were overwhelmingly devoted to the merit-based scholarship, and in particular, to high-school graduates matriculating at four-year public schools. The other 45 percent of awards flowed to technical schools as HOPE grants, but these institutions received a relatively small proportion of total aid owing to their low tuition.

Georgia's lottery, which was instituted primarily to fund HOPE and a universal pre-K program, has been extraordinarily successful. Because lottery sales far outpaced all early projections, the legislature expanded scholarship eligibility and award generosity. Initially, the scholarship was restricted to students from households with incomes less than $66,000, but the income cap was raised to $100,000

Table 6.4
Numbers of HOPE Awards
and Dollars of Aid, by Institution Type, 1993–2002

Institution Class	Number of Awards	% of Total	Aid in Millions of Dollars	% of Total
4-Year Schools	526,033		942.00	
Public	389,452	32.0	840.09	53.7
Private	136,581	11.2	101.91	6.5
2-Year Schools	144,061		279.43	279.43
Public	109,362	9.0	237.48	15.2
Private	34,699	2.8	41.95	2.7
Technical (DTAE) Schools	547,078	44.9	342.86	21.9
HOPE Program Total	1,217,172		1564.3	−8.6

Note: Of the 34 HOPE-eligible DTAE schools, 13 offer associate's degrees.
Source: Cornwell and Mustard (2003).

in 1994 and removed entirely in 1995. Also in 1995, the value of the private-school award was raised from $1,000 to $1,500, and then to $3,000 the next year. In 1996 and 1997, legislation made it easier for nontraditional students to qualify, and in 1998, home-school students were allowed to earn the scholarship retroactively to their freshmen years if they met the collegiate grade-point average criterion.

During this prosperous period the legislature also voted to use the lottery to fund other scholarships. Examples include the Public Safety Memorial Grant (1994), the Georgia Military College Scholarship (1995),[7] the PROMISE Teacher Scholarship,[8] the HOPE Teacher Scholarship (1996),[9] and the Scholarship for Engineering Education (1998).[10] Two features distinguish these "add-on" programs from HOPE. One is the increased use of service-cancelable loans instead of direct grants. The second is a requirement to work or serve in Georgia after graduation.

The last significant legislative expansion of the HOPE program occurred in 2001 when the Pell "offset" was removed. In the beginning, HOPE payments (both scholarship and grant) were reduced (offset) dollar-for-dollar for any Pell aid received by the student. Eliminating the offset ended one of the most common criticisms of HOPE. Now, low-income students who qualify for both Pell and HOPE can "stack" their awards, providing an even more powerful incentive to attend a Georgia college or university. As an indication of the impact of this program change, the state estimated that removing the Pell offset would require roughly $23 million in additional funds to provide Pell recipients with HOPE scholarships, but eventually distributed $87.8 million to 56,879 Pell-eligible students in 2002 alone (Seligman, Milford, O'Looney, and Ledbetter, 2004).

Figure 6.1
Lottery allocations to education versus educational expenditures, FY 1994–2009

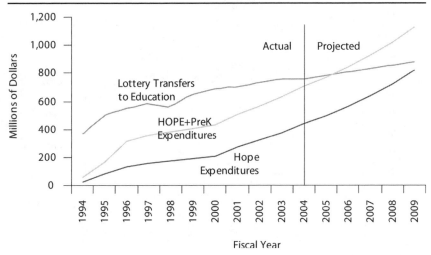

Source: Seligman (2003).

Notes: 1994 fiscal year runs from July 1, 1993–June 30, 1994. The values for 2004 and following are projections. The lottery projections include a 3.2 percent annual growth rate, which was the most favorable growth rate the commission considered. The educational projections were based on the number of students who are expected to utilize the resources.

Recently, there has been increasing concern that program expenditures will outstrip lottery revenue. Figure 6.1 compares the growth in the lottery funding for education with the expenditures on the HOPE and pre-K programs, projected through 2009. In its first year the lottery generated $1.12 billion in revenue and transferred $363 million to education. Since then, lottery transfers to education have grown rapidly since its inception, rising to almost $800 million in 2004. Despite the success of Georgia's lottery—its revenues grew over 200 percent in its first 10 years—it has not kept pace with the rise in expenditures by the programs the lottery is designated to fund. As illustrated in Figure 6.1, the sum of HOPE and pre-K spending is expected to match lottery resources by 2006. HOPE expenditures alone are projected to absorb almost all of the lottery funding by 2009. Cornwell, Mustard, and Sridhar (forthcoming) review the range of options the state has considered to ensure the financial stability of HOPE. Thus far, legislative action has been limited to minor adjustments in the high school grade-point average computation for HOPE eligibility and a contingency plan to reduce the book allowance in the event the difference between resources and expenditures dips below a set threshold.

State Appropriations

Given Georgia's population and economic growth in recent years, it is not surprising that state-appropriated higher education spending also rose; however,

Figure 6.2
Higher education expenditures in Georgia, 1989–2002 (in 2004 dollars)

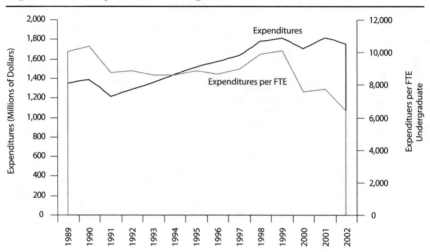

Source: NASSGAP.

these expenditure data reflect HOPE disbursements, which exceeded $2 billion through 2002. Figure 6.2 depicts the trends in real total and per undergraduate full-time equivalent (FTE) expenditures by the state from 1989 to 2002. After the recession that opened the decade, total spending increased from $1.21 billion (2004 dollars) in 1991 to $1.82 billion in 2001.

Although there was substantial growth in total allocations during this period, there was a pronounced drop in funding per FTE student. In 2004 dollars, this amount dropped 15.5 percent between 1990 and 1991 from $10,379 to $8,768. Between 1991 and 1999, there was some slight growth to $10,134. However, the large increase in the number of students and the decrease in funding with the last recession generated a sharp reduction from 1999 to 2002. In those three years, expenditures per FTE student dropped 36.7 percent (or $3,721) to $6,413, which was the lowest during the entire period. Later we examine some of the implications of this recent substantial decrease in aid in terms of faculty hiring and salaries.

This decline in state support can be illustrated alternatively by examining its share of the University of Georgia's total revenue. Figure 6.3 shows how the state's contribution (excluding HOPE) to higher education spending changed by charting the trends in revenue shares at UGA since 1987. The pattern is obvious: the state's share has steadily dropped, forcing the university to rely more heavily on tuition and private contributions. The share of UGA's total revenue accounted for by the state fell from 53.1 percent in 1987 to 34.7 percent in 2003, a pattern

Figure 6.3
Total revenue by share, University of Georgia, 1987–2003

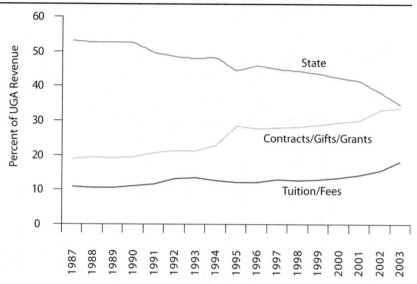

replicated across U.S. public higher education. Many large state universities (e.g., the Universities of Michigan and Virginia) now receive less than 15 percent of their funding from the state. Georgia is distinctive only because the decline in the state's share has been slower than the nation's as a whole.

Tuition, Fees, and Need-Based Aid

Table 6.5 presents a more comprehensive account of Georgia's recent tuition policy. Average tuition and fees at Georgia's four-year and two-colleges are reported with those of the other Southern Regional Education Board (SREB) member states and the U.S. and SREB medians for the academic years (AY) 1995 and 2002. These data provide a different perspective on the pattern of rising tuition at UGA depicted in Figure 6.3. Real tuition charges increased for Georgia residents, but in percentage terms the increases fell well below the regional and national medians. Real in-state tuition at Georgia's four-year schools rose only 16 percent AY1995 to AY2002, compared with 41 and 25.3 percent in the SREB and U.S. medians. In addition, Georgia's percentage increase and AY2002 level were the third lowest in the SREB. As a result, in AY2002, the average in-state tuition at Georgia's four-year schools, $2,576, amounted to only 79.2 percent of the SREB median and only 69.1 of the U.S. median.

Table 6.5
Real Tuition and Fees, Georgia versus the SREB and US, AY1995–2002

State/Region	Four-Year, In-State			Four-Year, Out-of-State			Two-Year		
	1995–96	2002–03	Pct Change	1995–96	2002–03	Pct Change	1995–96	2002–03	Pct Change
United States Median	$2,974	$3,728	25.3	$8,250	$9,998	11.6	$1,493	$1,952	19.9
SREB States Median	2,308	3,253	41.0	7,262	9,670	23.2	1,179	1,488	20.1
Georgia	2,221	2,576	16.0	6,004	8,606	16.1	1,330	1,522	6.0
Alabama	2,386	3,532	48.1	4,539	6,752	31.6	1,485	2,040	34.2
Arkansas	2,322	3,458	48.9	4,509	6,989	37.2	1,057	1,600	50.0
Delaware	3,852	4,873	26.5	9,952	12,021	7.4	1,568	1,806	36.3
Florida	2,119	2,696	27.2	7,897	12,172	36.1	1,265	1,583	12.9
Kentucky	2,322	3,126	34.6	6,282	8,076	24.8	1,155	1,536	24.0
Louisiana	2,377	2,515	5.8	5,432	8,433	35.0	1,249	1,490	18.7
Maryland	3,842	4,974	29.5	7,850	11,118	23.5	2,223	2,553	9.5
Mississippi	2,811	3,536	25.8	5,814	8,041	43.4	1,143	1,402	28.3
North Carolina	1,907	2,795	46.6	9,938	11,597	16.3	657	1,128	73.3
Oklahoma	1,964	2,346	19.5	4,563	5,475	12.2	1,338	1,626	11.1
South Carolina	3,607	4,704	30.4	7,598	10,310	25.7	1,179	2,136	75.6
Tennessee	2,277	3,454	51.7	7,145	10,412	36.0	1,214	1,735	34.9
Texas	2,110	3,278	55.3	8,898	9,818	1.0	843	1,088	14.0
Virginia	4,740	4,277	-9.8	10,709	11,754	11.6	1,684	1,488	-7.5
West Virginia	2,416	2,816	16.5	5,634	6,815	12.8	1,533	1,560	3.5

Source: SREB; tuition and fees expressed in terms of constant 2002 dollars.

Figure 6.4
Georgia's grant aid per FTE undergraduate and rank among all states, 1989–2002 (in 2004 dollars)

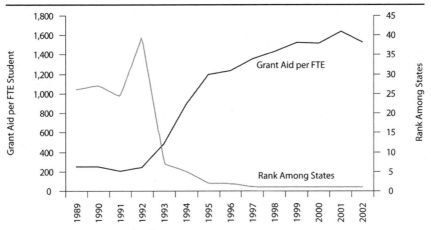

Source: NASSGAP.

This pattern is repeated in the state's two-year tuition and fees. Between AY1995 and AY2002, the average tuition of Georgia's two-year schools rose only 6 percent, which was the third smallest increase in the SREB and far below the regional and national hikes. In AY2002, Georgia remained in the bottom third of the SREB in terms of the cost of attending a public two-year college.

Charges to out-of-state students attending Georgia's four-year colleges increased at the same rate as in-state charges over the period. However, a 16 percent hike in nonresident tuition and fees exceeded the increase in U.S. median charges by 4.5 points. Georgia's increase still lagged behind the rise in median SREB out-of-state tuition. Georgia's out-of-state tuition and fees are more closely in line with the region's and nation's than its in-state charges. In AY2002, its nonresident tuition was 89 and 86 percent of the SREB and U.S. medians, respectively.

The relatively modest tuition increases that occurred in recent years can be explained in part by the introduction of the HOPE program in 1993. As noted earlier, USG schools' tuition is set centrally by the state's BOR. Because HOPE's award level is tied to tuition, the program constrains the BOR, because tuition increases translate into larger claims on lottery revenues. Evidence presented by both Cornwell et al. (forthcoming) and Long (2004) confirms that HOPE did not raise tuition in Georgia's public colleges and universities.

Not surprisingly, HOPE dramatically changed the state's grant aid. Figure 6.4 plots Georgia's grant aid per FTE undergraduate and its rank among the states on this measure over the period 1989–2002. In the late 1980s and early 1990s, Georgia's grant aid per FTE was relatively constant at slightly less than $250, which placed

Figure 6.5
Georgia's grant aid as a percentage of higher education expenditures and its rank
among all states, 1989–2002

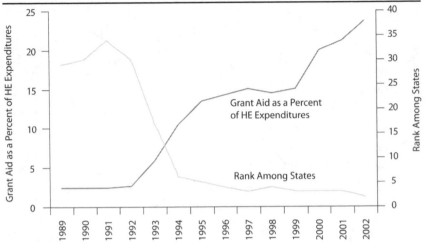

Source: NASSGAP.

the state between 25th and 39th in the United States. In 1992, the year before
HOPE's introduction, Georgia was 39th. This changed dramatically in 1993; in the
program's first year the state rose to seventh in grant aid per FTE, with about $500
per FTE. When the income cap was raised to $100,000 in 1994, Georgia moved up
to fifth, at nearly $900 per FTE. The state jumped to second after the income cap
on HOPE was removed in 1995 ($1,200 FTE). Since 1997, Georgia has distributed
more grant aid per FTE than any other state in the nation. In each year since 1999,
the state disbursed more than $1,500 in grant aid per FTE undergraduate.

Although not plotted separately, these trends are almost identical for grants
per FTE student. In 1992–1993, the year before HOPE, Georgia distributed 0.198
grants per FTE student, which ranked 24th among the states. In only three years
the state experienced an unprecedented change. By 1995–1996, the first year after
the income cap was removed, Georgia's rate rocketed to an astonishing 0.984, far
above second-place Vermont, which had 0.648 grants per FTE. All other states
distributed less than 0.50 per FTE. Georgia has held first place in this ranking
every year since 1994 (NASSGAP Annual Reports). This broad impact of the
HOPE program explains its substantial political support and the difficulty that
legislators face when considering reducing its generosity.

The impact of HOPE is reinforced in Figure 6.5, which shows Georgia's grant
aid as a percentage of higher education expenses. By 1995, state-sponsored grant
aid covered more than 15 percent of college costs, on average, and Georgia leaped
into the top five states in this category. By 2002, its grant-aid share of college
expenses had risen to almost 25 percent.

Georgia's impressive rise to the top ranks of state-sponsored grant aid is due to HOPE, which has no means test. A common argument against merit aid is that it reduces a state's commitment to need-based assistance, thus compromising the ability of needy students to succeed in college. Historically, however, Georgia has provided very little need-based aid—only about $25 to $30 per FTE before HOPE and $10 per FTE since then. In the year before HOPE, the state provided $4.9 million of strictly need-based grants, and $26.0 million of total aid (NASSGAP, *Annual Survey Reports*, 1993, Table 1, p. 40). By AY1997, Georgia provided more aid per full-time undergraduate and had a larger fraction of undergraduates who received aid than any other state in the nation (NASSGAP, *Annual Survey Reports*, 1998, Tables 12–13). So, in a state such as Georgia that never had a strong commitment to need-based aid and where substantially increasing need-based assistance is unlikely to be politically feasible, a large-scale merit-aid program may significantly increase the total funding available to low-income students. Singell, Waddell, and Curs (forthcoming) showed that even when the Pell offset existed, HOPE raised the enrollment of Pell-eligible students.

Faculty

In contrast to the enrollment growth depicted in Table 6.3, the faculty sizes of USG institutions exhibited a very different trend. Table 6.6 reports the number of faculty employed in each USG institution class at each rank in 1993 and 2002, and the percentage change over the period. As shown in the first row, the total number of USG faculty decreased 1.4 percent between 1993 and 2002. Overall, there was small growth in the number of full and associate professors, but assistant professors and non-tenure–track faculty declined markedly. A different trend occurred in research institutions, however, where a drop in the total number of faculty was accompanied by a sharp rise in non-tenure–track appointments. In 2002, research institutions employed one more professor than they did in 1993, but 8.6 percent fewer associate and 7.7 percent fewer assistant professors. Two-year college faculty sizes experienced the largest percentage decrease (23.2), in part owing to the relative price effects of HOPE on the four-year–two-year enrollment margin.

The most recent data for all institutions in the system are available only through 2002 and conceal the significant change in the number and composition of faculty that occurred in the last few years. The number of tenured and tenure-track faculty at UGA peaked in 2001 at 1,767 (*University of Georgia Fact Book*). In the next three years the number of full professors dropped by 4.6 percent and the number of associate professors increased by 1 from 509 to 510. Tight hiring restrictions significantly limited the hiring of assistant professors and their number fell by 15.8 percent. In contrast, during the same three-year period the number of instructors and lecturers increased 38.2 percent and 82.4 percent, respectively. Even this substantial increase in non-tenure–track faculty did not offset the drop among

Table 6.6
Number of Faculty in the "Corps of Instruction"
by Institution Type and Rank, 1993 and 2002

Institution Class	1993	2002	% Change
USG Total	8,995	8,870	−1.4
Professor	2,677	2,745	2.5
Associate	2,491	2,609	4.7
Assistant	2,976	2,780	−6.6
Other	851	736	−13.5
Research Universities	4,123	3,993	−3.2
Professor	1,512	1,513	0.0
Associate	1,302	1,190	−8.6
Assistant	1,130	1,043	−7.7
Other	179	247	38.0
Regional Universities	1,004	1,069	6.5
Professor	222	291	31.1
Associate	245	266	8.6
Assistant	389	408	4.9
Other	148	104	−29.7
State Universities	—	2,527	—
Professor	—	734	—
Associate	—	751	—
Assistant	—	869	—
Other	—	173	—
State Colleges	2,501	231	—
Professor	753	39	—
Associate	621	68	—
Assistant	929	101	—
Other	—	—	—
Two-Year Colleges	1,367	1,050	−23.2
Professor	190	168	−11.6
Associate	323	334	3.4
Assistant	528	359	−32.0
Other	326	189	−42.0

Table 6.7
Real Faculty Salaries by Institution Type and Rank,
1993 and 2002 (in 2002 dollars)

Institution Class	1993	2002	% Change
USG Total	54,860	63,689	16.1
Professor	68,115	87,174	28.0
Associate	54,920	62,944	14.6
Assistant	47,013	52,094	10.8
Research Universities	64,009	77,580	21.2
Professor	76,921	101,609	32.1
Associate	60,888	72,902	19.7
Assistant	56,144	62,583	11.5
Regional Universities	47,875	53,488	11.7
Professor	59,985	70,511	17.5
Associate	49,830	55,526	11.4
Assistant	42,184	47,449	12.5
State Universities	—	53,885	—
Professor	—	68,175	—
Associate	—	55,553	—
Assistant	—	46,182	—
State Colleges	47,784	50,975	6.7
Professor	56,868	67,903	11.8
Associate	48,573	55,168	13.6
Assistant	42,525	45,638	7.3
Two-Year Colleges	42,399	45,585	7.5
Professor	51,816	57,909	11.8
Associate	45,309	49,444	9.1
Assistant	38,591	42,160	9.2

Source: University System of Georgia.

tenured and tenure-track faculty, and the total number of instructional faculty decreased from 1,835 in 2001 to 1,769 in 2004, a reduction of 3.6 percent.

Table 6.7 complements Table 6.6 with the salary data for 1993 and 2002 by institution class and professorial rank. Overall, real faculty salaries in USG institutions rose 16.1 percent between 1993 and 2002. Underlying these gains are

Table 6.8
Faculty Salaries by Institution and Rank 1994 and 2004 (in 2004 dollars), Ranked by Percentage Change of Professor Salaries

Institution	1994–2005			2004–2005			Percent Change		
	Professor	Associate	Assistant	Professor	Associate	Assistant	Professor	Associate	Assistant
Louisiana State University	75.6	55.7	48.3	92.8	67.1	59.9	22.8	20.5	24.0
U of Maryland	93.0	63.6	54.9	111.0	76.3	75.2	19.3	20.0	36.9
U of North Carolina	95.2	68.7	56.7	112.7	77.2	65.8	18.4	12.4	16.0
U of Florida	81.7	57.9	52.4	96.0	69.1	59.5	17.5	19.4	13.6
U of Virginia	101.3	67.4	55.7	118.1	78.1	64.1	16.5	15.8	15.1
U of Oklahoma	77.8	56.7	46.3	89.7	62.0	51.7	15.4	9.3	11.7
U of Arkansas	73.4	56.7	49.6	84.5	63.0	54.6	15.1	11.1	10.1
U of Texas	75.6	56.1	46.7	86.0	65.4	59.9	13.8	16.6	28.4
U of South Carolina	81.2	60.4	52.3	92.1	65.7	59.2	13.4	8.7	13.3
U of Georgia	82.7	59.5	51.0	92.8	64.7	57.7	12.2	8.7	13.2
U of Tennessee	83.1	62.7	55.1	91.1	68.9	58.3	9.6	9.9	5.9
U of Mississippi	76.2	58.8	51.1	83.2	65.1	54.5	9.2	10.8	6.6
U of Alabama	81.3	60.7	51.4	88.0	64.0	52.3	8.2	5.5	1.8
U of Kentucky	83.7	62.1	53.8	90.0	64.1	57.7	7.5	3.3	7.3

Source: Chronicle of Higher Education.
Note: Salary data are only for the main campus of the flagship institutions in the SREB.

two clear patterns. First, salary increases were concentrated in the higher ranks. The salaries of assistant professors rose 10.8 percent, whereas associate and full professor pay jumped 14.6 percent and 28 percent, respectively. Second, salary growth rates were positively correlated with the scope of the institution. Faculty at the state's research and regional universities received average hikes of 32.1 and 17.5 percent, whereas those at state and two-year colleges received much smaller increases.

Table 6.8 puts the USG salary data in a regional context, comparing the growth in pay between 1994 and 2004 by rank in the SREB flagship institutions.[11] UGA generally ranks in the bottom third in real salary growth during the 1994–2004 period, with full, associate, and assistant professor pay rising 12.2, 8.7, and 13.2 percent, respectively. With the exception of full professor pay, where UGA ranks sixth in the region in 2004, the state's flagship is in the bottom third in salary levels. When comparing salaries across institutions, it is helpful to consider compositional effects. Part of the gap between UGA and some of the top institutions is that it has neither a medical nor an engineering school. The universities with the highest full professor salaries, Virginia, North Carolina, and Maryland, have one or the other or both.

Furthermore, examining only the first and last years obscures the substantial volatility in faculty salaries during the period. For example, UGA salaries experienced the third fastest growth rates until 1999 and the second slowest growth rates after 1999. Real salaries peaked at UGA and Georgia Tech in the 2002–2003 academic year. In the next two years, real salaries at UGA dropped 2.7 percent for professors, 4.5 percent for associates, and 0.6 percent for assistants. At Tech during the same period, real salaries dropped 1.5 percent for professors, 1.4 percent for associates, and 2.5 percent for assistants. Although the higher education systems in all states were affected negatively in the most recent economic slowdown, the impact was disproportionately large in Georgia. This decrease in faculty contemporaneous with an increase in enrollment increased the ratio of undergraduate students to tenured and tenure-track faculty by nearly 13 percent between 1998 and 2003.

ASSESSING THE OUTPUTS

Now we assess some of the primary outputs of Georgia's higher education system, namely enrollments, retention, and graduation rates. Again, the influence of the HOPE program permeates this discussion.

Enrollments

First, recall the enrollment data presented in Table 6.3 that show strong growth in USG institutions since 1995. In percentage terms, the greatest gains occurred at state colleges and two-year schools, but the enrollment in every institution class rose by at least 11 percent. Table 6.3, however, does not indicate whether these enrollment increases stand out when compared to the region or nation.

Table 6.9
Financial Aid for First-Time Freshmen HOPE and Pell, Fall 2001

Class of Institution	First-Time Freshmen from Georgia	No HOPE/Pell		HOPE and Pell		HOPE/No Pell	
		No.	%	No.	%	No.	%
Research Universities	6,836	27	0.4	5,617	82.2	1,045	15.3
Regional Universities	3,880	116	3.0	2,547	65.6	820	21.1
State Universities	8,067	454	5.6	4,915	60.9	1,728	21.4
State Colleges	1,069	140	13.1	501	46.9	196	18.3
Two-Year Colleges	7,358	1,023	13.9	2,855	38.8	1,240	16.8
System Total	27,210	1,760	6.5	16,435	60.4	5,029	18.5

Note: First-Time Freshmen from Georgia is defined as the subset of first-time freshmen who graduated from Georgia High School since 1993 plus freshmen receiving HOPE according to Georgia Student Finance Commission records.

Source: Data are from the Georgia Department of Education, 2002.

Cornwell et al. (forthcoming) compare college enrollments in Georgia with those in the other member states of the SREB through the first five years of HOPE. First, they show that the program increased total freshmen enrollment in Georgia colleges and universities by almost 6 percent, with the gains concentrated in four-year public and private schools. Second, they demonstrate that at least two-thirds of the increased enrollment of freshmen recently graduated from high school is due to the scholarship's incentive to remain in state for college; however, recent-graduate freshmen represent only about 40 percent of the total four-year-school enrollment increase. Third, in examining HOPE's effects on enrollment by race, they find that the scholarship increased white enrollment by about 3.6 percent and black enrollment by about 15 percent. Correspondingly, they report a significant 2.7 percentage-point rise in the black share of total (white + black) enrollment in Georgia. Much of the increased enrollment of blacks was accounted for by the state's HBCUs, whose enrollments rose 23 percent during the same period because of HOPE.

There are a couple of things to keep in mind when extrapolating from Georgia's experience with HOPE to other states adopting merit scholarship programs. First, it will be easier to retain academically accomplished high school graduates if highly selective colleges are located within the state. Over the last five years, Georgia (with Georgia Tech and the University of Georgia) is one of only four states that have at least two universities in the top 20 of the *U.S. News and World Report* rankings of national public universities (U.S. News & World Report, 2002). Second, the retention of black students likely depends on the size of the black population and number of HBCUs in the state.

Also important is the treatment of Pell aid. As mentioned earlier, with the elimination of the offset, Georgia's aid to Pell eligibles rose sharply, an effect that differed significantly by institution class. Table 6.9 presents the data on the numbers of Georgia-resident freshmen receiving either HOPE or Pell aid in fall 2001 by institution class. As indicated at the bottom of the last column, 18.5 percent of freshmen received both HOPE and Pell in fall 2001; however, Pell recipients represent a relatively small fraction (less than 16 percent) of total enrollment at the three research universities. Fewer than 1 percent of students enrolled at these institutions received Pell but not HOPE, whereas 15.4 percent received both. Low-income students make up an even smaller share at flagship schools, UGA and Georgia Tech, where only about 10 percent qualified for Pell.

Student Quality and Sorting

The concentration of Pell recipients outside the state's research universities raises questions about how enrollment may be stratified by income and student quality, and whether HOPE contributed to that stratification. UGA and Georgia Tech, which enroll the smallest percentage of Pell recipients, are by far the most selective of the state's public universities.

Overall, HOPE's influence on enrollment is not captured entirely by the decline in the number of students leaving the state; the composition of leavers also changed. Figure 6.6 plots the SAT series for freshmen enrolled in Georgia institutions and those of high school seniors in Georgia and the rest of the United States. The increases in SAT scores of Georgia freshmen stand out, rising about 60 points after HOPE. The SAT scores of the comparison groups increased by 30 points for Georgia high school seniors and by 20 points for high school seniors throughout the United States. Between 1993 and 2000, Georgia's rate of retaining students with SAT scores greater than 1500 climbed from 23 to 76 percent.

The overall increase in student quality depicted in Figure 6.6 does not address how the increase was shared across institution classes. Using data obtained from Peterson's covering the period 1989–2001, Cornwell et al. (2005) estimated HOPE's influence on both the mean and variance of student quality by comparing Georgia colleges to their SREB counterparts in terms of several common measures of academic achievement, including SAT scores and class rank. They show that the greatest gains in quality occurred at the state's most selective universities, where SAT verbal and math scores jumped by 14.3 and 9.4 points because of HOPE. Further, the scholarship increased these schools' percentage of students from the top 10 percent of their high school class by 7.6 percentage points. In contrast, the least selective schools experienced no statistically significant effect from HOPE on any measure of student quality. Finally, Cornwell and Mustard (2005) report that HOPE reduced the variance of SAT math and verbal scores in the most selective institutions, but had no impact on the variances at any other

Figure 6.6
SAT scores of Georgia college freshmen versus U.S. high school seniors and Georgia high school seniors, 1990–2003

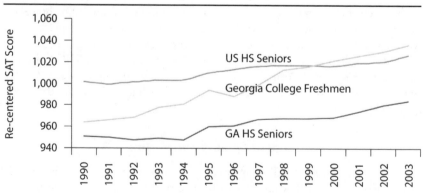

Source: National data are from the College Board and the Georgia data are from the University System of Georgia.

institution type. Their results provide strong evidence that HOPE exacerbated the stratification of enrollments by student quality.

Retention and Graduation

Policies that encourage college attendance are important insofar as they increase the number of college graduates. This raises questions about the performance of Georgia's colleges and universities in terms of student retention and graduation. Figure 6.7 plots the institution-specific and system-wide (which account for transfers between schools) one-year retention rates for first-time, full-time freshmen who enrolled in USG schools between 1984 and 2001. Until 1993, both rates varied within fairly narrow bands: 66 to 67.8 percent for specific institutions and 73.2 to 75.8 percent across the system. They reached their nadir in 1993, the year HOPE started. After 1993, retention rates rose steadily through the end of the period to 80.4 percent across the system as a whole. UGA stands out with the highest retention rate, a remarkable 90.7 percent in 2001. Dynarski (2005) showed that HOPE played an important role in increasing retention rates depicted in Figure 6.7.

Table 6.10 presents the retention rates for the fall 2003 cohort of first-time freshmen by institution class. Throughout the USG slightly more than 76 percent

Figure 6.7
USG first-year retention rates first-time, full-time freshmen fall 1984–2001

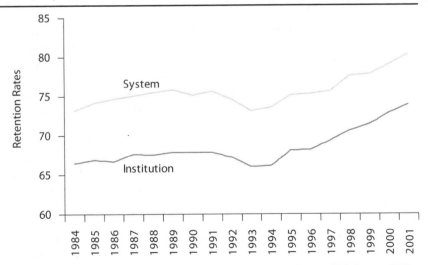

Source: University System of Georgia, Student Information Reporting System; SRA, January 2003.

Table 6.10
USG One-Year Retention Rates First-Time Freshmen, Fall 2003 Cohort

Institution Class	Institution-Specific Rate	System-Wide Rate
USG System	76.8	82.7
Research Universities	90.7	93.4
Regional Universities	78.4	86.6
State Universities	73.5	80.9
State Colleges	66.5	70.8
Two-Year Colleges	65.2	72.1

Source: University System of Georgia, Student Information Reporting System, Retention Rate Report.

of students returned to their same institutions and almost 83 percent returned to the system. The retention rates are highest for the most selective schools and decline systematically as the selectivity and scope of the institution decline.

Figure 6.8 plots the four- and six-year graduation rates for students who matriculated at UGA between 1987 and 2000. Between 1987 and 1989, the four-year rate was about 30 percent. Through 1991, the six-year rate hovered between 62 and 64 percent. During the period both rates increased significantly and peaked in the last year in our sample for the matriculating class of 2000. For that class the four-year rate was 45.6 percent and the six-year rate was 73.6 percent. This increase in retention rates is due in part to HOPE's role in increasing the quality and preparation of UGA's incoming students.

Retention rates and their implication for students persisting to graduation are important, but it is also essential to examine how HOPE affects students' academic choices along the way. After all, state-sponsored merit scholarships have proliferated, justified in part as inducements for academic achievement. Although their GPA requirements for eligibility and retention encourage students to apply greater effort toward their studies, they also encourage other behavioral responses like adjusting course loads and difficulty. Cornwell, Lee, and Mustard (2005) examine student responses to the eligibility and retention rules associated with the HOPE Scholarship. Using data on undergraduates who enrolled at the University of Georgia between 1989 and 1997, they estimated the effects of HOPE on enrollment, withdrawal, and completion, and the shifting of course credits to the summer, treating out-of-state students as a control group.

They found that HOPE reduced the probability of full-course load enrollment and enrolled credit hours and increased the probability of course withdrawal

Figure 6.8
UGA graduation rates by matriculating year 1987–2000

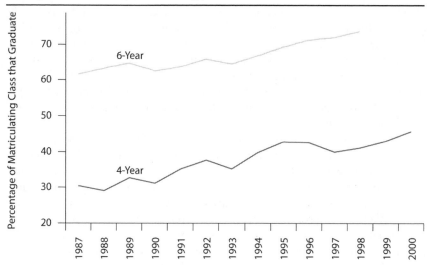

Source: UGA Fact Book.

and withdrawn credits for Georgia-resident freshmen. Together these responses amount to a 9.3 percent reduction in the likelihood of completing a full load and almost a 1-credit drop in completed credits. The credit-hour decline means that resident freshmen completed more than 3,100 fewer courses between 1993 and 1997 than they would have in the absence of HOPE. Whether these course-load adjustments constitute a delay in academic progress or intertemporal substitution, however, is unknown, as the evidence is mixed.

The diversion of course-taking to the summer is an example of adjusting course difficulty, as the average GPA of UGA freshmen is 10 to 15 percent higher in the summer than in the fall, even though the typical summer-school enrollee has a lower SAT score and HSGPA. HOPE increased summer-school credits completed by Georgia residents by 63 percent and 44 percent in the first two summers after matriculation. Summer-school results suggest that, to the extent intertemporal substitution occurs between the first and second years, summer enrollment accounts for most of it.

In sum, they conclude that HOPE's grade-based retention requirements lead to behavioral responses that partially undermine its objective to promote academic achievement and encourage greater effort. Although responses such as taking fewer courses per term may enhance human capital investment, the option to slow one's progress toward degree completion existed before HOPE.

CONCLUSIONS

Since the 1980s and especially over the last 15 years, Georgia has generally outpaced the nation in population and economic growth. Its growing population has increased the demand for college in the state, and its expanding economy has helped mitigate some of the challenges in meeting that demand. Across the United States, state shares of higher education funding have steadily fallen, putting pressure on tuition and other financing sources. Qualitatively, the pattern in Georgia has been similar but far less dramatic, so it remains a relatively high-subsidy, low-tuition state.

This broad characterization of Georgia and its higher education sector would likely hold in the absence of the HOPE program, but few of the details and changes of the last 15 years can be fully understood without an accounting of the program's effects. Since its introduction in 1993, HOPE has become the single most prominent feature of Georgia's higher education system, and currently presents state policymakers with one of their most important political issues. Its prominence has also been felt well beyond Georgia, as many states have followed with HOPE-like programs of their own, leading to a significant rise in state-sponsored merit aid.

As this chapter has described, the effects of HOPE are seen in both the inputs and outputs of the state's colleges and universities. On the input side, HOPE has transformed higher education finance in Georgia, affecting tuition policy and faculty hiring. First, through HOPE the state has sharply increased funding to students in exchange for funding to institutions. Thus although the state has reduced its real allocations to institutions, grant aid as a percentage of higher education expenses has grown substantially. In 1995, state-sponsored grant aid covered about 15 percent of college costs. By 2002, the grant-aid share of college expenses rose to almost 25 percent. In the late 1980s and early 1990s, Georgia's grant aid per FTE was ranked between 25th and 39th in the United States. Every year since 1997, Georgia has distributed more grant aid per FTE than any other state.

Second, HOPE has played a significant role in limiting the tuition growth in Georgia, other budgetary problems notwithstanding. Because scholarship and grant award levels are tied to tuition, there has been substantial political pressure to keep tuition increases small in an effort to preserve the program's financial footing. Real in-state tuition at Georgia's four-year schools rose only 16 percent between 1995 and 2002, much less than the increases of 41 and 25.3 percent in the SREB and United States, respectively. In 2002, the average in-state tuition at Georgia's four-year schools was $2,576, which amounted to only 79.2 percent of the SREB median and only 69.1 of the U.S. median.

Third, reduced state support and limits on tuition increases have led to significant changes in the composition of college faculties, particularly at its research universities. Most notably, there has been a pronounced shift from tenured and tenure-track faculty to lecturers and instructors in delivering classroom instruction. For example, between 2001 and 2004, the number of UGA full professors declined 4.6 percent and the number of assistant professors declined 15.8

percent, and the number of instructors and lecturers increased 38.2 and 82.4 percent, respectively. Occurring during a period of expanding enrollments, this compositional change substantially increased the ratio of undergraduate students to tenured and tenure-track faculty.

On the output side, HOPE has influenced enrollment, student quality, retention, and graduation. First, HOPE has contributed to enrollment growth in Georgia, in the range of 6 percent through the first five years of the program. Second, and perhaps more significantly, HOPE has increased enrollments by encouraging the state's higher achieving students to stay home for college. Because the best of these students are likely to attend one of the flagship institutions, these universities have experienced considerable increases in the freshmen SAT scores relative to their out-of-state peers. Although smaller by magnitudes, many other four-year schools have seen their freshmen SAT scores increase as well. Third, related to improvements in student quality, data indicate that HOPE is leading to gains in retention and graduation rates. A caveat to these gains is in order though, because evidence suggests the scholarship is affecting student academic choices in ways that may undermine HOPE's incentive for achievement (for example, by inducing more course withdrawals and diversion of course taking to the summer).

Finally, looking to the future, two important issues confront the state. The first is ensuring the long-term financial stability of the HOPE program. Although the current resources from the lottery are sufficient to pay for the HOPE and pre-K programs, the projected growth rate in the demand for them far exceeds the projected growth rate in lottery sales. Some attempts have been made to address this issue, but the efforts have been modest, because the strong political support for HOPE leaves little room for compromise. The second issue is reconciling Georgia's historic policy of low tuition with its more recent practice of cutting the state's share of higher education funding. Together, these actions have constrained faculty hiring and compensation, making it increasingly difficult to compete for talent in a highly competitive academic labor market and maintain institutional reputations that enhance student selectivity.

NOTES

1. Georgia Institute of Technology, Georgia State University, Medical College of Georgia, and the University of Georgia.
2. Georgia Southern University and Valdosta State University.
3. Albany State University, Armstrong Atlantic State University, Augusta State University, Clayton State University, Fort Valley State University, Georgia College and State University, Georgia Southwestern State University, Kennesaw State University, North Georgia College and State University, Savannah State University, Southern Polytechnic University, and State University of West Georgia.
4. Dalton State College and Macon State College.
5. For example, UGA tuition and fee charges are $2,314 per semester for the 2005–2006 academic year. Tuition and fee charges vary widely at the state's public institutions, but the book allowance is the same.

6. "Awards" do not equal "recipients" because a single recipient receives an award each year she qualifies and, in the case of the grant, she can receive multiple awards within the same year, depending on the nature of the vocational training program.

7. In return for the scholarship, recipients must serve for two years after graduation in the Georgia National Guard.

8. Students who received the PROMISE Teacher Scholarships agreed to teach after graduation in a Georgia public school up to a maximum of four years.

9. The HOPE Teacher Scholarship provide forgivable loans to recipients who teach in a Georgia public school in critical shortage fields.

10. The SEE provided service-cancelable loans for a maximum of $17,500 for a student's program of study and required students to work in an engineering-related field in Georgia after graduation.

11. There are 16 members of the SREB. Delaware was not a member for this entire period, so we exclude the University of Delaware. Data for the University of West Virginia were not available for the entire period, so it is also excluded.

CHAPTER 7

Changing Priorities and the Evolution of Public Higher Education Finance in Illinois

F. King Alexander and Daniel Layzell

I n March 2005, during the 24th annual David Dodds Henry Lecture at the University of Illinois at Urbana-Champaign, President Constantine Curris of the American Association of State Colleges and Universities stated that "ulti-mately, success in renewing the covenant between the public and its universities will depend on how well our work in teaching and learning, scholarship and cre-ative endeavor, and engagement with our fellow citizens is received by those who bear the burden of taxes and make personal sacrifices to sustain our work." This challenge faces all of public higher education today and is particularly relevant in the state of Illinois, where its greatest son, President Abraham Lincoln, once described public universities as the "public's universities."

Nearly a century and a half after President Lincoln made this statement, pub-lic higher education in Illinois is confronting significant challenges as a result of another economic recession that has created profound state fiscal difficulties and other state spending priorities. These challenges have been triggered by the convergence of unparalleled economic and demographic forces. Despite the state's long-standing policy goal of providing a wide array of affordable postsecondary education opportunities to students of all ages, public higher education in Illi-nois is facing increased competition and demands for limited state resources from rapidly growing mandatory funding obligations for Medicaid, other state-funded health care programs, and state retirement systems. Together, these obligations will cost more than the state anticipates in additional tax receipts, requiring an additional $1 to $1.5 billion. Medicaid alone, according to Kane and Orszag, has been called "the biggest challenge casting a shadow on public higher education's future" (2003, p. 33). In addition, there is an increasing realization among key state policymakers that the state's system for funding K12 education is in serious need of reform given its comparatively high reliance on local property taxes and the resulting inequities created among school districts because of this funding system. Currently, Illinois has one of the most property-tax reliant educational systems in the nation, and various proposals are being debated in Springfield and across the state that would reduce local property tax reliance for K12 funding and conversely increase its reliance on state income and sales taxes. These factors will make it difficult at best for public higher education to be a principal beneficiary of any new state tax revenues that might become available during the next decade, not to mention existing state revenues. Complicating this scenario is an increasing sense among state policymakers in Illinois, and nationally, that higher education can shift the financial burden to students, parents, and other revenue sources during periods of economic downturn (Lingenfelter 2004).

The growing pressures for limited state resources also comes at a time when higher education has become an economic necessity for individual opportunity resulting in rising enrollments and unprecedented demand. In the next decade Illinois forecasts indicate a 12.5 percent increase in the annual number of high school graduates and an additional 57,000 new undergraduate students enrolling in colleges and universities across Illinois (IBHE 2004, Carnevale and Fry 2000). Perhaps more significant is the fact that these students will be increasingly diverse and also are likely to be more at-risk academically given the current pattern of results in state standardized tests among elementary and high school students in Illinois (IBHE 2004). This will place further strain on the ability of public colleges and universities to handle the influx of additional students without compensatory state funding to support them.

These demographic pressures also are compounded by growing concerns regarding the ability of our nation to produce an educated and globally competitive workforce. As noted by Lawrence, "Increasingly, Illinoisans will vie for high-paying, knowledge-based jobs with bright, highly motivated workers in India who can sit at their computers and partner with intelligent, inventive women and men in Ireland to develop new products and ingenious means of marketing and distributing them" (2005, p. 12). This environment has generated an intense competition for high-quality faculty, more sophisticated technology, and universal access to knowledge-based training. Numerous reports during the last decade have already highlighted the overall competitive decline of public universities when compared to their private university counterparts in the academic marketplace (Alexander 2001, Orszag and Kane 2003). This relative decline in competitive capability has been of particular concern for research universities in Illinois such as the University of Illinois and Southern Illinois University, but has also impacted other public universities throughout Illinois as well.

This potential for diminished funding places at risk the state's ideal of broad, affordable access to postsecondary education and an overall concern for the quality of academic programs for public college and university students. The convergence of these economic and demographic forces has led some observers to forecast a pessimistic outlook for the support of public higher education in Illinois in the coming years. This chapter examines these developments by looking at the long-term and short-term financial trends for public higher education in Illinois. The chapter also highlights many of the more pressing issues impacting public higher education in Illinois by discussing the current and historical context of Illinois's system of higher education. Finally, this chapter provides alternative projections for the future of public higher education in Illinois based on three possible scenarios.

Current Status and Historical Context

Comparatively, Illinois is a very large, wealthy, and diverse state. It is currently the most populated state in the Midwest and the nation's fifth largest state, with approximately 12.5 million people. Also, the high school graduation and college attendance rates are consistently above the national average. In 2002, approximately 58 percent of high school graduates in Illinois entered higher education institutions during the next year (NCES 2003). This represents a slightly higher college attendance rate than the national average of 56.6 percent. Further, Illinois residents are above the national average on educational attainment, with 26.1 percent of residents over 25 years old having completed a bachelor's degree or higher compared to the national average of 24.4 percent Illinois also has the second highest level of attainment among all Midwestern states (U.S. Census 2000).

Despite its above-average college going rate and level of educational attainment, Illinois is also one of the nation's leading net exporters of higher education students. In 2000, freshmen leaving the state of Illinois to attend college outnumbered the students coming to Illinois by almost 10,000 (Mortenson 2003). For nearly two decades Illinois has consistently ranked as one of the nation's top states in the exportation of college students, trailing only the state of New Jersey in this category. The beneficiaries of this educated human capital outflow away from Illinois have been many neighboring states throughout the Midwest and the South such as Michigan, Wisconsin, Indiana, Iowa, and Kentucky. This pattern does not appear to have had significant impact on the state's overall level of educational attainment to date, but it does raise concerns regarding the future economic competitiveness of the state and the capacity of the Illinois higher education system to address the educational needs of a growing and more diverse student population. To better understand Illinois's current higher education system, it is important to briefly discuss the current structure within the context of its development over the last half-century.

Current Status

Illinois has a large and diverse system of higher education composed of 9 public universities on 12 campuses, 48 community colleges, 98 private not-for-profit, and 29 proprietary institutions that enrolled just over 800,000 students in total in fall 2004 (IBHE 2004). In the public two-year sector, Illinois is near the national average in the number of two-year institutions and the postsecondary enrollment in these institutions is significantly above other states as a percentage of all students enrolled. Currently, public community colleges constitute more than 45 percent of all higher education student enrollments. Among all states, Illinois trails only California in the proportion of its population enrolled in two-year institutions; however, the number of public four-year universities has always been comparatively low and enrollment in this sector constitutes only 25 percent of the total higher education population in Illinois. This represents one of the smallest four-year public university enrollments as a percentage of the total student population in the nation. In the private sector, however, the number of four-year institutions is above the national average and the enrollments at these institutions also give the private sector (both not-for-profit and proprietary) a large share of the student base constituting almost 30 percent of all higher education students in Illinois.

As shown in Table 7.1, total enrollment across all sectors grew by 67,700 students or 9.2 percent between fall terms 1990 and 2004. Enrollment growth by sector varied significantly, however, with the most rapid growth during this period occurring in the proprietary and private not-for-profit sectors, whereas the public university and community college sectors experienced only limited growth. As indicated in Table 7.1, enrollment in both the public university and community college sectors actually declined between 1990 and 2000, before rebounding during the past few years. It should also be noted that the relatively rapid growth in proprietary institution enrollment in Illinois during this period has been driven

Table 7.1
Total Enrollment in Illinois Higher Education by Sector Fall 1990 to Fall 2004

Fall Term	Public Universities	Community Colleges	Private Not-for-Profit Institutions	Proprietary Institutions	Total Headcount
1990	198,481	352,898	167,657	13,794	732,830
1995	192,532	337,716	176,855	14,472	721,575
2000	193,783	340,101	186,346	22,719	742,949
2004	201,448	362,771	202,134	34,170	800,523
Change: 1990–2004					
Number	2,967	9,873	34,477	20,376	67,693
Percent	1.5	2.8	20.6	147.7	9.2

Source: Illinois Board of Higher Education Fall Enrollment Surveys.

in part by the increasing number of proprietary institutions operating within the state.

Figure 7.1 provides an overview of the percentage distribution of total enrollment by sector in Illinois during this period. As noted earlier, approximately 70 percent of Illinois students are enrolled in public higher education, with almost half in the community college system. The overall share of students enrolled in private higher education (both not-for-profit and proprietary), however, has increased steadily during this period from 24.5 percent in fall 1990 to 29.5 percent in fall 2004.

The politics of these enrollment dynamics by sector have always played a significant role in the development of the higher education system in Illinois. Perhaps not surprisingly, the current structure has been based on a long-term effort to encourage both access to and choice among these many higher education sectors through both planned policy and budget actions. This strategy included the establishment of a comprehensive community college system in the early 1960s to augment the public universities and the development of a large need-based student financial aid program that was initiated in the late 1950s to primarily support private institutions.

Figure 7.1
Distribution of enrollment in Illinois higher education by sector, fall 1990 to fall 2004

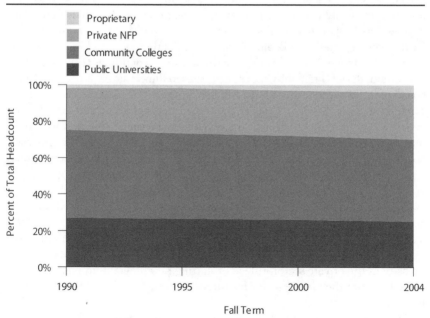

Source: Illinois Board of Higher Education Fall Enrollment Surveys (various years).

Historical Context

Legacies help to explain present state policies and challenges. In Illinois, most public universities were started in rural areas (as teachers colleges), and private institutions were established across the state, primarily in the Chicago area. Like most other states, the growth and development of public higher education in Illinois was relatively modest until after World War II and the impact of the GI Bill. Even after World War II, interest in higher education issues among state political leaders was largely of a parochial nature with little attention given to a statewide higher education policy framework or educational delivery system.

A more systemic focus on the role and purpose of higher education in Illinois took root in 1961 with the establishment of the Illinois Board of Higher Education (IBHE), a statewide coordinating board. The IBHE's initial focus was on improving access for Illinois's growing college-age population. Its first master plan published in July 1964 led to establishing the Illinois community college system as well as providing the foundation for the state's overall structure for higher education, which has been called the "system of systems." The system of systems was put together as a structure to improve the capacity of smaller public four-year institutions to compete for resources with the University of Illinois and Southern Illinois University, and to help coordinate the state's allocation of resources to address the rapidly growing demands for higher education across Illinois (Richardson, Bracco, Callan, and Finney 1999).

The "system of systems" included four public university governing boards with responsibility for 12 public universities. The governing boards included the board of governors (responsible for five universities), the board of regents (responsible for three universities), the Board of Trustees of Southern Illinois University (two campuses), and the Board of Trustees of the University of Illinois (two campuses). In addition, the 48 community college campuses in Illinois are governed by 39 local boards of trustees who work with the Illinois Community College Board (ICCB) in carrying out their missions. However, the "system of systems" was eliminated in the mid-1990s as the result of action by the governor and General Assembly to restructure higher education. Legislation was adopted that abolished two of the university boards (the board of governors [BOG] and the board of regents [BOR]), established separate boards of trustees for seven of the BOG/BOR institutions and moved one of the BOR institutions under the control of the University of Illinois.

The organization of the public sector and its subsequent growth raised concerns among private institutions forcing them to intensify their lobbying efforts in the late 1960s to seek state funding to help subsidize the cost of enrolling Illinois students attending private institutions. They also asked that the state maximize capacity in the private sector instead of starting new programs in public institutions. In return the private sector institutions agreed they should be involved in IBHE master planning.

The decisions made in the 1960s to use the capacity of private colleges and universities rather than building new four-year institutions and to create a statewide system of community colleges to accommodate most of the increases in new students at the lower-division undergraduate levels are important legacies that contributed to the shape and eventual challenges of contemporary Illinois higher education. To fully comprehend the challenges facing Illinois higher education, and particularly the public sector, it is essential to understand the dynamics of institutional or sector politics. In many ways, the history of higher education finance and the challenges facing public colleges and universities in Illinois is as Ferguson (2001) stated, "that the nexus between economics and politics is the key to understanding the modern world" (p. 60).

The remaining sections of this chapter analyze long-term and more recent higher education funding trends and attempts to forecast how these trends could impact support for public higher education in the coming years.

TRENDS IN ILLINOIS HIGHER EDUCATION FUNDING

In analyzing trends and patterns in Illinois higher education funding, it is important to place Illinois within a national context, as well as to examine changes in key components of the state's overall investment in higher education over time. Tax funds allocated annually for higher education in Illinois emanate from two primary sources, state appropriations, which constitute the lion's share of government revenues to colleges and universities, as well as other higher education-related programs and activities (e.g., student aid), and local appropriations to public community colleges, which constitute more than $600 million annually and represent an increasingly larger share of community college budgets in Illinois.

Illinois also is a relatively wealthy state, ranking 12th in the nation in per capita income. When comparing appropriations of state tax funds for higher education per $1,000 of personal per capita income, however, Illinois falls considerably below the national average ranking 32nd overall in tax effort (Palmer 2004). The Grapevine data are consistent with other reports regarding the below-average public support of higher education in Illinois. According to the recent state higher education finance report prepared by the State Higher Education Executive Officers higher education support per capita in Illinois is 98.7 percent of the national average or $6 less per capita than the national average of $417 (SHEEO 2004).

In analyzing tax support trends in greater depth by institutional sector, interesting distinctions emerge in tax effort by institutional sector. In the four-year public university sector, tax effort support was above the national average, ranking 15th overall in 2002. Despite the appearance of well-supported public university system, the primary reason that Illinois tax effort is considerably higher than the national average for public universities is the relatively low number of public university students in the public four-year sector as mentioned earlier. With only 25 percent of the total higher education population, public universities in Illinois appear to be underenrolled compared to other states. This is one important consequence of the decisions made in the 1960s regarding how Illinois would provide future higher education access.

Tax effort support of private higher education colleges and universities in Illinois is among the highest in the nation. In fact, Illinois ranked fourth in the nation in 2002 in tax effort for private four-year colleges and universities. In aggregate, state support for private higher education in Illinois (including student aid and direct institutional grant program support) has typically represented between 8 and 10 percent of the total state general fund spending on higher education each year (Figure 7.2). The primary means of providing taxpayer assistance to private sector institutions involves a combination of direct grant programs and indirect tuition support of students through a comparatively heavily state financed student aid system. As mentioned previously, the concept of promoting "access and choice" has historically been a key theme of Illinois state higher education policy and finance decisions. One of the primary mechanisms by which the state has pursued this policy has been through MAP (Monetary Assistance Program), a need-based student financial aid program administered by the Illinois Student Assistance Commission. The state appropriation for MAP in fiscal year 2005 totaled $339.6 million, ranking it fourth among all states in spending on need-based financial aid. Funding for MAP reached its high point in fiscal year 2002 ($372 million) before the most recent state fiscal difficulties. MAP eligibility is limited to Illinois residents enrolled in undergraduate study at an approved Illinois public university, community college, private not-for-profit college or university, or proprietary institution. MAP covers tuition and fees only, and the maximum award that students are currently eligible to receive is just under $4,500 annually depending on their determined need and cost of attendance.

Figure 7.2
State funding for Illinois private education as a percent of total state general fund (GF) spending on higher education for fiscal years 1990 to 2005

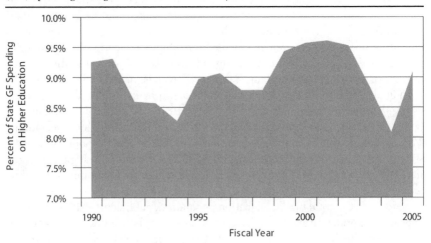

Source: Illinois Board of Higher Education records.

Funding for MAP is a significant portion of the overall state higher education budget in Illinois and has actually grown faster over time than the higher education budget on average. As noted in Figure 7.3, MAP as a percentage of total state general fund spending on higher education has grown from 10 percent in fiscal year 1990 to almost 16 percent in fiscal year 2005. A series of policy and programmatic changes were put in place during this period as well for MAP to strengthen the program including a funding supplement limited to the lowest income students (which primarily benefits students at community colleges) and the expansion of MAP eligibility to include students at proprietary institutions.

Approximately 51 percent of MAP funds currently are allocated to students enrolled at an Illinois public university or community college with the balance of 49 percent going to students at Illinois private institutions (both not-for-profit and proprietary). Public university and college students, however, constitute more than 72 percent of the eligible students receiving MAP awards. These figures indicate considerable differences in actual awards received by students attending lower cost public institutions and those attending higher cost private institutions. It should be mentioned, however, that in fiscal year 1990, 58 percent of MAP funds went to students enrolled in private institutions and 42 percent went to students at public universities and community colleges. The recent changes have occurred because of rapid growth in public university student tuition and fees and recent legislative support to implement formulaic changes that would more proportionately benefit lower-income community college students.

Figure 7.3
MAP as a percent of total state general fund spending on higher education for fiscal years 1990 to 2005

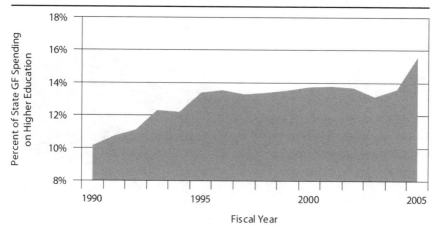

Source: Illinois Board of Higher Education records.

Long-Term Funding Trends

Figure 7.4 shows the trend in state appropriations for higher education operations and grants between fiscal years 1990 and 2005, both in current and inflation-adjusted dollars.[1] During this period, state general funds support for Illinois higher education grew from $1.6 billion to $2.4 billion. When accounting for inflation, however, state support actually declined by 1.8 percent since fiscal year 1990. As indicated in Figure 7.4, much of the gain in state support since the early 1990s was lost during the last three fiscal years. It should be noted, however, that expenditures in other areas of state government benefit higher education as well, such as the significant general fund support provided each year for the state employee group health insurance program (almost $1.0 billion in fiscal year 2005.)

Figure 7.5 shows the cumulative percentage change in state appropriations for higher education by sector, adjusted for inflation. Significant resources have been invested in the State Universities Retirement System since the mid-1990s in response to a statutory change to improve the long-term financial condition of all state-funded retirement systems.[2]

Between fiscal years 1990 and 2005, state support for the Illinois Student Assistance Commission (ISAC) increased by $95 million when accounting for inflation, or 32 percent. Virtually all of the funds appropriated to ISAC are for direct student assistance (98.8 percent), the majority of which is through MAP. MAP funds are sent to colleges and universities on behalf of students and thus support institutional expenditures for educational programs. The additional funds

Figure 7.4
State appropriations for higher education operations and grants (1990 to 2005)

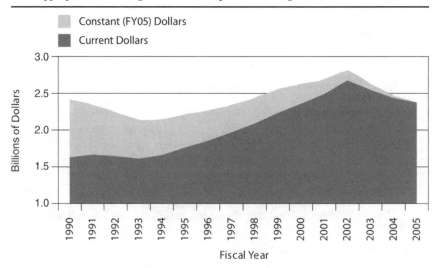

Source: Illinois Board Higher Education records.

provided for MAP since fiscal year 1990 have supported a number of program enhancements: extension of eligibility for part-time students and students attending proprietary institutions, formula changes to target additional resources to students from families with low incomes, and increases in the MAP maximum award and funding to cover tuition and fee increases.

State funding for public universities in fiscal year 2005, when adjusted for inflation, was $224.1 million less than in fiscal year 1990, or 14.7 percent. Funding for community colleges (including funds for adult education and postsecondary career education) is slightly above fiscal year 1990 levels owing primarily to the additional investment made in fiscal year 2002 for adult education. When these funds are excluded, inflation-adjusted state general fund support for community colleges in fiscal year 2005 was $33.3 million less than in fiscal year 1990, or 10 percent.

Figure 7.5
Percent change in state appropriations for higher education by sector, fiscal years 1990 to 2005 (in FY 2005 dollars)

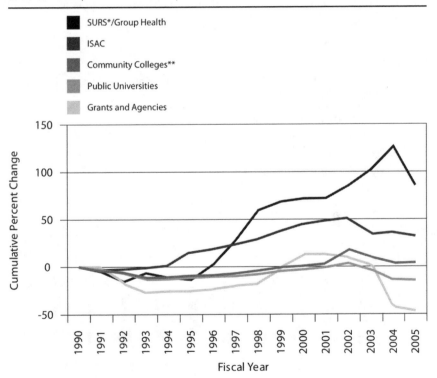

*Includes state general funds and state pensions fund. Group health insurance payment appropriated directly to CMS in FY 2005.

**Includes adult education and career and technical education.

Source: Illinois Board of Higher Education records.

State support for grant programs and agencies in fiscal year 2005 was $54.1 million less than in fiscal year 1990 when adjusted for inflation, or 47.2 percent. In large part, this reflects reductions in support for the Higher Education Cooperation Act grant program in fiscal year 2003, and the elimination of funding for the Illinois Financial Assistance Act grant program ($20.6 million) in fiscal year 2004, which provided capitation grants to eligible Illinois private colleges and universities based on the enrollment of Illinois resident undergraduate students.

Recent Funding Trends

As seen in Figures 7.5 and 7.6, the state's difficult fiscal situation in recent years has had an impact on funding availability for higher education, beginning in fiscal year 2002 when higher education was asked to place $25 million (or approximately 1 percent) in general funds appropriations in reserve to assist the state with a mid-year budget deficit. In addition, public universities were requested to contribute $45 million from their own resources that year to cover a portion of the cost of the state employee group health insurance program, a practice that has continued each fiscal year since that date.

Figure 7.6
Annual change in weighted average undergraduate tuition and fees by sector, fiscal years 1995 to 2005 (estimated)

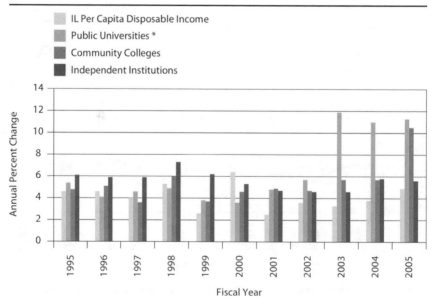

*Reflects annual change in average tuition and fee rate for continuing students.
Source: Illinois Board of Higher Education records.

Table 7.2
State Funding for Higher Education Operations and Grants

	FY2002 Appropriations	FY2004 Appropriations	FY2005 Appropriations	FY2002 to FY2004		FY2004 to FY2005	
				Dollar Change	Percent Change	Dollar Change	Percent Change
Public Universities	$1,502,910.9	$1,303,764.7	$1,304,875.4	(199,146.2)	(13.3)	1,110.7	0.1
Community Colleges	333,659.9	293,567.0	299,419.8	(40,092.9)	(12.0)	5,852.8	2.0
Grants to Colleges	331,103.5	291,345.4	297,198.2	(39,758.1)	(12.0)	5,852.8	2.0
Illinois Community College Board Administration	2,556.4	2,221.6	2,221.6	(334.8)	(13.1)	—	—
Adult Education/Postsecondary Career and Technical Education Grants	39,005.3	46,155.2	46,257.2	7,149.9	18.3	102.0	0.2
Illinois Student Assistance Commission (ISAC)	423,752.3	398,354.9	391,600.8	(25,397.4)	(6.0)	(6,754.1)	(1.7)
Monetary Award Program/IIA	374,728.3	345,899.8	345,899.8	(28,828.5)	(7.7)	—	—
Other Grant Programs	42,520.0	46,270.9	39,985.2	3,750.9	8.8	(6,285.7)	(13.6)
ISAC Administration	6,504.0	6,184.2	5,715.8	(319.8)	(4.9)	(468.4)	(7.6)

(Continued)

Table 7.2
(Continued)

	FY2002 Appropriations	FY2004 Appropriations	FY2005 Appropriations	FY2002 to FY2004		FY2004 to FY2005	
				Dollar Change	Percent Change	Dollar Change	Percent Change
Grant Program	97,256.0	46,915.3	40,568.3	(50,340.7)	(51.8)	(6,347.0)	(13.5)
Illinois Financial Assistance Act	22,169.1	—	—	(22,169.1)	(100.0)	—	—
Health Education Grants	21,708.3	17,000.0	17,000.0	(4,708.3)	(21.7)	—	—
Institutional Grants	53,378.6	29,915.3	23,568.3	(23,463.3)	(44.0)	(6,347.0)	(21.2)
Other Agencies	21,245.1	18,463.4	19,937.1	(2,781.7)	(13.1)	1,473.7	8.0
Illinois Mathematics and Science Academy	16,526.7	14,359.2	15,832.9	(2,167.5)	(13.1)	1,473.7	10.3
State Universities Civil Service System	1,441.2	1,253.6	1,253.6	(187.6)	(13.0)	—	—
Board of Higher Education	3,277.2	2,850.6	2,850.6	(426.6)	(13.0)	—	—

Subtotal - Institutional/ Agency Operations and Grants	2,417,829.5	2,107,220.5	2,102,658.6	(310,609.0)	(12.8)	(4,561.9)	(0.2)
Retirement/Transfer to CMS Health Insurance Reserve Fund*	258,146.1	329,594.9	273,250.7	71,448.8	27.7	(56,344.2)	(17.1)
Higher Education Total	$2,675,975.6	$2,436,815.4	$2,375,909.3	(239,160.2)	(8.9)	(60,906.1)	(2.5)

* Includes State General Funds and State Pension Fund. Health insurance finding (14.8 million) appropriated directly to Department of Central Management Services (CMS) in fiscal year 2005.

The higher education budget changes in fiscal years 2003 and 2004 were more significant in magnitude. Table 7.2 presents the cumulative change in state funding by sector/program for higher education operations and grants between fiscal years 2002 and 2004. Overall, state appropriations for higher education operations and grants declined by $239.2 million, or 8.9 percent during that two-year period. During this same period, higher education's share of state general fund appropriations in total declined from 11.5 to 10.4 percent. In addition, higher education was asked to place $55 million and $30.6 million of state general funds appropriations in reserve in fiscal years 2003 and 2004, respectively, to assist the state in addressing its ongoing fiscal difficulties. There were also significant reductions in state funding for institutional operations (public universities and community colleges) in both fiscal years 2003 and 2004.

The fiscal year 2005 state budget provides $2.1 billion in state general funds support for higher education operations and grants (excluding retirement), a net decrease of $4.6 million or 0.2 percent from fiscal year 2004 appropriated levels. As highlighted in Table 7.2, the fiscal year 2005 budget is a departure from the trends noted earlier, by largely maintaining (and in some cases increasing) state funding for higher education institutions and agencies, although funding was reduced or eliminated for some higher education grant programs and initiatives.

Despite the recent stabilization in state funding, public colleges and universities in Illinois will have to continue to look to student tuition and fee revenues as a primary source of future funding growth to address increasing enrollment demands and to maintain educational quality and competitiveness. As Figure 7.6 indicates, student tuition and fee increases at public universities and community colleges since fiscal year 2002 have nearly doubled the increases of previous years. The next section discusses more closely the funding patterns at Illinois public community colleges and universities over the last several years.

PUBLIC HIGHER EDUCATION FUNDING PATTERNS

State appropriations are, of course, just one source of funding for public university and community college operations. Public universities also receive support for general operating costs from student tuition (i.e., university income funds), and community colleges receive similar support from local property taxes and student tuition, in addition to other more restricted revenue sources in both sectors (e.g., federal grants that support research projects, fees that support residence halls and other auxiliary operations, private gifts that support scholarships and academic departments). However, state funding provides a critical and irreplaceable core of support for both sectors in delivering high quality instructional programs and other services for students. For public universities, state general funds appropriations and university income funds (i.e., student tuition) are the primary sources of funding for general support of educational and related activities. For community colleges, the primary sources of funding for general support of educational and related activities are state general funds appropriations, local property tax

Figure 7.7
Trend in educational and related revenues at Illinois public universities fiscal years
1990 to 2005 * (in FY 2005 dollars)

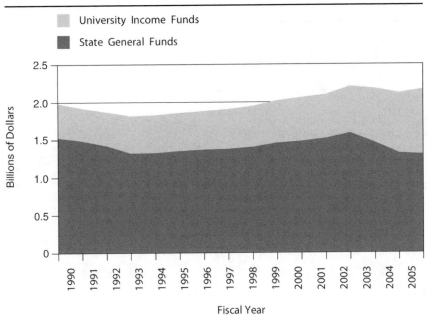

* University Income Funds for FY 2005 are estimated.
Source: Illinois Board of Higher Education records.

revenues, and student tuition and fees.[3] Other institutional operating revenue
sources (e.g., federal grants and contracts, auxiliary enterprise revenues, private
gifts) are typically restricted to the support of specific activities (e.g., sponsored
research projects, scholarships, debt service on bond revenue facilities).

Figures 7.7 and 7.8 show the inflation-adjusted trend in total educational and
related revenues at Illinois public universities and community colleges, respectively, between fiscal years 1990 and 2005 by source. During this period, total
educational and related revenues increased by 9.2 percent at public universities
and by 42.7 percent at community colleges, when adjusted for inflation. As indicated, total educational and related revenues for public universities were at their
highest in fiscal year 2002, while they have grown steadily for community colleges
during this period. In both sectors, however, support from nonstate sources has
increased at a greater rate since fiscal year 1990, with the most rapid rate of growth
in these sources since fiscal year 2000. State general funds support for public universities as a percent of total educational and related revenues declined from 77.0

Figure 7.8
Trend in educational and related revenues at Illinois community colleges, fiscal years
1990 to 2005* (in FY 2005 dollars)

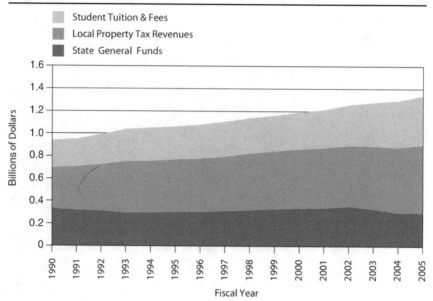

Fiscal Year

* Local property tax revenues and student tuition and fees amounts for FY 2004 and FY 2005 are
estimated.
Source: IBHE and ICCB records.

to 60.2 percent during this period. For community colleges, state general funds
support as a percent of total educational and related revenues declined from 35.4
to 22.3 percent during this period.[4]

As noted earlier, institutional competitiveness in the academic marketplace
is of keen interest to Illinois public universities for both enrollment capacity
and educational quality concerns. The IBHE has analyzed the competitiveness
of full-time faculty salaries at Illinois public colleges and universities relative to
their unique comparison (i.e., "peer") groups on an annual basis since the mid-
1980s. Figure 7.9 shows the range (highest and lowest) and average of weighted
average faculty salaries at public universities in relation to each public university's comparison group median faculty salary since fiscal year 1990. As noted,
on average, Illinois public university salaries have been below the median each
year (95.7 percent on average in fiscal year 2004). Further, although a few public
universities have been above their individual comparison group medians, the
majority of institutions have been below their median. Not surprisingly, most

Figure 7.9
Range and average of Illinois public university weighted average full-time faculty salaries as a percentage of comparison group medians, fiscal years 1990, 1995, and 2000–2004

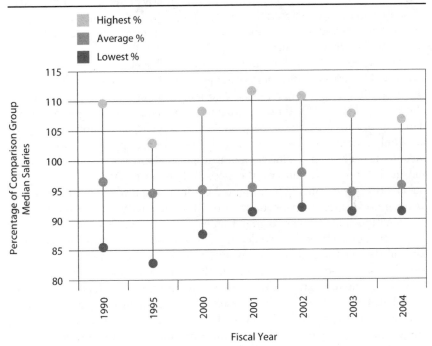

Note: The fiscal year 2004 faculty distribution among ranks was used to determine weighted average faculty salaries for all years to minimize the impact of annual changes in faculty mix on the trend analysis.
Source: IBHE Faculty Salary Studies (various years).

Illinois public universities have made enhancing faculty and staff compensation a top institutional budget priority in recent years.

WHAT NEXT?: ALTERNATIVE PROJECTIONS BASED ON THREE POSSIBLE SCENARIOS

Forecasting future funding trends for public higher education with any degree of precision is a difficult task at any time, but especially at this point in the twenty-first century when considering the unpredictability of current economic conditions in Illinois and throughout the nation. By analyzing previous fiscal trends and the resulting impact on public higher education in Illinois, however, this chapter outlines three broad, alternative economic scenarios for the future and the potential consequences that could occur in the next decade if these scenarios are realized. These predictions are based on both the intended and unintended consequences of previous budgetary fluctuations for public higher education in Illinois and the responses to such conditions. These alternative forecasts are intended to illustrate a likely range of possible scenarios for public higher education and their relative impacts and outcomes should any of these scenarios become reality and they should be viewed as such.

As shown in Table 7.3 the "most likely scenario" or economic possibility does not provide a very promising outlook for public higher education in Illinois. This scenario is based on a continuation of current economic instability and limited ability to address the fiscal needs of public higher education institutions or students. In this most likely category, public colleges and universities will experience only minimal to modest funding changes in state appropriations over the next decade at best, averaging approximately from 0 to 1 percent annual growth. Judging by previous conditions, the most likely result is a series of responses by public universities ranging from limited enrollment growth to enrollment caps at some universities. This scenario also will undoubtedly lead to a consistent continuation of moderate to high tuition increases that could average from 10 to 15 percent annually for the next decade. The most optimistic consequence of this most likely scenario will be that institutional aid packages awarded to students will also increase somewhat as a result of these tuition increases.

In this economic scenario the public community colleges will also face significant challenges that will most likely result in moderate increases in property taxes, moderate tuition growth in the range of 6 to 9 percent annually, and continued enrollment growth with more lower-income and full-time students seeking admission. The most likely scenario will also impact state student aid programs by forcing further changes in the MAP formula to target financial aid to lower income students while receiving only moderate increases in overall program funding.

The two additional possibilities for public higher education in Illinois as shown in Table 7.3 are made based on a potential "best case scenario" and a "worst case scenario." The best case prediction presents a very optimistic view and is contingent on a strong state economy and resulting state revenue growth that will support 2 to 4 percent average increases in state appropriations for public higher education during the next decade. If this scenario comes to fruition, public universities will most likely experience significant enrollment growth throughout Illinois while student tuition and fee rates will increase only at annual rates of 5 to 8 percent. For public community colleges the additional revenues in this scenario would result in only low to moderate tuition and local property tax growth. State student aid programs (especially MAP) would also be a beneficiary of the additional funding available. This essentially means that private colleges and universities would also receive more state support.

In the worst case scenario for public higher education in Illinois, average annual changes in state appropriations would fall by at least 1 to 5 percent per year over the next decade. This would have detrimental consequences on public higher education

Table 7.3
2005–2015 Possible Fiscal Scenarios for Public Higher Education in Illinois

Sector/Program	Best Case Scenario (2% to 4% Average Annual Change in State Appropriations)	Most Likely Scenario (0% to 1% Average Annual Change in State Appropriations)	Worst Case Scenario (−1% to −5% Average Annual Change in State Appropriations)
Public Universities	High enrollment growth Low to moderate tuition growth (5–8% annually)	Moderate enrollment growth Enrollment caps in selected academic programs Moderate to high tuition growth (10–15% annually) Movement toward surcharges for higher cost/higher demand programs (e.g., engineering, business, nursing)	Low to flat enrollment growth Enrollment caps at selected institutions and academic programs Pressure to eliminate and consolidate academic programs Significant tuition growth (>15% annually)
Public Community Colleges	Low enrollment growth Low to moderate tuition growth (4–6% annually) Low to moderate property tax growth	Moderate enrollment growth Moderate tuition growth (6–9% annually) Moderate property tax growth	High enrollment growth (driven in part by caps and tuition increases at public universities) Pressure to establish selected baccalaureate programs at selected community colleges Moderate to high tuition growth (10–15% annually) Moderate property tax growth

in Illinois and the growing numbers of students seeking postsecondary education opportunities. For public universities, continued appropriation declines would result in the following consequences: low to capped enrollment growth, elimination and consolidation of academic programs, and significant tuition and fee increases to help backfill lost state funds needed to support institutional operating costs. The consequences for public community colleges would not be much better. Community colleges in Illinois would likely experience rapid enrollment pressures driven in part by the tuition increases and possible enrollment caps implemented by the public universities. They would also experience moderate to high tuition and property tax increases to support their expanded educational and student needs. In addition, it is possible that there would be increased public pressure for the establishment of limited baccalaureate programs at public community colleges as the demand for greater access permeates the higher education landscape in Illinois.

The impact of the worst case scenario on the Monetary Assistance Program and other student aid programs would be detrimental as well. This scenario would most likely result in flat funding at a time when tuition rates are rapidly increasing. However, a positive impact would be that there would most likely be additional formulaic changes that would provide more assistance to help lower income students attend lower cost colleges such as public community colleges and lower cost public universities.

CONCLUSION

These three scenarios provide a window into the future of public higher education in Illinois in the next decade. The unpredictability of this environment remains an important challenge in itself as public universities and community colleges struggle to plan for the future to both maintain educational quality and provide access for an increasing number of students from across the state. Regardless of which (if any) of these scenarios become reality, it is evident that the compact between state government and public higher education has entered a new era in Illinois. The state will likely remain the primary financier and stakeholder of public higher education in Illinois, but it is also likely that the growing demands for higher education across the state will outstrip the state's ability to adequately fund those demands forcing public community colleges and universities to become more tuition-reliant and/or seek other funding arrangements with the state. Absent any significant influx of new state revenues, it is also possible that state government itself will look to other means and mechanisms for allocating the limited resources available for public higher education to maximize access and choice for state residents. In any event, to paraphrase David Breneman (2004), state policymakers and public higher education leaders must make a conscious and deliberate decision on what characteristics and desired outcomes are most important for Illinois's system of higher education rather than allowing it to happen by "inaction or default."

NOTES

1. State appropriation data for higher education operations and grants presented in Figure 7.5 and subsequent figures in this report include State General Funds and State Pension Fund (SPF) amounts, owing to a significant shift in State Universities Retirement System (SURS) funding sources in fiscal year 2005 from General Funds to the SPF to meet statutory funding requirements for the system. Between fiscal years 1990 and 2004, total SPF support for SURS ranged from $3.7 million to $16.7 million annually, representing 6.9 percent of total SURS funding on average during this period. The SPF appropriation for SURS in fiscal year 2005 totals $222.6 million, or 81.5 percent of total funding provided to the Syste m to meet the required funding level.

2. The amount shown for retirement on Figure 7.6 also includes $14.8 million appropriated to the Board of Higher Education for transfer to the state Group Health Insurance Fund in fiscal years 2002 through 2004, as well as general funds support for community college retirees' group health insurance ($3.3 million in fiscal year 2005). The funding for employee health insurance costs was appropriated directly to the Group Health Insurance Fund in the fiscal year 2005 budget, which accounts in part for the downward trend in this line from fiscal year 2004 to 2005. The reduction in required state support for SURS in fiscal year 2005 also reflects the infusion of funds to all state retirement systems from the $10 billion pension bond sale authorized in 2004 through Public Act 93–0002.

3. These revenue sources are referred to as "educational and related revenues" for the purposes of this chapter.

4. The ability of community college districts to generate local property tax revenue can be "capped" through the state Property Tax Extension Limitation Law (PTELL), and 14 of the 39 districts currently fall under this limitation. Community college tuition and fee rates are also limited under state law to no more than one-third of per capita instructional costs, although no district currently faces this limitation.

CHAPTER

Michigan Public Higher Education: Recent Trends and Policy Considerations for the Coming Decade

Stephen L. DesJardins, Allison Bell, and Iria Puyosa

Michigan's postsecondary education system has evolved into a "comprehensive, high-quality, and quite autonomous system . . . whose diversity of institutions, enrollment, and breadth of programs rivals that of most other large states" (Peterson and McLendon, 1998, pp.148–149). The last 30 years have been a particularly interesting and exciting time for public higher education in Michigan with the growth and refocusing of existing universities, legal cases that have significantly affected institutions of postsecondary education, and considerable challenges in financing public higher education. Looking forward there is considerable work to be done if Michigan hopes to continue to provide high quality higher education. The purpose of this chapter is to examine some of the more important events that shaped public higher education in Michigan over the last 25 to 30 years, and to look forward to where the state may be headed in the next decade.

FACTS ABOUT THE STATE OF MICHIGAN

Michigan is a state of nearly 10 million people, the eighth most populace state in the nation, whose population is centered in the southeastern part of the Lower Peninsula. The racial mix of the state is 78 percent white, 14 percent African American, 2 percent Asian American, 1 percent American Indian, and 4 percent Latino/a (of any race) (U.S. Census 2000). The state's population is projected to grow by 3 percent from 2000 to 2015, below the national rate of 13 percent. During the same period the number of high school graduates is projected to decline by 1 percent (Measuring Up 2004). U.S. Census projections estimate that by 2015, Michigan will have a college-age population (18–24 years) of 936,107 individuals, only 0.4 percent higher than the 2000 college-age population of 932,137. The college-age population is expected to decline between 2015 and 2025, and by 2025 the number of individuals in this age group will have declined by nearly 8 percent compared to 2000 (U.S. Census Bureau 2002). The only age group projected to grow over this period is those over 65.

Per capita income in Michigan ranked 20th (in 2001) at about $29,500, but more disconcerting is that the income change relative to the average in the United States is negative (nearly 12%) and 47th among the states (Cherry Commission 2004). In 1999, 14 percent of households had incomes lower than the official poverty threshold ($15,000), and individuals living in poverty accounted for 11 percent of the population and more than 13 percent of Michigan's children (those less than 18 years old).

Michigan's high school graduation rates are slightly higher than the 70 percent national average, but well below the best states that graduate nearly 90 percent of their students. Of the students who do graduate from high school, however, only about one-third are considered "college ready" compared to more than 50 percent in other states (Cherry Commission 2004). Currently, Michigan ranks 34th nationally in educational attainment in the United States (Cherry Commission 2004). Among the population 25 to 34 years old, about 26 percent of Michigan residents hold a bachelor's degree or higher, compared to nearly 28 percent in the United States as a whole (Cherry Commission 2004). This should not be surprising because in the past, Michigan residents could move from high school to the manufacturing industry into jobs that provided a standard of living well above the average of the typical high school graduate in other states. The days of this being a viable option are virtually gone as the auto industry continues to lose market share to foreign competition and with it the jobs that provided an avenue to the middle class for a generation (or more) of Michigan's citizens. Given this change in the labor market options of individuals and the increase in service sector jobs, many of which require a college education, participation in postsecondary education will become even more important for Michigan's citizens in the coming years.

Regarding postsecondary education participation, Michigan ranks moderately well compared to other states. The state has about 650,000 (headcount) students enrolled in postsecondary education (i.e., public/private/two-year/four-year; Cherry Commission 2004). About 39 percent of the state population between 18 and 24 years attends a postsecondary institution compared to nearly half in leading states (Measuring Up 2002). However, there are significant gaps in postsecondary education participation among socioeconomic and racial groups, with low-income and minority populations attending and completing at much lower rates than their white and more affluent counterparts (Cherry Commission 2004). Michigan also lags behind the nation in the number of people holding college degrees. Nationally, about one-fourth of the population holds a four-year degree compared to about 23 percent in Michigan. About 45 percent of students entering Michigan's colleges and universities do not complete a bachelor's degree, and low-income and minority students do even less well on this measure. A recent report by Wayne

State's Center for Urban Studies (Metzger, 2004) found that Michigan's college graduation rate ranks 35th in the nation, down two places from its 2000 ranking. Michigan's public NCAA Division I schools have six-year graduation rates as high as 84 percent at the University of Michigan-Ann Arbor, and as low as 38 percent at Eastern Michigan University (Chronicle of Higher Education 2004).

One of the long-term impacts of gaps in educational participation and completion is that Michigan will be a less attractive place for businesses to locate, especially the so-called knowledge-based industries. Policy analysts in Michigan estimate that the state needs to increase postsecondary education enrollment to about 850,000 by 2015 to match participation rates of leading states in order to produce the *number* of educated individuals that will be necessary to fuel the Michigan economy in the future and to prepare its citizens for the *types* of work that are likely to be available in the coming years.

MICHIGAN'S POSTSECONDARY EDUCATION SYSTEM

Michigan has 109 institutions of higher education: 15 public four-year institutions, 30 public two-year institutions (including one tribal community college), 56 private four-year institutions, and 8 private two-year institutions. In this chapter we provide a detailed examination of the 15 public four-year universities that include the three large research institutions: the University of Michigan at Ann Arbor; Michigan State University (MSU) located in Lansing, the state capitol; and Wayne State University (WSU). The University of Michigan at Ann Arbor is the state's flagship institution, and the University also has two branch campuses located in Dearborn and Flint, whose missions and profiles more closely resemble the state comprehensive universities. Michigan State University, which was initially chartered as a land-grant institution, has evolved into a very large research-oriented university. Located in metropolitan Detroit, Wayne State University has a different profile than the typical research institution, as it has traditionally served a large number of students from low-income and minority backgrounds, and to do so, its tuition has often been set at levels to achieve this goal.

The state comprehensive universities include Ferris State University (FSU), Grand Valley State University (GVSU), Lake Superior State University (LSSU), Oakland University (OU), and Saginaw Valley State University (SVSU). These institutions have varied missions but historically have focused on undergraduate education, although as we demonstrate later in the chapter, some of these institutions are now more fully engaged in graduate education.

There is a group of institutions that began as "normal" schools or teaching colleges and are known by some as "directional" institutions because of the geographic reference in their name (Ogren 2005). These institutions include Central, Eastern, Northern, and Western Michigan Universities, and although their focus remains teacher education, their missions are now more comprehensive than in the past. Michigan is also home to one specialized institution of higher education, Michigan Technological University (MTU), that specializes in engineering and technology and is especially well known for its programs in geological and mining engineering. With the exception of MTU located in Houghton, and its higher education neighbors Northern Michigan University 100 miles to the east, and Lake Superior State University (LSSU, a former branch of MTU) located in Sault Ste. Marie, all of Michigan's public universities are located in the Lower Peninsula.[1]

Michigan also has a system of local community colleges (CCs) and private colleges and universities, although they are not the focus of this chapter. The CC system has 28 institutions that in 2000–2001 enrolled more than 400,000 citizens either full- or part-time. In full-year equivalent (FYE) terms, however, this equates to about 110,000, whereas in 1992–1993, FYE enrollments peaked at about 130,000, and in the last few years FYE enrollments have remained relatively stable (Public Sector Consultants 2003). CCs have three major funding sources: property taxes (36%), state aid (33%), and tuition and fees (27%), and these institutions spend about 46 percent of their budgets on instruction (MCCA 2002). Similar to the public four-year universities, CCs are negatively affected in times of state fiscal constraint, and they have also turned to raising tuition to generate additional revenues. From 1990–1991 to 2000–2001, the in-district community college tuition rose an average of 4.1 percent a year (Public Sector Consultants, 2003). In 2005, in-district students attending Michigan CCs paid an average tuition of about $60 per contact hour, out-of-district students are paid an average tuition of about $100, and out-of-state students paid almost $122.

Community colleges have a potential source of increased revenue that their public and private four-year counterparts do not have: they can go to the voters to ask for an increase in local property taxes to support them. In fact, community college advocates have attempted to redraw some of Michigan's tax districts to increase the potential for revenue from property taxes (Public Sector Consultants 2003). This idea, however, has gained little momentum given negative reactions from voters and some legal restrictions regarding the creation of new taxes.

Michigan is also home to more than 30 private colleges and universities (not including religious seminaries). Private colleges and universities in Michigan enroll about 15 percent of the full-time-equivalent (FTE) enrollments in the state, and they take pride that they enroll about 19 percent of their students from underrepresented ethnic groups (Bracco 1997). The majority of Michigan's private institutions have religious affiliations, and there are no private universities or colleges with a national reputation similar to those of the University of Michigan and Michigan State University. Without considering the discounts often offered by these institutions, tuition varies sharply among private colleges and universities, ranging from a low of about $11,000 to a high of more than $23,000.

GOVERNANCE ISSUES

State Educational Governance

Michigan is one of only two states (the other being Delaware) that is not governed by a "buffering" agency such as a coordinating or governing board

(McGuinness Jr. 1997). The decentralized system of institutional governance is often called a planning agency model (McGuinness, Jr 1997) in that each of Michigan's public institutions has its own governing board and is responsible for negotiating appropriations with the legislature and the planning and management of the institution. (However, a single board of regents oversees all three of the University of Michigan campuses). All of the governing boards have nine members, which includes eight elected trustees and the institution's president who serves as an ex-officio member. The boards of the Big Three institutions (University of Michigan, Michigan State University, and Wayne State University) are elected by the public in statewide partisan elections and serve eight-year terms. The governor appoints the board members governing the rest of the public four-year institutions, and each of Michigan's public two-year community colleges has a regionally elected governing board.

All of Michigan's four-year institutions have constitutional autonomy. Constitutional autonomy allows institutional governing board's total control of management and planning, free from state government impositions. Among the most important rights derived from their constitutional autonomy is the freedom to set tuition and the right to decide how their state appropriations will be spent. The University of Michigan was granted constitutional autonomy in 1850, making it the first institution in the country to be accorded such status. Delegates to the 1850 constitutional convention argued that the university had experienced poor enrollment and growth since its creation in 1817 because of continual political intervention (Peterson and McLendon 1998). As other public universities were created and subsequent state constitutions adopted, constitutional autonomy was retained for public institutions because it was perceived as the most effective method of governance to protect against such political interference (Ferris State University 2003).

Although each institution has its own governing board, the governing boards often interact with the State Board of Education. This Board also includes eight elected members who are chosen in statewide elections and, like the public governing boards members, serve for eight-year terms. The governor also serves as the ninth member in an ex-officio, nonvoting capacity. Depending on the makeup of the board and the political realities of the times, the governor may have considerable control over the activities of the board. For instance, in 2004 Governor Granholm was successful in having the Superintendent of the Board removed because of policy differences.

The Michigan Constitution of 1963 charters the State Board of Education to serve as the general planning and coordinating body for all public education, including higher education, and to advise the legislature regarding institutions' financial requirements. The scope of the power of the board and the legislature, however, has, at times, been unclear. The state supreme court has ruled on several occasions against the board of education's actions that conflict with the institutional autonomy of universities (see Peterson and McLendon, 1998, for details). Ironically, the state board of education has more authority over private postsecondary institutions than public institutions because the former operate under charters granted by the state. This legal arrangement has implications for planning and management of private institutions. For example, private institutions are required to present a petition to change their charter each time they want to add a degree program (Bracco 1997).

In addition to the legal governance arrangements discussed previously, the 15 public four-year universities in Michigan have established a voluntary organization known as the Presidents Council. The Presidents Council began informally in the late 1940s when the presidents of Michigan's public colleges and universities began meeting to "discuss the challenges of a rapidly growing public higher education system" (Presidents Council 2005). The Presidents Council was established in 1952 and today is composed of the presidents or chancellors of the 15 public institutions. The council's activities include taking positions on the state budget for higher education, monitoring legislation affecting higher education, collecting and disseminating cross-institutional data and reviewing academic programs, and lobbying before state agencies and the legislature on their members' behalf. An extensive committee structure of representatives from each campus provides attention to a variety of academic and policy issues and provides recommendations for consideration by the member institutions (Presidents Council 2005). As evidence of its utility in providing comparative institutional data, some of the data and information provided below is a product of research done by the Presidents Council.

THE POLITICAL CONTEXT

Severe economic problems in the early 1980s led the new governor, James Blanchard (D), to look "increasingly to the state's research universities as an engine of economic growth and development" resulting in "a program of research grants intended to stimulate economic growth through university-based research and development initiatives" (Peterson and McLendon, 1998, p.161). In the mid 1980s, Blanchard increased state appropriations to higher education institutions, in fact, 1987 was the peak year for appropriations to public universities (in real dollars) since then.

In 1991, John Engler (R) was elected governor and a recession early in his first term posed funding problems for many of Michigan's public universities. Even though appropriations for higher education were slightly lower during the first years of Engler's administration, he was able to increase student financial aid in his first budget. This reflected his free market philosophy of making financial aid portable by putting money in the hands of students and allowing them to choose an institution. During his first term, Engler also increased state support to the growing community college sector in an effort to promote training for the labor market.

In 1994, Engler won a second term and he was bolstered by new majorities in both the Senate and House of Representatives, the first time the Republicans controlled both houses and the governorship for many years. At the same time, citizens voted in a new board of regents for the University of Michigan, composed of four Republicans and four Democrats. Given the split based on political affiliation, the board was unable to reach an agreement to elect a new chair (Bracco 1997). In October 1995, Michigan's President James Duderstadt announced his resignation, and Governor Engler took the opportunity to confront higher education's institutional autonomy by threatening to end the direct election of trustees to the Big Three (Michigan, Michigan State, and Wayne State) and to replace this system with one in which trustees were appointed by the governor. Engler failed to garner enough political support for this proposal, however, and it is questionable whether he would have prevailed because of the constitutional autonomy granted to institutions.

In another clash between Engler and the higher education sector, the governor vetoed state appropriations for Highland Park Community College, which forced the closing of this Detroit-based institution that had traditionally served a predominantly African American student body. Engler also engaged public universities on issues such as institutional affirmative action policies, same-sex domestic partnerships benefits, and insurance coverage for abortion procedures at university clinics and hospitals. On grounds of institutional autonomy granted by Michigan's constitution, the state Attorney General Frank Kelley (D) ruled unconstitutional a law cutting funds for public universities that extend benefits to domestic partners or provided insurance coverage for abortion procedures. A similar law that applied to community colleges was upheld, however, because these institutions lack the constitutional status of their university counterparts.

The turn of the century brought a new governor to Michigan. Jennifer Granholm (D), who had been state attorney general under Engler. She took office in the midst of a downturn in the economy after the burst of the dot-com bubble and the shock to the economy (and country) by the terrorist attacks of 9/11. Granholm's agenda was to diversify Michigan's economy by attracting knowledge-based industries, but she seems to realize that to do so Michigan must possess a workforce capable of staffing such industries. In 2004, she commissioned a group of academic, business, and labor leaders to consider what it would take to move Michigan toward a more diversified, knowledge-driven economy, and the role that postsecondary education would play in this process. The Lt. Governor's Commission on Labor and Economic Growth, also known as the Cherry Commission, so named for her Lt. Governor who chaired the commission, recently finished their work and has made a number of recommendations that will promote the governor's agenda. As seen later in the chapter, this report has important implications for postsecondary education policy in the next decade.

Regarding the governor's interaction with institutions of higher education, her first term has been a difficult one, as large state budget deficits have been the norm. To balance the state budget, a legal requirement, Granholm has had to cut state spending dramatically, and higher education has taken a particularly big hit. To gauge the public's sentiment regarding where to cut government spending, Granholm held a series of town hall meetings around the state, and she found little support for higher education; citizens were more concerned with other budget items (K12 education, Medicaid, and locking up criminals), so the governor acted accordingly, cutting higher education appropriations.

Notwithstanding the recent state budget problems and the subsequent cuts in state appropriations to postsecondary institutions, Governor Granholm has called on these institutions to play a more central role in preparing the state to compete in the coming decades. In her most recent State of the State message she said:

> Today, all children in Michigan—not many, not most—but all must grow up knowing that their education will not end in high school. Whether it is a four-year college degree, or a two-year associate degree, or other forms of technical training after high school, continued learning will be a requirement for all who seek a good-paying job in this new century.

RECENT ISSUES AFFECTING MICHIGAN HIGHER EDUCATION
Economics

Michigan's tax base has been dependent on manufacturing, especially the automotive sector. This was a real benefit to the state when the Big Three automakers (General Motors, Ford, and Chrysler) provided most of the cars for the world market (about 80 percent in 1950). But their share of the world automobile market has fallen to below 25 percent, and their domestic market share has also dropped from about 90 percent in 1970 to less than 50 percent of the new car market today. This decline has had a negative impact on Michigan's economy and thus the tax revenue generation capacity of the state. To balance the state budget (a requirement), lawmakers have focused on state spending reductions, and postsecondary education has been targeted for reductions in the (nominal) rate of growth of state appropriations and more recently in real cuts to the funding provided to institutions of higher education.

The availability of funds for higher education has also been constrained as a result of the school finance reform undertaken in 1994 when voters approved Proposal A. This law cut local property taxes by more than two-thirds, placed an annual cap on property (taxable) value increases, and replaced this source of local school funding by increasing the state sales tax from 4 to 6 percent. Before Proposal A, school funding was comprised of 63 percent local funds and 37 percent state funds; after implementation of the provisions of Proposal A, school funding is now comprised of 21 percent local funding and 79 percent state/federal funding (Weill et al. 2003, Michigan League for Human Services 2004). Even though Proposal A includes no General Fund requirement, each fiscal year since Proposal A's implementation, sizeable General Fund transfers have been needed to finance the School Aid Fund. The largest such transfer was $668 million in 1995 and the lowest was $198 million in 2002. The increased burden of financing K12 education has negatively affected higher education funding as lawmakers have shifted discretionary funding from postsecondary education to help fund their new obligations to the K12 system. By 2002, K12 funding was commanding 60 percent of the state's budget, with the remaining revenues going to such items as Medicaid and public safety. The higher education sector's share of the general fund is now only about 12 percent, down from 23 percent as recently as 2000 (Michigan League for Human Services 2004).

Student Financial Aid Trends and Policies

Between 1980 and 1985, student financial aid policies became quite controversial. Federal student aid declined during the 1980s, as funding began to switch from grants to loans. In an attempt to offset some of the reductions in federal support to students, states increased financial aid by about 44 percent, and institutional sources of aid increased by 65 percent (College Board 1988). In addition to changes in governmental support, student aid programs were increasingly under public scrutiny owing to the escalating default rates in the Guaranteed Student Loan programs. Although most institutions involved in the default loan scandal were private, less than four-year (especially proprietary) institutions and community colleges serving urban populations, a growing distrust in the postsecondary system was undermining public support for student federal aid in general. On the other hand, concern with declining student aid and its impact on college access, especially for low income and minority students, was growing. Despite rising costs to students and reduced federal support, in the late 1980s Michigan's need-based aid declined slightly and merit aid programs for students were small or did not exist. In an attempt to deal with rising tuition and declining aid availability, then Governor James J. Blanchard (D) proposed that parents be allowed to purchase certificates redeemable for four-year tuition at any of the state's 15 public universities. This proposal resulted in the creation of the Michigan Education Trust (MET) in 1987, a program designed to address middle-class parents' concern about access to postsecondary education. The first program of its kind in the country (an IRS Section 529 prepaid tuition program), the MET allows individuals to purchase contracts that guarantee a semester, year, or multiple years of tuition at Michigan public institutions. In the first year of its existence, more than 40,000 people signed up for the plan, and since then about 35,000 more have enrolled. For a variety of reasons, mostly related to rapid increases in tuition, a number of these prepaid tuition programs have had solvency problems. Michigan's program has been adjusted from time –to time by changing contract criteria and tweaking the pricing to ensure it is actuarially sound. The assets currently invested in these contracts total about $1 billion.

Michigan residents also have a Section 529 college savings plan available to them. The Michigan Education Savings Program, which began in 2000, offers tax-free growth, and these investments are tax deductible up to a $10,000 limit for joint filers and $5,000 for those filing single. Those with family incomes below $80,000 and who meet certain other criteria are eligible for a $1 to $3 matching grant. These investments are managed by TIAA-CREF and multiple investment options (with different degrees of risk) are available. Morningstar investment group rates the program as one of the best in the country because of its diversification options, many age-based options, and low management costs.

In fiscal year 2000, Michigan's budget for student financial aid went up dramatically. The Michigan legislature—controlled by Republicans—approved a merit-based scholarship program initially proposed by Governor Engler. Funds for the Michigan Merit Award Scholarship Program came from the tobacco lawsuit settlement. The lawsuit settlement payments funding the merit program amounted to more than $1.1 billion during the 1998–2001 payment years. The merit program was fully operative in 2000, and in FY 2003 its budget allocation was about $64 million (more on this later). If the program remains as is, however, the budget allocation could grow as more students become eligible.

The program awards $2,500 to students attending in-state public institutions and $1,000 to those attending private in-state or any out-of-state institution. Scholarships are awarded to students who score at Level 1 (exceeds Michigan standards) or Level 2 (meets Michigan standards) on all four portions of the Michigan Educational Assessment Program (MEAP) test, which is a state-designated high school test. The MEAP tests are criterion-referenced and designed to measure knowledge of the state's curricular frameworks in four subject areas: mathematics, reading, science, and writing (Heller and Rasmussen 2001). More than 195,000 students have qualified for a Michigan Merit Award scholarship since the program began in 2000.

In 2000, a coalition of groups headed by the American Civil Liberties Union of Michigan filed suit (*White et al. v. Engler et al.*), alleging that the MEAP program violates Title VI of the Civil Rights Act of 1964, and the 14th Amendment to the U.S. Constitution because of the apparent racial disparities in the distribution of MEAP scholarships (Heller and Rasmussen 2001).

Early in her first term, Governor Granholm appeared to be committed to keeping the merit scholarship program. During recent state budget negotiations, however, she has tried to change the program to help balance the state budget. Among proposed changes she offered for discussion with the Michigan legislature were adding 40 hours of community service during high school to the academic eligibility criteria, reducing the award level by $500, limiting awards to students attending in-state institutions, eliminating the $500 supplement for students who exceed Michigan standards on the middle school MEAP tests, withholding distribution of the award until after students finish two years of postsecondary education, and reducing the amount of Pell grants received from the $2,500 award. The last proposal was controversial, as it would exclude most low-income students from taking advantage of the merit award because they are likely to receive Pell awards that are larger than the MEAP maximum. Currently, none of the other proposals appeared to have traction with Republican legislators, who see the popular merit program as "theirs."

In January 2005, Governor Granholm approved legislation that will eventually replace the existing high school MEAP tests with a new test called the Michigan

Merit Examination, which will be ready for use in spring 2007. Also, starting in academic year 2006, students will need to do 40 hours of community service to be eligible for the Michigan Merit Award. In addition to the money allocated to fund the 2006 Michigan Merit Award, an additional $2.6 million has been earmarked to support the transition from the MEAP to the new Michigan Merit Examination.

Racial Conflicts and Affirmative Action

During the late 1980s and early 1990s, a number of issues pertaining to the racial climate at two of the Big Three campuses were evident. Racial tensions at Michigan State University and the University of Michigan increased, and some observers attributed the negative climate to affirmative action policies that were being used by these institutions. Because of the negative climate, the Board of Regents of the University of Michigan approved a new student conduct code that allowed expulsion sanctions for students who committed discriminatory acts on campus (Anonymous 1988).

The University of Michigan's well-publicized legal fight regarding its affirmative action policies also began in the late 1990s, when two class-action lawsuits were filed against it alleging that racial preferences were given for undergraduate and law school applicants. The two cases, *Grutter v. Bollinger*, involving the admissions policy of Michigan's law school, and *Gratz v. Bollinger*, involving the admissions policy of the university's undergraduate College of Literature, Science, and the Arts, were heard by the U.S. Supreme Court in 2003. The justices upheld the Michigan law school's admissions policies by a 5-to-4 vote, endorsing the claim that enrolling a racially and ethnically diverse student body provides educational benefits. In the *Gratz* case, the court ruled 6 to 3 against Michigan's undergraduate admissions policy, because the majority of the justices ruled that the policy treated whole groups of applicants differently based solely on their race, and that the undergraduate admissions system was not tailored to achieve educational diversity. Since then, Michigan and other institutions around the country have taken the ruling in the *Gratz* case to mean that the Supreme Court decisions allow the use of race as a factor to achieve educational diversity, but the selection system must be targeted specifically toward this goal and a more holistic admissions approach is required. Changing to a more holistic approach in admissions has been costly for the University of Michigan. It now requires an essay as well as the traditional admissions criteria from the more than 20,000 undergraduate applications received during each admissions cycle, costing the University an additional $2 million.

TRENDS IN MICHIGAN'S PUBLIC UNIVERSITIES

We now examine some general trends in enrollment, tuition, faculty numbers and salaries, state appropriations, and student aid. Given the highly decentralized nature of Michigan's higher education system, obtaining comparative information on these institutions is difficult. In other states that have state governing and coordinating board structures, comparative information is much easier to obtain. So the mere compilation of the information presented in this discussion is a major accomplishment. Information is culled from federal sources (e.g., Integrated Postsecondary Education Data Survey [IPEDS]), state fiscal agencies (e.g., the HEIDI database, a state fiscal agency tool; state financial and policy reports), the Presidents Council, and institutional sources. Where possible we provide data beginning in the late 1970s or early 1980s and follow trends through the early 2000s. Our objective is to provide a profile of the public four-year higher education system in Michigan over the last 25 to 30 years.

Enrollment

In Michigan's 15 public universities, total student enrollment (in headcounts) are at a record level at nearly 289,000 as of 2004. Although headcounts are interesting, in most cases we report FYEs given that there are substantial numbers of part-time students attending some of these institutions and this group is growing, and because FYEs are often used as a measure of instructional activity.

From the 1976–1977 to the 2001–2002 academic years, the total *undergraduate* (resident and nonresident) FYE enrollments rose 14 percent, from just over 160,000 students to almost 190,000 students. After a slight decline in enrollment in the late 1970s, there was an increase that coincided with the severe recession in the early 1980s and yet another counter cyclical increase during the recession of the early 1990s. Since about 1995, undergraduate enrollments have increased at a fairly rapid pace.

Resident FYE undergraduate enrollments exhibit a similar (though more pronounced because of scaling) pattern given that resident student FYE enrollments are a large proportion of total undergraduate enrollments. Specifically, throughout the 1977 to 2002 observation period, resident students accounted for at least 85 percent (in recent years) of undergraduate enrollments and as high as 90 percent in earlier years.

Except for a slight decline in the early 1980s, nonresident enrollments have been increasing and, of late, at a faster rate than in earlier years. This is not surprising given reductions in state appropriations as institutions find additional revenues by enrolling more out-of-state students who pay higher tuition.

The figures noted here suggest that institutions have been increasing nonresident enrollments relative to the proportion of resident student enrollments, and this is especially true at the Big Three institutions—Michigan State University, University of Michigan, and Wayne State University. Nonresident enrollment at these institutions has been on the rise, increasing from about 10 percent of undergraduate enrollments in the late 1970s to almost 20 percent around the turn of the century. This increase has been driven by the University of Michigan-Ann Arbor and to a lesser extent Wayne State. The nonresident enrollment at

Wayne State University made up about 2 percent of their student body in the 1976–1977 academic year, and that proportion increased to nearly 10 percent by the 2001–2002 academic year (but on a small base). Nonresidents made up about 10 percent of the total undergraduate enrollment at Michigan State University in the late 1970s, and this proportion has been fairly constant over the last 25 years, declining slightly (to less than 10 percent) in recent years. The nonresident proportion of total undergraduate enrollments at the University of Michigan-Ann Arbor campus accounted for about 20 percent in 1977–1978 but had increased to about 35 percent of the total undergraduate enrollment in 2001–2002. Large percentage increases in FYE nonresidents have also taken place in nearly all the other public institutions as they search for sources of new tuition.

Compared to other public universities in the state, the Big Three consistently enroll the most undergraduate students. Michigan State continues to have the largest enrollments (around 33,000 FYE); however, their numbers are actually slightly lower in the 2001–2002 than in the 1976–1977 academic year. Enrollment at the University of Michigan-Ann Arbor campus has been fairly constant over the observation period, increasing slightly from about 22,000 to 24,000 in recent years. Enrollment at Wayne State University, although consistently above the state average for all universities, has declined during the observation period from about 19,000 to about 14,000. This decline is attributable to a deliberate policy change in the mid 1990s when they decided to focus more on graduate education and decided to reduce the number of undergraduates they serve. The nonresident student population at the directional universities has consistently been less than 10 percent of their total enrollments during the 1976–1977 to the 2001–2002 academic year. However, there has been a noticeable increase in the number of nonresident students these institutions have attracted.

The comprehensive state universities serve the smallest proportion of nonresident undergraduates, typically attracting less than 5 percent of their undergraduates from outside the state of Michigan. In recent years, however, a number of the directional and comprehensive universities have begun to look outside Michigan's borders for undergraduates. For instance, Central and Northern Michigan Universities have increased their nonresident student enrollment by 224 and 166 percent, respectively, from a base of 146 and 377 students, respectively, in 1977. According to enrollment managers at Northern Michigan University, since the mid-1990s, they have made recruitment in Wisconsin and especially the urban areas of Illinois a high priority and claim to have had substantial success in attracting students from these states.

Total undergraduate enrollments (in headcounts) by race/ethnicity have increased quite dramatically since the early 1980s. African American enrollments are up to nearly 14,000 students and Asian student representation is nearing the 7,000 mark. Latino/a enrollments have also increased and are now approaching 4,000. The number of American Indians served has remained relatively flat, although this may change as tribes invest more of their gambling revenue into the education of their children.

Graduate student enrollments have exhibited an interesting pattern over the last three decades. In the late 1970s, the Big Three enrolled about 25,000 (FYE) graduate students. The number of graduate students educated by these institutions fell until the late 1980s and then began to rise until the mid 1990s and has remained relatively constant since then at about 22,000 students. A similar pattern emerges for the directional institutions that now enroll about 10,000 graduate students. What is interesting is the increase in graduate student enrollments among the comprehensive institutions. Since the mid 1980s, when they enrolled about 2,500 graduate students, this sector of public higher education has seen a steady increase in the number and percent of all graduate students educated in Michigan's public institutions. Comprehensive institutions now enroll about 8,000 graduate students and have increased their share from about 7 percent of the total educated in public institutions to about 19 percent in recent years.

Tuition

Not unlike other public universities in the country, in general tuition rates at the public universities in Michigan have been increasing. Data that track tuition back to 1984 from the IPEDS was used to display tuition trends. These data have been adjusted using the Higher Education Price Index (HEPI) to reflect 2002 dollars. In-state undergraduate tuition averaged less than $3,500 in 1984 (adjusted to reflect 2002 dollars) and rose to about $4,900 by 2002. Out-of-state tuition is generally two to three times higher than in-state tuition for each of the years, regardless of institution type.

Of the Big Three institutions, the out-of-state to in-state tuition ratio has been consistently the highest at the University of Michigan-Ann Arbor. The University of Michigan-Ann Arbor also has the highest in-state tuition of all the Big Three institutions. The gap between the three in terms of in-state tuition has widened. Michigan State University and Wayne State University had similar tuition rates in 1984, but by 2002, Michigan State University's tuition was considerably higher than Wayne State's resident tuition. For a period during the late 1990s, WSU's real tuition for resident students actually decreased, but since then has rebounded. The University of Michigan's in-state tuition has increased about 50 percent from 1984 to 2002 (but as we will see later, this has been coupled with increases in financial aid). Michigan State University's tuition has increased almost as much as Michigan's, about 48 percent during the same period.

Real out-of-state tuition at the Big Three institutions has generally tracked the in-state tuition patterns, however, to a more dramatic extent. From 1984 to 2002, the University of Michigan-Ann Arbor's out-of-state tuition increased 53 percent, from about $14,340 to about $22,004. Michigan State University's nonresident tuition increased 44 percent, from $9,159 to about $13,214. Finally, Wayne State University's out-of-state tuition increased from the late 1980s until the late 1990s and has decreased slightly or remained constant since then.

Tuition at the directional institutions is generally lower than that of the Big Three institutions. In-state tuition levels (in real terms) for all four directional institutions were similar in 1984 at about $3,000. The in-state tuition rates at each of the four institutions show a pattern similar to that of the Big Three: A decrease for a few years in the early to mid 1980s, followed by a quite rapid increase that peaked in the late 1990s and was followed by a short period of decline. The period of decline coincides with these institutions holding constant their nominal rates, which results in a decline in the real value of their tuition rates as the general level of prices rise. Since 2000, these institutions' real rates have again risen. Also interesting is the relative differences in tuition at each of the directional institutions. The differences became more pronounced in the mid-1990s, and by 2002 Western Michigan University had the highest real tuition at almost $4,500; Eastern Michigan University's in-state tuition was slightly lower at about $4,000, followed by Central Michigan at just under $4,000; and Northern Michigan University had the lowest in-state tuition rate in 2002 at about $3,500.

In real 2002 dollars, nonresident tuition levels at the directional institutions were between $6,000 and $8,000 in 1984. Similar to the in-state tuition rates, the nonresident rates declined slightly from 1984 to 1986. At this point, the pattern of out-of-state tuition rates began to diverge within this group of institutions. Nonresident tuition rates at Central Michigan University, Eastern Michigan University, and Western Michigan University all underwent periods of increase that were almost exactly the same until about 1998, when Western Michigan's rates began to increase more rapidly. By 2002, Western Michigan's out-of-state tuition was almost $12,000, whereas the nonresident rates at Central and Eastern Michigan remained similar at about $10,000.

Trends in tuition at the comprehensive institutions in Michigan are similar to the tuition trends at the Big Three and the directional institutions. In the late 1980s, both in-state and out-of-state tuition increased. These increases continued until the mid-1990s, when rates started to decline for a short period. Ultimately, tuition levels in the period from 1984 to 2002 at Michigan's comprehensive institutions increased. Real in-state tuition levels increased anywhere from 3 percent at Saginaw Valley State University to more than 60 percent at Grand Valley State University during this period. The percent increases in out-of-state tuition levels ranged from 9 percent at Saginaw Valley State University to more than 50 percent at Michigan Technical University.

Faculty

As one might expect, the trends in the number of faculty employed by institutions of higher education mirror the overall enrollment trends. Since the late 1970s, faculty FTEs have increased from about 13,000 to about 17,000. The Big Three institutions employ the largest number of faculty, although their share of all faculty has decreased relative to the other two types of institutions. Faculty at the directional institutions have typically composed about 13 percent of the total faculty in the public university sector during the observation period, yet the proportion of the total faculty in the Michigan higher education system that are employed in the comprehensive institutions has increased to more than 20 percent of the total. The latter group has seen the largest increase in faculty numbers; however, many of the new hires have been short-term hires or non-tenure–track faculty (Prince 2003).

Ranked faculty have declined as a percent of all faculty in all three institutional groups being examined. In the late 1970s ranked faculty accounted for more than 70 percent of faculty in the Big Three institutions, but this percentage has declined to about 60 percent in recent years. This decline is almost solely due to declines in the percentage of ranked faculty at Wayne State University. Our analysis shows that institutions have increased their use of nonranked faculty over the years, and Prince (2003) suggests that this is the case stating, "Much of the growth in FTE faculty during this period, at both the major research universities and the other twelve institutions, was in the number of unranked faculty members" (Prince 2003, p.23).

Salaries

Total faculty compensation (in 2002) dollars in Michigan's 15 public universities has increased from about $800 million to about $1.2 billion from fiscal year 1977 to the 2002 fiscal year, a nearly 50 percent increase. This increase seems dramatic, but it is only slightly higher than the increase in faculty numbers over the same period. When one examines average faculty compensation (adjusted to 2002 dollars using the Detroit CPI) by institution type, the trends at each of the three types of institution are fairly similar to one another. In the early 1980s, there was a period of decline in faculty salaries that was followed by a period of increase from the mid-1980s to the early 1990s. During this time, the Big Three had the highest average faculty salaries, and the directional and comprehensive institutions had much more similar compensation levels. The gap between these two groups widened slightly throughout the late 1980s. In the early 1990s, the average compensation at the comprehensive institutions increased, which brought the salaries at these institutions much closer to that of the directional institutions. By 2002, the average faculty salary at the Big Three institutions was about $75,000, compared to about $64,000 at the comprehensive institutions, and closer to $60,000 at the directional institutions. These averages are undoubtedly affected by many factors, including disciplinary and academic rank differences among institutions, and the proportion of tenure and tenure-track faculty employed.

State Appropriations

As discussed earlier in the chapter, the recession of the late 1970s and early 1980s severely impacted the state budget and therefore state appropriations for higher education. Overall, Michigan appropriations for higher education declined in the early 1980s (in real and nominal terms). In the mid 1980s, state appropriations rose slightly, peaking in 1987. Indeed, when weighted by FYE students, state appropriations in 1987 were slightly larger than in recent years (Prince 2003); that is, the trend has declined since 1987. The declining trend in state appropriations has been exacerbated in recent years, as state budget deficits have negatively affected higher education appropriations.

Michigan's public universities have dealt with these fiscal constraints by belt-tightening activities, increasing tuition rates, and enrolling more nonresidents who pay two to three times more tuition than their in-state counterparts. When state appropriations are reduced institutions make up for these losses in part by increasing tuition. Other strategies have also been used, however. In the mid 1990s, some institutions (MSU in particular) were successful in maintaining funding by agreeing to keep tuition increases at or below the rate of inflation. This may have been a wise political strategy, at least in the short term, as other institutions (University of Michigan) who did not hold down tuition rates were widely criticized. Institutions that increased nonresident enrollments to make up for losses in state appropriations (in particular the University of Michigan) were also criticized and lost some political support within the state.

Regarding the University of Michigan, they have absorbed more than their share of cuts in appropriations during times of reduction. The contribution of state appropriations to their general fund has declined from nearly 59 percent in 1978 to approximately 32 percent by 2002 (Prince 2003). The university has made up for this loss in revenue by increasing indirect cost recovery revenue (research grants), as well as increasing tuition/fee revenues by increasing overall enrollments and the proportion of out-of-state undergraduate and graduated students. In comparison, state appropriations cover about 60 percent of Wayne State University's general fund, even while its undergraduate enrollment has declined (by design) and its tuition levels have remained relatively constant. Revenue streams at Michigan State University have followed a pattern similar to the University of Michigan's, but about 45 to 50 percent of MSU's general fund is derived from state appropriations.

The University of Michigan-Ann Arbor has consistently had the highest level of state appropriations, even though they have experienced about a $50 million reduction in recent years. In real terms the amount appropriated in 2002 was slightly less than the 1977 state appropriation. Conversely, Michigan State had a slightly higher appropriations level (in real terms) in 2002 than in 1977. Wayne State's appropriations, although experiencing some fluctuations, were about the same in 2002 as they were in 1977 (in real terms).

Appropriations made to the directional institutions (in nominal and real terms, respectively) display patterns similar to those of the Big Three. Of these four institutions, Western Michigan University has consistently had the highest (nominal) amount appropriated at about $120 million, and Northern Michigan has consistently had the lowest level of state appropriations, less than half of Western

Michigan's funding levels. Although the fluctuation in appropriations for each of these schools has been dramatic, in 2002 each was appropriated at least as much (in real terms), if not more, than they were appropriated in 1977.

Appropriation levels to the comprehensive institutions in the state also exhibit patterns similar to those described previously. Appropriations to Ferris State, Michigan Tech, and Oakland University have been consistently commensurate with the appropriations to the directional institutions. Particularly noteworthy is the dramatic increase in appropriations to Grand Valley State University (GVSU), especially since the mid 1990s. In nominal terms GVSU's state appropriations have increased sixfold, and in real terms they have nearly doubled from 1977 to 2002. This is the most dramatic increase in state appropriations of all the Michigan public universities. Explanations for this increase in appropriations include the growth in this institution resulting from the increased demand for higher education in the western part of the state, and in recent years the institution has benefited from having legislators from this (mainly Republican) region who have powerful positions in the House and Senate.

Another way to represent the distribution of state appropriations for the Big Three is by weighting the figures just mentioned by the number of resident students served. The University of Michigan-Ann Arbor has the highest state appropriation per student, followed by Wayne State, and then MSU. Although Ann Arbor's appropriations are the highest, they have experienced a significant decline beginning in the late 1980s. Conversely, Wayne State's appropriations have increased since the early 1990s, in part resulting from the change in mission (discussed previously) in which the institution now focuses more heavily on graduate student education.

Student Aid

Before fiscal year 2000–2001, most state financial aid was disbursed in the form of competitive scholarships that had a substantial need component. Beginning in FY 2001, however, the Michigan Merit Awards were available for students, and nearly $47 million was awarded that year, which tripled state financial aid from the previous fiscal year. By FY 2003, these merit-based awards were more than $64 million, accounting for about 65 percent of all state aid to students in Michigan's universities. This is a substantial change in what has historically been a nearly purely need-based program to what is now dominated by a large merit program.

General fund expenditures from Michigan's universities for undergraduate financial aid have increased at an annual rate of about 9 percent, from about $35 million in FY 1986 to about $161 million in FY 2003. The growth in this form of financial aid was greater than that of tuition over the same period, which grew at an annualized rate of 6.8 percent. (During the same period per capita personal income grew by 4.2 percent.) The growth in aid over this period has been quite consistent across the 15 institutions, starting from an average of $220 in FY 1986 to $828 (in nominal terms) by FY 2003, an annualized rate of about 8 percent.

The state averages mask the substantial variation in the average amount for each institution, with a high of $1,720 (in FY 2003) at the University of Michigan-Ann Arbor campus, more than double the state average, whereas MSU provides $622, about $200 less than the state average, and the low average amount of aid being $449 at Oakland University (Jen 2004).[2]

Tuition discounts are predominant not only in private higher education these days but are also increasingly used by public institutions. From the mid 1980s to the mid 1990s, the average discount[3] among Michigan's Big Three declined from an average of about 39 percent to about 31 percent and then was flat until the turn of the century. Since then the discount has steadily increased and the average in FY 2003 was about 37 percent, reflecting a state average tuition rate of $5,570 and an average aid package of $2,072 (in FY 2003). The average aid package at the University of Michigan-Ann Arbor in the same time period was $2,928 on a "sticker price" of $7,960, and their discount rate has remained relatively stable since the mid 1980s. Michigan State's (Wayne State's) average discount has increased in recent years, and in FY 2003 their average aid package was $1,865 ($2,176) on a posted tuition of $6,454 ($5,104).

DISTINGUISHABLE PATTERNS

Enrollment growth over the last 25 to 30 years has been mostly in the directional and comprehensive universities. The former saw their enrollments grow from the end of the 1980s through the early 1990s, whereas the latter's enrollment increases have taken place since the mid to late 1990s. Especially noteworthy are the large increases in resident student enrollments at Grand Valley State and Saginaw Valley State Universities. Although the Big Three's total enrollments have remained relatively constant (or declined slightly), the mix of enrollments at these institutions has changed over time. Wayne State has, by design, increased the number and percentage of graduate students it serves (a more than 300 percent increase in graduate student enrollments from 1997 to 2002). The University of Michigan-Ann Arbor campus has increased the number of undergraduate students enrolled and increased its percentage of nonresident students. MSU's enrollment levels have remained fairly stable, but the percentage of graduate students served has declined slightly over the last 25 years or so. Another evident pattern is the increase in the teaching of graduate students in the comprehensive institutions. Comprehensive institutions now account for about 20 percent of graduate enrollments, up from 10 percent of all graduate students taught in the state in the early to mid-1980s.

In the early 1980s, state appropriations declined sharply because of a severe economic recession in the state. After that there was a recovery in appropriations, leading to the peak in state appropriations in the late 1980s, and since then funding from the state has declined. The Big Three institutions have incurred the most dramatic declines since the peak in funding in 1987. In fact, in real terms, appropriations to the Big Three institutions in 2002 were lower than the levels of funding in the late 1970s. To compensate for decreases in appropriations, institutions have implemented a number of strategies including increasing funding from other sources (e.g., research), increasing tuition and nonresident enrollment, and decreasing their use of permanent, ranked faculty.

In the process of writing this chapter, a discernible pattern has emerged. Poor economic conditions lead to a decline in general fund revenues. Then policymakers have the unenviable task of figuring out how to balance the state budget year in and year out. During the last 25 years, they have done so in a number of ways, one of which is reducing the rate of growth in higher education appropriations, or in recent years actually cutting (in real terms) funding to universities. Reduced funding tends to lead to increased tuition at affected institutions and uses of enrollment management techniques that attempt to maximize net tuition revenue by enrolling more nonresident students or "leveraging" financial aid (a form of price discrimination). Raising tuition and/or increasing out-of-state enrollments are likely to produce negative reactions among legislators, who then threaten to or actually do carry out another round of appropriations cuts. This cycle appears to be destructive and is not sustainable if Michigan wants to continue to have the high-quality postsecondary system it is known for and will need if it wants to be competitive in the coming years.

LOOKING FORWARD

Whether affordability is as big a problem as perceived by some higher education stakeholders, it is nonetheless one of the biggest challenges facing Michigan postsecondary education. Critics note that an average income family in Michigan needs to devote about 22 percent of its income to pay for college expenses (less financial aid) while attending a community college, whereas the national average is only 15 percent. Attending a public four-year college requires about 32 percent of a Michigan family's income, but the national average is only half that rate at 16 percent. The state investment in need-based financial aid is low when compared with most states; it ranks 34th and the average loan amount that a Michigan undergraduate student borrows each year is $3,011 (Measuring Up 2004). So there is considerable pressure from legislators to hold down or even reduce the costs to families who aspire to public higher education in Michigan. The problem is that the state is struggling to provide funding for a number of important social objectives, and higher education is not a high priority in some political circles.

Preparation for college is also seen as a critical issue, as only 32 percent of Michigan students graduate from high school having the required coursework and minimal test scores for being admitted to a selective four-year college (Cherry Commission 2004). Only 40 percent of Michigan high school students take at least one upper-level math course (e.g., algebra or above) (Measuring Up 2004), and nearly 35 percent of all college freshmen need to take at least one remedial course (Cherry Commission 2004). Notwithstanding such weakness in preparation, 80 percent of freshmen at four-year colleges return for their sophomore year

(Measuring Up 2004), however, community college retention is relatively poor, and fewer than 20 percent of Michigan's full-time students at these institutions graduate within three years (150 percent of "normal" time, Cherry Commission 2004). Four-year colleges have more success in graduating students; 54 percent of their students graduate within six years (also 150 percent of "normal" time) of college entrance (Measuring Up 2004). If Michigan aspires to enter the knowledge-based economy, it must do a better job of preparing their children for postsecondary education, and providing life-long learning for adults, so that the citizens of the state will be prepared for the jobs that will be available in the coming years.

Launching the Knowledge-Based Economy in Michigan

Regarding Michigan's ability to enter the knowledge-based economy, in the 2002 New Economy Index developed by the Progressive Policy Institute, Michigan ranked 23rd overall. The state ranked low (30th) in information technology jobs, but high in the educational attainment of the manufacturing workforce (7th). The state is doing well both exporting manufactured goods (11th) and attracting foreign investment (14th); however, Michigan scores poorly (40th) in economic dynamism indicators, which are measures of entrepreneurship. A positive sign is that Michigan industries invest high in research and development (10th), but according to this report the state does not have enough high-tech jobs (36th) (Atkinson 2002).

To move Michigan ahead on the knowledge-based economy, in 2004 Governor Granholm appointed a bipartisan commission chaired by Lieutenant Governor John D. Cherry, Jr. The Cherry Commission was charged with preparing a set of recommendations for (1) building a dynamic workforce of employees who have the talents and skills needed for succeeding in the twenty-first century economy, (2) doubling the percentage of Michigan citizens who attain postsecondary degrees or other credentials that link them to economic success, and (3) improving the alignment of Michigan's institutions of higher education with emerging employment opportunities in the state's economy.

The Cherry Commission identified three competitive advantages that make the state a likely candidate to develop a knowledge-based economy: (1) a high level of R&D expenditures as percent of the Gross State Product, (2) a high percent of science and engineering degrees granted each year, and (3) a high number of patents issued (Cherry Commission 2004). The commission divided its work into four areas: preparation, participation, completion, and economic benefits, providing recommendations in each of these areas.

The main recommendations of the preparation group are (1) to develop rigorous high school curriculum standards; (2) to establish a new statewide test that measure students' performance against Michigan standards and that may also be used as a college entrance examination; and (3) to refashion high schools by implementing research-based reforms such as small schools, K16 mergers, and thematic schools.

The participation group made the following recommendations: (1) make postsecondary education the educational attainment standard, (2) organize community compacts for increasing postsecondary education by 5 percent annually over the next 10 years, and (3) implement a new dual enrollment funding system to ensure that 50 percent of Michigan students earn college credits while in high school (by 2015).

The completion group made the following recommendations: (1) ask postsecondary education institutions to produce an annual report of their efforts to enhance student completion, (2) expand the geographic coverage of Michigan postsecondary education institutions, and (3) create (by 2006) a statewide transfer wizard to smooth the progress of transferring from two- to four-year institutions.

The economic benefits group made the following recommendations: (1) create K16 partnerships for offering courses that help to develop entrepreneurial skills; (2) call Michigan businesses and foundations to fund scholarships for Michigan students, especially for those pursuing science and engineering degrees; and (3) channel investment into the Michigan Technology Tri-Corridor, which extends from Detroit to Ann Arbor and westward to Grand Rapids (Cherry Commission 2004). The state has provided incentive grants to fund high technology and life science-related investments in this corridor. Not surprisingly the corridor is home to some of the most important higher education institutions in the state and all three of the state's large research institutions.

The Cherry Commission also identified several critical factors affecting participation in postsecondary education including (1) high school preparation; (2) financial problems encountered by students; (3) poor knowledge about how to navigate the higher education system; (4) geographic, physical, and cultural barriers to higher education; (5) low expectations among some citizens that diminish student aspirations; and (6) increased demands placed on working adults (Cherry Commission 2004). The Commission's recommendations addressed all but one of the barriers to access noted previously: financial problems. Because of the state structural fiscal constraints, Michigan is not able to increase substantially financial aid for needy students. Thus, colleges and universities may have to channel institutional aid to serve such need. As noted previously, the University of Michigan has taken the leadership in providing institutional aid to its students, especially students from low- and middle-income students. The University has announced another initiative to increase access to students from underrepresented groups. The program, named M-PACT, will commit $3 million a year to need-based aid to reduce the loan burden of undergraduate resident students. The program has been seeded with $9 million from private gifts, but the university will launch a major fundraising initiative to raise $60 million to sustain this effort over time (Coleman 2005). Although the university has been and continues to support needy students, they are also reacting to aid policies that their private (e.g., Princeton, Harvard, Yale) and public peers (e.g., North Carolina, Berkeley) have implemented to make education at their institutions more affordable for needy students. Targeting more aid to needy students is a growing trend among elite institutions like those mentioned previously. If this becomes the norm, the question is whether other institutions in Michigan (and elsewhere) will have the financial resources to commit to this effort.

Another suggestion being floated in some policy circles is to create a multiyear strategy to achieve aggregate per-student appropriations that at least meet the average of the Great Lakes region and their competing states. Michigan's per-student average level of support is about $1,000 lower that neighboring states and its close competitors. Combining increased public support with institutional savings will go a long way toward restraining tuition increases, increasing quality, and expanding accessibility. It is unclear, however, where the dollars to fund this proposal would come from.

Another recommendation of the Cherry Commission is for the State of Michigan to establish a unit record student tracking system to improve the information available about Michigan's institutions of education. This system will resemble those established in other states such as Florida and Missouri. The system will contain information on students as they progress through the K12 ranks and into the postsecondary education system. Also available will be information about social (e.g., welfare dependence, incarcerations) and labor market outcomes (e.g., occupation employed in, weekly earnings) for students after they leave our schools and universities. Establishment of this system may improve our collective understanding of the link between K12 education and success in higher education and/or the labor market. Another benefit of establishing such a system is the ability to establish (with more precision) the social benefits of formal education because actual earnings is available rather than using proxies such as the average earnings differences between high school and college graduates. One of the criticisms of public higher education has been that they have not documented the benefits that accrue to the state by the provision of state subsidies to students and institutions. Such a system has the potential of improving our understanding of the return that accrues to the state from its support of postsecondary education. Currently, it appears that this system will be created, as funds now appropriated to this effort and a team of policymakers and academics are being assembled to design and implement the system (and the first author of this chapter is part of this team).

It appears that Michigan's current leadership is committed to move the state from being dependent on manufacturing—especially the auto industry—and to take a lead position in the knowledge-driven economy. For instance, state and academic policymakers appear interested in developing the capacity to compete in the area of life sciences research and manufacturing, and the state has provided tax credits and seed money for this effort. At the same time politicians realize that having a labor force educated in these areas is also necessary, so to be successful, universities are ramping up their efforts in the area of life sciences. Whether this enterprise is a success will in many ways depend on the postsecondary institutions in the state, especially the Big Three, playing a critical role in training the scientists who will work in this area. The universities cannot do this alone, however; they will need to have continuing financial and political support from Lansing.

CONCLUSIONS

Every decade the Presidents Council assembles a group of business and labor leaders to examine the state of Michigan's public universities. In 2002, this group was
again convened and their effort culminated in a report. In this report the Commission Chairman Paul Hillegonds noted, "We must look beyond the current
budget issues and find ways to make higher education available and affordable for
more people in Michigan. The future growth of this state depends on our ability
to remain competitive and that takes an educated workforce" (University Investment Commission 2003). The Commission called for a long-term strategy to meet
the challenge of building economic security and social progress in Michigan. In
the report the Commission also proposed a new compact between the state and its
public universities with shared responsibility for strengthening Michigan's world-
class higher education institutions and achieving greater numbers of people with
four-year degrees, especially in segments that are currently underrepresented in
universities. The report also urged Governor Granholm to convene a statewide
summit of university, political, business, labor, and civic leaders to assist in fash-
ioning a long-term higher education development strategy. The Cherry Commission was established to do so and, as mentioned previously, has made a number
of recommendations that are now being implemented to more closely align the
economy of the state and the postsecondary sector. It seems that an alliance of
labor, business, political, and academic leaders is quite serious about improving
the state's capabilities to be competitive in the twenty-first century, and the postsecondary education system will play an important role in this process. Only time
will tell, of course, whether there will be the financial and political wherewithal
to make this plan a reality.

NOTES

1. More information about the 15 public institutions can be found at http://www.pcsum.
org/universities.html. For more information about the CCs see http://www.mcca.org/.
The private colleges contact is Edward Blews at blewse@aol.com.

2. The University of Michigan's per-student aid figure may be overstated because these
figures are based on resident student enrollments, and the Ann Arbor campus has substantially more nonresident students than other state universities (see Jen, 2004, Appendix A
for more details).

3. The discount is calculated by taking the difference between the posted tuition rate
and the average amount of federal, state, and institutional aid provided by the institution
(tax credits available are not included).

CHAPTER

North Carolina's Commitment to Higher Education: Access and Affordability

Betsy E. Brown and Robert L. Clark

North Carolina has been committed to providing affordable college education to its citizens for more than 200 years. The state has placed access to quality higher education at the top of its policy agenda. Today, all public, four-year institutions of higher education are organized into a single system, the University of North Carolina (UNC). The 16 campuses of UNC are located throughout the state to provide access to citizens in all geographical areas. The institutions are diverse and varied in their missions, but all are dedicated to the objective of producing a more educated citizenry for the state.

In this chapter, we examine the current organizational structure of UNC and its constituent institutions and the way in which key indicators of productivity, excellence, and funding have evolved over the last two decades. We begin with a description of public higher education in North Carolina and the way in which it is currently managed and financed. Next, we consider important aspects of UNC as they relate to undergraduate and graduate students. Finally, we assess some of the important changes in the faculty. All of these indicators are considered within the context of the current fiscal environment of the state.

ORGANIZATIONAL STRUCTURE OF UNC

The University of North Carolina in Chapel Hill (UNC-CH) was chartered in 1789 as the first public university in the United States. UNC-CH was the only public university to graduate students in the eighteenth century. Today, UNC is a multi-campus university system composed of 16 constituent institutions granting baccalaureate, masters, doctoral, and professional degrees. Among the most important constitutional and statutory mandates that govern the University of North Carolina is Section 9, Article IX of the Constitution of the State, which states "The General Assembly shall provide that the benefits of The University of North Carolina and other public institutions of higher education, as far as practicable, be extended to the people of the State free of expense."

The current structure of UNC was established in 1971 when the 16 public institutions of higher education were reorganized into the single system of the University of North Carolina. The stated purpose was "to foster the development of a well-planned and coordinated system of higher education, to improve the quality of education, to extend its benefits, and to encourage an economical use of the state's resources." The UNC system is governed by a 32-member board of governors elected by the two houses of the North Carolina General Assembly. The board has responsibility for approving degree programs, setting enrollment levels, establishing tuition and fees, and submitting the university's budget request to the governor and General Assembly. In addition to the 16-campus university system, North Carolina has a system of 58 public community colleges and institutes governed by a separate board. These institutions offer two-year college degrees, providing technical, vocational, and college transfer programs.

The president of the University of North Carolina is responsible for carrying out the educational policies adopted by the board of governors. The president, who is appointed by the board, manages the professional staff in the Office of the President and the day-to-day operations of the university. Each of the campuses has a board of trustees appointed by the board of governors and the governor of North Carolina and has a chancellor as its chief executive officer. The local boards are responsible for searching for new chancellors and submitting a short list of candidates to the president. The president then submits a recommendation to the board to be confirmed as a campus chancellor. The president works with the chancellors of the 16 universities to carry out the mission of the university system and the separate missions of each institution.

In recent years, the board of governors has given greater flexibility and authority to the campus boards to manage their campus budgets, appoint new faculty and administrators, and set compensation for academic and administrative personnel, in compliance with the policies and procedures of the board of governors. The boards of trustees are also responsible for the management and oversight of academic policies, awarding of degrees, budget administration, endowments and trust funds, admissions and financial aid, student services and student activities, intercollegiate athletics, campus safety, and parking.

The governance structure of the University of North Carolina is recognized by most stakeholders as a model that "works." This assessment may be the result of the "balance of powers" in the appointment of the board and the campus boards of trustees. The tension between centralization and autonomy that is inherent in any large state university system has been lessened because the authority and responsibilities of each unit are continuously evaluated and revised as appropriate. An example of change in governance in response to evolving educational interest is the board of governor's delegation of authority to the campuses in 2003 for hiring, promotion, and setting compensation for most employees. The delegation of these areas of responsibilities requires each institution to submit its personnel policies to the board of governors for their review.

Of course, the main areas of contention are over funding formulas and the budgetary allocations to the individual campuses and, more recently, tuition levels set by the board of governors. The primary challenge is to provide the differential funding for the research campuses of UNC-CH and North Carolina State University (NCSU) to allow them to remain competitive for nationally prominent research scholars while funding other campuses at a level that allows them to develop and expand their programs consistent with their missions. In the 1990s, the board of governors first permitted institutions to propose their own tuition charges in addition to any across-the-board increases and, in 1999, identified several institutions as "focused growth" campuses to receive additional funding to accommodate an expected increase in student enrollment.

UNC's Constituent Institutions

The 16 UNC constituent institutions vary widely in their missions, size, emphasis on research, and degree programs. The universities represent six different Carnegie classifications and are geographically located throughout the state. The individual institutions are:

1. Specialized Institutions
   North Carolina School of the Arts (NCSA)
2. Baccalaureate Colleges—General
   Elizabeth City State University (ECSU)**
   Winston-Salem State University (WSSU)**
3. Baccalaureate Colleges—Liberal Arts
   University of North Carolina at Asheville (UNCA)
4. Master's (Comprehensive) Colleges and Universities
   Appalachian State University (ASU)
   Fayetteville State University (FSU)**
   North Carolina Central University (NCCU)**
   University of North Carolina at Pembroke (UNCP)***
   University of North Carolina at Wilmington (UNCW)
   Western Carolina University (WCU)
5. Doctoral/Research Intensive Universities
   East Carolina University (ECU)
   North Carolina Agricultural and Technical State University* (NC A&T)**

University of North Carolina at Charlotte (UNCC)

University of North Carolina at Greensboro (UNCG)

6. Doctoral/Research Extensive Universities

North Carolina State University (NCSU)

University of North Carolina at Chapel Hill (UNC-CH)

* In 2004, North Carolina A&T State University met the criteria for classification as a Doctoral/Research Intensive University.

** Historically Black Universities.

*** Historically Native American-serving University.

The diverse size and missions of the campuses, represented by their six Carnegie classifications, make generalizations from composite data difficult. With differentiated missions, the campuses have different academic programs, funding and expenditures per student, tuition and fee levels, mix of undergraduate and graduate programs, and emphasis on research. In addition, the university includes institutions with different histories. UNC-CH was the first state-supported institution in the state and is generally classified as the "flagship" institution of the system. NCSU was established as the agricultural and technical land grant institution for the state but now is a fully diversified university and the largest institution in the UNC system. The University of North Carolina at Greensboro (UNCG) was initially established as the state's "Women's College" but is now a coeducational research-intensive institution. In addition, five UNC institutions are historically black universities (Elizabeth City State University, Winston-Salem State University, Fayetteville State University, North Carolina Central University, and North Carolina Agricultural and Technical State University, an 1890 land grant institution) and one, the University of North Carolina at Pembroke, is an historically Native American-serving institution.

In this chapter, data reported for all UNC institutions are generally reported according to Carnegie classification, with data from the two doctoral/research extensive universities reported separately from the doctoral/research intensive, master's, and baccalaureate universities. In some cases, data from the North Carolina School of the Arts (NCSA) are excluded. NCSA, a conservatory-style institution that also includes high school students, does not award tenure to its faculty, and has an academic program based primarily on performance rather than the academic study of the arts. When NCSA data are included, they do not include high school enrollment. Unless otherwise noted, all data in the text and tables have been provided by the UNC Office of the President.

State Appropriations

Similar to trends in other states, the proportion of total state appropriations going to education and higher education in particular has been declining. In 1985,

67.8 percent of the state budget was allocated to education (K12, community colleges, and UNC). By 2004, the educational share of state spending had declined to 55.8 percent. During the same period, the share of state expenditures going to UNC declined from 17.2 percent to 11.8 percent of all state appropriations. These funds are provided to UNC and then allocated by the board of governors to the individual campuses.

Funding for UNC institutions is based on a formula that includes differential funding rates by discipline and level of student. For example, science and engineering programs are funded at a higher dollar amount per student credit hour (SCH) than humanities, and master's and doctoral programs receive greater funding per student than undergraduate programs. These differences in programmatic funding result in different funding levels for each institution. Appropriations per student full-time equivalent (FTE) for each campus and all of UNC are shown in Table 9.1.

Between 2000–2001 and 2004–2005, total UNC state funding per FTE student (defined as 12 hours for undergraduate and 9 hours for graduate students) declined. Overall funding per FTE declined from $9,535 in 2000–2001 to $8,708 in 2003–2004 before rising to $9,172 in 2004–2005. Adjusting for inflation, the real value of state appropriations per FTE in 2004 was 11 percent lower than per student funding in 2000. The decline in state funding reflects the adverse financial status of the North Carolina state budget. In response to looming deficits in the state budget, the legislature and the governor sharply reduced funding for virtually all state agencies. Funds for projected enrollment growth at UNC were appropriated each year; however, other reductions in the university's budget offset these increased enrollment funds.

Funding per FTE student varies dramatically across UNC campuses, as shown in Table 9.1. Individual campus differences reflect increases in enrollment, changes in program mix such as additional doctoral programs, diseconomies of scale, and, in the case of campuses such as ECSU, UNCP, and WSSU, special "focused growth" funding (see "Enrollments").

One measure of funding by which North Carolina can be compared to other states is the proportion of total state personal income that is allocated to higher education. *Post-Secondary Higher Education Opportunity*, which tracks a number of measures of state support for universities and students, has compared states based on the appropriation of state tax funds for higher education operating expenses per $1,000 of personal income for the state. According to this measure, North Carolina ranked fifth nationally in 2005, appropriating $11.05 per $1,000 of personal income, compared to an average of $6.91 for all states. Appropriations per $1,000 of personal income between 1976 and 2005 declined by 34.7 percent nationally, and appropriations in North Carolina declined by 22.6 percent, the 13th lowest decline in the United States (*Postsecondary Higher Education Opportunity*, 2005a). Reductions in state funding have had a serious impact on University budgets, but by this measure and others, UNC has fared better than its counterparts in many other states.

Table 9.1
Appropriations per Budgeted Average Annual FTE Student

Institution	1993–1994	2000–2001	2001–2002	2002–2003	2003–2004	2004–2005
Appalachian State University	5,142	7,311	6,991	6,618	6,801	6,933
East Carolina University, AA	5,059	7,213	6,994	6,853	6,661	7,421
Elizabeth City State University	8,546	11,236	11,247	11,786	10,826	11,868
Fayetteville State University	6,281	8,413	8,529	8,417	8,727	8,033
North Carolina A & T State University	6,659	8,614	8,326	7,812	7,610	7,778
North Carolina Central University	6,571	8,631	8,335	8,421	8,251	8,339
North Carolina State University	7,631	10,774	10,469	10,231	9,696	10,267
UNC-Asheville	6,263	8,440	8,415	7,817	7,820	8,242
UNC-Chapel Hill, AA	7,832	10,756	10,583	9,841	9,371	10,143
UNC-Charlotte	4,655	6,813	6,639	6,336	6,241	6,955
UNC-Greensboro	5,523	8,223	8,058	7,802	7,923	8,304
UNC-Pembroke	6,459	8,964	9,153	9,039	8,645	9,013
UNC-Wilmington	4,929	6,737	6,520	6,154	5,879	6,339
Western Carolina University	5,909	8,089	8,003	8,034	7,963	7,867
Winston-Salem State University	7,690	10,761	10,664	10,629	9,938	10,678
Total UNC	6,897	9,535	9,324	8,910	8,708	9,172
Total UNC in 2004 Dollars	8,830	10,310	9,846	9,261	8,908	9,172

Total Revenues and Income Sources

Despite their decline in recent years, state appropriations still represent the largest single source of funding for UNC. In 2002–2003, state appropriations represented 30.8 percent of the UNC budget. Table 9.2 provides a detailed picture of the revenues sources and indicates that 17.5 percent of all revenues were from grants and contracts, 11.9 percent from tuition and fees, and 13.4 percent from endowment income and gifts.

Although state funding for UNC has declined in recent years, one source of revenue, sponsored programs, has grown dramatically over the last 10 years. In FY 2004, the University of North Carolina attracted more than $1 billion of external support for research and sponsored programs. This represents an 8 percent increase over the previous year, contributing to a five-year gain of 69 percent. Funding for the university's research and public outreach activities comes from state, local, and federal government; business and industry; and associations, foundations, and other not-for-profit organizations. Federal funding accounts for approximately two-thirds of the university's awards, and UNC remains successful in competing for these awards. UNC-CH (17th nationally in 2004) and NCSU (62nd nationally) are consistently among the top 75 institutions in the country. In the most recent survey of federal funding obligations to HBCUs, NC A&T was among the top five institutions receiving federal support for science and engineering and was ranked seventh for total R&D support among all HBCUs. The National Institutes of Health are the largest source of federal research funds, with 2004 awards exceeding $300 billion. In addition to the federal funds for research, awards from

Table 9.2
UNC Sources of Revenue 2002–2003

State appropriations	30.8%
Grants and contracts	17.5%
Auxiliary enterprises	15.4%
Tuition and fees	11.9%
Gifts, investment income, capital grants and gifts	13.4%
Hospitals	8.9%
Federal appropriations	0.5%
Independent operations	0.2%
Other Sources	1.4%
Total Revenues	$5.4B

Source: IPEDS.

foundations accounted for 10 percent of this external funding, and grants and contracts from state and local governments represented 9 percent.

UNDERGRADUATE STUDENT OUTCOMES
Tuition and Fees

Costs to attend UNC institutions have traditionally been among the lowest in the country. In the last five years, however, tuition and fees for students entering UNC have risen substantially. Reflecting both board of governor-approved and campus-initiated increases, the rate of increase has been much higher than the average for similar institutions around the country. For resident undergraduates at UNC-CH, tuition and fees rose from $2,211 in 1998–1999 to $3,856 in 2002–2003. This amounted to a 74.4 percent increase in only five years. In contrast, the national average of tuition and fees for flagship campuses rose only 26.7 percent. As a result, the cost of attending UNC-CH for North Carolina residents, which was 59.9 percent of the average cost at other flagship institutions in 1998–1999, increased to 82.5 percent in 2002–2003. A similar increase was noted in tuition and fees for nonresident students at UNC-CH, for whom costs increased from $11,377 or 108.8 percent of the national average in 1998–1999 to $15,140 in 2002–2003, when these costs were 114.3 percent of the national average. Tuition and fees have continued to increase over the last two years, to $4,359 for resident students and $17,467 for nonresident in 2004–2005 at UNC-CH.

The cost for residents attending comprehensive universities in the UNC system rose from $1,757 to $2,677 or 52.4 percent during the same five-year period, increasing the cost of attending these institutions from 60.2 percent to 72.0 percent of the national average. Nonresident costs of attending comprehensive UNC campuses soared from $8,857 to $11,534. Tuition and fees have continued to rise for all classifications of UNC institutions through 2004–2005, although the board of governors voted not to increase resident tuition and fees across the board for 2005–2006; campus-based tuition increases were approved only for nonresident students and graduate students, and required fees for all students were increased for most campuses. The rapid increase in the cost of higher education in North Carolina is a cause for concern and threatens to undermine the state's historic commitment of low-cost access to quality higher education to citizens of the state.

Enrollment

Despite state budgetary problems and reductions in funding, UNC's enrollment continues to grow, increasing by 12 percent between 2001 and 2004, when enrollment reached 189,614. Table 9.3 shows the enrollments separately by institution for each of the last four years. NCSU has the largest enrollment, with a head count of 29,957 in 2004 followed by UNC-CH (26,878); six campuses have headcounts of less than 6,000. Projections are that total enrollment will rise to 235,180 in 2012 or an increase of 24 percent between 2004 and 2012. Thus, UNC is expected

Table 9.3
Fall Headcount Enrollments, 2001-2012

Institution	2001	2002	2003	2004	2012 (projected)
ASU	13,762	14,178	14,343	14,653	16,731
ECU	19,412	20,577	21,756	22,767	28,500
ECSU	2,004	2,150	2,308	2,470	3,578
FSU	5,010	5,308	5,329	5,441	6,603
NCA&TU	8,319	9,115	10,030	10,383	15,867
NCCU	5,753	6,519	7,191	7,727	9,938
NCSA	789	817	792	788	923
NCSU	29,286	29,637	29,854	29,957	36,500
UNCA	3,293	3,391	3,446	3,574	3,717
UNC-CH,AA	25,494	26,028	26,359	26,878	28,871
UNCC	18,308	18,916	19,605	19,845	28,430
UNCG	13,775	14,453	14,870	15,329	18,683
UNCP	3,933	4,432	4,722	5,027	6,786
UNCW	10,799	10,918	11,079	11,574	13,641
WCU	6,863	7,033	7,561	8,396	10,210
WSSU	2,992	3,495	4,102	4,805	6,202
Total UNC	169,792	176,967	183,347	189,614	235,180

to have almost 30,000 more students in the next six years. Finding the resources to maintain educational quality while providing appropriate access to the growing number of qualified students will be a major challenge for UNC.

Higher education enrollment growth in North Carolina is a result of demographic factors and an increased college-participation rate (the percentage of high school graduates pursuing higher education at a two- or four-year institution). The number of high school graduates in North Carolina is projected to increase by 118 percent from 1992 to 2012. This increase in high school graduates, fueled in part by dramatic increases in North Carolina's Hispanic population, will push the demand for enrollments in UNC to higher levels. Although high school dropout rates remain high for North Carolina (41 percent from ninth to twelfth grade), the college-participation rate in North Carolina rose from 52 percent in 1990 to 65 percent in 2000. The state rate is above the national rate of 58 percent and is the highest among the 12 most populous states.

The UNC-going rate for North Carolina high school graduates increased from 25 percent to 31 percent in the decade 1993–2003, with comparable increases for white, African American, and Native American students. The rate is expected to stay around 30 percent for the near term. The increased college-going rate resulted, in part, from efforts by the university, community colleges, and independent colleges in the state, including programs such as GEAR-UP, to reach middle-school students, and a comprehensive Web site, CFNC.org, which contains extensive information to assist students and their families to plan, apply, and pay for college.

The combination of increases in high school graduates and increases in the college participation rate will continue to place enrollment pressure on UNC in the coming decade. In anticipation of dramatic enrollment increases from 2000 though 2012, the university conducted a study of the capacity for growth at each institution. This study revealed significant capacity of seven institutions (the five HBUs, UNC Pembroke, and Western Carolina University) that were designated as "focused-growth institutions." At the same time, the University decided to restrain growth at the North Carolina School of the Arts and UNC Asheville (the liberal arts campus of UNC) in recognition of their special missions. The other seven UNC institutions were given more moderate enrollment targets than the seven focused growth institutions. They have met these targets through a combination of on-campus growth and increased delivery of courses through various modes of distance learning.

Additional state funding for the focused-growth institutions has been received from the state over several years to assist them in meeting expected enrollment growth and building capacity in areas such as recruitment, fundraising, and academic program development. The focused-growth institutions received approximately $28 million in recurring and $8.6 million in one-time additional funding between 1999 and 2004. These funds accounted for a 10 percent average increase in funding per student in 2004–2005. As a group, these institutions have increased their enrollments dramatically since 2001, with a combined enrollment increase of 8.4 percent in a single year from 2002 to 2003. Their enrollment grew 36.3 percent from 1999 to 2004, compared to an increase of 17.8 percent for UNC overall for the same period. Focused growth institutions are projected to increase enrollment between 2002 and 2007 by 30 to 45 percent and by 45 to 75 percent between 2002 and 2012. In addition, these institutions have increased their fundraising (which grew from $15 million to $25 million between 2001 and 2003) and their competitive grants (up 175 percent from 1999 to 2004).

UNC's enrollment projections were accompanied by analysis of the physical capacity of campuses to accommodate dramatic enrollment growth. By comparing the number of students projected to enroll at UNC and community college campuses to the estimated capacity at each institution, the state's public higher education sector was able to make the case for dramatic expansion of campus facilities necessary to accommodate an increased number of students. The combination of these analyses with strong support from governmental and business representatives resulted in approval by North Carolina voters of a $3.1 billion bond issue in 2000, the largest higher education bond issue in the United States. UNC's share of the bond issue, $2.5 billion, has resulted in an aggressive construction program on every UNC campus.

Retention and Graduate Rates

Measures of the success of educational institutions include the rate at which students continue to make academic progress and ultimately graduate from the university. Freshman to sophomore retention rates for all students at each of the UNC institutions from 1997 to 2003 are shown in Table 9.4. This rate has remained relatively stable during this period at 80 to 81 percent for all of the institutions combined and 90 to 95 percent for UNC-CH and NCSU. The retention rates are slightly above the national average for each type of institution. Freshman to sophomore retention rates for both blacks and whites have remained relatively stable at approximately 80 percent, with the retention rate for whites tending to be about 2 percent higher than the rate for blacks since 1992.

Four-year graduation rates for UNC institutions tend to be above the national average for comparable types of institutions (Table 9.5). UNC-CH has by far the highest four-year graduation rates, ranging from 65 to 70 percent for recent cohorts, with UNCW's rate reaching more than 42 percent and NCSU's nearly 40 percent for the 2000 cohort. Given the large number of part-time students at some of these institutions, a more useful measure is the four-year graduate rate for full-time students. The four-year graduation rate for full-time students enrolled in UNC is nearly 60 percent compared to 35 percent for all students. The overall UNC six-year graduation rate averages about 57 percent, compared to a national average of 55 percent; six-year graduation rates for each of the universities tend to be higher than comparable institutions nationwide.

Financial Aid

Need-based financial aid from campus, federal, and state sources has, to some extent, offset recent increases in tuition and fees at UNC institutions. The expansion of grants and scholarships has kept public higher education in North Carolina affordable to most students. In particular, a program of state need-based financial aid requested by the board of governors and partially funded by the General Assembly has increased at the same time as tuition and fees and has offset some of the increase in the price of higher education for needy students and families.

Between 1997–1998 and 2004–2005, state need-based financial aid from a variety of programs increased from approximately $40 million to $128.6 million, an increase of 247 percent; aid from this source is expected to increase to $144 million in 2005–2006. These funds go to students at community and independent colleges, as well as UNC campuses, and have been a significant addition to federal and campus-based financial aid. According to the North Carolina State Education Assistance Authority (NCSEAA), higher education in the state is more affordable for most students than it was in 1999–2000 and compared to national trends (NCSEAA 2003).

NCSEAA has begun to track the net price of college at UNC institutions (a weighted average price for in-state students at all UNC campuses including tuition, fees, room, board, housing, personal expenses, and transportation)

Table 9.4
One-Year Retention Rates: 1997–2003 Cohorts

	1997 (%)	1998 (%)	1999 (%)	2000 (%)	2001 (%)	2002 (%)	2003 (%)	1996–2002 Nat'l Average (%) (by institution type)*
NCSU	87.8	88.0	88.9	88.7	90.1	90.2	90.2	84.6
UNC-CH	94.8	93.9	93.9	95.0	94.7	95.3	95.2	—
ECU	78.2	79.0	76.4	78.0	76.7	76.6	78.7	75.4
NCA&T	76.7	75.5	72.3	76.6	76.0	73.0	73.1	—
UNCC	78.7	73.3	73.1	77.7	76.4	75.7	77.1	—
UNCG	73.9	74.0	73.9	74.9	73.8	75.5	76.9	—
ASU	82.9	81.1	84.7	83.2	81.6	83.0	84.2	74.6
FSU	72.8	74.2	72.6	71.0	73.9	73.4	72.7	—
NCCU	77.2	77.0	72.3	78.5	81.8	78.2	77.7	—
UNC-P	71.0	66.6	67.4	68.6	72.2	67.2	67.1	—
UNC-W	78.3	80.0	79.8	81.8	83.9	85.6	85.7	—
WCU	67.5	69.6	71.5	69.4	70.9	69.1	73.9	—
ECSU	76.4	72.9	77.3	81.5	73.2	74.9	76.2	70.1
NCSA	72.6	77.4	79.6	75.2	74.3	74.6	76.9	—
UNC-A	77.0	77.8	76.8	79.8	77.8	77.8	79.6	—
WSSU	68.0	72.9	71.8	73.1	78.3	76.7	78.7	—
UNC Total	81.1	80.6	80.3	86.6	81.5	80.9	81.8	79.5

* Six-year average, 1996–2002. CSRDE, University of Oklahoma.

Table 9.5
Four-Year Full-Time and Traditional Graduation Rates: 1997–2000 Cohorts

| | Four-Year Full Time Rate | | | | Four-Year Rate UNC | | | | |
	1997 (%)	1998 (%)	1999 (%)	2000 (%)	1997 (%)	1998 (%)	1999 (%)	2000 (%)	National Average* (%)
NCSU	46.2	48.1	53.7	55.6	26.5	29.7	35.5	36.9	36.6
UNCCH	83.8	82.3	84.9	78.9	69.4	66.7	70.5	65.3	—
ECU	48.5	48.8	48.1	50.6	24.5	25.7	25.3	27.6	25.0
NCA&T	53.8	50.2	49.1	41.2	26.3	23.6	22.7	19.3	—
UNC-C	49.8	50.7	54.0	54.6	22.0	21.4	23.5	25.8	—
UNC-G	58.7	59.0	60.0	62.0	27.2	26.2	28.2	29.7	—
ASU	57.3	51.7	56.4	56.3	32.9	29.7	35.3	34.2	22.8
FSU	45.5	32.3	55.2	39.4	18.0	12.1	24.4	14.2	—
NCCU	62.7	55.2	50.9	42.5	28.4	27.5	22.8	22.5	—
UNC-P	53.9	57.9	51.5	52.1	20.4	21.3	18.7	20.1	—
UNC-W	64.1	66.5	69.3	70.1	35.3	37.3	40.7	42.7	—
WCU	56.1	54.6	50.1	55.4	25.3	22.7	22.6	24.6	—
ECSU	58.1	58.1	51.9	57.9	31.4	28.6	27.4	30.1	27.1
NCSA	96.2	98.7	97.6	97.6	44.6	48.2	52.1	49.7	—
UNC-A	63.7	55.8	56.1	61.7	29.1	25.3	28.1	30.9	—
WSSU	52.7	45.1	43.4	37.8	24.1	21.8	21.4	18.6	—
UNC Total	60.3	59.0	53.7	55.6	33.4	32.7	34.8	34.7	30.2

* Three-year average, 2000-2003. CSRDE, University of Oklahoma.

compared to family income and financial aid. The NCSEAA study looks at the impact of price increases on five income quintiles, from the lowest to the highest income families. Over five years (1997–1998 through 2001–2002), net price for all quintiles increased 25 percent; for the lowest income quintile, grant aid increased 44 percent while borrowing increased only 1 percent. Remaining need after grant aid remained relatively stable (within the increase in the consumer price index) and, according to NCSEAA, was within the capacity for students in all income groups to meet through work and low-interest loans. Remaining need after grants *and* loan aid was approximately $1,200 and $2,200 for the lowest two income quartiles and was reduced to $0 for the three highest income quintiles. During the same period, the percent of the net price of college attendance paid by families in the lowest income quintile after grants and loans decreased from 28 to 24 percent.

Another important measure of affordability is student debt on graduation. For students attending North Carolina institutions in 2001–2002 who had at least one educational loan over four years studied by NCSEAA, average cumulative debt was $15,048, an amount that (depending on various studies) is between 11 and 14 percent less than the national average. This level of indebtedness would require repayment of approximately $150 per month for 120 months in the first 10 years after graduation.

According to *Postsecondary Higher Education Opportunity*, North Carolina's college participation rate for low-income students (defined as Pell grant recipients) has increased at a much higher rate than nationally. Although the state's 24.6 percent college participation rate for these students in 2002–2003 was near the national average (24.7 percent), North Carolina's increase in participation between 1997 and 2002 was 3.8 percent, compared to an increase nationally of only 0.9 percent (Mortensen 2005).

In 2003, UNC-CH announced the Carolina Covenant, a commitment to make it possible for low-income students to graduate debt-free. To be eligible, a family's annual income may not exceed 200 percent of the federal poverty standard, and the family must also qualify for federal student financial aid. Eligible students will graduate debt free if they work on campus 10 to 12 hours weekly in a federal work-study job throughout their four years, instead of borrowing, with the rest of the student's financial need met through a combination of federal, state, university, and private grants and scholarships. UNC-CH was the first public institution in the nation to make such a pledge. It is unlikely that other UNC campuses will be able to make such a commitment to low-income students in the near future.

Transfers

In 1996, the University of North Carolina and the North Carolina Community College System established a Comprehensive Articulation Agreement governing the transfer of credits from community colleges to university campuses. A Transfer

Articulation Committee made up of representatives from both higher education systems oversees the transfer agreement, which includes a general education transfer core. This 44-semester-hour core, if completed successfully by a community college student with a 2.00 GPA, is transferable as a block across the community college system and to all UNC campuses. The agreement also allows for graduates of two-year associate in arts and associate in sciences degree programs, who are assumed to have completed the general education requirements of the receiving institution, to transfer to UNC campuses with junior status.

The Transfer Advisory Committee has developed premajor agreements for majors that have significant "transfer traffic" from community colleges to the university campuses. UNC publishes a Transfer Student Academic Performance Report each year that is sent to each community college as a means of assessing their students' success after transfer and the effectiveness of the Transfer Articulation Agreement. The Transfer Articulation Agreement has also been endorsed by more than 20 independent colleges in the state as a guide for community college students interested in transferring to non-UNC institutions.

Each fall semester, approximately 4,500 students transfer from North Carolina community colleges to UNC campuses. Approximately 1,800 additional students transfer into UNC institutions each spring semester. Based on the annual Performance Report, these students are successful in the period after their transfer. For example, in 2002–2003, community college transfer students achieved a mean grade point average of 2.70 at UNC institutions after two semesters. Recently, in response to a request from the community college system, the Transfer Advisory Committee has developed a Transfer Assured Admissions Policy, which ensures that community college students who meet all transfer and admission requirements, but are not admitted to their first-choice UNC campus, are directed to the CFNC.org Web site and provided information regarding space availability at other UNC campuses. Although for 2004–2005 fewer than 40 qualified community college students were not admitted to their UNC campus of choice, this program should ensure an even higher number of successful transfers.

GRADUATE STUDENT OUTCOMES
Enrollment

At the same time that UNC institutions have seen a dramatic increase in undergraduate enrollment, graduate enrollment has also increased, from 34,225 to 39,580 from 2001 to 2004, at rates comparable to the increase in undergraduate enrollment. Enrollment in master's and doctoral programs increased 17 percent from 2001 to 2004, higher than the undergraduate increase of approximately 12 percent.

In 2004, graduate enrollment represented slightly more than 20 percent of total UNC enrollment; UNC-CH and NCSU enrolled 44 percent of all UNC graduate students, with three doctoral/research intensive institution (ECU,

UNCC, and UNCG) accounting for an additional 33 percent. NC A&T achieved doctoral/research intensive status in 2004 and has the highest graduate enrollment among UNC's historically black universities. Comprehensive institutions enroll significant numbers of master's students, with more than 1,000 master's-degree students enrolled at ASU, NCCU, UNCW, and WCU in 2004.

Graduate Tuition

Graduate tuition and fees at UNC institutions, like undergraduate costs, have increased dramatically in recent years. Costs for resident graduate students at UNC-CH represented 54.8 percent of the national average in 1998–1999 but, by 2002–2003, had increased to 78.3 percent compared to other flagship universities. Nonresident graduate tuition at UNC-CH, already 110.5 percent of the U.S. average in 1998–1999, was 121.9 percent by 2002–2003, reaching $15,692. Tuition at UNC comprehensive institutions (primarily for master's degrees) increased at a somewhat slower rate between 1998–1999 and 2002–2003, increasing from 57 percent to 67.6 percent of the U.S. average for resident graduate students and from 119.8 percent to 122.8 percent for nonresident graduate students in the same period.

Tuition and fees have increased for graduate students, and enrollment has continued to increase as well. However, high rates of tuition and fees and limited tuition waivers, which are budgeted by the General Assembly and allocated to institutions based on graduate enrollment, may reduce support for graduate students, as discussed next, particularly for graduate teaching assistants supported institutionally rather than by grant funds.

Use of Graduate Students as Instructors

Teaching assistants are a significant component of the faculty cohort at UNC-CH; at other UNC institutions, teaching assistants deliver a smaller proportion of instruction. According to the Delaware Study, in which UNC has participated since 1999, for 1999–2000 through 2001–2002, two-thirds of the 491 teaching assistants assigned fall semester sections were at UNC-CH. Teaching assistants made up only 6 percent of faculty system-wide; however, they made up 15 percent of faculty at UNC-CH, 7 percent at UNCG, and a lower percentage (from 1 to 4 percent) at the other institutions.

In addition to the Delaware data, UNC also collects data on the training, monitoring, and evaluation of graduate teaching assistants (GTAs). According to the most recent report, 10 UNC institutions employed GTAs in 2002–2003. Reports from these institutions indicate that, for those institutions making considerable use of teaching assistants, GTAs are provided seminars in teaching effectiveness either at the departmental or institutional level, are supervised by full-time faculty members, and receive feedback on their teaching. International GTAs are tested for fluency in English, are provided English as a Second Language instruction at most institutions, and are not assigned their own lecture or laboratory sections until their fluency is adequate for effective instruction.

Institutional reports reflected a slight decline in the number of sections taught by GTAs in 2002–2003 from reports for 2001–2002. The decline has been attributed initially to the high cost of tuition waivers for graduate students, particularly those from out of state, as tuition rates have increased. The apparent decline in the number of graduate assistants at UNC institutions is being closely monitored by the Office of the President. Although departments and institutions are committed to providing instructional or research experience to their graduate students, the costs of hiring part-time instructors or postdoctoral researchers may be lower than the cost of hiring graduate students with stipends and tuition remissions.

FACULTY TRENDS
Composition of Faculty

The number of faculty employed by UNC is increasing as a result of rapid enrollment growth. In 2003, UNC employed a total headcount, full- and part-time, of 14,603 faculty, up from 12,767 in 2000. In 2003, the number of full-time faculty, tenure-track and non-tenure–track, was 11,405, compared to 10,041 in 2000. In 2001, UNC conducted a comprehensive study of hiring trends, driven primarily by concern about increases in the percentage of non-tenure–track faculty (both full-time and part-time) at UNC institutions. In its report, the committee noted that from 1990 to 2000, the percentage of non-tenure–track faculty increased at UNC institutions but that non-tenure–track faculty made up a smaller percentage of total faculty at UNC institutions and had increased at a slower rate compared to national increases.

Data indicate that UNC has a much lower percentage of part-time non-tenure–track faculty and a slightly higher percentage of full-time non-tenure–track faculty compared to national data. In 2000, *part-time* non-tenure–track faculty made up 21 percent of faculty at UNC institutions, compared to 43 percent among all U.S. institutions and 34 percent among four-year institutions, as reported in the *1999 National Study of Post-Secondary Faculty* (U.S. Department of Education 2001). The UNC percentage of *full-time* non-tenure–track faculty in 2000 was 23 percent, compared to 18 percent at all U.S. institutions with tenure systems and 21 percent at four-year institutions offering tenure.

Non-tenure–track faculty have increased at UNC institutions at a slower rate than the increase nationally. Data from UNC institutions indicate that, from 1990–2000, *part-time* non-tenure–track faculty (including participants in UNC's Phased Retirement Program) increased from 15 percent to 21 percent, while *full-time* non-tenure–track faculty increased from 19 to 23 percent. Combined, part-time and full-time non-tenure–track faculty increased at UNC institutions from 34 to 43 percent over 10 years, an increase of 9 percentage points compared to a national increase of 20 percentage points in roughly the same period (Table 9.6).

Table 9.6
Combined Part-time and Full-time Non-Tenure–Track Faculty in the United States and at UNC

	1987	1990	1992	1995	1998	2000
US	41%	—	53%	—	61%	—
UNC	—	34%	—	37%	—	43%

Source: NSOPF: 99, Chronicle of Higher Education, May 4, 2001, and UNC Office of the President.

Between 1990 and 2000, UNC institutions saw a decline in tenured and tenure-track faculty paralleling the increase in non-tenure–track faculty. Among all UNC faculty, the percentage of tenured faculty in 2000 was 42 percent, declining from 47 percent in 1990. The percentage of tenure-track faculty in 2000 was 15 percent, down from 19 percent in 1990. When these two groups are combined, the percentage of these "tenure-stream" (tenure-track and tenured) faculty declined from 66 percent in 1990 to 57 percent in 2000.

In the years since the UNC Report on Non-Tenure–Track Faculty in 2001, the trend toward hiring more non-tenure–track faculty has continued, with tenure-stream faculty making up a smaller percentage of total UNC faculty. The pattern of these changes, however, is not consistent across all types of faculty appointments. In fall 2003, the percentage of *non-tenure–track part-time* faculty was unchanged since 2000 (21 percent), while the percentage of *full-time non-tenure–track* faculty increased to 25 percent, up 2 percentage points since 2000. Combined, non-tenure–track faculty increased by 3 percentage points to 46 percent of all UNC faculty in 2003. At the same time, the percentage of *tenure-track* faculty actually increased slightly at UNC institutions, from 15 percent to 16 percent, while *tenured* faculty percentages decreased by 4 percent, to 38 percent in 2003.

The combination of a decreasing proportion of tenured faculty, a higher proportion of tenure-track faculty, and an increase in full-time non-tenure–track faculty may reflect increased retirements or resignations among tenured faculty, with tenure-track and full-time non-tenure–track faculty hired both to replace these tenured faculty and meet growing enrollments at UNC institutions. In 2000, the University of North Carolina predicted these trends, projecting that UNC institutions would have to hire more than 10,000 new faculty between 2001 and 2010 to replace retiring faculty members and meet enrollment growth. The increase in full-time, non-tenure–track as opposed to tenure-track faculty replacements, however, continues the downward trend in tenure-stream faculty, which declined by 3 percentage points, from 57 percent in 2000 to 54 percent in 2003.

The Delaware Study tracks the proportion of teaching at various levels of the curriculum assigned to four categories of faculty. (Before 1999, the University employed its own methodology for tracking faculty-teaching load; data on teaching loads were collected from academic departments in categories that are not comparable to the Delaware data.) Combined data for fall semesters from 1999–2000 through

2001–2002 indicate that, except for lower-division undergraduate classes, tenure-track faculty members (tenured and probationary, which made up 64 percent of instructional staff) taught between 56 and 58 percent of sections, all SCHs, and undergraduate SCHs. Tenure-track faculty members taught 50 percent of lower-division undergraduate SCHs over these three years. When the category of "Other Regular" faculty (i.e., full-time non-tenure–track faculty and administrators who teach) are added to tenure-track faculty, these full-time university employees made up 81 percent of faculty and taught between 73 and 77 percent of sections, SCHs, undergraduate SCHs, and lower-division SCHs. Two other Delaware categories ("Other Supplemental" or part-time faculty and Teaching Assistants) made up 19 percent of faculty but taught between 22 and 24 percent of sections, SCHs, and undergraduate SCHs and 27 percent of lower-division SCHs.

As with other measures, composite numbers reflecting who teaches students at UNC institutions do not reflect the significant differences among faculty teaching assignments at institutions with diverse missions and academic programs. At UNC-CH, for example, tenure-track faculty made up 66 percent of faculty and taught 50 percent of sections, 54 percent of SCHs and 49 percent of undergraduate SCHs but only 39 percent of lower-division SCHs. Teaching assistants made up 15 percent of faculty but taught 37 percent of lower-division SCHs. "Other Regular" and "Supplemental" faculty made up 19 percent of UNC-CH faculty and taught 24 percent of undergraduate SCHs but only 9 percent of lower-division SCHs, reflecting the important role teaching assistants play in the instructional program at this research-extensive institution.

Faculty Salaries

To continue to provide quality higher education to the citizens of North Carolina, UNC must maintain nationally prominent faculty at its campuses. To recruit and retain quality faculty, universities must offer competitive salaries and benefits. Historically, salaries by rank in the UNC system have been at or below the national averages compared to similar public institutions. Table 9.7 reports average faculty salary by rank for each campus in 2003. The table also compares UNC annual salaries to the national average of comparable institutions nationally, using data from the AAUP salary study. With the exception of salaries at UNC-CH, all of the other doctoral institutions have average salaries below the national average of professor in public doctoral universities. The shortfall in salaries compared to the national average for professors at public institutions ranges from 4 percent at NCSU to 16 percent at ECU. At the lower ranks, salaries at NCSU exceed the national average. A review of all of the salary data for each of the three classifications would support the generalization that salaries at UNC campuses tend to be below the national average for public institutions.

Over the last six years, salary increases for faculty have been relatively small in nominal terms and in many cases lagged behind the rate of inflation. Table 9.8 presents average salaries by campuses for all tenured and tenure-track faculty (assistant

Table 9.7
Annual Salary by Rank at UNC Campuses and National Averages, 2003

Doctoral	School	Professor	Associate Professor	Assistant Professor
	UNC-CH	106,262	74,112	61,843
	NCSU	90,934	67,275	59,607
	ECU	79,691	61,031	53,500
	UNCG	81,436	59,845	51,582
	UNCC	84,003	62,393	53,831
National Doctoral				
	Public	94,606	66,275	56,277
	Private	122,158	78,863	68,218
Masters				
	ASU	70,953	58,872	49,832
	FSU	68,217	57,227	52,593
	NC A&T	72,059	61,641	59,104
	NCCU	78,087	61,314	51,447
	UNCP	72,516	52,303	45,846
	UNCW	71,889	56,876	49,547
	WCU	67,613	56,067	48,384
National Masters				
	Public	74,872	59,365	49,795
	Private	82,344	60,207	43,201
Baccalaureate				
	ECSU	61,481	52,826	46,797
	UNCA	69,804	52,027	44,837
	WSSU	63,219	55,287	53,024
National Baccalaureate				
	Public	68,996	55,887	46,387
	Private	82,344	60,207	43,201

professors, associate professors, and professors) for 1998 through 2003. During this period, the consumer price index rose by 12.9 percent; thus, to maintain the real level of income, faculty salaries needed to rise by 12.9 percent. Average salaries at half the campuses increased by more than the rate of inflation, but half the campuses had salary increases that fell below this amount. At the upper end, ECU, NC A&T, and UNC-CH had increases in their average annual compensation of 18 percent, whereas UNC-P and Elizabeth City had the smallest increase in average salaries. Between 1998 and 2003, the average real salary of faculty of all ranks at NCSU declined by 0.7 percent, and the average real salary at UNC-CH rose by 4.5 percent.

For UNC-CH and NCSU, specific comparisons to peer institutions may be more important than these comparisons to national averages. Each of these institutions benchmark their programs to a group of 15 comparable universities. We examined salary data for tenured and tenure-track faculty by rank for UNC

Table 9.8
Average Annual Salary, All Ranks,* 1998 to 2003

NC School	1998	1999	2000	2001	2002	2003	Percent increase 1998–2003
ASU	$53,123	$56,120	$58,173	$59,628	$61,754	$61,311	15.4
ECU	$52,708	$55,549	$59,423	$61,056	$62,203	$62,662	18.9
ECSU	$50,473	$51,278	$53,307	$53,725	$54,930	$54,857	8.7
FSU	$52,812	$54,763	$57,501	$58,617	$57,544	$58,388	10.6
NC A&T	$54,482	$56,236	$60,015	$60,001	$61,252	$64,622	18.6
NCCU	$55,008	$57,865	$61,072	$62,021	$63,329	$63,807	16.0
NCSU	$68,460	$71,054	$75,880	$77,221	$78,194	$76,757	12.1
UNCA	$50,148	$51,538	$53,193	$54,078	$54,507	$55,793	11.3
UNCCH	$74,099	$79,547	$84,778	$85,876	$87,319	$87,448	18.0
UNC-C	$56,437	$59,310	$63,318	$66,538	$66,553	$66,113	17.1
UNCG	$56,519	$58,767	$61,091	$63,148	$63,925	$63,821	12.9
UNCP	$54,219	$55,565	$58,368	$57,895	$57,894	$55,497	2.4
UNCW	$52,797	$55,602	$58,273	$58,414	$60,499	$59,906	13.5
WCU	$51,091	$53,495	$55,147	$55,352	$55,045	$56,325	10.2
WSSU	$51,175	$53,854	$55,747	$56,466	$58,608	$56,807	11.0
Change in CPI							12.9

* Assistant Professor, Associate Professor, and Full Professor.

doctoral/research extensive campuses and their peer groups. In 2003, NCSU's average salary for professors was below 14 of their 15 peer institutions and was essentially the same as the 15th institution. The average salary of associate professors at NCSU was higher than only one of their peers; at the assistant professor level, the average salary for NCSU faculty was higher than three of their peers. For all ranks together, the average salary at NCSU was 10 percent lower than the average at its peer institutions. UNC-CH fared somewhat better, with the average salary for all ranks being greater than 6 of the 15 peer institutions.

Employee Benefits

The most important employee benefits provided by the state of North Carolina to UNC faculty are health and retirement benefits. The N.C. State Employees Health Plan, which covers UNC employees, appears to be comparable to those offered by other institutions; however, faculty must pay a higher proportion of total health care expenses than employees at other institutions. UNC pays the full cost of employees' premiums. The UNC Office of the President estimates that the average proportion of premiums for employees paid by other institutions is 91 percent. However, UNC pays nothing toward the premium for dependent coverage. On average, other universities pay approximately 64 percent of these costs. Because of the relatively high cost of dependent coverage, UNC lags behind other universities in the number of dependents enrolled in the health plan. UNC pays 76 percent of premiums, which is lower than the estimated 81 percent subsidy at other universities. In addition, UNC requires faculty to cover a higher percentage of out-of-pocket costs for deductibles, co-insurance, and co-payments. Thus, faculty end up paying 20 percent of total costs compared to 14 percent at other universities. UNC does extend health insurance to eligible retired faculty under the same terms as provided to active employees, a valuable employee benefit.

Newly hired UNC faculty have a choice between participating in the Teachers and State Employees Retirement System or selecting one of four Option Retirement Plans (ORPs). The state plan is a defined benefit plan that determines benefits based on a formula of 1.82 percent of final salary average per year of employment. Average earnings are based on the employee's highest four consecutive years of earnings. The plan has a five-year vesting requirement. The normal retirement age is 65 with 5 years of service; however, the plan also provides unreduced retirement benefits with 30 years of service regardless of age or at age 60 with 25 years of service. Early retirement with reduced benefits is available at age 50 with 20 years of service or age 60 with 5 years of service.

This retirement plan is somewhat less generous and requires higher faculty contributions than many defined benefit plans offered to faculty at other public universities. In 1999, a report by the UNC Office of the President recommended that legislation be sought to increase the benefit formula multiplier to 2.0 percent, to decrease the employee contribution rate to less than 4.0 percent, and to reduce the final average salary period to three years; however, the legislature has taken no action on these recommendations.

The ORPs are defined contribution plans in which the employee contributes 6 percent of salary and the employer contributes 6.84 percent of salary. UNC ORP employer contribution rates are significantly lower than the average rates of peer institutions, but the combined employer and employee contribution rate is slightly higher than the average of peer institutions. Based on the 1999 study, the average employee contribution rate to optional retirement programs at other institutions was 3.71 percent, compared to the UNC ORP employee contribution rate of 6.0 percent. The average employer contribution rate at other universities was 8.48 percent, compared to the UNC ORP rate of 6.84 percent. Thus, the same salary employment offers at UNC tend to be worth less in total compensation than such offers of employment by UNC peer institutions because of the lower value of the pension plan.

The UNC ORP five-year delayed vesting period is not competitive with peer institutions. By design, portability is a key feature of an optional retirement program, and immediate vesting of employer contributions is the norm across the country. The five-year vesting period is often confusing to newly hired faculty members and is cumbersome for UNC to monitor and administer. UNC leaders are currently attempting to get authorization to institute a one-year vesting period for employer contributions to ORPs.

CONCLUSIONS

North Carolina has a long history of support for its colleges and universities. Higher education has been a major public priority in the state, and the university system continues to be a source of pride. Access to a university education for qualified students "free of expense . . . as far as practicable" has been an historical goal. Recent state budgetary shortfalls, however, have resulted in reduced funding for UNC, higher tuition for its students, and a real and relative decline in average faculty salaries. The university has had significant and important reductions in funding, but the adverse impact has not been as severe as in many states and has been accompanied by unprecedented growth in campus construction. The focused growth initiative has resulted in increased quality and capacity at seven institutions and allowed for more effective management of enrollment growth at all UNC campuses.

As the population of North Carolina continues to grow, the number and proportion of high school graduates seeking admission to UNC are increasing dramatically. The university and the state must find the funds to support an additional 30,000 students over the next decade. The university must also address declines in faculty compensation to retain UNC's quality and competitiveness in light of the challenge of recruiting and retaining 10,000 new faculty in the first decade of the twenty-first century. Managing enrollment increases and finding new sources of funds are the two major challenges facing UNC.

CHAPTER

State Support for Public Higher Education in Pennsylvania

Donald E. Heller

The Commonwealth of Pennsylvania, like many other states in the northeastern region of the United States, is characterized by a postsecondary education structure that relies on a strong and wide-ranging private sector.[1] The state has 256 Title IV-eligible institutions of higher education, including 67 public institutions, 103 private nonprofit institutions, and 86 proprietary colleges. Collectively, these institutions enroll more than 630,000 students, and in fiscal year 2001, they spent more than $14 billion annually on educating them, conducting research, and providing service to their communities, the state, and beyond (Chronicle of Higher Education 2004).

In fiscal year 2005, Pennsylvania appropriated just over $2 billion for higher education, including direct appropriations for both public and private institutions, as well as for student aid (Center for the Study of Education Policy 2004). Pennsylvania is one of a handful of states that provides direct appropriations to private colleges and universities, a sum that totaled more than $80 million that year.

Pennsylvania is a state that historically has pursued a "high tuition/high aid" policy, with relatively high tuition and one of the nation's largest need-based grant programs. Pennsylvania was one of the first states to create a need-based grant program in 1963. In 2002–2003, the state had the nation's third largest grant program for undergraduate students, trailing only those of California and New York (National Association of State Student Grant & Aid Programs 2004). Yet even with this aid, Pennsylvania was graded "F" in the category of affordability of higher education in the *Measuring Up 2004* report card issued by the National Center For Public Policy and Higher Education (2004).

In this chapter, I provide an overview of trends in enrollment and funding of Pennsylvania's public institutions of higher education over the last two decades. I then turn to an analysis of these trends given the historical and political context of the state and conclude with a look toward the future.

THE STRUCTURE OF PUBLIC HIGHER EDUCATION IN PENNSYLVANIA

The public system of higher education in Pennsylvania has a tripartite structure. Four universities are designated as "state-related" universities: The Pennsylvania State University, the University of Pittsburgh, Temple University, and Lincoln University. These four institutions, although legally public institutions, enjoy a great deal of autonomy from the state government. They have self-perpetuating boards of trustees that are subject to limited control or oversight of the state legislature or governor.[2]

Although these four institutions receive public funding, the state laws governing their operation and administration are minimal. For example, they are generally free from most state purchasing regulations that guide other state agencies, and they are not subject to state public records laws to the same extent as are other state agencies. This degree of autonomy is highly unusual among public institutions of higher education across the nation. The board of each institution has full tuition-setting authority.

Penn State, the University of Pittsburgh, and Temple University are all doctoral-granting institutions, with the first two being members of the prestigious Association of American Universities. Lincoln University is a master's granting and historically black institution. Penn State is a multi-campus system governed by a single board and president, and includes the flagship research university campus for the state (University Park), as well as separate campuses in Hershey for the medical school and Carlisle for the law school (Dickinson College of Law, a formerly private institution that merged with Penn State in 2000). Penn state has 21 additional campuses, offering a range of programs from associate's to master's degrees. The University of Pittsburgh also has four satellite campuses. Each of these state-related institutions receives a lump-sum budget from the state, with distribution of the appropriation made within the institution.[3]

The next tier of public institutions are grouped together into the State System of Higher Education (SSHE). These 14 universities, many of which started as normal schools, are primarily comprehensive institutions, with a limited number of doctoral programs. The state system is governed by a single chancellor and board of governors, with a president as the chief executive officer of each campus. The governor of the commonwealth appoints the 14 members of the SSHE board, which includes four state legislators (Colbeck 2001). The SSHE board sets tuition rates for each of the institutions.

The third tier is the state's 14 community colleges. Each is governed by a local district board, and receives roughly equal levels of financial support from both the state and local or county property taxes. Given its geographic size and population, Pennsylvania has relatively few community colleges. For example,

Massachusetts—a state with a large private sector of higher education, an area less than one-quarter of Pennsylvania's and a population just over half—has 15 community colleges whose enrollments total approximately 82 percent of Pennsylvania's (U.S. Census Bureau 2005, National Center for Education Statistics 2005).

Unlike most of the other 50 states, Pennsylvania has no statewide governing, coordinating, or planning board with responsibility for public institutions of higher education. The state department of education provides some data collection and reporting functions, and is responsible for licensing and approval of degree programs and private institutions in the state, but in general its functions and responsibilities are much more limited than in other states.[4]

ENROLLMENT IN PUBLIC HIGHER EDUCATION IN PENNSYLVANIA

In the 2000–2001 academic year, approximately 336,000 students were enrolled in public institutions in higher education in Pennsylvania.[5] Figure 10.1 shows

Figure 10.1
Headcount enrollment by public sector in Pennsylvania. Numbers in parentheses are annual growth rates

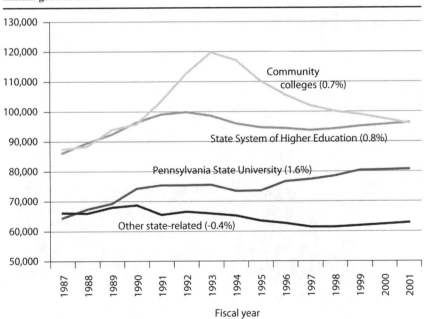

Fiscal year

Source: Quantum Research Corporation (2005).

the distribution of enrollments in each public sector. Enrollments at Penn State grew 1.6 percent per year, from approximately 64,000 in 1987 to almost 81,000 in 2001. Some of this growth was fueled by the merge of the former Williamsport Area Community College into Penn State as the Penn College of Technology in 1990. Throughout this period, the proportion of Penn State students attending the flagship campus at University Park declined slightly from 54 percent of the total in 1987 to 50 percent in 2001.

Enrollments at the other state-related institutions, which totaled approximately the same as Penn State in 1987, declined during this period. Enrollments at the SSHE institutions grew in the late 1980s, then declined in the early 1990s followed by growth in the latter half of that decade. The community colleges in Pennsylvania saw rapid growth through the early 1990s, increasing their enrollments by more than one-third, before declining in the rest of that decade.[6] The gains in the late 1980s and early 1990s were not made by taking enrollments from the other sectors, as enrollment in the other sectors grew or were flat during

Figure 10.2
Enrollment of first-time freshmen in public institutions as a proportion of high school graduates in Pennsylvania

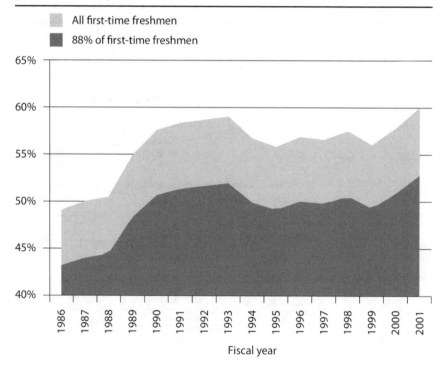

Source: Author's calculations from National Center for Education Statistics (2005, 2005); Quantum Research Corporation (2005).

this period. Rather, the enrollment gains in the community colleges were largely accomplished through the enrollment of new students.

Figure 10.2 shows the enrollment of first-time freshmen students in Pennsylvania's public institutions, as a proportion of public high school graduates in the state. This measure is only a rough estimate of the market share garnered by the public institutions, as it does not take into account migration of high school graduates out of state or to private institutions, or the migration of out-of-state students into the public institutions. However, data from the National Center for Education Statistics (2005) Integrated Postsecondary Education Data Survey (IPEDS) surveys indicate that of the first-time freshmen enrolling in Pennsylvania public institutions in the fall of 2000 who had graduated from high school in the previous year, 88 percent were Pennsylvania residents. This proportion was the same level as in the fall of 1986. So migration patterns were changed little during this time period. The dashed line in Figure 10.6 represents the approximately 88 percent of the freshmen students who were Pennsylvania residents.

Figure 10.2 demonstrates that the public institutions' "market share" of Pennsylvania high school graduates increased in the late 1980s and early 1990s. This was followed by a small decline, then stability in the late 1990s, and an increase in the early part of the twenty-first century.

FINANCING PUBLIC HIGHER EDUCATION IN PENNSYLVANIA

State Funding for Public Institutions

The Grapevine project at Illinois State University has for more than 40 years provided excellent comparative data on state appropriations for higher education (Center for the Study of Education Policy, various years). Analysis in this section is drawn from those annual reports, starting with fiscal year 1981.[7]

Figure 10.3 shows the state appropriations to Penn State, the other state-related institutions, the State System of Higher Education, and community colleges from the 1980–1981 fiscal year to 2004–2005.[8] The patterns of appropriations for the four-year sectors are similar: high growth during the 1980s, followed by a downturn in the recession of the early 1990s, when constrained state revenues led to level funding or actual cuts in appropriations. Appropriations recovered after that recession, but then were cut again in the most recent recession.

During this period, Penn State saw the highest growth rate in funding among the four-year sectors, with a 5.1 percent annual increase over this period, compared to 4.1 percent for the other three state-related institutions and 3.3 percent at the SSHE. As a basis of comparison, the consumer price index over this same period (September monthly) increased 3.5 percent annually (author's calculations from Bureau of Labor Statistics 2005).

The effect of the most recent recession is readily apparent in Figure 10.3. At the state-related institutions, appropriations were cut for three consecutive years, beginning in fiscal year 2002, with funding not yet having returned to the peak levels enjoyed in 2001. The SSHE was level-funded in 2002 and then also saw its appropriation cut in the next two years.

Funding for the community colleges grew at the fastest rate during this 25-year period, increasing at an annual rate of 7.0 percent. The community colleges were also more buffered from the effect of the two recessions, as they saw only small cuts in the earlier recession and have actually seen a large increase in funding in the most recent recession.

The periods before and after 1990 were two different eras in funding for higher education in Pennsylvania. Table 10.1 shows the annual rates of growth in each sector during these two periods, as well as for the entire 25-year period. In every sector, the rate of increase in appropriations slowed in the most recent 15 years compared to the 1980s. In each of the four-year sectors, the growth rate was cut by at least two-thirds.

The impact of this change can be seen in Figure 10.4, which shows the actual appropriations along with what funding for higher education would have been if

Figure 10.3
Appropriations for public higher education institutions in Pennsylvania ($thousands). Numbers in parentheses are annual growth rates

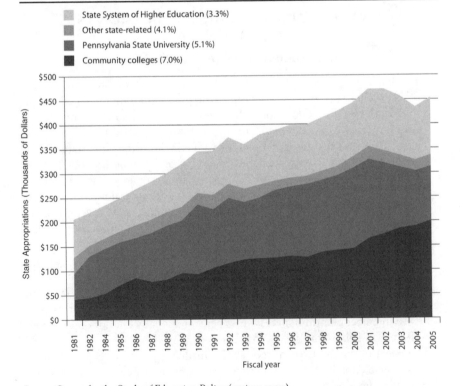

Source: Center for the Study of Education Policy (various years).

Table 10.1
Annual Rate of Change in Appropriations by Sector

	1981–1990 (%)	1990–2005 (%)	1981–2005 (%)
Penn State	10.7	1.9	5.1
Other state-related	8.2	1.7	4.1
State System of Higher Education	5.8	1.8	3.3
Comm. colleges	9.7	5.3	7.0

Source: Figure 10.1.

Figure 10.4
Projected funding for public higher education institutions in Pennsylvania, based on
1981 to 1990 growth rates ($ thousands)

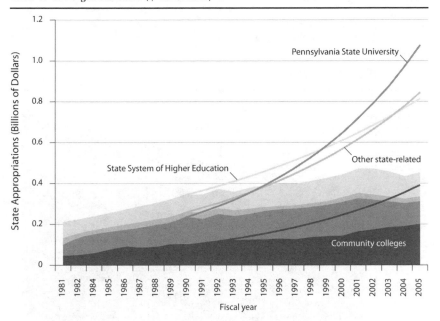

Source: Author's calculations from Figure 10.3.

the rates of growth seen in the period from 1981 to 1990 were continued for the subsequent 15 years. For each sector, the period from 1981 to 1990 is the same for both the shaded area and the line. Starting in 1991, the lines show what the funding levels would have been if the annual rates of growth from 1981 to 1990 were maintained through 2005.

As can be seen in Figure 10.4, the slowdown in rates of growth after 1990 had a major impact on the level of appropriations in each sector. Funding for Penn State today would be more than three times the current appropriation level if it had continued to grow at the rate enjoyed during the 1980s (10.7 percent annually). In the other three sectors, appropriations would be approximately twice their current levels.

Data on enrollments and appropriations can be combined to examine funding per student in each of the sectors. Figure 10.5 shows these amounts. The multi-campus structure of Penn State leads to an unusual per-student funding situation compared with that of most other states. In other states, the flagship research university or university system generally receives a higher per-student level of

Figure 10.5
Appropriations per student. Numbers in parentheses are annual growth rates

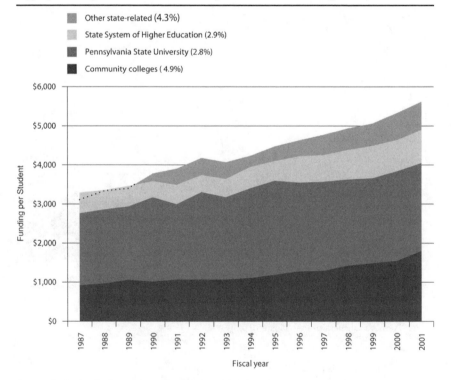

Source: Author's calculations from Figures 10.1 and 10.3.

appropriations, in recognition of the more complex missions (mix of teaching, research, and service) of those institutions. Because Penn State has campuses with such differentiated missions (from those offering only associate's degree programs to medical and law campuses), its level of per-student funding is lower than the other four-year institutions in the state.[9]

Penn State also saw the slowest growth in per-student funding among the four sectors. This has caused the gap between it and the other four-year sectors to widen over the period. For example, in 1987 the per-student funding at the other state-related institutions was approximately $350 higher than at Penn State. By 2001, this gap had increased to $1,600. Even though Penn State's appropriation grew more than those of the other state-related institutions over this period (84 compared to 72 percent, respectively), Penn State's enrollments also grew faster, thus helping to contribute to the increase in the size of the funding gap between the two sectors.

The growth in per-student funding shown in Figure 10.5 has undoubtedly slowed or declined since 2001. As shown in Figure 10.3, the fiscal situation in Pennsylvania has led to declines in funding in the four-year sectors, while enrollments have generally been stable. This is not true in the community colleges, however, where state appropriations continued to increase in the last few years.

Tuition Charges and Financial Aid

As noted earlier, Pennsylvania has historically been a "high tuition/high aid" state. Correspondingly, tuition charges at the public institutions in the state are high compared to national averages. Figure 10.6 shows the average tuition charges in three of the public sectors in the state.[10]

Tuition grew fastest at Penn State-University Park, averaging 8.2 percent annually from 1981 to 2005 (as noted earlier, the consumer price index increased an average of 3.5 percent annually during this period). In 2005, Penn State surpassed the University of Vermont for the first time to become the most expensive public flagship university in the nation. Tuition in the other two sectors also grew at rates far in excess of inflation. The faster rate of growth in the Penn State tuition helped to increase the gap between it and tuition in the other sectors. The ratio of Penn State tuition to tuition in the SSHE institutions increased from 1.4 in 1981 to 1.8 in 2005, and the ratio of Penn State to community college tuition increased from 2.3 to 4.1 over the same period. The relationship between tuition prices in different types of public institutions has been found to have an impact on the distribution of enrollments across sectors (Kane 1995; Heller 1999).

Even though tuition in Pennsylvania increased far in excess of inflation, the increases were not that different from those in the rest of the nation. The average annual increase nationally in both four-year sectors was 7.9 percent from 1981 to 2005, and 7.0 percent in community colleges (Washington Higher Education Coordinating Board 2005).

Figure 10.6
Average tuition charges for in-state students in Pennsylvania public institutions.
Numbers in parentheses are annual growth rates

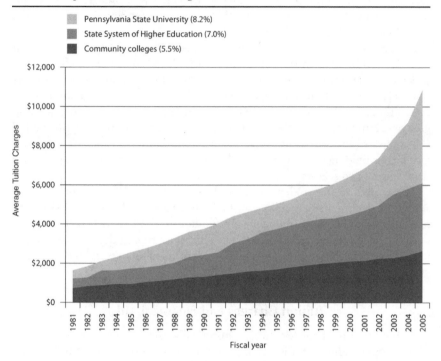

Source: Washington Higher Education Coordinating Board (2005).

The relationship between tuition in Pennsylvania and the rest of the nation can be seen in Figure 10.7. In 1981, tuition in all three sectors was more than 160 percent of the national median. The ratio of Penn State to the national average, which started at 194 percent, rose to more than twice the average in 1988, but then declined through most of the 1990s. The relatively large increase in tuition in recent years (tuition increased more than 50 percent from 2001 to 2005) helped push Penn State tuition to more than twice the national average again in 2005.

In both the state's comprehensive universities in the SSHE and in the community colleges, tuition rates steadily declined in relation to the national average during the last 25 years. In the 2004–2005 year, tuition at SSHE was 141 percent of the national average, and at the community colleges it was 118 percent.

As described in the beginning of this section, Pennsylvania's tuition is not just higher than the national average, but it also maintains a policy of providing need-based grants that is more generous than in most other states. In an earlier study, I examined the relationship between states' tuition-pricing policies and their state

Figure 10.7
In-state tuition as a percentage of the national median

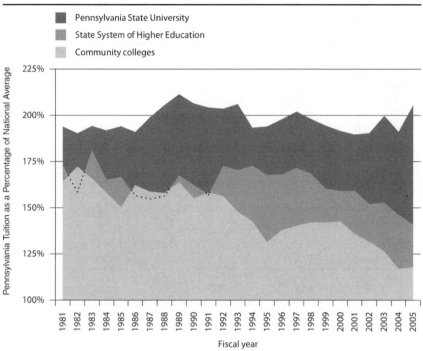

Fiscal year

Source: Author's calculations from Washington Higher Education Coordinating Board (2005).

financial aid policies (Heller 2000). In that study, Pennsylvania stood out as among four states (including Vermont, New Jersey, and New York) that were the most aggressive in pursuing a high tuition/high aid policy.

Pennsylvania does have one of the nation's oldest and largest need-based grant programs, but funding for it has not kept pace with enrollment and tuition increases. Table 10.2 shows changes in enrollment, tuition prices, and funding for the state's need-based grant program in fiscal years 1981 and 2003. Although the increase in total spending on need-based grants increased at a rate roughly on par with the tuition increases, once the increase in enrollment is factored in, the grant spending on a per-student basis did not keep pace with the tuition increases in any of the three sectors.[11]

The financial need of students and their families also grew during this period. The median income of four-person families in Pennsylvania increased from $24,814 in 1980 to $64,310 in 2002, or 4.4 percent annually (U.S. Census Bureau 2005). As the growth of family incomes does not keep pace with changes in college costs, this helps lead to an increase in financial need.

Table 10.2
Enrollment, Tuition, and Grant Funding, Fiscal Years 1981 and 2003

	1981	2003	Annual change
Tuition			
Pennsylvania State University	$1,641	$7,396	7.1%
State System of Higher Education	1,216	4,969	6.6
Comm. colleges	724	2,252	5.3
State need-based grants			
Spending on undergraduate grants	$79,879,000	$348,788,000	6.9
Undergraduate enrollment (public and private institutions)	354,245	565,220	2.1
Grant spending per student*	$225	$617	4.7

* For all students, not just those receiving grants.

Source: Figure 10.6, National Association of State Student Grant & Aid Programs (2004), Quantum Research Corporation (2005), and National Center for Education Statistics (2005)

In recent years, Penn State has increased its spending on institutional aid to help offset the increases in tuition prices that have been imposed in response to the appropriation declines. Between the 2000–2001 and 2003–2004 academic years, spending on institutionally funded grants at Penn State increased 39 percent. In comparison, federal and state aid (loans and grants combined) received by Penn State students increased 25 percent and 7 percent, respectively, during the same period (Office of Planning and Institutional Assessment 2005). The difficulty that many Penn State students faced in financing their educations without additional help, however, is reflected in the fact that private loan volume at Penn State—those loans outside of the federal programs—increased more than 600 percent during the same period (Griswold 2005).

ANALYSIS OF FUNDING TRENDS

The higher education financing trends seen in Pennsylvania are not anomalous to those of the rest of the nation. In another publication (Heller in press), I have documented the shifting of the burden for paying the costs of public higher education from state taxpayers to students and their families. In 1980, approximately 48 percent of the current fund revenues received by public postsecondary

Figure 10.8
Annual change in total state and higher education expenditures in the United States

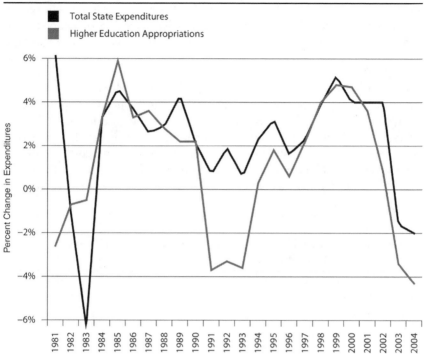

Source: Center for the Study of Education Policy (various years) and National Association of State Budget Officers (various years).

institutions nationally came from state and local government appropriations; by 2000, this had dropped to 35 percent. Funding for higher education declined from 12 percent of total state budget expenditures in 1987 to 9 percent in 2004 (Heller 2004).

This relative disinvestment on the part of states can be seen when one examines the relationship between changes in higher education appropriations and total state expenditures. Figure 10.8 shows the annual change in appropriations and total expenditures since 1981. The interesting pattern is that since 1987, in every year with the exception of three, states have increased their overall spending more than they have their higher education spending, or cut overall spending less than they cut higher education spending.[12]

As described in Table 10.1, Pennsylvania public higher education enjoyed robust growth in appropriations in the 1980s, followed by a large slowdown in the subsequent 15 years. This trend mirrored the general pattern nationally, where appropriations grew 7.2 percent annually from 1981 to 1990, and only 3.2 percent annually from 1990 to 2005 (Center for the Study of Education Policy various years). But the slowdown in growth in Pennsylvania was even greater than among all states. Figure 10.9 shows the appropriations for all four public sectors in Pennsylvania and all appropriations nationally, indexed to a common base in 1981. The shaded areas show the actual appropriations, and the lines show the projected appropriations if the 1981 to 1990 growth rates had been maintained through 2005.

Pennsylvania increased appropriations at a rate slightly higher than the nation in the 1980s and, beginning in 1990, began to increase appropriations at rates much higher than the nation. This pattern continued until the late 1990s, at which time rates of growth in Pennsylvania began to slip below that of the rest of the country. The lines show that growth in appropriations in Pennsylvania would have outpaced the rest of the nation if the growth rates of the 1980s had been maintained over the subsequent 15 years. Appropriations

Figure 10.9
Projected funding for public higher education in Pennsylvania and in the
United States, based on 1981 to 1990 growth rates

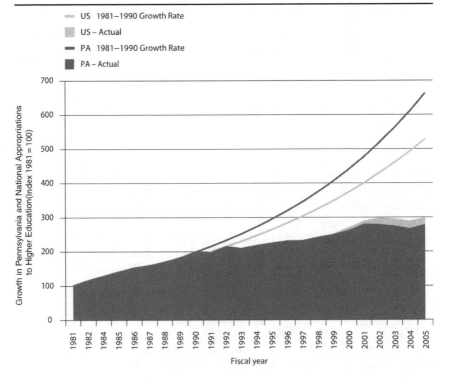

Source: Author's calculations from Figure 10.4 and Center for the Study of Education Policy (various years).

in the United States would have been approximately five times greater in 2005 than 1981 if these earlier rates would have been maintained, but in Pennsylvania appropriations would have been almost seven times greater under a similar growth scenario.

As the states have stepped back from their funding of higher education, students and their families have shouldered more of the burden. Revenues from tuition and fees at public institutions nationally increased from 13 percent of total revenues to 18 percent between 1980 and 2000 (Heller in press).

This shifting of the burden from public sources to students and parents has been seen in Pennsylvania public higher education as well. Table 10.3 shows the state appropriations and tuition and fee revenues received by each of the four public sectors in fiscal years 1985 and 2000. In 1985, Penn State received $0.94 in state appropriations for every dollar received from students and their families. By 2001, it was receiving only $0.51 from the state for every dollar paid by students and families. In 1985, the SSHE institutions received $1.94 from the state for every dollar paid by students; by 2001, the state was receiving more in the form of tuition and fee revenues than it was receiving from the state. Only in the community colleges were state (and local) appropriations greater than tuition revenue in 2001.

The shifting of the burden of paying for college from public resources to students and their families, and the impact this has on college access—particularly for students from lower-income families—has been well documented in recent years.[13] College prices that rise at rates faster than increases in the ability of families to pay them have a deleterious effect on the participation of students from

Table 10.3
Revenues from Appropriations and Tuition and Fees, Fiscal Year 1985 and 2001
($ millions)

	Penn State	State System of Higher Education	Community Colleges
1985			
A. State and local appropriations	$163	$248	$96
B. Tuition and fee revenues	173	128	56
Ratio of A to B	0.94	1.94	1.71
2001			
A. State and local appropriations	$316	$454	$258
B. Tuition and fee revenues	620	477	191
Ratio of A to B	0.51	0.95	1.35

Note: Data from all of the other state-related universities in 2001 were not available.
Source: Author's calculations from National Center for Education Statistics (2005).

poorer families. This is true whether you measure tuition as the sticker price, or as the net price after subtracting financial aid.[14]

In examining the higher education policy environment in Pennsylvania, one can find examples of government attempts at addressing issues of funding, costs, and affordability. The nature of the public-private mix of higher education institutions in the state has no doubt been an important catalyst to the development and continued expansion of the state-operated student aid program. A 1985 gubernatorial-appointed panel noted that:

> The philosophy which led to the Commonwealth's decision to provide extensive student assistance is that Pennsylvania should continue to have a tuition-based system of financing higher education. The Commission concurs in this philosophy and has sought ways to improve access and excellence while not deviating from this policy. (Subcommittee on Higher Education 1998)

A guiding principle articulated by this panel was that "Pennsylvania's unique mixture of public and private higher education institutions has served its citizens well and should be preserved" (p. 7). This, along with the fact that the state has long provided direct appropriations to a number of purely private institutions, is an acknowledgment of the importance of both public and private institutions of higher education in meeting the human capital and other economic needs of the state.[15]

This same panel raised concerns about the affordability of higher education in the state, a concern echoed in later legislative panels (Subcommittee on Higher Education 1998, Task Force on Higher Education Funding of the Pennsylvania House of Representatives 1994). The 1998 panel recommended that:

> the General Assembly should implement a long-term strategy for awarding higher levels of appropriations to Pennsylvania's community colleges, the State System of Higher Education, Lincoln University, The Pennsylvania State University, The University of Pittsburgh, and Temple University based upon achieving performance measures, developed in conjunction with the Master Plan, to increase cost efficiencies and to reduce the price of education (tuition and fees) to the students at these institutions. (p. 5)

This same group echoed the philosophy of the 1985 panel when it noted that:

> policy in Pennsylvania has evolved to promote both financial access and choice in postsecondary education. . . . in states where access to education has been the priority (largely Southern and Western states with relatively few independent institutions), state subsidies have kept public tuition low. In essence, policies in Pennsylvania have spread subsidies across institutions and students to provide a number of choices for students in selecting the postsecondary institutions that best meets their expectations. (p. 8)

The impact of these policy recommendations on college participation is hard to gauge. Figure 10.7 demonstrated that since 1985, tuition prices at the SSHE institutions and community colleges in Pennsylvania have declined relative to national averages, whereas prices at Penn State moved within a fairly narrow band around a price that is approximately twice that of other public flagship institutions nationally. So one could argue that the affordability of Pennsylvania's public institutions, at least as measured by the sticker price of tuition, has not worsened relative to other states.

There are a number of counter arguments, however. First, it should be acknowledged that Pennsylvania started as a very high tuition state (more than 50 percent greater than the national average in all sectors in 1981), and although some gains relative to the rest of the nation have been made at the community colleges and SSHE institutions, tuition is still high. One could argue that rather than a concerted effort on the part of the state, the gains are more likely the result of other states increasing their prices at faster rates in recent years. Tuition as a proportion of median incomes of four-person families rose in all sectors between 1981 and 2002, from 6.2 percent to 11.5 percent at Penn State, 4.6 percent to 7.7 percent at the SSHE, and from 2.7 to 3.5 percent in the community colleges (author's calculations from Washington Higher Education Coordinating Board 2005, U.S. Census Bureau 2005). These changes understate the magnitude of the problem, as tuition prices since 2002 have increased 47 percent at Penn State, 23 percent at the SSHE institutions, and 17 percent at the community colleges. Although the state-level income data from the Census Bureau is available only for years as recent as 2002, it is unlikely that median incomes in the state have risen at rates anywhere near these.

Second, although Pennsylvania does have one of the nation's largest need-based grant programs, and it has resisted the development of broad-based merit aid programs that has been the trend in about a quarter of the states (Heller and Marin 2002, 2004), as shown earlier funding for the grants has not kept pace with either the growth in college costs or the financial need of the state's students. This has been especially true in the most recent years, when the maximum grant has been frozen at $3,300 since the 2001–2002 academic year, and tuition prices have risen at the rates described in the previous paragraph.[16]

It also should be acknowledged that the state's dependence on private institutions, almost all of whom have prices greater than the options in the public sector, places a larger demand on the grant program. The grant amount that students receive is sensitive to the cost of attendance at the institution they attend, but the maximum award of $3,300 is well below the price in every sector in the state.[17] A task force created by the grant agency in 2004 looked at the structure of the awards as their value eroded in recent years. One proposal that the panel considered was whether to put in place different maximum award amounts for different sectors (Financial aid agency proposes boosting college grant awards 2005). This would allow students in private institutions to receive larger maximum awards than those of students in public institutions.

Third, other measures of college affordability and participation demonstrate that Pennsylvania has lost ground in these measures, particularly when one examines them from an equity perspective. The National Center For Public Policy and Higher Education (2004), in its *Measuring Up 2004* report card on higher education in the states, gave Pennsylvania a grade of "B" in college participation that year and noted that the state's performance had been largely stable over the previous decade. However, the report noted that:

> Over the past decade, among the young adult population (ages 18 to 24), the gap in college participation between whites and minority ethnic groups has widened substantially. Young adults who are white are twice as likely to attend college as young adults who are from minority ethnic groups. (p. 7)

This gap between racial groups is much larger than the national figures, where the college participation rates of black and Hispanic youth, although still lagging behind those of their white counterparts, are not nearly as low (National Center for Education Statistics 2003). The *Measuring Up* report also notes that the gap in college participation between students from high-income and low-income families in the state has also widened over the last decade.

Measuring Up gave Pennsylvania a grade of "F" in its measure of the affordability of higher education, which takes into account the price of both public and private institutions, as well as the availability of state need-based aid. This was a decrease from a grade of "D+" in 2002, and "C" in 2000. The report notes as a major reason for this decline in affordability the rise in the proportion of family income needed to pay for college in each sector (described earlier in this chapter), commenting that:

> The state is a top performer in the very high investment it makes in need-based financial aid. Nonetheless, the share of income, including financial aid, needed to pay for college is very large compared with other states. (National Center For Public Policy and Higher Education 2004)

The Future of Higher Education Funding in Pennsylvania

Like many other states in the Northeast, the college-age population of Pennsylvania is not growing nearly as rapidly as many other parts of the country. The number of high school graduates is projected to peak at 143,250 in 2008, 3 percent more than in 2005 but less than the number who graduated in 1988 (Western Interstate Commission for Higher Education 2003). From that peak, the number of high school graduates is projected to decline steadily to approximately 125,000 in 2018.

So the challenge for state policymakers is not how to meet the needs of an expanding population, but rather, how to ensure that the existing population will be able to afford a postsecondary education. The recent past in the state has demonstrated that when state funds grow slowly, or are actually cut, the public institutions generally have responded by increasing tuition prices to make up all or part of the difference. In many cases, this has been an explicit policy decision on the part of the institutions, whose boards have the authority to set their own tuition levels. In announcing its tuition levels for the 2002–2003 academic year, Penn State stated in a press release:

> A higher than usual tuition increase of 13.5 percent for the 2002–2003 academic year was approved by Penn State's Board of Trustees today (July 12) to make up for two years of cuts in state appropriation and significant cost increases. . . . "Sadly, tuition is at a level higher than any of us would like," said Penn State President Graham B. Spanier. "However, we remain strongly committed to providing a high quality education for our students. Despite aggressive internal budget reductions and reallocations that have saved more than $87 million over the past decade, the costs of providing a quality education have far outpaced our own aggressive reduction and reallocation program and the steady erosion of state support. That leaves tuition as the only means to bridge the financial gap." (The Pennsylvania State University Department of Public Information 2005b)

As Penn State's president noted, the university had undertaken a large-scale effort to cut costs. But this was not enough to offset the decline in state support. Even in the face of these financial pressures, the university still maintained a commitment to increase spending in certain areas. For example, raising faculty salaries at Penn State, which had long lagged behind those of other institutions in the Big Ten, remained a priority for the university even in the face of the financial pressures it faced (The Pennsylvania State University Department of Public Information 2005a).

There is little likelihood that future governors and legislatures of the state will make major changes to higher education funding patterns. A return to better fiscal times may provide some room for healthy increases in funding (as were seen after the last recession of the early 1990s), but the glory days of the 1980s, when appropriations grew at much higher rates, will likely never be seen again. From the perspective of a governor or legislator, it is hard to see the major impact of rapidly escalating prices. At a macro level, enrollments continue to be healthy, and institutions appear to be thriving. But below the surface, often unseen by state policymakers, there are some troubling trends. For example, at Penn State, the proportion of undergraduates who come from low-income families declined from 18 to 13 percent between 1998 and 2004. Borrowing by students in private loan programs, many of which offer terms that are not nearly as generous as the federal loan programs, increased sevenfold at Penn State, from $6.7 million to $47.6 million, in the three years between 2001 and 2004 (Griswold 2005). The gaps in participation between racial majority and minority students, and between rich and poor, that were documented by the *Measuring Up* report often do not receive the scrutiny from policymakers that results in meaningful legislative action.

At regular intervals, the funds appropriated to the private institutions in the state (totaling $82 million in 2005) have come under scrutiny. Many in the public sector would like to see that money redirected to their institutions, but doing so would have little impact. Redistributing that sum to the public institutions would increase their 2005 appropriations by 6 percent. One could argue that this would help to control the future growth of tuition prices, but it would do little to make up for the increases that have already occurred.

Other state funding policies have rankled the public institutions. In 2001, Pennsylvania began a program that rewarded postsecondary institutions that graduated at least 40 percent of their Pennsylvania resident bachelor's degree recipients within four years. Colleges were provided an unrestricted grant of almost $700 for each recipient, with the amount totaling $6 million that year. The program received much criticism when the first round of grants were awarded entirely to private institutions, as none of the public colleges in the state qualified. A spokesman for the SSHE remarked that, "We don't believe we're failing our students because it may take them an extra semester or two to graduate. We're giving our students an opportunity" (Selingo 2001).

The private college lobby in the state, led by the Association of Independent Colleges and Universities of Pennsylvania, has historically maintained much influence with policymakers. It is unlikely that there will be a major threat to the support these institutions receive from the state. Largely through its influence, the proposed changes to the state's need-based grant program, which would create larger awards for students attending private institutions, may become a reality. This may come about even though the private institutions in the state enroll fewer lower-income students than do the public sectors. In the 1998–1999 academic year, 22 percent of undergraduates in private institutions were Pell grant recipients, compared to 29 percent at public four-year institutions and 27 percent in community colleges.[18] The state's long history of relying on the private sector for meeting the postsecondary needs of its citizens appears likely to continue into the future.

The notion of higher education as the "balance wheel," as described by Hovey (1999), appears to be well entrenched in Pennsylvania as in much of the rest of the nation. As one of the few agencies of state government that can generate significant revenues through user fees, governors and legislators have been more than willing to cut funding to higher education, or to increase it at rates well below that of other parts of state government. There is little to indicate that this will change in the future in Pennsylvania.

NOTES

1. Although legally a commonwealth, Pennsylvania will be referred to throughout this chapter as a state for clarity of presentation.

2. The governor and secretary of education are ex-officio members of these boards. Some of the trustees in these institutions are elected by specific constituencies, such as alumni.

3. The medical schools of Penn State, the University of Pittsburgh, and Temple University receive separate line-item appropriations from the state. These amounts, which totaled $20.2 million in fiscal year 2005, are not included in the appropriations discussed in the next section.

4. Pennsylvania's higher education structure can best be compared to that of Michigan, which also has no statewide board with responsibility for higher education. See Pennsylvania Department of Education (2005) for more on the department's role with respect to postsecondary education.

5. The enrollment figures presented in this section are from the National Center for Education Statistics Integrated Postsecondary Education Data System (IPEDS) surveys and represent headcount enrollments in Title IV-eligible institutions in the fall of each fiscal year.

6. The reason for the enrollment spike in the community colleges in the early 1990s is unknown. However, the data were compared to another source (National Center for Education Statistics 2005) for consistency and were found to be comparable.

7. Data for 1983 were not available.

8. Since 1986, the Thaddeus Stevens College of Technology, a public two-year college of technology, has received a separate line-item appropriation from the state. This appropriation totaled just over $10 million in 2005. It has been included here with the community colleges.

9. The appropriation to Penn State is a lump sum for the entire university, so it is impossible to allocate it among the campuses. Approximately half of Penn State's enrollment is at the flagship campus in University Park.

10. The PSU rate is the tuition charge at the main campus at University Park. The tuition data from the Washington Higher Education Coordinating Board are for three sectors in each state: public flagship, comprehensive institutions, and community colleges. The charges shown are tuition and all mandatory fees for in-state (in-district, for community colleges) students.

11. Extending the analysis out to more current years would show an even more dramatic increase in prices relative to grants. Between 2003 and 2005, tuition prices at Penn State, the state system institutions, and the community colleges increased 47 percent, 23 percent, and 17 percent, respectively, whereas spending on need-based grants was largely stagnant.

12. In the three exception years—1990, 1998, and 2000—state spending for higher education grew at a rate less than 1 percent more than that of overall state expenditures.

13. See, for example, McPherson and Schapiro (1991), Mumper (1996), Kane (1999), Advisory Committee on Student Financial Assistance (2001), Heller (2002), Advisory Committee on Student Financial Assistance (2002), and Kahlenberg (2004).

14. See Jackson and Weathersby (1975), Leslie and Brinkman (1988), and Heller (1997) for reviews of the literature that address this question.

15. As described earlier, in fiscal year 2005, the appropriations to private institutions totaled approximately $82 million, or 4 percent of the state's total appropriation for higher education (Center for the Study of Education Policy 2004). Most of these line-item appropriations are for specific programs not offered by public institutions in the state, or offered in only limited areas or with limited enrollment.

16. Students have received little help during this period from other sources of aid. The maximum Pell grant has risen only 8 percent since 2002, and limits in the federal loan programs and tax credits have not increased. Borrowing in private loan programs has more than doubled during this period, however, from $4.7 billion in 2002 to $10.6 billion in 2004 (College Board 2004).

17. The Pennsylvania Higher Education Assistance Agency, which administers the grant program, recently announced that the maximum grant would be increased to $3,500

in 2005–2006, the first increase in four years (Financial aid grant awards for 2005–2006 school year increased in 2005).

18. These percentages were calculated by the author using data on Pell grant recipients by institution provided private by the U.S. Department of Education and undergraduate enrollment data (Quantum Research Corporation 2005).

CHAPTER 11

The Changing Accessibility, Affordability, and Quality of Higher Education in Texas

Lisa M. Dickson

Recent changes in admissions criteria, tuition levels, and costs have affected the accessibility, affordability, and quality of higher education in Texas. During the 1990s, public colleges and public universities in Texas transitioned from a college admissions process that allowed for affirmative action to a percent plan. The changes in college admissions affected the accessibility of higher education in Texas. The affordability of higher education in Texas has been threatened by significant increases in the average tuition and fees listed for public universities in Texas. Recent changes in college admissions and costs may have also affected the quality of higher education in Texas.

The end of affirmative action and the institution of a percent plan affected the cultural accessibility of higher education and the geographic accessibility of higher education. Higher education is defined, in this study, as being culturally accessible if students are encouraged to pursue higher education. Higher education is defined, in this study, as being geographically accessible if students can obtain a high quality education locally. The end of affirmative action in Texas decreased the cultural accessibility and geographic accessibility of higher education for some Hispanic students and black students[1] However, the percent plan increased the cultural accessibility of higher education for students in the top 10 percent of their high school class. Students who may not have considered college previously are now being encouraged to apply and to attend college. Therefore the end of affirmative action and the institution of a percent plan reduced the accessibility of the state flagship institutions for some students and increased the accessibility for others.

The financial accessibility of higher education in Texas is defined by how affordable higher education is in Texas. During the 1990s, the average tuition and fees listed for public universities in Texas doubled in real terms. Two sets of analyses are conducted to assess whether the increases in tuition represent decreases in the affordability of higher education. First, the changes in listed tuition are compared to the changes in median family income in Texas. If tuition and fees increased faster than median family income, then higher education in Texas may have become less affordable. Second, the amounts and types of financial aid students receive today are compared to the amounts and types of financial aid students received in the past. If students are borrowing more money in loans, then higher education in Texas may have become less affordable.

The quality of higher education in Texas may have been affected by both changes in college admissions and changes in the financing of public universities in Texas. The changes in college admissions may have affected the quality of higher education in Texas because it affected who enrolled at the state flagships. Students are a quality input into higher education because of peer effects. The financial structure of public universities in Texas may have affected the quality of higher education because it may have affected the demand for tenured and tenure-track faculty. Tenured faculty and tenure-track faculty constitute a quality input into higher education because faculty produce research and teach students. In this study, I analyze the trends in the employment of tenured and tenure-track faculty at public universities in Texas to assess whether the quality of higher education has changed. In addition, this study presents the trends in six-year graduation rates and freshman retention rates at several public universities in Texas.

CHANGES IN ADMISSIONS CRITERIA

The 5th Circuit Court decision in Hopwood v. University of Texas in 1996 ended the use of race in college admissions decisions and financial aid decisions in Texas.[2] In the year after the Hopwood decision, minority applications, minority acceptance rates, and minority enrollment fell at the state flagship institutions.[3] In 1997, the Texas state legislature passed a law that guarantees students who graduate in the top 10 percent of their high school class acceptance to any public college or public university in Texas.[4] Because high schools are highly segregated in Texas, the top 10 percent plan effectively encourages racial and ethnic diversity without explicitly using race as an admissions criterion.

The admission benefits for Hispanics or blacks under affirmative action have been shown to be larger than the admission benefits for Hispanics or blacks under a percent plan (Long 2004). The smaller admission benefits from the percent plan can be understood by considering the effects of the percent plan for students outside the top 10 percent of their high school class. Hispanic students or black students outside the top 10 percent of their high school class are not helped by the percent plan, but they may be helped by an affirmative action policy.

The end of affirmative action in Texas also eliminated the use of race as a factor in financial aid decisions. The University of Texas at Austin (UT-Austin) and Texas A&M at College Station (Texas A&M) instituted new financial aid programs in response to this limitation. UT-Austin started the Longhorn Opportunity Scholars program in 1998. This program offers scholarships of $4,000 to high school graduates who graduate from qualifying high schools.[5] Texas A&M started the Century Scholar program in 1999 and modeled it after the Longhorn Opportunity Scholar program. High schools that qualify for either program tend to enroll a larger proportion of Hispanic students and black students than high schools that do not qualify for the scholarship programs.[6] The Longhorn Opportunity Scholar Program and the Century Scholar Program increased the affordability and cultural accessibility of the state flagships for a select group of students.

The percent plan and the new financial aid programs had limited success in boosting Hispanic enrollment and black enrollment at the state flagships. Figure 11.1 shows the shares of first-time undergraduates by race enrolled at the two state flagships in 1995 and 2002. In 1995, race could be used in college admissions. In 2002, race could not be used in college admissions and students in the top 10 percent of their high school class had to be accepted to every public college and

Figure 11.1
The percentage of entering freshmen who graduated in the top 10 percent of their high school class

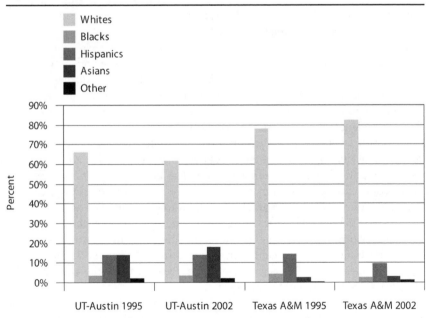

Source: The Texas Higher Education Coordinating Board is keeping a record of the number of students in the top 10 percent of their high school class in Texas who apply to and attend universities in Texas. This information is available for all universities in the First-Time Undergraduate Applicant, Acceptance and Enrollment Information Reports produced by the Texas Higher Education Coordinating Board.

public university in Texas. By 2002, the share of Hispanic students and black students in the freshman class at UT-Austin slightly surpassed the pre-*Hopwood* levels, and the share of Hispanic students and black students in the entering freshman class at Texas A&M were lower than the pre-*Hopwood* levels.

Although Figure 11.1 shows little change over time, this stagnation occurs at a time of a fast growing minority population. The percent of high school graduates who were Hispanic was 29.2 percent in 1995 and increased to 33.1 percent in 2002.[7] The percent of high school graduates who were black was 12 percent in 1995 and increased to 13.3 percent in 2002.[8] Against this backdrop, the percent plan and the financial aid initiatives at the state flagships appear to be a failure (Tienda, Leicht, Sullivan, Maltese and Lloyd 2003).

The increasing discrepancy between Hispanic enrollments and black enrollments at the state flagships and the racial composition of the state may be due to decreases in the share of minorities applying to college, decreases in the admission probabilities for minorities, or decreases in the enrollment probabilities for minorities. After the *Hopwood* decision, the percent of in-state students who applied to the state flagships who were minorities declined.[9] Minority students also experienced a decrease in admission probabilities at the state flagships but also showed offsetting increases in enrollment probabilities.[10] These results taken together suggest that the increasing discrepancy between minority enrollment and the minority composition of high school graduates is due to decreases in the share of minority students applying to college.[11]

The Texas percent plan offers a unique opportunity to study racial differences in enrollment preferences. The Texas percent plan affords this opportunity because it greatly simplifies the matching game between students and colleges. Usually, the college admissions process can be thought of as a two-sided matching game. Students choose which colleges to apply to and colleges choose whom to admit. Because students choose colleges and colleges choose students, it is often difficult to determine whether where students attend is due to students' preferences over colleges or is due to colleges' preferences over students. The Texas percent plan greatly simplifies the college admissions problem because it limits the ability of public colleges or public universities in Texas to choose students. Public colleges and public universities may still choose whom to offer financial aid, but public colleges and public universities in Texas must accept students who graduate in the top 10 percent of their high school class. Therefore the resulting allocation of students in the top 10 percent of their high school class at public colleges and public universities in Texas is due to students' preferences for the characteristics of colleges and for offers of financial aid.

Although the Texas percent plan guarantees acceptance to students in the top 10 percent of their high school, it does not guarantee that all students who are guaranteed admission will attend college. While the percent plan was in place, approximately 50 public high schools reported that less than 10 percent of the students took either the SAT or the ACT (Dickson 2006). This suggests that some students are not taking advantage of the opportunity offered to them by the

Texas percent plan. Recent research also suggests that Hispanic students who are guaranteed admission (in the top 10 percent) are less likely to apply to four-year institutions than white students, black students, and Asian students who are guaranteed admission.[12]

Because all students who graduate in the top 10 percent of their high school class are guaranteed acceptance to any public university in Texas, we can create a preference ranking of where students choose to attend given that they are all allowed to choose any public university in Texas.[13] The ranking allows a comparison of how students of different races and ethnic groups choose where to enroll given that they attend a public university in Texas.[14] Table 11.1 shows the 10 most preferred public universities in Texas separated by race and ethnicity. The ranking uses all information on enrollments for students in the top 10 percent of their high school graduating class at public universities in Texas between 1998 and 2003.

Table 11.1 reveals that 58 percent of students in the top 10 percent who choose to enroll at a public university in Texas enroll at the state flagships. The preference rankings by race, however, show dramatic differences in the enrollment rates by race and ethnic group. Approximately 70 percent of Asians in the top 10 percent of their high school class who choose to attend a public university in Texas enroll at the state flagships. In comparison, approximately 46 percent of Hispanics in the top 10 percent of their high school class who choose to attend a public university in Texas enroll at the state flagships. The comparable numbers for whites and blacks are 63 and 31 percent, respectively.

The preference rankings within each race or ethnic group do not correspond directly to the standard measures used to assess university quality. The state flagships are generally considered to be the highest quality universities in Texas by the standard measures. For instance, *U.S. News and World Report* currently ranks the University of Texas at Austin as 47th among national universities and Texas A&M at College Station as 62nd among national universities. Whites rank Texas A&M at College Station above UT-Austin even though *U.S. News & World Report* ranks UT-Austin above Texas A&M at College Station. Blacks and Asians both rank the University of Houston above Texas A&M at College Station, but the University of Houston is considered to be a third-tier university by *U.S. News & World Report*.

Because students are automatically accepted to any public university in Texas, it would seem natural that the preference rankings should correspond to the selectivity of the universities in Texas. We might expect students who are guaranteed acceptance to attend the most selective universities. Yet the rankings suggest that the students do not necessarily prefer the most selective universities, and the Hispanic ranking and black ranking actually reveal that the students prefer less selective institutions. The University of Texas at El Paso and the University of Texas at San Antonio are ranked number three and four, respectively, in the Hispanic ranking, but both universities are considered to be "less selective" by *U.S. News and World Report*. In the Hispanic ranking,

Table 11.1
Revealed Preference Rankings by Race and Ethnicity

Total Ranking		White Ranking		Hispanic Ranking		Black Ranking		Asian Ranking	
University	Share (%)	University	Share (%)	University	Share (%)	University	Share (%)	University	Share (%)
UT-Austin	30.41	Texas A&M	36.19	UT-Austin	29.49	UT-Austin	20.43	UT-Austin	60.16
Texas A&M	28.24	UT-Austin	27.12	Texas A&M	16.29	U of Houston	13.25	U of Houston	13.08
Texas Tech	6.87	Texas Tech	9.24	UT-El Paso	9.35	Texas A&M	10.69	Texas A&M	9.97
U of Houston	5.18	University of North Texas	4.16	UT-San Antonio	8.32	Prairie View A&M	10.04	UT-Arlington	5.68
University of North Texas	3.68	Stephen F. Austin	2.80	U of Houston	7.50	Texas Southern	7.32	UT-Dallas	3.18
UT-Arlington	2.86	Texas State	2.61	Texas State	3.84	University of North Texas	6.89	University of North Texas	1.59
Texas State	2.65	U of Houston	2.34	Texas Tech	3.22	UT-Arlington	5.25	Texas Tech	1.45
UT-San Antonio	2.54	UT-Arlington	2.26	Texas A&M–Kingsville	3.00	Stephen F. Austin	5.02	UT-San Antonio	1.22

Stephen F. Austin	2.34%	UT-Dallas	1.96%	Texas A&M International	2.72%	Sam Houston State	3.35%	Lamar University	0.84%
UT-El Paso	1.98%	Sam Houston State	1.42%	Texas A&M-Corpus Christi	2.66%	Texas State	3.33%	Stephen F. Austin	0.43%
N = 66625		N = 42766		N = 12284		N = 4264		N = 6782	

Note: The ranking is calculated by the author using information from the Texas Higher Education Coordinating Board's first-time undergraduate applicant, acceptance, and enrollment information. All students in the top 10 percent of their high school class are admitted to any public university, and I calculate the ranking using information from students who choose to attend any public university in Texas. I am unable to provide a ranking that incorporates the decision to enroll in higher education outside of the state because of data limitations. The rankings provided in this table uses information for all years between 1998 and 2003.

these "less selective" universities are both ranked higher than universities that are considered to be "selective" (University of Houston and Texas Tech) by *U.S. News and World Report*. Prairie View A&M receives almost 10 percent of the black students in the top 10 percent who choose to remain in the state; however, Prairie View A&M is considered by *U.S. News and World Report* to be in the "least selective" category. Texas Southern receives 7 percent of the black students in the top 10 percent but is considered to be "selective" by *U.S. News and World Report*. Yet the black ranking suggests that black students prefer Prairie View A&M to Texas Southern.

Universities that receive a large proportion of the top 10 percent students who are minorities are those that already enroll a large proportion of minorities. UT-El Paso and UT-San Antonio receive 9.35 and 8.32 percent, respectively of the Hispanic top 10 percent students who enroll in any public university in Texas. The undergraduate enrollment at UT-El Paso and UT-San Antonio in 1999 was 71.6 percent Hispanic and 46.1 percent Hispanic, respectively. Two historically black universities are ranked numbers four and five by blacks. Prairie View University receives 10.04 percent of the black top 10 percent students who enroll in a public university in Texas and this university's undergraduate enrollment was 92.5 percent black in 1999.[15] Texas Southern University receives 7.32 percent of the black top 10 percent students who enroll in a public university in Texas and this university's undergraduate enrollment was 88.4 percent black in 1999.[16]

Because of the large percentage of top 10 percent students choosing to attend the state flagships, the share of available spaces in the freshman class for students

Figure 11.2
First-time undergraduates at the state flagships by race and ethnicity

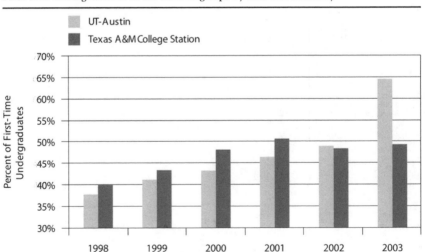

Source: Texas Higher Education Coordinating Board Statistical Reports.

outside the top 10 percent of their high school class has declined dramatically. Figure 11.2 shows the percent of freshmen who enrolled at each flagship who graduated in the top 10 percent of their high school class. Between 1998 and 2003, the share of entering freshman at UT-Austin in the top 10 percent of their high school class in Texas increased from 38 percent of the freshman class to 65 percent of the freshman class. At the same time, the share of entering freshmen at Texas A&M in the top 10 percent of their high school class in Texas increased from 39 percent of the freshman class to 49 percent of the freshman class.

Parents, policymakers, and the public have been concerned by the increase in the share of the entering freshman classes at the state flagships taken up by students who were guaranteed acceptance. The first concern is that the state flagships are now less accessible to students outside the top decile of their high school class. The second concern is that some students who are admitted under the percent plan are not academically prepared to study at the state flagships. Research suggests, however, that students admitted under the percent plan perform well at the state flagships.[17] The performance of the students in the top 10 percent of their high school class may be partially due to investments made by the state flagships.[18]

The percent plan may have inadvertently affected the quality of higher education in Texas by changing the incentives of high school students. Students may choose to maximize class rank while sacrificing their performance on other measures of student quality. For example, students enrolled in high schools where high school class rank is computed without regard to class difficulty may take easier classes to promote their rank. This may cause students to be less prepared than they would be if college admissions were based on multiple criteria. Students in the top 10 percent of their high school class may also be less likely to invest time in studying for the SAT or the ACT. Therefore the percent plan may have reduced the average SAT or ACT scores at the state universities compared to what they would be if students did not know they were guaranteed acceptance.

CHANGES IN THE AFFORDABILITY OF HIGHER EDUCATION IN TEXAS

The affordability of higher education is dictated by the listed tuition and fees, the amounts and types of financial aid available to students, and the family income available for students. In the 1990s, the average listed tuition and fees for public universities in Texas increased faster than the national average. At the same time, the amounts and types of financial aid available to students changed as a result of changes in federal laws, state aid, and institutional aid. In this section of the study, I examine the effects of the rising tuition on affordability.

In the last decade, the average tuition and fees in Texas increased faster than the national average, but the level of tuition and fees in Texas is still slightly below the national average. Figure 11.3 shows the time trend in tuition and fees for universities, community colleges, and technical colleges in Texas.

Figure 11.3
Average tuition and fees listed for public higher education institutions in Texas

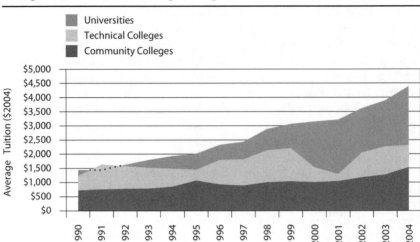

Notes: The average tuition levels are deflated using the consumer price index and the amounts listed are in 2004 dollars. The tuition levels are for in-state residents and can be found in the College Student Budgets produced annually by the Texas Higher Education Coordinating Board.

The figure reveals that the average tuition and fees listed for an in-state student at a public university in Texas doubled, adjusted for inflation, between 1990 and 2000. The figure also reveals that the average tuition levels for community colleges and technical colleges have also been increasing but at a slower rate than the tuition levels at public universities. The real tuition levels at community colleges increased by 32 percent between 1990 and 2000.

To assess the affordability of these increases for the population, we consider how the tuition increases compare to family income. The listed tuition and fees at public universities in Texas have been increasing faster than the median family income in Texas. The average tuition for a full-time equivalent student at a doctoral research university in Texas increased from 3.4 percent of median family income in 1990 to 7.5 percent of median family income in 2000.[19] At the same time, average tuition for a full-time equivalent student at a comprehensive university in Texas increased from 2.6 percent of median family income in 1990 to 4.8 percent of median family income in 2000.[20] These statistics suggest that higher education is becoming less affordable for the typical Texas student.

Students who cannot afford the increases in tuition at public universities in Texas may be receiving financial aid in the form of grants, scholarships, loans, or work-study programs. The number of students at public universities in Texas receiving need-based financial aid increased from 154,598 (38 percent of total enrollment) in 1996 to 189,184 (41.5 percent of total enrollment) in 2002.[21] At

Table 11.2
Enrollment of Public High School Graduates in Public Higher Education in Texas

	Enrolled in Texas Public Universities	Enrolled in Texas Public Two-year Colleges	Not Located in Texas Public Higher Education	Total
1996	37,928	53,174	80,881	171,983
1997	39,055	57,129	85,682	181,866
1998	41,849	60,140	95,197	197,186
1999	41,631	61,977	99,785	203,393
2000	44,433	63,461	105,031	212,925
2001	45,751	65,543	104,022	215,316
2002	57,345	65,720	102,102	225,167
2003	59,014	70,550	108,545	238,109

Source: Texas Higher Education Coordinating Board "High school graduates enrolled in higher education"

the same time, the average amount of money students enrolled at public universities in Texas received in need-based financial aid also increased by $1,000 (adjusted for inflation) between 1996 and 2002.[22] The average amounts and types of financial aid received by students differ by the race and ethnicity of the students. In 2002, 66 percent of black students enrolled received need-based financial aid and 58 percent of Hispanic students enrolled received need-based financial aid.[23] In 2002, 36 percent of white students enrolled received need-based financial aid and 41 percent of Asian students enrolled received need-based financial aid.[24] Most of the financial aid received by students in Texas is from the federal government (83 percent).[25]

The type of financial aid a student receives matters to both the student and the state. Students prefer scholarships and grants to loans or work-study programs. Scholarships and grants do not need to be repaid. Scholarships are merit-based and grants are need-based. Loans are used to transfer the costs of the education to the student rather than it being a burden for the parents to pay. In the last few years, the average amount of financial aid students receive in the form of loans has increased. McMillion et al. (2005) found that the median borrower at public universities in Texas in 1992 borrowed $5,250 compared to $13,621 in 2002. The increasing loan burden reinforces the idea that higher education in Texas has become less affordable.

The loan burden for students has increased as a result of changes in the eligibility for loans and low amounts of grant aid. The 1992 Reauthorization of Higher Education Act changed the federal financial aid system.[26] Two of the changes in the federal financial aid policy can help to explain the increase in the median borrower's indebtedness. First, the 1992 Reauthorization of Higher Education Act increased the amount of money that could be borrowed through the Stafford loan program. Second, the 1992 Reauthorization of Higher Education Act made unsubsidized loans available to students. The amount of grant aid available to Texas students has increased recently, but the amount of grant aid in Texas is by far the lowest in the six largest states.[27]

Although higher education in Texas appears to have become less affordable, the number of students enrolling in public higher education in Texas has steadily increased. Table 11.2 shows the number of public high school graduates enrolling in public universities in Texas, public two-year colleges in Texas and high school graduates not enrolled in public higher education in Texas. The number of public high school graduates enrolled in public universities in Texas increased from 37,928 in 1996 to 59,014 in 2002. The number of public high school graduates enrolling in public two-year colleges has increased from 53,174 in 1996 to 70,550 in 2003. The paradox of decreasing affordability and increasing enrollment is part of a national trend. Heller (2001) discussed the national trends in prices and enrollments.

WHY HAS TUITION INCREASED IN TEXAS?
State Appropriations

The rising tuition in Texas is part of a national trend. The average tuition charged by public universities for an in-state student increased by 80 percent between 1988 and 1998.[28] Mumper (2001) discussed four possible explanations for the rising tuition at public universities in the country: decreases in state appropriations, increases in spending on Medicaid and prisons, increases in the costs of quality inputs, and irresponsible spending by colleges. McPherson, Schapiro, and Winston (1989) suggested that universities may be raising tuition because they know that students will pay for the increase in tuition with federal financial aid.

The increasing tuition levels in Texas do not appear to be directly related to decreases in state appropriations. In the last 15 years, the amount of state appropriations (adjusted for inflation) has been steadily increasing. Figure 11.4 shows the trends in state appropriations per full-time equivalent (FTE) student for all public universities in Texas. The figure shows that in the mid 1980s, state appropriations per FTE student at public universities in Texas fell by 22 percent in real terms. Since 1985, state appropriations in Texas have been increasing in real terms; however, the real amount of state appropriations given to public universities in Texas today is lower than the real amount of state appropriations given to public universities in 1985.

Case Study of the Finances at the State Flagships

Because the increases in tuition do not appear to be directly related to state appropriations, this study presents an analysis of the finances at the state flagships.

Figure 11.4
State appropriations per FTE student at public universities in Texas

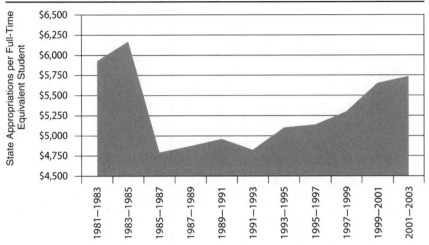

Notes: The state appropriations are deflated using the consumer price index (CPI) for all goods and all dollar amounts shown are in 2001 dollars. The state appropriations are deflated using the first year of the state appropriations. State appropriations are reported per biennium because the Texas state legislature meets once every two years. Data are available from the Texas Higher Education Coordinating Board's statistical reports.

The tuition and fees at the state flagships increased significantly between 1997 and 2003. The tuition and fees for an in-state resident at UT-Austin in 1997 was $3,157 (in 2003 dollars) and this increased to $5,721 (in 2003 dollars) in 2003. This represents a real increase of $2,564 (81 percent). At Texas A&M, the tuition and fees for an in-state resident increased from $2,910 (in 2003 dollars) in 1997 to $4,937 in 2003. This represents a real increase of $2,027 (70 percent). The tuition and fees for out-of-state residents are considerably higher at each of the state flagships. In 2003, an out-of-state resident at UT-Austin is charged $12,261, and an out-of-state resident at Texas A&M is charged $11,477. To determine why tuition and fees increased, this study presents an analysis of the revenues and expenditures at the state flagships.

Table 11.3 presents the revenues and expenditures for each of the state flagships in 1997 and 2002. The revenues and expenditures exclude auxiliary enterprise expenditures or revenues. All of the monetary values in Table 11.3 are presented in 2002 dollars and are presented for a FTE student. The percent columns in Table 11.3 show the fraction of either total revenues or total expenditures each category represents. For example, state appropriations per FTE in 1997 represented 28 percent of total revenues.

Table 11.3 reveals that revenues for the state flagship have increased significantly since 1997. The total revenues per FTE student increased at UT-Austin by $3,278

Table 11.3
Finances for the State Flagships in 1997 and 2003

	The University of Texas at Austin						Texas A&M at College Station					
	1997		2003				1997		2003		
	Dollars	Percent	Dollars	Percent			Dollars	Percent	Dollars	Percent
Revenues per FTE										
State appropriations per FTE	6,153	28	5,929	23			6,952	45	6,133	32
Tuition and fees per FTE	3,716	17	4,739	19			3,176	20	4,771	25
Gifts, grants and contracts per FTE	7,229	33	7,644	30			2,547	16	3,220	17
Other revenues per FTE	5,141	23	7,204	28			2,906	19	5,010	26

Total revenues per FTE	22,238	100	25,516	100	15,581	100	19,134	100
Expenditures per FTE								
Instruction per FTE	7,295	34	8,704	36	7,435	51	7,985	46
Research per FTE	5,897	28	6,546	27	1,651	11	1,547	9
Scholarships and fellowships per FTE	1,916	9	1,863	8	1,814	12	2,150	12
Other expenditures per FTE	6,123	29	7,207	30	3,807	26	5,867	33
Total expenditures per FTE	21,231	100	24,320	100	14,706	100	17,549	100

Notes: The dollar values presented are all in 2003 dollars. The other revenues per FTE include state remissions and exemptions, returns on investment, sales and services. The other expenditures include academic support, student services, plant operations and maintenance. The data is available from the Texas Higher Education Coordinating Board's Data and Performance Reports.

and total revenues per FTE increased at Texas A&M by $3,553. Increases in revenues at both flagships are due to increases from tuition and fees, gifts, grants and contracts, and other revenues. At both state flagships, the real amount of state appropriations has fallen. At the University of Texas at Austin, it has fallen from $6,153 to $5,929 and has fallen from 28 percent of all revenues to 23 percent of all revenues. At Texas A&M, it has fallen from $6,952 to $6,133 and has fallen from 45 percent of all revenues to 32 percent of all revenues.

The total amount of expenditures at the state flagships has also risen significantly since 1997. The total expenditures per FTE increased by $3,089 at UT-Austin and by $2,843 at Texas A&M. Increases in expenditures at the UT-Austin appear to be due to an increase of $1,409 spent on instruction, $649 spent on research, and $1,084 spent on other goods. The amount of expenditures on scholarships and fellowships per FTE student at UT-Austin has actually declined since 1997. Increases in expenditures at Texas A&M appear to be due to an increase of $550 on instruction, $336 on scholarships and fellowships, and an increase of $2,060 on other goods.

The increase in expenditures may be partially due to the increasing prices of goods bought by higher education institutions. Each year, the Research Associates of Washington calculates the Higher Education Price Index (HEPI). The HEPI calculates the increases in the prices of goods that higher education institutions purchase. Between 1961 and 1998, the HEPI increased by 0.8 percentage points more per year than the consumer price index (CPI).[29]

TRENDS IN THE EMPLOYMENT OF TENURED AND TENURE-TRACK FACULTY IN TEXAS

Instruction is the largest expenditure category at the state flagships. Increases in expenditures on instruction may be due to the universities hiring more faculty members or may be due to the universities paying higher salaries to the current faculty. In this section of the study, I analyze the trends in the employment of tenured and tenure-track faculty in Texas. The purpose of this analysis is to determine how public universities spend their money on instruction and to determine whether public universities in Texas have been able to attract and retain tenured faculty.

Figure 11.5 shows the trend in average salaries paid to each faculty rank for all faculty employed by any public university in Texas. Between 1996 and 2003, the average salary paid to full professors in Texas increased from $76,915 dollars to $85,774 (in 2003 dollars). This represents an increase of 11.5 percent over an eight-year period. Average salaries increased between 1996 and 2002 and then decreased slightly in 2003.

The average salary for faculty employed at public universities in Texas is lower than the national average for faculty employed at any public university. When using the data for all ranks, the average faculty member earns $61,965 in Texas, which can be compared to the national average of $63,421.[30] When separating

Figure 11.5
Average salaries for faculty at public universities in Texas

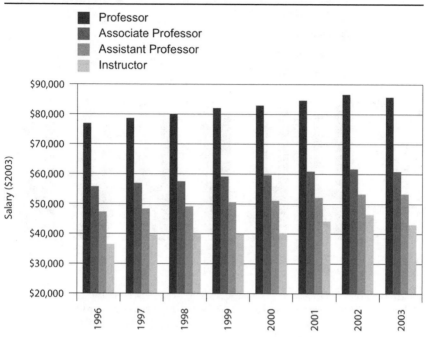

Notes: Data come from the statistical reports produced each year by the Texas Higher Education Coordinating Board. The weighted average salaries presented are deflated using the consumer price index (CPI) for all goods and are presented in 2003 dollars. The year 1996 refers to the 1996-1997 school year.

the data by rank, it becomes apparent that assistant professors in Texas and full professors in Texas earn more than the national average. Assistant professors earn almost $300 more in Texas, and full professors earn $1,667 more than the national average.[31]

Public universities in Texas have witnessed a decline in the fraction of tenured faculty. This may be a result of the average salaries at public universities in Texas being lower than the average salaries at other universities (both public and private). Professors may be choosing to seek out higher paid employment; however, public universities could also be reducing the fraction of tenured faculty to reduce costs. In this section, I do not distinguish between these two forces.[32] Between 1996 and 2003, the share of tenured faculty employed by public universities in Texas fell from 33 to 29 percent. At the same time, the share of non-tenure–track faculty employed at public universities in Texas increased from 50 to 53 percent.

As a result of the decreasing share of tenured and tenure-track faculty, the fraction of semester credit hours taught by tenured faculty at public universities

Figure 11.6
Percentage of undergraduate semester credit hours taught by faculty type

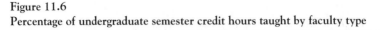

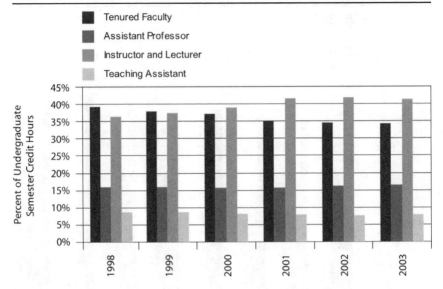

Source: The share of undergraduate credit hours taught by faculty rank is calculated by the author from information collected using the Texas Higher Education Coordinating Board Prep Query Tool.

in Texas has declined. The decrease in the share of semester credit hours taught by tenured, tenure-track, and nontenured faculty at public universities has been concentrated at the undergraduate level. Figure 11.6 shows the trends in the share of undergraduate semester credit hours taught by tenured, tenure-track, and nontenured faculty at public universities in Texas. During the last six years, the share of undergraduate credit hours taught by tenured faculty decreased by almost 5 percent, from 39 to 34 percent. The share of undergraduate credit hours taught by instructors and lecturers has increased by almost 5 percent, from 36 to 41 percent over the same period.

TRENDS IN OUTPUTS

The decline in the share of undergraduate credit hours taught by tenured faculty may have adversely affected the quality of the public universities in Texas. One way to assess whether the quality of public universities in Texas changed is to analyze trends in output. Two measures of output often used to describe the quality of universities are the graduation rate and the freshman retention rate. In this section of the study, I analyze trends in the six-year graduation rate and the freshman retention rate to determine whether public universities in Texas have changed in quality.

In Texas, the six-year graduation rate is recorded for all public universities. Table 11.4 shows the six-year graduation rates for the 1991 cohort and the 1996 cohort. For most of the universities shown, the six-year graduation rate increased.

Table 11.4
Six-year Graduation Rates at Public Universities in Texas

	1991–1997	1996–2002	% Change
UT-Austin	64.7	71.8	7.1
Texas A&M	66.3	74.6	8.3
Texas Tech	43.5	51.3	7.8
U. of Houston	37.2	37	−0.2
U. of North Texas	34.4	38.4	4
UT-Arlington	26.7	36.4	9.7
UT-El Paso	21.7	24.7	3
UT-San Antonio	23	25.5	2.5
Prairie View A&M	27.3	33.6	6.3
Texas Southern	10.4	18.4	8

Source: Texas Higher Education Coordinating Board Data and Performance Reports.

Table 11.5
Freshman Retention Rates at Public Universities in Texas

	1996–1997	2001–2002	% Change
UT- Austin	87.2	90.7	3.5
Texas A&M	86.5	89.4	2.9
Texas Tech	78.4	82.3	3.9
U. of Houston	74.4	78.5	4.1
U. of North Texas	69.8	71.7	1.9
UT-Arlington	63.3	65	1.7
UT-El Paso	63.1	64.3	1.2
UT-San Antonio	56.3	59.9	3.6
Prairie View A&M	58.9	69.2	10.3
Texas Southern	53.3	63.1	9.8

Source: Texas Higher Education Coordinating Board Data and Performance Reports.

Texas A&M at College Station records the highest graduation rate at 74.6 percent for the 1996 cohort. The second highest graduation rate is 71.8 percent for the 1996 cohort at UT-Austin. Texas Tech reports a graduation rate of 51.3 percent for the 1996 cohort, but for the rest of the universities listed the graduation rate is less than 40 percent. The largest gain was at UT-Arlington where the graduation rate increased by 9.7 percentage points.

The freshman retention rate at most of the public universities in Texas also increased between 1996–1997 and 2001–2002. Table 11.5 shows the freshman retention rate at some of the public universities in Texas. UT-Austin maintains the highest freshman retention rate, with Texas A&M following close behind. There is a considerable range in the freshman retention rates. The freshman retention rate at Texas Southern is almost 28 percentage points lower than the freshman retention rate at UT-Austin.

The output measures suggest that the quality of the schools as captured by these measures has increased. In the past few years, there have been large increases in the six-year graduation rate and increases in the freshman retention rates for public universities in Texas. These numbers suggest that for now the slight decreases in tenured faculty do not appear to be negatively impacting student outcomes.

CONCLUSION

Higher education in Texas has faced several challenges. It has had to attempt to help a diverse population without the use of race as a criterion in admissions or as a factor in financial aid decisions. In addition, higher education institutions has had to accept students in the top 10 percent of their high school class whether or not the students were prepared for a college education. In addition, higher education in Texas has been challenged with increasing costs. Higher education in Texas has dealt with these challenges with some success and with some failure.

The accessibility of higher education in Texas changed differentially for students of different races and ethnicities, as well as for students of different high school class ranks. The end of affirmative action reduced the cultural accessibility and geographic accessibility of higher education for minority students. The percent plan and population growth also reduced the accessibility of the state flagships for students outside of the top 10 percent of their high school class. Meanwhile, the percent plan increased the accessibility of the state flagships for students in the top 10 percent of their high school class. For students in the top 10 percent of the poorest high schools in the state, the accessibility and affordability of the state flagships greatly increased. The Texas percent plan guaranteed access to the state flagships for these students, and the state flagship universities offered large amounts of financial aid to these students.

The affordability of college education in Texas for the average student appears to have decreased. The rising costs and the increased expenditures made by public universities in the state led to increasing tuition and fee levels. The tuition and fees levels increased faster than the national average, faster than average price levels, and faster than the median family income in Texas. As a result of these increases, more students are receiving need-based financial aid and more students are borrowing more money in the form of loans.

The changes in admissions criteria may have adversely affected the quality of higher education in Texas. The change to a statewide policy based on one admissions criterion distorts incentives for students. Students who are enrolled at the most competitive high schools in the state may prefer to be enrolled at lower quality high schools. At high schools where class rank is not based on the difficulty of classes undertaken, students may choose to take easier classes. This reduces the academic quality of the student. Students who know they will be automatically accepted may be less likely to study for the SAT or the ACT, and this may lower the average scores for the entering freshman. As this is a criterion used by *U.S. News & World Report* in its rankings of universities, it is possible that these decreased incentives may slightly reduce the ranking of the public universities in Texas.

In recent years, it also appears that the quality of education as measured by the percent of faculty that are tenured and tenure-track has declined at public universities in Texas. There has been a corresponding decline in the share of undergraduate semester credit hours taught by tenured and tenure-track faculty, and this may have adversely impacted the quality of the universities as perceived by the students. However, the current output measures (six-year graduation rates and freshman retention rates) do not appear to have been affected yet.

Current research also reveals some troubling facts. First, not all students who are guaranteed acceptance to college appear to apply to college. This may be due to preferences, but if it is due to the lack of affordability of college, then this represents a problem. Also, minorities who are guaranteed acceptance to the state flagships are less likely to enroll than nonminorities who are guaranteed acceptance to the state flagships. This may be due to student preferences, but if it is due to discouragement and/or the increasing cost of a higher education, then this constitutes another problem that needs to be remedied.

NOTES

1. See Chapa and Lazaro (1998); Tienda, Cortes, and Niu (2003).

2. The ruling itself does not apply directly to financial aid decisions. However, the Texas state attorney general at the time interpreted the decision to apply to financial aid decisions, and this led to the end of the use of race in financial aid decisions at public colleges and public universities in Texas.

3. See Chapa and Lazaro (1998), Card and Krueger (2004), and Texas Higher Education Coordinating Board statistical reports.

4. The Texas percent plan differs significantly from the California and Florida percent plans because students in the top 10 percent of their high school class can choose where they wish to attend.

5. Information on high schools that qualify for the Longhorn Opportunity Scholarship program is provided in Dickson (forthcoming).

6. Tienda and Lloyd provide information on the Longhorn Opportunity Scholars Program and the Century Scholar program.

7. Texas Education Agency

8. Ibid.

9. See Tienda, Leicht, Sullivan, Maltese, and Lloyd (2003); Tienda, Cortes, and Niu (2003).

10. Tienda, Leicht, Sullivan, Maltese, and Lloyd (2003).

11. Dickson (2006) demonstrates a significant decrease in the percent of minority high school students taking either the SAT or the ACT after the Hopwood decision in Texas.

12. Approximately 71 percent of Hispanic students in the top 10 percent of their high school class apply to four-year institutions, compared to 80 percent of white students in the top 10 percent, 88 percent of Asian students in the top 10 percent, and 79 percent of black students in the top 10 percent (Tienda, Cortes, and Niu 2003).

13. Avery et al. (2004) provide a national revealed preference ranking.

14. In Texas, there are 35 public universities: UT-Arlington, UT-Austin, UT-Dallas, UT-El Paso, UT-Pan American, UT-Brownsville, UT- Permian Basin, UT-San Antonio, UT-Tyler, Texas A&M, Texas A&M at Galveston, Prairie View A&M University, Tarleton State University, Texas A&M at Commerce, Texas A&M at Corpus Christi, Texas A&M at Kingsville, Texas A&M at International University, Texas A&M at Texarkana, West Texas A&M University, University of Houston, University of Houston at Clear Lake, University of Houston—Downtown, University of Houston—Victoria, Midwestern State University, University of North Texas, Stephen F. Austin State University, Texas Southern University, Texas Tech University, Texas Woman's University, Angelo State University, Lamar University, Sam Houston State University, Texas State University (formerly called Southwest Texas University), Sul Ross State University, and Sul Ross State University—Rio Grande College.

15. Texas Higher Education Coordinating Board statistical report.

16. Ibid.

17. Bucks (2004) provides an analysis of the academic performance of whites and minorities at the state flagship institutions before and after the end of affirmative action.

18. UT-Austin maintains the Connexus program for Longhorn Opportunity Scholars. The program provides academic advisors for the students and free tutoring for the students in some subjects. In addition, the program places the students in smaller classes for a few subjects. These types of initiatives may have helped to boost the performance of Longhorn Opportunity Scholars.

19. See Texas Higher Education Coordinating Board "Financing Higher Education."

20. Ibid.

21. See Texas Higher Education Coordinating Board's statistical reports.

22. Ibid.

23. Texas Higher Education Coordinating Board statistical reports

24. Ibid.

25. McMillion et al. (2005).

26. A discussion of the Reauthorization of the Higher Education Act is provided by the National Center for Education Statistics in "Paying for college: Changes between 1990 and 2000 for full-time dependent undergraduates."

27. McMillion et al. (2005).

28. Mumper (2001) documents the increases in tuition at public universities. Ehrenberg (2002) documents some of the trends in tuition at the selective private colleges in the United States and discusses some possible explanations for the increasing tuition levels.

29. Research Associates of Washington.

30. Texas Higher Education Coordinating Board report on "Average faculty salary in public universities in Texas and the ten most populous states for fiscal year 2002."

31. Ibid.

32. Ehrenberg and Zhang (2004) estimate demand equations for faculty members and show how the demand for faculty is affected by the average salaries of different types of faculty members. Nagowski (2004) investigates the relationship of average salaries and the turnover of associate professors and finds that institutions with higher average salaries maintain lower faculty turnover rates.

CHAPTER 12

Higher Tuition, Higher Aid, and the Quest to Improve Opportunities for Low-Income Students: The Case of Virginia

Sarah Turner

Rising costs and substantial fluctuations in state fiscal policy during the last two decades has created a sharp tension for selective state universities between objectives of excellence and the mission of providing collegiate opportunities for state residents from all backgrounds. With increased claims on state coffers from programs such as Medicaid and persistent voter pressure for reduced tax burdens, colleges and universities have not been successful in proclaiming the long-term benefits associated with investments in higher education to substantially increase resources from state sources in good economic times. In bad economic times, public universities are increasingly hard hit, as higher education is one of the few discretionary items in state budgets (Kane and Orszag 2003). Faced with the realities of limited funding from public sources in the twenty-first century, public colleges and universities in many states have been forced to reexamine the traditional balance between public subsidy and private tuition payments.

In Virginia, the selective public colleges and universities have taken proactive steps to change the "terms of trade" with the state. Faced with stagnant state funding and severe cutbacks during economic contractions, selective public institutions in the state of Virginia are shifting to high tuition coupled with high student aid. Under the Restructured Higher Education Financial and Administrative Operations Act [SB 1327 and HB 2866, "Restructured Higher Education Act"],[1] public colleges and universities in the state of Virginia have new latitude to enter into a "contract" with the state in which greater autonomy in tuition-setting and purchasing is granted in exchange for a somewhat smaller expectation of future state support. Loosely coupled with this initiative is a new emphasis on increasing the opportunities for students from modest economic circumstances to attend the state flagship institution. The University of Virginia has put forward an aggressive plan known as AccessUVa to increase public information, recruiting, and need-based financial aid for low income students.

What is unambiguous in the discussion to date is that, with more autonomy, these selective public institutions, including the University of Virginia, will raise "sticker price" or posted tuition, particularly for in-state students who currently receive substantial discounts. In short, the selective public universities propose to adopt a high-tuition, high-aid model to raise revenue and provide access to low-income students, while increasing the overall level of resources available to promote excellence in teaching and research. Even in the absence of higher tuition, low-income students are dramatically underrepresented at the University of Virginia and the other selective public universities in the state, raising concerns that yet higher tuition would further reduce opportunities. Can a high-tuition strategy really increase opportunities for low-income students?

The first part of this chapter shows how variation in tuition levels and state funding at the University of Virginia during the last decade has brought about a call for a restructuring of the state-university financial arrangement. The second section sets forth the "terms" of the Restructured Higher Education Act and AccessUVa, discussing how these policies are likely to affect "sticker price" and price net of financial aid for students from various economic circumstances. (Note that although both graduate and undergraduate education are affected by the Restructured Higher Education Act, the focus of this analysis is on undergraduate education.) The third section turns to the evaluation of these policies in the context of the broad discussion of the tradeoffs associated with high-tuition, high-aid public policies. Whether the Restructured Higher Education Act coupled with AccessUVa can yield improvements in long-term financial stability and enrollment of low-income students through a high-tuition, high-aid strategy is the key question.

Several caveats necessarily preface this discussion. First, although the legislation has been approved by the General Assembly and became law on July 1, 2005, state universities negotiated management agreements with the Commonwealth in November 2005, which must yet be approved by the General Assembly before going into effect in July 2006.[2] Institutions such as the University of Virginia that are pursuing the highest level of autonomy had to negotiate management agreements with the secretary or secretaries designated by the governor before November 15, 2005, and these agreements must be approved by the General Assembly in the their 2006 session; the full provisions will not come into effect until July 1, 2006. Thus there is considerable room for change. Second, the following analysis focuses specifically on the tuition revenue and financial aid components of the legislation; many other significant dimensions of the legislation for the operation of the university cover employment and contracting relations. Although the analysis here concentrates on the case of the University of Virginia, there are important lessons from this experience for tuition and aid policy in other states.

STATE APPROPRIATIONS AND TUITION POLICIES IN THE LAST DECADE: EVIDENCE OF UNDERFUNDING

The Virginia Case

For the University of Virginia, more than a decade of fiscal uncertainty and cycles of "boom" and "bust" have been a clear motivation for a change in the relationship with the state. Cyclical fluctuations in Virginia have been particularly sharp, owing to the structure of state politics and the cycles of the local economy. With a one-term limit on the governor's tenure, tuition policy has been used as a potent and symbolic political lever.[3] Moreover, with a growing high-tech sector in the DC corridor, Virginia benefited substantially from the tech boom but also experienced a more painful contraction in 2000 and 2001 and the events of September 11, 2001 touched the Virginia area.

That the University of Virginia has been underfunded over the course of the last decade is not just administrative rhetoric, but a reality borne out by the data assembled by the State Council of Higher Education of Virginia (SCHEV, the coordinating board for higher education in the state). With a stated goal of maintaining the salaries of public colleges and universities at the 60th percentile of peer group norms, the University of Virginia has fallen short in all but one year since this policy was articulated in 1989 (University of Virginia, Board of Visitors, Finance Committee, 2005, p. 18).

Appropriations from the state combined with revenues from student tuition and fees are the primary sources of support for broad-based education and general expenses at the University of Virginia and other public institutions in the state. Both variables have been subject to cyclical variation and political intervention. The trend in state general fund appropriations to the University of Virginia is shown in Figure 12.1, represented in constant (2004) dollars. From 1988 to 2004, real state appropriations fell from nearly $185 million to about $120 million. During this time, funding cycled to a similar low of about $126 million in the academic year beginning in 1995 before rebounding to a local peak of $172 million in 2000.

If one thinks of the state appropriation as having characteristics similar to an endowment payout for a private university, the implication is that year-to-year variation in the state appropriation has been larger than the realized variation in endowment returns for private universities. At a 5 percent real rate of return, the fluctuation in state funding would imply a decline in endowment value from $3.45 billion to $2.39 billion between 2000 and 2004, which is an appreciably larger swing than observed by most market funds. What is more, rather than incurring the full weight of year-to-year fluctuations in endowment, private universities generally "smooth out" cyclical fluctuations with spending rules that provide for additional spending in tough years countered by additional saving in more robust periods.

The overall impact of the decline in the real value of state appropriations is magnified when considered in the context of rising overall higher education costs. Figure 12.2 illustrates the trends in state appropriations relative to educa-

Figure 12.1
State Appropriations from General Fund to the University of Virginia

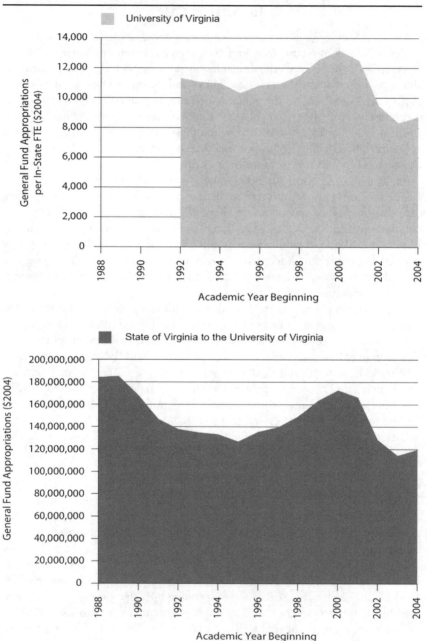

Source: State Council of Higher Education for Virginia, SCHEV Research Data Warehouse.

tion and general expenditures at the University of Virginia, which covers the core current operating and academic expenditures including faculty salaries. Visible is the marked drop in the state-supported share from about 62 percent of education-general expenditures in 1988 to only about one-third in 2004; the reduction is yet more marked when the full University of Virginia current budget is used in the denominator. The evidence would seem to support an often repeated quip among public university administrators that their institutions have gone from "state-funded to state-supported to state-located."

Tuition, the other major source of operating support for the University of Virginia, does move countercyclically, but variations have not been sufficient to offset fully declines in state appropriations. Tuition is by statute a variable under the control of the Board of Visitors, but the political realities have been far different. Moves to raise tuition by an institution outside the expectations of the governor and the state legislature can be countered with retribution in appropriations. What is more, "tuition" has at times been used as a political variable. Figure 12.3 shows the nominal and real trend in tuition and fees at the University of Virginia over the last two decades. What is visible is considerable variation, including the recent five-year period in which tuition and fees were reduced by 20 percent, frozen, and then increased by nearly 28 percent.[4] Surely,

Figure 12.2
General fund state appropriations relative to education-general expenditures

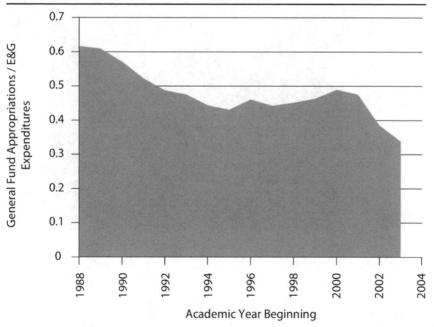

Figure 12.3
Tuition and fees, University of Virginia, constant dollar

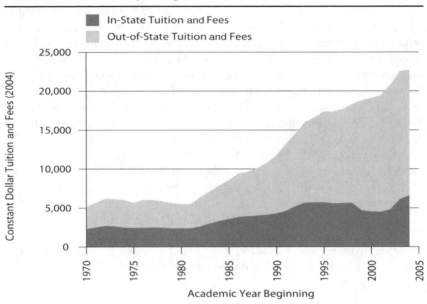

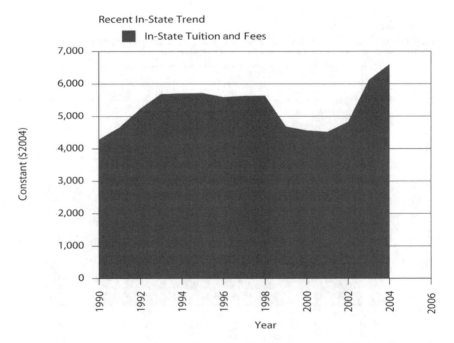

Source: University of Virginia, Institutional Assessment and Studies, Data Catalog http://www.web. virginia.edu/iaas/data_catalog/institutional/historical/historical.htm.

many other public universities have faced similar cycles, although the case of the University of Virginia is extreme.[5]

At least at the University of Virginia, sharp fluctuations in posted tuition rates do not appear to have had a significant impact on enrollment demand. In 2004, the University of Virginia received more than 15,000 applications and made offers to less than 40 percent of these candidates. The university has consistently faced circumstances of excess demand, like other selective public and private universities, and changes in tuition price at the undergraduate level bears little overall relation to enrollment levels. Of course, demographics and the increase in the size of the college-age cohort are partly at issue, yet there is a substantial *positive* correlation between real tuition and the number of applications received for both in-state and out-of-state students. How demand—conditional on both family income and student achievement—can be expected to adjust with changes in tuition is a key question to be considered in evaluating the new policies at the University of Virginia.

For the University of Virginia, the status quo funding arrangement undermines institutional objectives because it limits the level of resources available for academic purposes while also increasing the volatility in funding. Both the low level of resources and the uncertainty in funding have limited institutional advancement. The effects of the level of resources should be obvious: if resources are used efficiently, adding resources increases output along dimensions of quality or quantity or both. The effect of uncertainty in funding is, perhaps, somewhat more subtle but no less significant. Universities facing significant uncertainty may not make long-term investments with high expected returns either because the institutions are credit constrained or because they are risk averse. Either way, the institution puts aside an investment with a positive expected return.

It should be no surprise that resource constraints produced visible effects on faculty hiring, class size, and course availability in the last decade. Commenting after deans froze hiring during the 2001 budget crisis, the student newspaper at the University of Virginia recorded the comments of various chairs of major departments (Hechtkopf 2001):

> Department heads are charged with adjusting plans to implement the freeze as directed by the deans. Many share the deans' fears concerning class number and size.
>
> "We have way too many students for the number of faculty," Fatton said of the government and foreign affairs department.
>
> He said three hiring searches for the department were canceled. That translates into 12 to 15 more courses that will have to be absorbed by the current faculty through larger class sizes or fewer course offerings.
>
> "Seminars aren't really going to be seminars," he added. "It affects the quality of the teaching."
>
> Economics Department Chairman David Mills said six searches initially were halted but that funding was restored to recover three.
>
> "Classes will be larger than ideal next year, and larger than they were a few years back."

The comments of the department chairs are not just idle speculation, but are reflected in demonstrable "excess student demand." In 2003, an extended story in the *Cavalier Daily* chronicled how the faculty hiring freeze created extraordinary excess demand in many departments (Lamesa 2003):

> Economics, which currently has only 22 faculty members but awarded 419 bachelors degrees in 2002, also suffered tremendously from the freeze, Economics Dept. Chair David Mills said.
>
> "Not hiring for the last two years—it'll take a decade to work ourselves out of the problem that creates," Mills said, adding that it is unclear how economics arrived at its present faculty shortage.

Similar problems persisted into 2005 (Keith 2005):

> Unfortunately, this situation has been all too common this year, as the realities of budget crunches and professor shortages have been manifested through severe overcrowding in many of the University's most popular courses. This overcrowding is not only a headache for many students, but also a detriment to the University's quality of education and academic reputation.
>
> The most direct consequences of the overcrowding of the courses are ultimately felt by students at the University. Indeed, because students in overcrowded departments are unable to enroll in many of their desired classes, large numbers of students have to fill out their schedules by roaming from class to class with a ream of course action forms and by joining electronic waitlists on ISIS [the course registration system at the University of Virginia]. Since this system offers little degree of certainty as to prospects for course enrollment, it is very difficult for students to plan their academic future.
>
> Moreover, because course overcrowding forces professors to give priority to students who need their class as a requirement for their major, students have difficulty enrolling in certain classes outside their major and the well-roundedness that is the foundation of the University's liberal arts education is harmed.
>
> While course overcrowding decreases the quality of education for current students, it also hurts the University's academic reputation. Indeed, as accounts of overcrowding reach prospective students through word of mouth or through publications such a *The Princeton Review*, it becomes more difficult for the University to attract strong students. Thus, course overcrowding hurts the University's academic reputation and makes its diplomas less attractive commodities to graduate schools and future employers.

A striking observation in the case of the University of Virginia is the demonstrated student support for somewhat higher levels of tuition in the face of severe resource limitations. Editorials in the student newspaper have, on more than one occasion, taken the position that students would benefit from higher tuition levels. To cite a few examples:

> While increases in tuition aren't a substitute for better funding from the state level, students should shoulder the increasing burden equally. (*Cavalier Daily* 2000).

More recently, the response to the stiff increase in tuition (11.2 percent) remained positive under an editorial of the title "A Prudent Tuition Hike" (*Cavalier Daily* 2003):

> Students, who understandably aren't pleased to pay more for their education, usually meet tuition increases with lukewarm receptions. However, in this case, students should applaud the Board [of Visitors] for the tuition increases. In light of recent budget cuts, the Board's decisions were—no pun intended—right on the money.

That the "customers" are on the record supporting higher tuition charges in exchange for increased academic resources is a clear sign that the combination of budget crisis and tuition freeze distorted the provision of collegiate services.

Because research universities rely on relatively long cycles to build staffing and programs, the "start-and-stop" cycle of state funding for the University of Virginia had particularly deleterious consequences. Bill Johnson, an economist at the University, described the impact of the funding cutbacks on the long-term quality of University programs in a *Washington Post* op-ed (Johnson 2003):

> Greatness in a university is very difficult to attain and easy to lose. At bottom, as Jefferson knew, academic greatness requires recruiting and retaining top faculty members, and providing them an environment in which to flourish. . . . highly cyclical revenue sources mandating "stop-and-go" hiring policies make it tough to maintain, let alone improve, faculties, especially in the hard-to-hire fields so crucial for national prominence. Truly outstanding scholars are scarce and difficult to hire. Moreover the best people are attracted to departments with able colleagues, so a department can collapse if a few leading faculty members leave. And, as Humpty Dumpty proved, it is hard to put the pieces back together again.

Thus, it is the inefficiency and erosion of quality caused by the feast-and-famine funding cycles that is a primary impetus for the exploration of a structural reform in the relationship between the university and the state.[6]

Public universities in Virginia are not alone in struggling with constrained levels of state support for higher education and limits on tuition increases, combined with considerable year-to-year uncertainty. During the last 15 years, these constraints have made it more difficult for flagship state universities to hold their ground and compete with elite private universities. With relatively fixed enrollment capacity and little control over tuition, universities have few operational degrees of freedom. Across the board, infrastructure demands and growing Medicaid commitments have increased demands on the state purse, essentially crowding out state expenditures on higher education.[7]

THE UNIVERSITY OF VIRGINIA: NEW STRATEGIES FOR TUITION AND AID

The starting point for a reconfiguration of the funding relationship between the state of Virginia and the public universities is a recognition that the unfunded gap in resources is structural, not transitory. A long-held position of state policymakers and higher education leaders was that cutbacks to higher education funding were cyclical, and eventually relatively high levels of state appropriations would return. Yet, policymakers in Virginia and elsewhere have increasingly adopted the view that the cutbacks to higher education are permanent, with dollars taken away "never coming back" (Breneman 2004).[8]

Add to this clear evidence that start-and-stop funding has long-term costs and the stage was set for considerable negotiation. That the Darden School, the Law School, and the University Hospital system already have considerable autonomy from state regulations provides something of a model.[9] The autonomy of the Darden School is described by Kirp (2003) as the "most autonomous—most 'private'—school in any American public university." Still, a wholesale "privatization" initiative for public universities in the state of Virginia would be highly unlikely because these institutions remain dependent on public subsidies for operating support.

Increased University Autonomy

The (formal) timeline for the Restructured Higher Education Act initiative extends from January 2004 when the presidents of the University of Virginia, the College of William and Mary, and Virginia Polytechnic Institute and State University (Virginia Tech) announced their intention to put forth a plan to redefine the relationship between these universities and the state through a proposal titled "Commonwealth Chartered Universities and Colleges Act." The initial proposal was the subject of considerable public discourse, resulting is some modification. By February 2005, the idea evolved to legislation. The Restructured Higher Education Financial and Administrative Operations Act (House Bill 2866 and Senate Bill 1327) passed the General Assembly. Virginia Governor Mark Warner attached some amendments, which largely related to the status of nonfaculty employees, to the legislation before returning it to the General Assembly for approval. The final legislation was approved by both houses of the General Assembly on April 6, 2005 and took effect July 1, 2005.[10] This left universities, including the University of Virginia, to negotiate a management agreement with the Commonwealth and to present a six-year plan, which must be approved by the General Assembly in 2006.

The initiative has evolved appreciably since it was introduced by the three large universities at the start of 2004 to include provisions for all 16 public colleges and universities in the state.[11] Although the institutional coverage has broadened (to include something for everyone), the scope of the autonomy offered to institutions such as University of Virginia has also been narrowed to a large degree. Rather than permanent autonomy, the university will develop a six-year academic and financial plan outlining tuition and fee projections and enrollment projections (including the mix of in-state and out-of-state students). In addition, the plan will include benchmarks related to the availability of opportunities for students from different economic circumstances and accountability standards.[12]

The motivating idea behind the initiative is the recognition that state resources sufficient to allow the University of Virginia to be competitive with peer institutions are unlikely to be forthcoming. At the same time, the university has substantial "excess demand" at the undergraduate level.[13] Autonomy to set tuition is the key provision of the proposal on the revenue side. (Overall, there are a number of other important dimensions of the policy, including the relaxation of state regulations governing contracting, building, and so forth.)

A key piece of the argument in favor of tuition autonomy (and, implicitly, higher tuition levels) is that students will be the beneficiaries of the increase in resources. Implicitly, students are "off their demand curves" when they are willing to pay more for a higher quality (or at least more resource intensive) offering. Evidence that many current students prefer the prospect of higher tuition to budget constraints of further reliance on state funding is provided by the support of the student council for the initiative.[14]

As the formal contract between the University of Virginia and the state has yet to be negotiated, the terms of the agreement are not yet settled. Still, the shape of the expected agreement appears to be in place. It is expected that the tuition and fee increases for in-state undergraduate students will be phased in over a five-year period to allow for full-funding of base adequacy (including the 60th percentile of the university's peer group). It is further expected that the state will achieve a goal of funding 67 percent of the cost of education for every in-state student over a five-year period. Explicit is the expectation of continued resources from the state general fund and an agreement that the "Commonwealth [agrees to] continue funding the College at the level the College would receive if this Charter Agreement had not been put in place."[15] To meet this target, it is expected that the appropriations from the state will increase by $52.6 million in 2009–2010, and net tuition revenues will increase by nearly $77 million (Exhibit B, 1/05 Board of Visitors; see Table 12.1 for full projections). In effect, the structural funding gap is to be closed through an increase in in-state tuition.

Although neither the proposed Charter agreement specific to the University of Virginia nor the Restructured Higher Education Act legislation makes the expected increases in tuition levels explicit, some indication is offered by the review of projections presented to the board of visitors. At the January 2005 board of visitors meeting, there was a substantial discussion of the long-term tuition plan, including explicit projections for the tuition levels needed to achieve funding targets over the next five years.[16] Annual tuition and fee increases of just below 10 percent for in-state undergraduates have been proposed, leading to an expected increase in total sticker price (including fees room and board) of about 8 percent per year. For out-of-state students, annual increases of just over 6 percent are expected. Table 12.2 lists undergraduate tuition projections based on the plan submitted to the state in October of 2005 assuming the state meets its funding commitments. Whether the realized tuition increases will be larger or more modest depends on the extent to which the state is able to fund its commitment to general fund appropriations.

Appendix Table 12.1
Revenue and Expenditure Projections for the University of Virginia

	2005–2006	2006–2007	2007–2008	2008–2009	2009–2010
Base State Educational and General	362,325,000	362,325,000	362,325,000	362,325,000	362,325,000
Incremental Funding Requirements					
Salary commitments	10,587,000	20,686,000	31,052,000	41,699,000	52,642,000
Base budget adequacy	–1,059,000	–2,069,000	–3,105,000	–4,170,000	–5,264,000
Net new general fund support	9,528,000	18,617,000	27,947,000	37,529,000	47,378,000
Interest earning on Net New General Fund	250,000	500,000	750,000	1,000,000	1,250,000
Other E&G Increases	92,000	187,000	285,000	385,000	488,000
Subtotal	372,195,000	381,629,000	391,307,000	401,239,000	411,441,000

Incremental funding requirements					
Salary commitments	12,689,000	26,248,000	40,453,000	55,337,000	70,935,000
Base budget adequacy	10,871,000	21,743,000	32,614,000	43,485,000	54,357,000
Subtotal incremental funding	23,560,000	47,991,000	73,067,000	98,822,000	125,292,000
Needs	385,885,000	410,316,000	435,392,000	461,147,000	487,617,000
Expected	372,195,000	381,629,000	391,307,000	401,239,000	411,441,000
Needed from tuition	13,690,000	28,687,000	44,085,000	59,908,000	76,176,000
Gross New Tuition Revenue	20,006,000	36,591,000	53,315,000	70,984,000	88,889,000
Increases in graduate financial aid	−1,232,000	−1,496,000	−1,774,000	−1,875,000	−2,192,000
Increases in undergraduate financial aid (AccessUVa)	−1,349,000	−3,525,000	−5,437,000	−7,723,000	−9,710,000
Net New Tuition Revenues	17,425,000	31,570,000	46,104,000	61,386,000	76,987,000

Table 12.2

University of Virginia Undergraduate Tuition Projections as Part of Six-Year Plan
(October 2005)

	2005–06	2006–07	2007–08	2008–09	2009–10
In-state under-graduate Tuition + Educational and General Fees	5,714	5,714	5,714	5,714	5,714
Non Educational and General Fees	1,419	1,495	1,570	1,648	1,730
Room and Board	6,389	6,389	6,389	6,389	6,389
Projected Total Sticker Price	13,522	13,598	13,673	13,751	13,833
Out-of-state under-graduate Tuition + Educational and General Fees	22,634	24,110	25,670	27,328	28,558

The most recent iteration of the Restructured Higher Education Act legislation makes clear that, with increased autonomy and higher tuition levels,
public universities must actively pursue efforts to enhance "access" and "affordability." The proposed legislation makes explicit the expected commitment to
financial aid policies sufficient to help families address increased tuition, stating that "Each such institution shall commit to the Governor and the General
Assembly to:

1. Consistent with its institutional mission, provide access to higher education for
   all citizens throughout the Commonwealth, including underrepresented populations, and, consistent with subdivision 4 of § 23–9.6:1 and in accordance with
   anticipated demand analysis, meet enrollment projections and degree estimates
   as agreed upon with the State Council of Higher Education for Virginia;
2. Consistent with § 23–9.2:3.02, ensure that higher education remains affordable,
   regardless of individual or family income, and through a periodic assessment, determine the impact of tuition and fee levels net of financial aid on applications, enrollment, and student indebtedness incurred for the payment of tuition and fees;[17]

Although numerical targets are not specified, there is a clear sense that demonstrable
shifts in the composition of the student body toward more affluent, full-pay students would be considered a breach of the terms of the contract. Nevertheless, it is
plainly unclear how the state or policy authorities will monitor the success of the
university in attaining the objective of equality of educational opportunity.

As the authorizing language is operationalized in a "draft" of an agreement between the University of Virginia and the state, considerable emphasis is placed on the recently initiated outreach effort known as AccessUVa. Described later in more detail, AccessUVa is not an outgrowth of the Charter initiative but rather a predecessor, as the first prong of the initiative implemented with the class entering in the fall of 2004, which guarantees that the university will meet 100 percent of need for a specific group of low-income students. Because the AccessUVa initiative is incorporated directly in the terms of the proposed agreement, aid and tuition policies become "coupled" in the policy process.

AccessUVa

Concern about the representation of low income students at the University of Virginia predates the initiative for fiscal autonomy,[18] but the cause has received new urgency with the formalization of the Restructured Higher Education Act. Much of the impetus for AccessUVa was driven by the concern over how the fiscally inevitable tuition increases in 2003 and 2004 would impact students eligible for financial aid. At the October 2003 meeting of the Board of Visitors, President Casteen asked staff to craft a plan that would address the impending financing challenges for low- and middle-income students at the university.

To much fanfare, the AccessUVa plan was announced in February 2004. AccessUVa is not a single financial aid initiative, but rather a portfolio of institutional policies intended to increase the representation of students from low and moderate incomes among University of Virginia undergraduates. The first prongs of the program are relatively easy to define and concern financial aid: first, students with family income below 200 percent of the poverty line (150 percent initially) are guaranteed that the loan portion of their aid packages will be replaced with grants; second, the university will address the concerns of moderate income families with financial need by capping the amount of expected debt at no more than the cost of education for one year ($14,520 for in-state students in 2004).[19] But beyond changes in the availability and distribution of financial aid, the AccessUVa program includes an aggressive outreach and public information campaign designed to get the word out that students from all economic circumstances have opportunities to attend the university.

Although the financial aid changes are well documented, it is more difficult to document the changes in recruitment strategies designed to increase the representation of students from relatively disadvantaged economic circumstances in the undergraduate class. These steps include:

- Increases in the number of visits to high schools from relatively low income areas that have traditionally not sent large numbers of students to the university
- Public service announcements on radio and in other media touting the openness of the University of Virginia to students with financial need[20]
- More aggressive assistance from the financial aid office in helping students to complete FAFSA forms and understand financial aid options

There is much enthusiasm and determination surrounding the objectives of AccessUVa at the university level, as discussions with staff reveal commitment from many offices.

Yet the barriers to the enrollment of low-income students at the University of Virginia have been persistent, even in periods of somewhat lower tuition. Research questions that remain open include how these initiatives ultimately affect application behavior, as well as matriculation and persistence at the university. Data from the State Council of Higher Education for Virginia identify just over 6 percent of students in the entering class of the fall of 2002 (the most recent year for which detailed data are available) with family income less than $30,000. What is more, working-class families are underrepresented at the University of Virginia, where one report placed nearly 60 percent of the incoming class with family incomes over $100,000 (Marklein 2004).

As public discussions of the Chartered Universities Initiative and later the Restructured Higher Education Act have progressed, the question of how the universities will maintain a commitment to helping low- and middle-income families finance college has been prominent. For example, an editorial in the *Virginian-Pilot* notes: "No matter how much Virginia wants revered colleges engaged in cutting edge inquiry, the state cannot neglect its primary duty of making college broadly accessible, both through affordable tuition and an adequate number of slots" ("A Pass-Fail Test for Charter Colleges" 2004).

The need for a transparent and public indication of University commitment to financial aid to gain broad-based support for the Restructured Higher Education Act has, in turn, strengthened support for AccessUVa within the university. In the end, aggressive financial aid strengthens the university's hand in negotiations for greater autonomy (including setting tuition). At the same time, efforts to gain public endorsement for greater institutional autonomy increase the visibility and internal support for policies such as AccessUVa. Thus the result is a set of policies coupling higher tuition with higher financial aid in long-term projections.

HIGH TUITION, HIGH AID: PROSPECTS AND PERILS

The combination of renegotiated institutional status under the Restructured Higher Education Act and AccessUVa represents an unambiguous shift to a high-tuition, high-aid policy at the University of Virginia. Some would argue that this is a first-best policy solution, which takes full advantage of student demand and the existing national market for higher education. A more reluctant group would come to support the policy only with the recognition that it is unlikely that increased public support will be forthcoming to allow for a competitive level of funding of the University of Virginia.[21]

The discussion of the tradeoffs between a high-tuition, high-aid strategy and across-the-board low tuition has surfaced in research and policy discussion for more than three decades. Late in the 1960s, Hansen and Weisbrod (1969) made the case that large state subsidies to support low tuition were both inequitable and inefficient. Instead, tuition should more accurately reflect cost of instruction, with public subsidies targeted to low-income students in the form of higher financial aid. The crux of the Hansen and Weisbrod argument, which derived in part from a study of the case of California, is that students from relatively affluent families are represented disproportionately in flagship universities that receive the largest per student appropriations from the state. To this end, the distribution of subsidies was inequitable, in the sense that they were concentrated among the relatively affluent, and inefficient in that these students would likely continue to enroll at selective public institutions if they were charged appreciably higher prices.

Much debate ensued, but no state adopted the high-tuition, high-aid model as explicit policy in the 1970s and, as noted by Breneman and Finn (1978), many leaders in higher education at the time maintained "that higher education, like elementary and secondary schooling, should be provided by a society at little or no cost to all who want it who are qualified." In turn, to the extent that substantial tuition growth occurred at public universities during the 1990s, it was far from a conscious shift in financing strategy but often a stop-gap funding response to state fiscal crises. That tuition hikes occurring at state institutions were often a response to local fiscal crisis left the goal of providing opportunities for low-income students frequently pushed to the side. Because tuition increases have not been consciously tied to a structural shift to a high-tuition, high-aid policy in recent years, opportunities for students from the most economically disadvantaged families may have eroded.

In weighing the tradeoffs between a low-tuition policy and a high-tuition, high-aid model, the political philosopher Amy Gutman (1987) noted:

> A morally troublingly risk of a high-tuition, full scholarship policy is that in times of austerity, the two parts of the policy may be decoupled, public or private universities retaining their high tuitions and giving up their full scholarships. The risk cannot be eliminated without doing away with democracy or the autonomy of universities, but it can be minimized by policies that tie levels of tuition to levels of support. . . . The commitment to economic nondiscrimination is thereby expressed by a single policy, rather than being the coincidence of two policies with independent rationales.

In a world in which relatively high tuition at public universities seems to have arrived as a matter of public policy necessity, the question is whether tuition and aid policy can be effectively recoupled in the public interest.

In evaluating the likely consequences of a shift to a high-tuition, high-aid policy at the University of Virginia, two significant questions of behavior come to the surface. The first is a politics question: Are contracts with the state enforceable over the long term? At issue is whether a change in politics or other circumstances facing the legislature or the governor could lead to a unilateral dismantling of the terms of the Restructured Higher Education Act, leaving selective public universities no better off (if not worse off) than under the counterfactual without this policy. Second, the strength of a high-tuition, high-aid policy is derived from the assumption of relatively inelastic demand and the capacity of the university to price discriminate to a substantial degree. Available evidence points to little change in demand in the neighborhood of existing prices, but it is not known whether this regularity will hold for high-achieving students as prices are pushed closer to levels charged by private providers. Moreover, even with the aggressive and well-placed efforts of AccessUVa, the problem of the underrepresentation of low-income students at selective institutions is nontrivial and "high aid" may be necessary but not sufficient to increase enrollment demand for these students.

Contracting with the State

It is clear that the question of whether an institution such as the University of Virginia can enter a nonrevocable contract with the state is not specific to higher education.[22] In this case, it is useful to restate the symbolic politics of public tuition policy. When times are good, governors find favor among constituencies when they can step in and "freeze" (or even better, reduce) tuition at public colleges and universities. Even in bad times, state politicians may try to limit tuition increases, essentially forcing a compromise between lower overall university revenues and somewhat higher tuition. What will be the reaction of a governor when faced with budget problems? When state appropriations fail to meet expectations, the terms of the agreement allow for yet greater tuition increases. If universities avail themselves of this option, will politicians abandon the political high ground and declare opposition (backed by budgetary or regulatory retribution) to greater-than-expected increases in tuition during times when families are likely already facing tough financial circumstances?

Eric Patashnik, a political scientist at the University of Virginia studying the political durability of policy reforms, suggests that there are fundamental barriers limiting the capacity of government agents to make long-term policy commitments. Patashnik identified two potential threats to the durability of the "charter" contract—the time consistency problem and political uncertainty. The "time consistency problem" captures the idea that incentives change as circumstances change: policy makers may agree to do X at time t but have an incentive to do Y at time t + 1. In addition, the cast of players in political office changes over time, and new governors or legislators may have explicit motivation to distinguish themselves from their predecessors or revoke policies established in the previous administration, particularly when "election" is taken as a mandate for change.

In this sense, there is inevitable concern that without more fundamental structural reform in the relationship of the university to the state, it will be difficult to guarantee the stability of contracts. For the University of Virginia, the key question is whether there are policy actions that will increase the cost to state politicians of reneging on the contract. Consistent and visible demonstrations that the outcomes under the arrangement provide significant general benefits to the state will make it more difficult for politicians to change the terms of trade without generating public objection.

Demand Adjustments

The effects of shifting to a high-tuition, high-aid policy at the University of Virginia necessarily depend on the nature of demand. With more than 14,000 applications last year for about 2,800 spaces, there is little argument that the university will continue to be able to fill its entering undergraduate class even if the in-state tuition price were to rise as high as that currently charged to out-of-state students. Because the production process in higher education depends on student inputs, however, the key question is how the new pricing strategy will affect the composition of the entering class. In short, achievement of equity and excellence depends not only on financial resources but also the capacity to recruit able students from a range of socioeconomic circumstances. Whether students are likely to face higher or lower college costs will depend on where they are in the income distribution.

Some students will definitely face a higher net price of attendance. How does this change behavior? To answer this question, we need to think about demand—and the elasticity of demand[23]—and how it varies among students. To be sure, there are some students who are quite inelastic in their demand for attendance at the University of Virginia, as they have established loyalty through family or they simply have a strong affinity for Mr. Jefferson's architecture. Other students weigh the University of Virginia option among a portfolio of other selective public and private universities. For each student, the question will be how does the price and quality of the University of Virginia compare to the student's best alternative. In all likelihood, the University of Virginia will remain less expensive than private options in absolute terms, yet relative prices will shift. Students who once chose the University of Virginia over private options such as Duke, the University of Pennsylvania, and Georgetown may now change their choice of college.

Consider which students are likely to be lured by these selective, private options or selective public options outside the state of Virginia. Students for whom the best private alternative is an institution less highly ranked than the University of Virginia may be relatively unlikely to change behavior (assuming the University of Virginia still dominates alternative in-state institutions). Students who have outside options at more highly ranked institutions, however, may be more likely to change behavior.[24] These students are also likely to be the most able. Evidence from other selective universities makes clear that the net price elasticity of demand is greatest among students at the top of the SAT distribution (Ehrenberg and Sherman 1984).

Thus, a well-placed concern is that tuition increases may have an adverse effect on the quality of the undergraduate student body.[25] Because peer effects are an important part of the "production process" at residential undergraduate institutions such as the University of Virginia, declines in the achievement of students caused by an increase in tuition would have deleterious effects on the quality of undergraduate education and, in turn, ranking of the institution (Winston 1999).

Estimating the magnitude of this potential effect at the University of Virginia is a nontrivial empirical challenge, and one should not be content with "turn down" surveys as an indicator of the potential effect.[26] Commonly available empirical evidence (in the form of "turn down" surveys) often fails to distinguish students by achievement or income. Moreover, the key question concerns the outside options available to students who enroll under existing policies as those who currently turn down the University of Virginia would most likely continue to do so with appreciably higher relative tuition levels.

A further challenge to forecasting the effects of the change in aid and tuition policies is that application behavior will likely adjust. Students who at present apply only to the University of Virginia or to the University of Virginia under Early Decision are likely to consider a wider range of options. Of course, one intended outcome of AccessUVa is to increase applications among students from relatively low-income families. The extent to which this group of students responds to the greater availability of aid remains to be seen.

The increase in price necessarily forces the University of Virginia into more active competition in the national higher education market. The result need not be a net loss of the most able students if the university is able to use additional resources to raise the quality of undergraduate offerings.

DISCUSSION

The success of the proposed high-tuition, high-aid model at the University of Virginia under the combined charter and AccessUVa initiatives will depend on the extent to which the institution is able to raise both overall quality and participation of low-income students under the new terms. Even with additional tuition revenues, neither outcome is certain. Concerns are twofold: first, it remains to be seen whether contracts or agreements with the state are truly enforceable as circumstance change; second, how potential students from different achievement groups and economic circumstances respond to changes in net price will determine the extent to which a high-tuition, high-aid strategy successfully increases opportunity and excellence at the University of Virginia.

Since the passage of the "Restructured Higher Education Financial and Administrative Operations Act," the University of Virginia submitted to the state in October 2005 a six-year operating plan and negotiated a management agreement with the Commonwealth. The six-year operating plan is direct in targeting efforts to improve affordability for low- and moderate-income students and AccessUVa is the centerpiece of this commitment, mentioned no less than 18 times in the current draft (University of Virginia 2006). The AccessUVa program and the goal of increasing the enrollment of low-income students is now embedded in the agreement with the Commonwealth.

There is good reason for policy analysts to be (cautiously) enthusiastic about the direction of tuition and aid financing at the University of Virginia. In the past, higher tuition has not been explicitly coupled with financial aid, leaving opportunities for low-income students often threatened by efforts to raise university resources. That the restructured universities initiative explicitly couples financial aid through AccessUVa with proposals to increase tuition may yield an outcome fostering both excellence and opportunity at the University of Virginia. It may thereby serve as a model for other selective state university systems.

NOTES

1. When this initiative was unveiled in January 2004 by the leaders of the University of Virginia, William and Mary, and Virginia Tech, it was known as the Commonwealth Chartered Universities and Colleges Act. As discussions progressed, the reference to the participating institutions as charter universities was formally dropped, although the description continues to appear in many background documents.

2. The legislation was introduced on January 21, 2005, as House Bill 2866 and Senate Bill 1327. The legislation was passed by the Virginia House of Delegates on February 21, 2005, and by the Virginia Senate on the next day. On March 31, 2005, Governor Warner introduced amendments to the legislation and returned it to the General Assembly for approval. On April 6, 2005, both the Senate and House passed the legislation. The legislation took effect July 1, 2005.

3. In the mid-1990s, then-Governor George Allen found that a tuition freeze at public colleges and universities was particularly attractive to middle-income voters, as he was able to portray leaders of public colleges and universities as raising the price of higher education out of reach of middle-class students. The next governor, James Gilmore, ran on a platform of cutting taxes and providing greater affordability of higher education and went yet further to push through legislation effectively requiring tuition cuts of 20 percent at public universities in Virginia. Proposals for cutting tuition (and taxes) were able to generate considerable bipartisan support in the General Assembly, as both Republicans and Democrats found political appeal in the argument of "a cheaper college education as the best way to elevate the poor and middle class" (Timberg, 1998).

4. Leonard Sandridge, Executive Vice President and Chief Operating Officer of the University of Virginia, in a talk to the faculty, notes: "Let me give you a history here—1996–97, we were required by the state to have zero increase in tuition. 1997–98, the state required a zero increase in tuition. 1998–99, a 1.2% increase required by the state. Get this one: 1999–2000, a tuition rollback of 20% for undergraduate in-state students. In 2000–01, a zero percent increase. 2001–02, a zero percent increase. By 2002–03, things are in pretty desperate condition around here. People are complaining about not being able to get classes, so the state gives us a formula that they tell the public is a 5% cap on tuition, but they don't tell you about the fine print. We applied that and the tuition and fees—The tuition component was up about 28%, but when you combined it with fees which didn't go up that much, we went up 21%. That was really a state formula and then this last year, tuition went up 23%. I got to tell you, gang, that's no way to run a railroad that way. We can't together accomplish what you expect and ought to expect from this place without having some ability to manage resources better than that. That's what this proposal for charter is all about." (U.Va. Community Briefing, Commonwealth Charter Status, November 12, 2004 http://www.virginia.edu/restructuring/eb041112.html.)

5. It should be noted that –unlike states such as California—a "low tuition" policy is relatively new at the University of Virginia. Only a decade ago, in-state tuition at the University of Virginia was nearly $1,200 higher than at peer public universities (*Cavalier Daily* 2000).

6. Quoted in the *Washington Post* (1/12/2004) Travis Reindl of the American Association of State Colleges and Universities notes, "The numbers just dictate it. If you're a university like U-Va and the state has become such a minority stakeholder, you can legitimately ask how much authority should they exercise over my business if they are only kicking in 10 percent of funding." Reindl goes on to note that the logic for such institutions is "we'd rather have less money we can count on than more money we can't count on."

7. An early note of this trend is found in Breneman and Finney (1997); Kane and Orszag (2004) have done considerable work to formalize this relationship.

8. Breneman (2004) wrote: "The severity of the cuts, coming after more than two decades of slow but steady relative decline in state support, has forced many education leaders to conclude that the old, often implicit, compacts between states and their universities—such as ensured access to public colleges and universities for the states high school graduates—have been abandoned. Hence, it is understandable that we are seeing efforts to establish a new relationship that gives the institutions control over setting tuition and freedom from specific state regulations."

9. As quoted in Kirp (2003), stirrings of potential greater autonomy for state universities can be found in the mid-1990s. One 1996 General Assembly report concluded: "as higher education changes the way it conducts business, the Commonwealth should consider changing its business relationship with higher education, develop[ing] a plan to grant selected institutions special independent status in state government [to free then from] stifling bureaucratic regulation"

10. Yet, it is not until July 1, 2006, that the University of Virginia or other state colleges will operate under a new management agreement. The terms of the legislation specify that universities (such as the University of Virginia) pursuing the highest level of autonomy must negotiate agreements with the secretary or secretaries designated by the governor before November 15, 2005, and these agreements must be approved by the General Assembly in the their 2006 session.

11. The legislation offers three levels of autonomy in which all institutions can qualify for freedom to manage salaries, purchasing and leasing, with the level of autonomy depending on each school's financial strength and ability to manage day-to-day operations. At the highest level (that covering the University of Virginia), institutions can negotiate individual autonomy agreements while retaining public status.

12. Significant provisions of the legislation affect the degree of autonomy that colleges and universities are afforded in procurement, personnel, and capital-project regulations. University administrators make the case that many state regulations pose unnecessary costs on higher education institutions, hampering efficiency in production. An example of the inefficiency created by state regulations is the requirement that all building projects (including those funded with private money) must go through a more than 15-month planning process, gain approval from the General Assembly, and adhere to all state building regulations. Such a process is not only time-intensive but often opens projects to lobbying efforts and political wrangling. Tebbs (2005) noted two examples of costly delays that might be avoided under more autonomous building regulations. In one case, the University of Virginia spent considerable time and resources on the question of whether a sprinkler system was necessary in the roof over a new pool at the Aquatics and Fitness Center,

while at William and Mary administrators were forced to engage in a dispute over whether illuminated exit signs were required in a four-post picnic shelter (with no walls).

13. For example, the proposal notes: "The key to the proposed legislation is enabling UVa to use its untapped 'market share' to produce additional revenues. The potential of the 'market share' is demonstrated by the fact that UVa, like William and Mary and Virginia Tech, annually receives many more applications for admission than it can accept. Yet the tuitions of these universities are substantially lower than those of comparable universities to which many of the same students are applying."

14. UV Student Council passed a resolution recommending "the General Assembly allow the University of Virginia Board of Visitors to be autonomous in its decision making with respect to the University's government and management, including determining tuition levels"

15. As proposed, there is also a modest "give back" where the chartered universities agree to accept a somewhat smaller rate of increase in general fund appropriations than universities at large. "Based on this state funding assumption, when an increase in state general funds is provided by the Commonwealth to public institutions of higher education for educational and general purposes, the Academic Division agrees to accept only 90% of the amount of the increase that it otherwise would receive if the University were not a Commonwealth Chartered University."

16. "University of Virginia Board of Visitors Meeting of the Finance Committee" February 3, 2005. Available from http://www.virginia.edu/bov/meetings/05feb/ %2705%20Feb%20Finance%20Comm%20Book.pdf.

17. House Bill No. 2866. Amendment in the Nature of a Substitute. Available from http://leg1.state.va.us/cgi-bin/legp504.exe?051+ful+HB2866H1.

18. Unlike some selective private universities that have been able to meet full financial aid for several decades, it was not until the matriculation of the Class of 2001 that the university was first able to commit to meeting the full needs of all aid-eligible students.

19. In January 2005, the University of Virginia announced the expansion of AccessUVa to expand opportunities for transfer students from the Virginia Community College System and to increase the cutoff for eligibility for relief from loans and work study those with family incomes less than or equal to 200 percent of the federal poverty level ($37,700 for a family of four).

20. Using the slogan "Got the Brains but not the Bucks? The Door is Open," the advertisements feature actor Shawn Patrick Thomas, a University of Virginia alumnus, and encourage general inquiries from potential students.

21. It is surely the case that there may be opponents to the general outline of the plan. To argue in opposition to increased tuition conditional on stagnant public funding is to make the case that the objective of low tuition serves a more significant policy objective than full-funding of universities at the target level. This position is not invalid, but it illustrates an unavoidable choice between low tuition and high resources per student.

22. For example, Moe (1990) underscored how "political uncertainty" is of fundamental importance in distinguishing the behavior of government entities from private institutions and, in turn, distinctly affects the organizational structure of public bureaucracies.

23. The elasticity of demand captures the proportional change in enrollment relative to a proportional change in net price. That this parameter may vary with student achievement or income is an important consideration in evaluating the expected adjustments to changes in tuition and financial aid policies.

24. The intuition comes from a model in which students make a choice between college quality and an outside good, conditional on the set of colleges to which a student is

admitted. A student for whom the University of Virginia is the most highly ranked insti-tution is, essentially, at a corner, but a student with more highly ranked options is not.

25. One institutional response may be to engage in "merit aid" in order to continue to recruit high-achieving students able to pay the full tuition. Such a policy would likely be expensive and potentially detrimental to educational objectives (see McPherson and Schapiro, 1998, for a full discussion of merit aid programs).

26. To illustrate, the meeting of the Finance Committee of the Board of Visitors of the University of Virginia looked to evidence on the schools chosen by those admitted to, but not attending, the University of Virginia in setting projections for tuition (Board of Visitors, February 2005). The report notes: "In-state applicants accepted by the University turned down our offer of admission to attend these institutions: William & Mary (126), Virginia Tech (64), Duke (32), UNC—Chapel Hill(24), Cornell (23), Virginia Com-monwealth (20), Richmond (15), Yale (14), Pennsylvania (12), MIT (12), Princeton (11), Harvard (10), Rice (10), and Georgetown (10). Out-of-state applicants accepted by the University turned down our offer of admission to attend these institutions: Duke (95), UNC—Chapel Hill (59), Pennsylvania (47), Georgetown (45), Cornell (41), Harvard (35), Yale (30), Dartmouth (28), Vanderbilt (28), Maryland (24), Notre Dame (23), Brown (22), Stanford (21), and Princeton (20)."

CHAPTER

Public Higher Education in Washington State: Aspirations Are Misaligned with Fiscal Structure and Politics

William Zumeta

Washington, a rapidly growing state of more than 6 million, is blessed with quality public higher education institutions. Its flagship campus, the University of Washington (UW) (enrolling on its main campus in Seattle more than 37,000 full-time-equivalent (FTE) students including more than 10,000 graduate and professional students), is one of the nation's leading research universities, topping all public universities for a number of years in federal research and training grants (ranking second among all universities).[1] It is ranked 20th in the world among all universities in overall quality in the recent, widely publicized ranking by the Shanghai Jiao Tong University Institute of Higher Education,[2] and it is home to five Nobel Prize winners named during the last 15 years (University of Washington 2005d).

Washington State University (WSU) (enrollment around 20,000 FTE including more than 4,000 graduate students on its main campus) is a mid-range land grant university located in the small farming community of Pullman near the Idaho border about 75 miles south of Spokane. It ranks 30th among the land grants—tied with the Universities of Arkansas and Kentucky—and 120th overall in the 2005 national university rankings published by *U.S. News and World Report* (*USNWR*).[3] Western Washington University, with about 11,500 FTE students in fall 2003 and located in Bellingham, a small city in the northwestern part of the state, is regarded as one of the better public "comprehensive" universities in the country. It was ranked 16th among Western colleges and universities in 2004 by *USNWR*[4] and, according to its Office of Institutional Research, attracts nearly 8,000 freshman applications per year. The Evergreen State College, founded in 1971 in Olympia, the state capital, is an innovative, even avant-garde public liberal arts college of approximately 4,100 students, featuring small classes taught by faculty without ranks who often teach in teams, extensive service learning programs, and highly individualized courses and majors.

In addition, the state is served by two other public comprehensives, Central Washington University (located in Ellensburg just east of the Cascade mountains and enrolling just under 8,700 FTE students), and Eastern Washington University, enrolling approximately 9,000 FTE in Cheney about 20 miles from Spokane (population about 180,000). These latter two campuses, in particular, have had difficulty drawing sufficient students to match their enrollment capacity at some points in the past, although this is not true at present. Thus, there are a total of just six public colleges and universities in the state and 63 percent of the total enrollments in these (58 percent of the undergraduates) are located at the two research universities. Compared to other states, the capacity of the comprehensive sector is quite small relative to the research universities.

Also, the state is blessed with a generally very good community and technical college system, enrolling some 260,000 (fall 2003 headcount) students at 34 campuses plus a number of satellite sites widely distributed around the state.[5] Thus, this two-year system enrolls more than 70 percent[6] of the students in the state, an unusually high percentage. Unlike in the majority of other states, the community and technical colleges in Washington do not receive any local property tax support; their public funding comes entirely from the state. Finally, there are 22 private nonprofit colleges in the state, enrolling about 39,000 students, and some 11 degree-granting for-profits.[7] This private sector has some small liberal arts colleges and a few modest-sized comprehensives but no universities with a range of doctoral programs. It has grown modestly in recent years with help from a generous state scholarship program for which private college students are eligible.

The quality of this *system*—the term is used loosely as the four-year institutions are autonomous with a coordinating board of modest influence and the two-year colleges have their own board—is in some ways remarkable, as it has been almost continuously under fiscal strain for many years. In this chapter I seek to explain a bit further the basic structural features of the system, including their roots and implications; survey more closely the recent policy, enrollment, and fiscal history; identify and weigh the implications of recent unfavorable trends and coping mechanisms; and briefly consider prospects for change in light of the political economy and culture of the state around higher education issues. In light of the special focus in this volume on flagship research universities, particular attention will be given to the University of Washington (UW) throughout. The analysis is supported by data developed primarily from authoritative sources within the state. Space permits only a small part of the database developed for this chapter to be depicted graphically or in tabular form.

EARLY HISTORY AND STRUCTURE

The University of Washington, founded in 1861, is the oldest university in the West Coast states and one of the oldest in the western part of the country.

Washington State University, the land grant institution, also dates to the nineteenth century (1890). The three regional comprehensives—Eastern, Central, and Western Washington Universities—like many other schools of this type, have roots in regional "normal schools" set up to train teachers in the early days.[8] Only The Evergreen State College is of fairly recent origin (1971). The local forces operating at the time these institutions were founded dictated their locations, but they are not well positioned relative to recent population growth patterns. Other than the UW, they are located in rather small cities and towns, meaning that most students must relocate to attend. This poses a problem for participation opportunities both for many recent high school graduates and even more for older would-be students and their employers seeking accessible postsecondary education.

The limitations of this historical configuration began to become clear when demand for higher education first burgeoned in the decades after World War II. Eventually, in 1967, the state responded by creating a community college system from "grade 13–14" programs that had been developed by some school districts— in some cases from earlier, autonomous junior college roots—and building it up rapidly. Indeed, this system grew remarkably from just 11,000 students in 10 colleges in 1960 to 191,500 enrolled in 27 colleges less than two decades later, in 1979 (Zumeta 1996, 12). Public four-year institution enrollments grew much more modestly during this period, from about 40,000 in 1960 to 83,000 in 1980 (Zumeta 1996, 12). The only four-year institution created over these years was Evergreen, a rather unusual school, a child of the 1960s in ethos, and by deliberate design uncommonly small for a public institution. Thus Washington's primary strategy for enhancing postsecondary participation in the 1960s and 1970s was community college expansion. Because participation is known to be closely linked to college proximity,[9] it is not surprising that the community colleges were spread widely across the state. Of course political factors also played a major role in spreading this form of wealth, and these colleges' broad distribution continues to be very important in strategic thinking about higher education in the state and the allocation of public resources to and within it.

Another historical element worth noting because it continues to play an important role today is attitudes toward system governance. In general, higher education policymaking in Washington has not benefited from vision and staying power from policymakers with a statewide perspective and deep knowledge.[10] Washington was one of the last states to move beyond system-wide management by means of voluntary meetings of institution presidents and direct influence from the legislature when it created the Council on Higher Education in 1969 (a few years thereafter renamed the Council on Postsecondary Education) to function as a statewide coordinating body. With a few short periods excepted (see preceding note), this body and its successor—now called the Higher Education Coordinating Board (HECB)—have not been terribly influential in higher education policymaking or financing decisions, largely because the major players have not truly wanted them to be. The six four-year institutions jealously guard their autonomy and work their own agendas and networks in Olympia. Unlike in most states, they continue to coordinate these activities to the extent they find necessary through a precoordinating board, voluntary Council of Presidents, with its own staff.

Moreover, structurally, the HECB has only limited influence over the community and technical colleges, which have long had their own statewide board. Although strengthened by legislation at various points, the HECB continues to have limited structural powers overall, notably with regard to budgets. Whether cause or effect of these historical weaknesses, appointments to the higher education board are much less sought after by leading citizens than appointments to the universities' boards of regents or trustees. This in turn further saps the board's capacity for influence. Only rarely have governors or legislative leaders provided much attention or leadership for this "system," and it has not usually lasted long. By and large, they have not seen higher education as particularly important[11] or problematic and so have devoted their attention to other matters, leaving higher education politics and policymaking most of the time to the machinations of the every day players—the institutions with their individual agendas, strengths, and weaknesses, and the generally weak coordinating agency.

HIGHLIGHTS OF THE ROLLERCOASTER PERIOD, 1980–2005[12]

We pick up the historical sketch around 1980, which proved to be a key turning point. Around that time Washington's economy, based in natural resources and Boeing, went into a tailspin, taking state revenues down with it and forcing a series of devastating budget cuts. There were repeated mid-term reductions in college and university budgets, cuts to base budgets, and painful and acrimonious program eliminations.[13] Enrollments were cut back sharply. Community college enrollment fell by more than 35 percent in just three years, to 123,800 students in fall 1982.[14] In the four-year institutions, reductions were much less severe and more gradual—from a peak of more than 83,000 students in 1980 to a low of 77,250 in 1986, a decrease of about 7 percent. These declines coincided with modest population growth so that the effects on participation rates were significant.

The New Higher Education Coordinating Board and the Birth of Branch Campuses

At this point, the state leadership undertook a notable effort to rebuild the system. The by then discredited Council on Postsecondary Education was terminated and replaced by the Higher Education Coordinating Board, which received the benefits of close gubernatorial attention to the initial board appointments and skilled, effective leadership by the chair, a respected business and public sector leader who was close to the governor. With this necessary precondition in place, the board undertook some policy studies and eventually a master planning exercise that helped buttress an emerging political consensus supporting reinvestment in higher education.[15] Although the business-oriented board was initially skeptical of the claims of the institutions about underfunding, they became quickly convinced that higher education was a key ingredient for the state's success in the already fast-moving global economy and that participation was far too low and the system poorly supported.

While calling for efficiency-oriented moves such as a rationalization of admission standards among the institutions, initial steps toward outcome-based accountability measures, and more flexibility in how the schools used their money, the board agreed that underfunding was the leading threat to quality. It found that per-student spending in Washington had fallen from thirtieth among the states in 1983–1984 to near the bottom of the heap by 1985–1986 (HECB 1987, cited in Zumeta 1996, 16). The board established formal peer comparison groups for each of the institutions and called for them to move up from their current place near the tail end in per-student funding comparisons to the 75th percentile by 1997. It broke this ambitious goal into four nearly equal-size chunks for the four biennia just ahead. Facilitated by the diversifying state economy's recovery from its doldrums of the early and mid-1980s, Governor Booth Gardner, a moderate Democrat, enthusiastically endorsed these recommendations, which were largely enacted for the 1989–1991 biennium, after an already strong gain in state support for higher education in 1987–1991.[16] In this environment, the legislature provided the money, but, always cognizant of Washington's rollercoaster economy and revenue structure, never endorsed the HECB's ambitious longer term financing goals.

Similarly, with respect to participation, the new HECB did its homework, and the result was a set of ambitious improvement goals. The board's research showed that the state's ranking in overall participation in higher education had fallen sharply during the first half of the 1980s. Participation at the community college level was still relatively high, but Washington ranked only 37th among the states at the upper division level and 36th in graduate/professional-level participation rates in 1986 (HECB 1987, 10). There were also wide differences from county to county in participation rates related to proximity to four-year institutions or, for the fast-growing counties in the western part of the state, to adequate capacity in these. The board also prepared long-range enrollment projections that foretold the worsening of these problems as the coming of age of the "baby boom echo" cohort loomed on the planning horizon.

After concluding that the existing campuses in the western part of the state did not want to expand very much and that those in the central and eastern regions could not well serve the students from the west—many of whom were determined to be "place-bound" by jobs and families—the board proposed and eventually sold the legislature on a somewhat novel solution. This was the creation of a network of five branch campuses located, by and large, near the largest pools of underserved students. The two new branches assigned to the UW were originally planned to grow to about 3,000 at Bothell (a fast-growing suburban area 18 miles northeast of the Seattle campus) and 3,500 at Tacoma by the mid-1990s, and to 4,800 at Bothell and 6,000 at Tacoma in 2010 (HECB 1988, 6; University of Washington 1988, 17).[17] Washington State University was also tasked to create a new branch campus at Vancouver (near Portland, Oregon) and to expand existing, limited programs at Spokane and the Tri-Cities area, which is near the scientific complex at the Hanford nuclear reservation.

Of interest, the branches were assigned to the two research universities, the powerhouses in state higher education politics, even though they were not designed to look much like research university campuses. Rather, the branches were specifically designed to meet the identified access needs of their regions without many other "frills." In particular, owing mainly to strenuous lobbying by the community college system and private institutions, the branches have been limited to enrolling only upper division students—the idea was to serve community college transfers and older students seeking to complete degrees—and providing certain master's programs in applied fields, such as business, teacher education, nursing, and computer fields, serving the local market. They have no independent research mission and only a limited set of majors, thus few of the characteristics of full service research universities. The branch campuses were set in motion by the 1989 legislature but, ever mindful of the uncertainties of state revenues, not before it cut back the HECB's enrollment projections, slowed the pace of planning, and provided limited funding for the first biennium in carefully controlled dollops.

The Early 1990s Downturn and Its Legacy

The early 1990s turned out very different from what the original HECB master planning had contemplated. As Washington's economy again slowed, higher education endured some mid-term budget cuts in the 1991–1993 biennium, followed by serious stringencies leading to another round of program elimination efforts in the succeeding two biennia. This occurred in spite of the enactment of $650 million in politically costly tax increases advocated by a newly elected Democrat governor, Michael Lowry, in 1993. Also, tuition was hiked annually by figures in the 10 to 15 percent range between 1991–1992 and 1994–1995 and, significantly, by the end of this period the institutions were permitted to retain their tuition revenues for the first time. Yet higher education faculty and other salaries were frozen for 2.5 years beginning January 1, 1993, and state appropriations actually declined in 1993–1995 compared to the previous biennium. Facing a growing young population knocking at college doors, the legislature insisted on enrollment increases nonetheless and the institutions complied. During the five years between 1990–1991 and 1995–1996, community and technical college enrollments grew by 17.5 percent to more than 118,000 FTE students, and four-year institutions gained 7.6 percent to just over 78,000 FTE.

Recognizing the need for salary and *funded* enrollment increases by this time, the 1995 legislature provided a one-time salary increase of 4 percent (with nothing in the second year of the biennium) and funding for 1,500 new enrollments in each of the two years, but only after 2.4 percent was cut from already stretched base budgets. The state also negotiated an arrangement whereby institutions would not raise tuition by more than 4 percent annually in this biennium. This meant, in effect, that the institutions cut programs, personnel, and nonsalary items to pay for the salary and mandated enrollment increases. When funds unexpectedly became available, the 1996 legislature added 3,365 more enrollment slots, funded roughly on an average cost basis, and provided one-time funding to start a statewide distance-learning network also targeted to increase access to higher education. But they did not restore the cuts in base budgets.

Thus the results of this period, in terms of both participation gains (in a state with a fast-growing young population) and especially per-student funding, were a far cry from what the HECB had in mind in the late 1980s. In spite of the enrollment gains, between 1990 and 1995, participation rates in Washington's four-year public institutions fell by 4 percent and the state remained mired at 49th place on this measure.[18] State appropriations per student system-wide plummeted from around $7,000 in 1990–1991 to $5,771 in 1995–1996, or 17.6 percent.[19] For the University of Washington, the decline was even steeper, from $11,708 in 1990–1991 to $9,394 at the nadir in 1996–1997 (−19.8 percent). According to a 50-state data series compiled by the State Higher Education Executive Officers (2004), the state's rank in total higher education expenditures per student (including those from tuition revenue) thus sank from 20th in 1990–1991 to 42nd in 1995–1996.

Perhaps the most important legacy from this period, however, was that of statutory fiscal limitation. When Governor Lowry took office in January 1993, he faced a rapidly deteriorating state revenue picture and had to make difficult choices about how to balance the 1993–1995 biennial budget. Being a fairly liberal Democrat, he chose the path of limited spending cuts and a substantial package of tax increases. This produced a firestorm of opposition and ultimately the passage of a citizen initiative (Initiative 601), placing stringent limitations on the growth of state expenditures and the enactment of new taxes and tax and fee increases. New taxes, such as a possible income tax (Washington is one of a handful of states without a state income tax), and increases in tax rates require a two-thirds vote in each house of the legislature.[20] Fee increases are governed by an inflation index with special procedures for new fees. Tuition increases are not subject to this provision but are separately controlled by the legislature.

Equally important, annual growth in state general fund expenditures is limited to the rate of inflation, as measured by the gross domestic product implicit price deflator, plus the rate of population growth, averaged over the previous three years. This is designed to rein in state spending during periods when Washington's rollercoaster economy is booming. But another effect is that, if expenditures are cut in a recession period, the base for future increases is simultaneously reduced, so there can be no "catch up" increases in the state budget. Also, coming out of a recession, both inflation and population growth rates for the previous years that figure into the formula tend to be depressed so the fiscal stringency is prolonged. In the long run, the I–601 index lags the economic growth rate so that it effectively reduces the size of public expenditures relative to the economy.[21] And it prevents the general fund's growth from keeping up with caseload growth in such fast-growing areas as Medicaid and long-term care, and, at times, prison populations and K12 education enrollments.[22] This clearly puts higher education enrollment growth and funding at grave risk, as support by the state for these other major functions is a matter of mandate of one sort or another.[23] In short, the state has placed itself in a kind of fiscal straitjacket and higher education is the function getting squeezed most tightly.

Boom and Bust in the Late 1990s and Early Twenty-first Century

As is commonly the case, for a few years higher education fared considerably better once the state's revenues belatedly emerged from the trough created by the recession of the 1990s and its aftermath. Governor Gary Locke, a moderate Democrat elected in 1996 when Lowry chose not to run again, made higher education something of a priority but a divided legislature and the state's proven resistance to public spending limited his latitude on the fiscal side. Given the surging population and growth in high school graduates, the priority in the late 1990s boom period continued to be increased enrollments and, for the governor, a new program of "Promise Scholarships" designed to reward with financial aid students from low- and moderate-income families with good grades. In addition, both the governor and legislature emphasized increased accountability measures (Zumeta 2001).

During the five years from 1995–1996 through 2000–2001, when state budgets were improving, enrollments continued to climb: by 8.5 percent in the two-year sector and by 8.6 percent in the four-year colleges and universities, with a considerable share of the latter growth at the UW and WSU branch campuses. The net effect was some modest gains in state funding per student, which increased (in 2005 dollars) from $5,771 in FY 1996 to $6,686 in FY 2001, or 15.9 percent, system-wide, but remained well below the $7,001 peak reached in FY 1991. For the UW, gains in appropriations per student were more modest: from a low of $9,394 in FY 1997 to $10,345 in FY 2001, or 10.1 percent. The 2001 figure remained 11.6 percent below the level reached 10 years earlier.

After the large tuition increases of the early 1990s, predictably there followed an effort to moderate tuition, the other main source of institutions' general revenue. As a share of institutional general revenue, tuition had jumped sharply from 18 percent in FY 1991 to 28 percent by 1995 for the UW and WSU, and by comparable amounts in the other sectors.[24] In nominal dollars, annual tuition and fees for resident undergraduates at the two research universities increased from $1,953 in 1990–1991 to $3,021 in 1995–1996, a compound annual rate of growth of 9.1 percent. Over the more prosperous succeeding five years (1995–1996 to 2000–2001), increases were much more moderate: a compound annual growth rate of 3.9 percent so that these charges stood at $3,649 in 2000–2001.[25]

Washington's economy suffered mightily in the downturn that began in the 2000–2001 period. The state's burgeoning software industry was hurt by the dot-com bust, and the Boeing Company was seriously affected by the decline in air travel after the terrorist attacks of September 2001. According to the Bureau of Labor Statistics, total employment in Washington fell by more than 5 percent between July 1999 and the low point in January 2002, with manufacturing employment particularly hard hit. Jobs grew sluggishly and erratically over the succeeding two years. Until recently, unemployment rates had been among the highest in the nation and state revenues suffered accordingly.

In higher education the results were predictable in the Washington context: continued enrollment growth but fewer state resources, with the cuts partly mitigated by large tuition increases. Between FY 2002 and 2004, the six four-year schools sustained an aggregate cut in state appropriations of 8.6 percent in nominal dollars with somewhat less than half the lost ground made up in the FY 2005 budget. The community and technical colleges' state funding decreased about 1 percent between FY 2002 and 2004, and in FY 2005 they received just 2.2 percent more than in 2002. Nonetheless, enrollments in the four-year institutions increased by more than 5,000 FTE (6.2 percent) in the fiscally difficult three years from FY 2001 to 2004. In the two-year colleges the gain was more than 10,000 FTE (7.9 percent). Tuition again turned sharply upward, with the compound growth rate between 2000–2001 and 2004–2005 for UW and WSU resident undergraduate tuition and fees reaching 7.0 percent.

Total educational expenditures on higher education per student statewide, composed of state appropriations plus tuition revenue, thus again fell by more than $1,000 (–13.3 percent) from its highest point in the late 1990s to FY 2003.[26] In terms of the national rankings on this measure constructed by SHEEO (2004), this pattern was just sufficient for Washington to maintain its place in the low forties among the 50 states from FY 1996 through 1999, after which it slipped further to 45th and below (46th in the latest year available, FY 2003). This is a far cry from the 20th ranking that the state had reached in the mid-1980s and again in FY 1991.

To sum up, in Washington in recent decades, given its odd tax structure[27] and self-imposed fiscal straitjacket, passionate tax resistance, and the difficult-to-control growth in costs of other state functions, higher education has been a priority only for short periods when policymakers felt the state could readily afford it. Within higher education, the main priority has been access, meaning creating more places within the system as cheaply as possible, and to a lesser extent providing financial aid to needy students to allow them to enroll.[28] This pattern has been reinforced by the political influence of the widely distributed community and technical colleges, who, although not particularly well funded per student, have been successful in maintaining their unusually large share of enrollment slots and associated funding even though the serious underparticipation problems of the state are at the upper division and graduate levels.

Since the temporarily successful effort at improving the per-student funding of the system in the early years of the Higher Education Coordinating Board—which was helped mightily by a strong economy and the fact that the baby boom "echo" cohort had not yet come of age—no sustained progress has been made on the "quality" (funding per student) issue. Indeed, in spite of sharp increases in tuition over time, this source of added revenue has, overall, just about offset declines in state funding, in inflation-adjusted, per-student terms. Moreover, in the face of the rapidly growing college-age population, the participation rate of prime age young people (17–22 years) at public four-year institutions is now little better than it was in the late 1980s.[29]

Prospects for the foreseeable future do not look greatly different. Washington's economy is improving, but, like many other states, it is faced with a persistent structural budget deficit; and there is little political interest in touching the "third rail" of Washington politics, the idea of a state income tax. Such a tax is the only obvious source of substantial additional revenue.[30] There has been some talk in recent times of creating a special fund for education (including K12) from existing revenue sources, but an initiative to this end was soundly defeated at the polls in 2004.

The newly elected governor, moderate Democrat Christine Gregoire, has Democrat majorities in both houses of the legislature (a rarity) but faces an uphill political climb from her hairline electoral victory—by 133 votes—in what is believed to be the closest gubernatorial election in American history. Given her past foci in public office and the primary concerns of most of her supporters, higher education might seem unlikely to be a priority issue for her beyond seeking to respond to the continuing pressures to expand student places in the system with limited resources and a special interest in biomedical research. Like many other Democrats, she has generally been a moderate-tuition supporter, which would limit one potential source of increased revenue that universities with considerable market power, like the University of Washington, might otherwise tap.

On the other hand, the UW recently floated a trial balloon calling for consideration in state policy circles of roughly doubling the research universities' resident undergraduate tuition while also providing more student financial aid. Notably, the governor (and the press) did not immediately shoot this down. Also, she recently appointed a blue ribbon commission on education policy and funding, which she chairs, suggesting that she may have learned that education investments are indeed crucial to the state's future. Although K12 issues seem most likely to dominate the agenda of this study group, its existence does provide what Kingdon (1995) calls a "policy window" that might allow higher education to get its case for higher funding priority or access to new revenue sources seriously heard. Absent this, the history recounted here would lead one to anticipate little more for higher education than modest "catch-up" funding as long as the economy continues to improve, accompanied by strong pressure to expand enrollment spaces.

IMPACTS OF THE LONG-TERM SQUEEZE

In this section I examine how the universities, in particular the University of Washington, have responded to the long-term fiscal squeeze described previously. These main themes are identified here: (1) a remarkable commitment to providing as much enrollment access as possible given the schools' circumstances; (2) efforts to avoid increasing student-faculty ratios, although some notable substitutions of nonladder for tenure ladder faculty have been made; (3) difficult, internally troublesome measures taken to ensure that limited salary dollars are used as efficiently as possible to protect faculty quality; (4) a strong commitment to sustaining the UW's crown jewel, its ability to attract federal research dollars; and (5) increasingly strenuous efforts to develop new sources of revenue. These latter measures can influence the ways and the pace at which different areas of the institution develop.

Figures 13.1 through 13.4 depict the trends back to around 1980 in real state appropriations per student, total educational resources per student, tuition levels, and enrollments for the UW, the state's six public universities in aggregate (including Evergreen State College for simplicity), and the 34 community and technical colleges as a group. The cyclical patterns described earlier are apparent as is the long-term real growth in tuition rates. Enrollments grew considerably beginning in the late 1980s but, as has been described, in light of rapid population growth not enough to overcome low participation rates at the upper division and graduate levels. Two-year college enrollments make up a growing share of the

Figure 13.1
General fund state dollars per FTE constant 2005 dollars

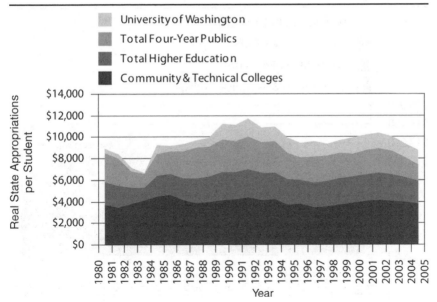

Source: Legislative Evaluation and Accountability Program, State of Washington

Note: Data before FY 1992 may not be completely comparable to current budget data but are the best available.

statewide total. Most important for present purposes, system-wide state appropriations per student are at about the levels of 25 years ago, and total educational
resources per student—in spite of the long-term tuition escalation—are below
early 1990s levels.

For the UW, the patterns are similar but not quite as unfavorable as the aggregate story, owing largely to its ability to boost its tuition revenue when permitted
to do so. Overall, the university's state support per student has declined significantly in real terms, tuition revenue has increased sharply, and in the aggregate,
real total expenditures per student in FY 2004 were at about the level of the early
1990s, down 5.2 percent from the peak reached in FY 2001. Meanwhile, the
university's FTE enrollment has increased from fall 1989 to fall 2004 by about
3,800 FTE at the main Seattle campus, and from zero to about 1,580 FTE at the
Tacoma branch and to 1,250 FTE at Bothell.[31] Although they have grown at
a modest pace, as indicated earlier the state has been much slower to fund branch
campus expansion than was originally planned.

Since 1989, the state has had in place official funding per student targets at
the 75th percentile of state-established peer groups of public universities. The
UW's peer group is called the "HECB 24."[32] In the years since 1989–1990, the

Figure 13.2
Total educational funding* per FTE constant 2005 dollars
*State appropriations plus tuition revenue

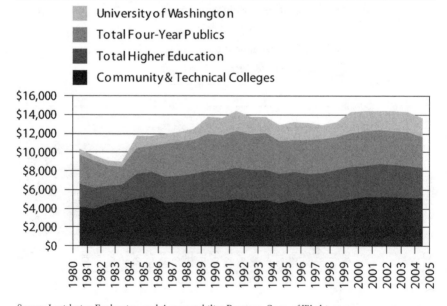

Source: Legislative Evaluation and Accountability Program, State of Washington.
Note: Data before FY 1992 may not be completely comparable to current budget data but are the best
available.

university's total funding per student (including tuition) has not come close to this target, although it remained around the middle of the pack through 1999–2000. By 2002–2003, the latest year for which this comparison is available, the UW's total funding per student had sunk below the 35th percentile of this varied group, ahead of only a few state universities, most of which are not closely comparable to it in assessed quality or graduate education emphasis (Table 13.1). The UW's total funding was more than $4,000 per student and 25 percent below the 75th percentile target. In terms of state support, the picture was even bleaker: the University would need a 65 *percent increase in state funding per student* to reach the 75th percentile target and led only three universities in the official peer group.

The UW and the other public institutions in Washington have generally been quite creative in coping with the difficult task of taking on more students with declining incremental resources, but there are consequences over a long period. The following sections provide evidence related to these coping strategies and their consequences.

Figure 13.3
Undergraduate resident tuition in constant 2005 dollars

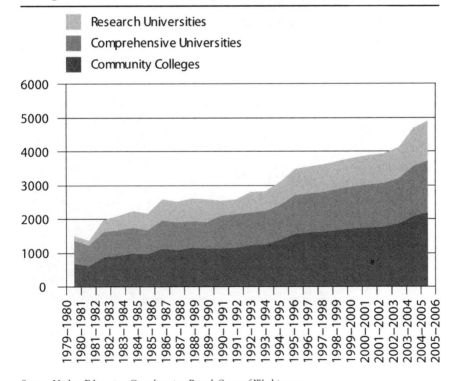

Source: Higher Education Coordinating Board, State of Washington.
Note: Technology fees charged at some institutions are excluded.

Nonresident Students and Tuition

Most of the attention in tuition policymaking for public universities focuses on charges to resident undergraduate students, but hard-pressed institutions may also seek to increase revenue by raising charges to nonresidents[33]—which are typically several times those for residents—and/or increasing the proportion of nonresidents in the student mix.[34] Some flagship public universities enroll as much as one-third or more of incoming freshmen from outside the state. As the flagship university in Washington and the one with the most visible national presence, the UW has by far the greatest scope to use this strategy. It has in fact done relatively little recruiting of students from outside the state. The proportion of incoming freshmen who were *not* Washington residents was in the 15 percent range through most of the 1980s and early and mid-1990s, crept up a few points by 2000–2001 with some additional recruiting efforts, and appears to have stabilized since then in the 18 to 19 percent range. The official target for freshman

Figure 13.4
Actual FTE enrollments

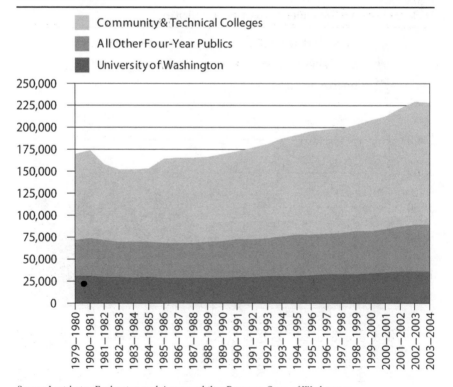

Source: Legislative Evaluation and Accountability Program, State of Washington.

Note: Data before FY 1992 may not be completely comparable to current data but are the best available.

Tabel 13.1
University of Washington State and Total Funding per FTE Compared to HECB 24
Peers, 2002–03

	Total $ per FTE	Appropriations $ per FTE	Percentile Ranking (%)	Rank by Total $/FTE
Cornell-Statutory	42,190	29,534	100.0	1
California-Los Angeles	25,550	19,285	95.8	2
Michigan-Ann Arbor	23,499	9,729	91.7	3
Minnesota-Twin Cities	23,188	15,204	87.5	4
North Carolina-Chapel Hill	22,699	16,221	83.3	5
California-Davis	22,535	17,308	79.2	6
California-San Diego	20,554	14,830	75.0	7
Kentucky	19,370	14,630	70.8	8
Pittsburgh	18,629	7,652	66.7	9
Iowa	18,415	12,044	62.5	10
Virginia	18,312	8,204	58.3	11
Illinois-Chicago	18,095	11,660	54.2	12
Ohio State	18,079	9,566	50.0	13
California-Irvine	17,469	11,896	45.8	14
Hawaii	17,318	13,245	41.7	15
Michigan State	16,947	9,760	37.5	16
Washington	16,388	8,866	34.6	17
Florida	16,140	12,624	33.3	18
Wisconsin-Madison	15,946	9,798	29.2	19
Utah	15,786	10,715	25.0	20
Arizona	15,729	10,928	20.8	21
Missouri-Columbia	15,528	9,554	16.7	22
Texas A&M	15,207	9,738	12.5	23
New Mexico	15,089	11,873	8.3	24
Cincinnati	13,865	7,550	4.2	25

Source: University of Washington, Office of Institutional Studies.

nonresidents is now 19.5 percent.[35] Compared to comparable leading flagship universities, these proportions are not large and the increases very modest. The UW Board of Regents and administration have long been philosophically committed to serving Washington residents primarily, admitting only enough nonresidents to reasonably leaven the student body. More recently, population gains have sharply increased pressures to serve Washington students.

Nonresident tuition rates were set by the legislature until recently and generally tracked resident rates closely during the 1980s and 1990s. Partly in recognition of the need for more revenue, the universities including the UW received authority over nonresident undergraduate and all graduate and professional tuition rates for six years, effective in 2003–2004. University of Washington policymakers have been aggressive in increasing nonresident undergraduate tuition since; the annual increases were 11.5 percent in both 2004–2005 and 2005–2006 compared to 6.4 percent and 7.0 percent, respectively, for resident undergraduates, whose rates are still set by the legislature. Still, the incremental revenue potential here is severely limited by the factors that limit the share of nonresidents. The legislature continues to jealously guard its control over resident tuition, limiting the UW's potential to exploit its considerable market power in this domain.

Faculty Salaries

Since 1990, the official benchmark for average faculty salaries at the University of Washington has been the 75th percentile of its state-sanctioned peer group, the HECB 24. Over time the UW has drifted further behind this benchmark, reaching a low point of 87 percent of the 75th percentile figure in FY 2000 followed by some gain to 91 percent by FY 2004. Of course, these patterns reflect the generally straitened recent circumstances of the peer public universities. Although official statistics relative to leading private universities are not compiled, as such comparisons are considered beyond the pale, the salary gap between private and public universities has been growing steadily in recent years.[36] The other public universities in Washington have also lost ground over this period relative to their official peer groups. Washington State University's average faculty salary was at 82 percent of its peer group's 75th percentile in FY 1990, improved to 87 percent by FY 1994, and fell back to 80 percent by 2004. The pattern for the comprehensive schools is similar, although not quite as unfavorable.[37]

At the University of Washington, annual faculty resignations are up by about two-thirds compared to the late 1990s.[38] The effort to remain competitive with too little funding for faculty salaries has led to a concentration of salary funds on the most market sensitive faculty: new hires at the assistant professor level and faculty who are able to attract and present higher salary offers from competitor universities.[39] The result is salary "compression"—relatively small gaps between average salaries by rank—and also wide differences in salaries at the same rank within departments.[40] Comparing the AAUP survey data for the University of Washington for 1992–1993 and 2004–2005, the ratio of average full professor to average assistant professor salary fell from 1.62 to 1.52, and the ratio of average associate professor to average assistant professor salary fell from 1.14 to 1.09 over the 12 years.

There is a great deal of unhappiness about such conditions within the senior faculty, and this is manifest in Faculty Senate attention to these matters. The major result of this was the adoption of a policy effective in 2000–2001 whereby, short of officially declared financial exigency, most faculty are virtually guaranteed at least a 2 percent base salary increase each year even if this means cuts elsewhere in the institution's budget. Also, the UW administration has recently announced that it will begin to address compression with an allocation to deans for this purpose of about 1 percent of the salary base for 2005–2006.

Student-Faculty Ratios and Faculty Mix

At the University of Washington, the overall student-faculty ratio appears to have changed little over the period for which comparable data are available (fall 1992–2003), remaining at around 9 to 1; however, there has been an appreciable difference in the respective growth rates of different categories of faculty. From fall 1990 to fall 2003, the number of tenure ladder faculty (assistant, associate, and full professors) increased from 2,512 to 3,041 (21.1 percent). Meanwhile, nonladder rank faculty[41] increased from 724 to 1,030, or 42.3 percent, about twice as fast. This produced a gain in the nonladder proportion of total faculty from 22.4 percent in 1990 to 25.3 percent in 2003. The differential pace of growth is at least a cause for concern.

The proportion of undergraduate credits taught by the different categories of faculty at the UW's Seattle campus has changed quite markedly over the most recent nine-year period for which data could be obtained, 1993–1994 through 2002–2003. The proportion of these credits taught by ladder faculty fell by about 15 percent, from 55.2 percent to 46.9 percent. The additional credits were picked up by faculty in the Instructor/Lecturer category (up from 18.6 to 27.8 percent, or nearly 50 percent) and the "Other Faculty" category, up from 9.5 percent to 12.2 percent.[42] The share assigned to graduate assistants *fell* from 16.6 percent to 13.1 percent.

Retention and Graduation Rates

According to a series from the State Office of Financial Management on freshman-to-sophomore retention (spring to fall) for the public four-year universities in aggregate from 1986 to 2003, trends in this measure seem to parallel funding cycles. The system-wide aggregate retention rate improved from 81.5 percent in 1986 to 87.2 percent in 1993, then dropped a bit but remained around 86 percent through 1998 before starting a steeper decline as funding fell off in the early 2000s. This aggregate retention rate had fallen to 83.2 percent by 2003.

For the University of Washington, retention data are available by freshman entry cohort as far back as 1984 (from the UW Office of Institutional Studies).

Retention to the second year for that cohort was 84.1 percent. There was rapid improvement to the 89–90 percent range over the next few years and small further gains so that retention was more than 90 percent for the 2000–2002 entry cohorts. The UW's increased admission selectivity in recent years has likely contributed to these gains, which have come in the face of serious resource limitations.

The UW made a concerted effort to improve its undergraduate degree completion rates beginning in the 1980s. Improvement has been considerable, with six-year bachelor's completion rates increasing from just over 60 percent for the 1984 entry cohort (i.e., by 1990) to nearly 72 percent for the 1993 entry cohort as of 1999. There has been some modest fallback from this peak in the last few years, but the rates for the most recent cohorts remain above 70 percent. It has been difficult to make further improvements in recent years, as the resources needed to fill faculty positions in popular major fields and to apply adequate resources to specific "bottleneck" courses have simply not been available. Indeed, some students are now allowed to graduate with surprisingly few upper division credits, which could point to a quality issue.[43]

Trends and Policies Regarding Community College Transfers

As already described, Washington depends heavily on its two-year colleges to meet demand for higher education and to keep state costs per student low. To make this strategy work at all satisfactorily, there must be capacity to accept would-be transfers at the universities and policies agreed on by all stakeholders to facilitate transfer. Since the mid-1980s, the community colleges and universities have had transfer agreements in place specifying the courses students must take at a community college to be eligible for automatic admission to a university provided their college GPA is 2.75 or greater. In recent years, some of the universities and colleges have jointly funded counselors located at the two-year campuses to assist students in preparing for transfer.

Data maintained by the State Office of Financial Management permit the calculation of trends in the number of community college transfers to the four-year public institutions in Washington and in the ratio of such transfers to the total community college "academic" enrollment in the prior year. (This is considered the best available series indicating students who are taking transferable academic courses applicable to an associate's degree.) The total number of transfers climbed fairly steadily through 1994–1995, but has since fallen off somewhat even though community college academic enrollments have continued to grow. Thus the "transfer rate," as roughly calculated here, increased from about 10 percent in the early 1980s to the 14 to 15 percent range during most of the 1990s before falling off to below 12 percent in 2002 and 2003. Limited capacity in the universities is almost certainly partly to blame.

The UW took in a steadily growing number of transfers for some years, particularly after 1990 when its two branch campuses came on line. Indeed, these and the WSU branches were designed specifically for students who had completed approximately two years of college work, as they do not accept freshmen.[44] After 1996, however, the UW sharply reduced the number of community college transfers it accepted at the Seattle campus,[45] so much so that total transfers to the three UW campuses remain well below the level of the mid-1990s.

The statewide transfer rate is almost certain to decline considerably further as the UW has announced that, owing to its upper division capacity limitations, it will terminate as of fall 2005 its participation in the longstanding agreement to accept all community college transfers who take prescribed general education courses and meet grade standards. As a result, competition for community college transfers to gain admission will become quite stiff even though the UW-Seattle guarantees to accept as many transfers as a proportion of all new entrants as before, that is, approximately 30 percent. It is expected that about half the would-be transfer students who would have been admitted under the old standards will no longer be able to be accommodated at the main campus. Even allowing for planned future growth at Bothell and Tacoma, as a large share of the would-be transfers from community colleges in the state are located in the Puget Sound region, the inability of the UW to accommodate anywhere near all of them probably means that many will not complete bachelor's degrees. This is causing considerable consternation. It is another manifestation of the system's limited resources at the upper division level and of the poor match of the capacity that is available to the geographic location of the needs.

The impending opening of the branch campuses to lower division entrants is one hopeful sign of response to the access crisis but will not directly address the problems at the upper division level. The situation is so dire that the community colleges have been authorized to begin piloting upper division programs in certain applied fields, and these schools are also encouraged to establish partnerships with the comprehensive institutions whereby community college facilities are used to offer upper division courses and programs under the auspices of the comprehensives. Legitimate questions can be raised about the limitations of these types of arrangements for producing bachelor's degrees meeting traditional quality standards, although they are surely better than providing no opportunities at all to place-bound students.

Racial/Ethnic Patterns in Enrollment

In light of the history described, it is worth examining trends in the representation of minority population groups in the state's institutions of higher education. Washington is not a particularly diverse state in terms of the usual categories most associated with historical disadvantage in American society: African Americans, Hispanic Americans, and Native Americans. According to data from the Office of Financial Management(a), among those ages 18 to 24, African Americans are estimated to account for 4.2 percent of the population, Native Americans/Alaska Natives 2.0 percent, and Hispanics 12.3 percent in 2004. The Asian American (7.8 percent of those ages 18 to 24) and Hispanic populations have been growing fairly rapidly. Data from the HECB for fall 1995 and fall 2003 show little change over this interval in the racial and ethnic distribution of enrollments in the state's public four-year institutions (2005, 20). Enrollments in each of the minority categories have grown but only the Asian and Hispanic numbers gained sufficiently to increase their representation among all students. The Asian-Pacific Islander share grew from 9.7 to 11.1 percent of all students over this period, but the Hispanic share gained only from 3.4 to 3.7 percent.

Progress in increasing minority representation was affected by the passage by popular vote in 1998 of Initiative 200, which made it unlawful for state institutions to take race or ethnicity into account in admissions and most financial aid decisions. Because such a change has its primary impact at selective institutions, the University of Washington-Seattle was most affected.[46] African Americans' undergraduate numbers were on a modest declining trend before I-200 but fell much more sharply when it first took effect—by nearly 20 percent between fall 1997 and fall 2000. In the latest years, the figures show some recovery but are still well below pre-I-200 levels. Numbers of Native American students grew during most of the 1990s but have fallen 28 percent since 1997. Hispanics' numbers increased until 1998 but have since fallen off by about 9 percent. Asian American students are much more numerous than the other groups, and their numbers have grown steadily except for a slight decline in 1998. Because total enrollment has been growing, the declines in percentages of the three historically underrepresented groups are even greater than those in the absolute numbers.[47]

The UW has made major efforts in outreach, redesign of admission procedures, and identification of ways to provide financial aid legally to minority students. It seems clear, however, that these measures have at best been able to arrest the decline in minority enrollments and representation precipitated by the previously mentioned policy changes.

Socioeconomic Mix of Enrollments

Tuition has increased very considerably in real terms over the years in Washington's public institutions. As noted earlier, the state has responded to this better than most, at least in the western United States, by supporting need-based student aid fairly generously. The proportion of undergraduates who are Pell grant recipients—a rough indicator of the proportion who are of low-income origin—has grown gradually over the years. According to data from the HECB, for the Washington public four-year institutions as a group, the Pell recipient proportion grew from 26.2 percent in 1991–1992 to 29.9 percent in 2002–2003, suggesting that students of very modest means at least were not being shut out of the system relative to others. For the UW, this proportion has also grown, from 22.2 percent in 1991–1992 to 26.0 percent in 2002–2003.[48] This trend is perhaps somewhat surprising in light of the steep long-term growth in tuition rates and the recent increases in selectivity.

Graduate and Professional Education Trends and Their Broader Impacts

Graduate education is a major emphasis of Washington's two research universities by virtue of their basic mission. It gets much less emphasis at the four comprehensive institutions, although all have several hundred graduate students at the master's level. In an era of great pressure to expand undergraduate enrollments but limited state support, it is notable that the two research universities both have increased their graduate enrollments significantly. At the UW, the rate of increase since 1991–1992 has been just slightly greater than that of undergraduates (22 percent vs. 20 percent), but at WSU graduate enrollments have grown at a much faster pace (64 percent compared to 15 percent). Thus, in 2002–2003, UW enrolled 26,087 FTE undergraduates and 10,876 FTE graduate students, whereas WSU had 15,892 undergraduates and 4,418 graduates. The growth in graduate students is not surprising given the earlier mentioned relative underdevelopment of graduate education in the state. Also, research universities are able to teach undergraduates relatively economically, particularly at the lower division level, largely because they use graduate students as relatively inexpensive factors in the education production process while also contributing to the latter's preparation.

Graduate students in the arts and sciences contribute to undergraduate education in this way but not much to the university's fiscal resources via tuition. A high proportion of graduate students in these fields have their tuition covered as part of teaching and research assistant compensation or via university fellowships, so net tuition revenue from this group is relatively small.[49] Graduate students in such fields as law, business, education, public affairs, public health, and the like contribute much less to undergraduate education, for there are few undergraduate programs in which to teach in most of these fields. The large majority of them pursue master's or professional degrees and generally do produce net tuition revenues, as financial aid in these fields is limited.

The UW has sought to take advantage of this latter pattern by acquiring from the state authority, as of 2003–2004, to set graduate and professional tuition and then fairly ambitiously ramping up rates where it believes the market will bear substantial increases. Thus, for example, tuition for state resident law (JD) students was doubled to $13,000 in just two years between 2002–2003 and 2004–2005; for MBA students tuition is planned to increase from $6,285 in 2002–2003 to $17,286 in 2006–2007.[50] Less ambitious plans are also in place for the various health professions schools. Policy discussions are underway about installing similar regimens in other fields, where demand may support substantial increases, and most of the incremental revenue would represent a net financial gain. Complex issues of incentives, the sharing of revenues between affected units and other parts of the institution, and how to monitor and mitigate effects on the student demographic profile remain, however. Potentially, such increased tuition revenue could be a source of significant self-generated funds for some programs as well as allowing for revenue sharing with parts of the university operating in more constrained markets. However, it also has potential for contention, can enlarge perceived inequities, and, if incentives are not managed carefully, can potentially make units less willing to collaborate.

Also of note is that the UW has increasingly turned to the development of new degree programs—mostly graduate-level programs in professional fields— that are financially self-sustaining or even profitable for their units. The central administration encourages this approach and has even reinvented its educational outreach unit to provide risk capital and infrastructure support. Since the late 1990s, several dozen degree programs have been created through UW Educational Outreach to add to a handful of preexisting programs run by individual units. Fully 20 percent of the University's graduate students are now in fee-based degree programs, up from just a few percent 10 years ago. This is beginning to present some internal complexities and tensions in terms of movement of students and faculty across the line between similar self-sustaining and state-subsidized courses. The net revenues from these programs can be a substantial help to units that control them, but generally core arts and science units are less well suited than those in professionally oriented fields to develop them.

Impacts of Research on Undergraduate Education

The University of Washington is the leading public university in the country at acquiring federal R&D and training grants, with a total of more than $756 million in FY 2004.[51] In addition to the academic stature this fact alone brings, the funds are crucial to both scholarly output and the attraction, training, and support of graduate students; but the impacts on undergraduate education are more ambiguous. Although research income has grown more rapidly than other sources—particularly than state support—in gross terms, it is no longer clear that the grant-supported R&D fully pays for itself.

During the past decade or more, the federal government has become increasingly strict and tight-fisted with respect to indirect cost payments,[52] and increasingly federal and other sponsors require matching funds from grant recipients. The indirect cost rates certainly do not fully cover the cost of replacing and upgrading research buildings and facilities. Because these needs must generally be funded from state or, increasingly, private sources, one wonders what the true opportunity costs are in terms of other ends the institution might pursue in seeking such funds and the energies that are poured into the science/grant competition. Another problem is that the cost of keeping up with competitors in the grant-intensive laboratory science fields often requires the university to find resources for costly start-up packages for incoming faculty—some of whom do little or no undergraduate teaching—by leaving vacant faculty positions unfilled. This may be related to the more rapid growth in nonladder (often temporary) faculty positions and the increases in the share of undergraduate teaching by such faculty noted earlier.

Perhaps in part in response to such concerns, the UW has in recent years taken explicit steps to increase participation of undergraduates in faculty research. The university has identified the percentage of undergraduates reporting substantial involvement in such experiences as one of its accountability measures before the state and had managed to increase this proportion from 20.7 percent in the mid-1990s to 24.2 percent by 2002–2003 (University of Washington 2005a). More broadly, the research-oriented environment at such an institution certainly creates opportunities for interested, ambitious undergraduates that cannot be matched by other types of schools. One wonders how the benefits and costs balance for undergraduates overall, however.

Major Investments in Private Funds Development

Finally, it should be noted that, like many other public universities, the UW has made large investments in its capacity for raising private funds.[53] As a result, total private voluntary support to the UW increased from just $6 million in 1977–1978, to $78 million in 1986–1987, and to $311 million by 2002–2003.[54] In just the short period from FY 1998 to 2003, gifts for current use (many for capital construction purposes) increased from 2 to 6 percent of the university's total income, and the institution is currently involved in a $2 billion capital campaign over eight years. To achieve these goals, spending on development activities has more than doubled just since FY 2001, from about $9.4 million to a projected $22.3 million in FY 2005.

Although the returns on investment are impressive, the institution is having some difficulty sustaining the development operation at its new level because general funds are so scarce, endowment returns have been sluggish in recent years, and donors are resistant to taxing schemes to support fundraising. Although certainly valuable, the whole activity has limited immediate benefits for the operating budget, as much of the gift income goes into capital, which the state has also funded poorly in recent years, and endowments that generate modest current returns and are usually for restricted purposes that do not always match the greatest needs.

CONCLUSION

This chapter has sought to recount the essentials of the history of the financing of public higher education in the state of Washington, to understand why things work the way they do in this policy arena, and to examine some of the consequences of the long-term underfunding of the system, especially for the state's flagship university and its students. Policymakers in the UW and the other public institutions in the state have proven themselves resourceful and remarkably dedicated to providing educational opportunities for as many students as possible to the best quality they can produce with the resources available. The quality, by national norms, is certainly not bad and is surprising given the modest public money invested.

It is hard to say definitively that the system is at the brink of a crisis. Yet, as has been shown, the UW finds it increasingly difficult to compete with the Harvards and Michigans of the academic world as salaries slip far behind, temporary faculty have to be substituted for those with a full stake in the institution, and an increasing share of resources must be obtained from sources that have the potential to create distortions, many of which work to the particular disadvantage of undergraduates in the liberal arts. The other public universities in the state appear to be in even worse shape, as they have less market power, fewer alternative sources of revenue, and faculty salaries that are even further behind their peers. In spite of the inadequate funding, the state continues to expect the universities to enroll more students, yet the increased enrollments are at best maintaining the state's low standing in comparative participation rates.

One might expect that this situation must eventually have political and economic consequences. But given Washington's continued attractiveness to already-educated in-migrants, the fact that high school graduate numbers will begin to level off in five years or so, and the deep-seated resistance to tampering with the state's regressive tax structure, a major shift in current patterns will not necessarily occur any time soon. The best hope for a change would be for the new governor to join with the technology and other modern economy business interests in the state—this would be a bipartisan coalition—to seize the issue of higher education investment and its intimate connection to economic and social development as a central one. They could make this the cornerstone for a leadership campaign to do what is necessary to convince the public and elected officials, particularly in the growing urbanized regions, that the tax structure and other revenue capacity of the state must be reexamined and restructured to permit well-planned, future-oriented investments such as in human capital. By broadening the coalition to include other constituencies who would benefit from increased investment and convincing the electorate that the investments are well thought out and will be managed responsibly, it might be possible to create sufficient momentum to overcome the many cultural and structural obstacles to change.

Perhaps Governor Gregoire's new task force on education policy and finance is the first step in this direction. Decisive action would probably need to occur soon enough to catch the early part of the upturn in the economic cycle while the memory of recent deprivation remains fresh. Later, as more or less ample money rolls in for a few years at the peak of the cycle in spite of the existing revenue structure, there will be little incentive to bear the costs of seeking to change it. Also, once the demographically induced surge in demand for higher education levels off about 2010, the impetus for change will be much weaker. A longtime observer must admit to some pessimism that all these stars will line up at just the right time to produce a sea change, but one should never abandon hope. The current alignment does present a fresh opportunity.

NOTES

1. According to the National Science Foundation: http://www.nsf.gov/statistics/profiles/data/cas_ranking.cfm.

2. Shanghai Jiao Tong University Institute of Higher Education, "Top 500 World Universities (1–100)," Shanghai Jiao Tong University, Institute of Higher Education, http://ed.sjtu.edu.cn/rank/2004/top500(1–100).htm.

3. *U.S. News and World Report* http://www.usnews.com/usnews/edu/college/rankings/brief/natudoc/tier1/t1natudoc_brief.php.

4. *U.S. News and World Report* (2004, 96).

5. Higher Education Coordinating Board (2005). This translates to about 138,200 full-time equivalent students.

6. This figure is for fall 2003 and includes public sector enrollments only. If private college enrollments are included the community colleges' share is still 63 percent of the total. In FTE terms, the community colleges' share of public sector enrollments is approximately 61 percent. Calculations are from data at Higher Education Coordinating Board, "Key Facts."

7. Data are from P. Mosqueda, Washington Higher Education Coordinating Board, May 2, 2005.

8. The roots of Eastern date to 1882, Central to 1891, and Western to 1893.

9. See Do (2004) and the literature cited therein.

10. There have been exceptions, notably the period of great system expansion in the 1960s and early 1970s that included the creation of the community college system and Evergreen State College spearheaded by Governor Daniel J. Evans; a short period in the 1970s when the economy was strong and the coordinating board was exceptionally influential and well led by James Furman and then Patrick M. Callan; and a period in the late 1980s under Governor Booth Gardner and Higher Education Coordinating Board Chair Charles Collins that will be described in some detail.

11. Western populism may play a role here: higher education was not a big priority on the frontier, and there remains some skepticism of educated elites in parts of the state and the legislature. This is not unique to Washington of course (Hofstadter, 1962). More generally, the fact that higher education's priority on the macro-agenda of state policymaking waxes and wanes is not altogether surprising in light of research findings on the nature of policy agenda setting (Baumgartner and Jones 1993; Kingdon 1995).

12. Much of the account of the 1980s and early 1990s in this section is drawn from research previously reported in Zumeta (1996).

13. There were also large tuition increases during this period, but at that time all tuition revenue went into the state general fund not to the institutions.

14. This occurred in part because most noncredit enrollments were no longer funded by the state.

15. Efforts by the institutions and their supporters played a crucial role, too; see Zumeta (1996), De Give and Olswang (1999).

16. State appropriations to higher education grew by about 15 percent in the 1987–1989 biennium over the previous one, and by nearly 18 percent in 1989–1991 (Zumeta 1996: 19, data from State Office of Financial Management).

17. Actual enrollments in fall 2004 were 1,250 at the Bothell campus and 1,580 at Tacoma according to data from the State's Legislative Evaluation and Accountability Program.

18. On the other hand, participation rates at the two-year college level, already fifth in the nation, improved during this period and the state's ranking moved up to fourth (Office of Financial Management 2005b).

19. The figures, from the Legislative Evaluation and Accountability Program, are in constant dollars adjusted to 2005 using the GDP implicit price deflator.

20. The legislature has at times voted to temporarily lift the two-thirds majority requirement. With Democrat majorities in both houses, it did so in 2005 (Shannon 2005).

21. The Office of Financial Management estimates that the I-601 fiscal growth factor grows at 85 to 95 percent of the growth rate of personal income (Moore and Lefberg 2005).

22. Ibid.

23. In addition to the well-known spending pressures created by mandated caseload growth and rapid inflation in such areas as health care and criminal justice, Washington's constitution declares that making "ample provision" for "basic education" is the *paramount duty* of the state. In contrast, higher education enrollments and funding levels per student are entirely discretionary.

24. This paralleled a similar jump during the economic downturn of the early 1980s, which was followed by a period of stability in this measure that lasted eight years, 1983–1991.

25. Patterns in the comprehensive and two-year college sectors over these periods were similar.

26. Compared to the highest point reached in FY 1991, total funding per student in FY 2003 was down more than $2,000, or 22.3 percent, in inflation-adjusted terms.

27. Lacking an income tax and with its longstanding estate tax recently declared unconstitutional, the state depends on a high sales tax, a "business and occupations" tax, which is essentially a gross receipts tax on businesses and professionals, a modest statewide property tax, stiff excise taxes, and a motley collection of fees and minor taxes. Taken as a whole, this tax structure is among the most regressive in the country (McIntyre et al. 2003).

28. As of 2002–2003, Washington ranked 13th among the states in state student aid grants provided per enrolled student and was first among the western states (National Association of State Scholarship and Grant Programs 2004, 23).

29. There were gains until 2000, but substantial declines in this measure in the years since. The participation rate of the next older age group (23–29-year-olds) is about where it was in 1980 (Office of Financial Management 2005a).

30. The 2005–2007 state budget provided for $480 million in new revenue via increases in "sin" taxes and a new version of the estate tax limited to large estates. There are predictions that even this limited tax package could lead to something like a replay of the 1993 enactment of Initiative 601 and Republican recapture of the legislature in 1994 that followed the tax increases of 1993.

31. Data are from the State Legislative Evaluation and Accountability Program. A considerable part of enrollment increases in recent years at the main campus have been unfunded by the state entirely—largely the product of an independent institutional commitment to respond to real enrollment demand and also of difficulty in forecasting varying yield rates from those admitted.

32. The HECB 24 consists of all public universities with medical schools in the Carnegie Foundation's (1994) Research I category. Some of the schools in this group are far below the UW in terms of standing in assessments of graduate program quality, extramural research support, and even proportion of graduate students.

33. The UW has recently sought to increase revenue from nonresident students somewhat by tightening the standards for establishing residency to make them more similar to nearby states.

34. Increasing the proportion of nonresidents may also serve academic goals by adding to the geographic and other diversity dimensions of the student body and, if the nonresident applicant pool is strong or can be improved, improving the average academic profile.

35. Data are from Timothy Washburn, Associate Vice-President for Enrollment, May 5, 2005.

36. See Ehrenberg (2004, 21). Full professor salaries at the University of Washington stood at around the 54th percentile among doctoral institutions in the 2004–2005 AAUP salary survey published in *Academe* (Curtis 2005). This was a considerable decline from the 60th percentile where they had been in 1992–1993. UW associate and assistant professors' rankings improved somewhat over this period, however. Compared to the leading private universities with which the university competes for faculty, as represented by the 95th percentile of the doctoral institutions' distribution, UW salaries had fallen as follows over these years: professor, from .784 to .726; associate professor, from .826 to .774; assistant professor, from .868 to .861. (Author's calculations from data published in Hamermesh, 1993, and Curtis, 2005).

37. The official comparison group for WSU is all public land grant universities classified as research universities by Carnegie (categories 1 and 2) with veterinary schools. The comparison group for Central, Eastern, and Western Washington Universities is all public colleges and universities classified as comprehensives (category 1).

38. Calculated from data in University of Washington, 2003–2004 Faculty Status Report.

39. As state funds for meeting competitive offers have recently been very limited, the standards for receiving such support from the central UW retention pool have become increasingly strict. Units can fund retention offers from internal funds, but this is difficult and contentious in a period of extended budgetary stringency. The university is also experimenting with ways of using extramural research funds to augment base salaries for those with grant support, because the UW is a leader in such funding; however, these funds are distributed unevenly across disciplines.

40. There are also many cases of lower rank faculty with higher salaries than their higher-ranking peers, usually because the former were more recently hired, a particularly vexing issue for morale and intraunit relations.

41. Included as nonladder faculty are the following titles: Lecturer Full-time, Lecturer Part-time, Senior Lecturer, Teaching Associate, Artist and Senior Artist in Residence, and Acting Instructor.

42. Other faculty includes the following titles: Clinical Faculty, Affiliate/Adjunct Faculty, Research Faculty, Emeritus/Retiree, Visiting Faculty, and Other Teaching Faculty. The changes over time were calculated by the author from "Faculty Teaching Workload By Faculty Home Department and Course Level" data provided by the UW Office of Institutional Studies.

43. A recent UW internal analysis shows a number of undergraduate majors where recent graduates have accrued fewer than 40 percent of their credits at the upper division or graduate level and some are below 30 percent. The proportion of all undergraduate credits that were at the upper division level fell by 2.3 percentage points, or nearly 5 percent, to 44.4 percent between 1993–1994 and 2002–2003 (author's calculations from "Faculty Teaching Workload").

44. This unusual arrangement was built into the branch campus designs at the insistence of the community college system, and to a lesser extent private colleges, who feared competition from more "full-service" universities. Under the current extreme enrollment pressures, the legislature agreed in 2005 to permit certain of the UW and WSU branches to begin accepting small numbers of freshmen and sophomores in autumn 2006.

45. The university increased the size of its freshman intake at Seattle at this time and also responded to what turned out to be a temporary decrease in transfer applicants.

46. The figures reported in this paragraph are from the University of Washington, Office of Institutional Studies. The latest year available at the time of writing was fall 2002.

47. These trends may also reflect the impact of the decline in community college transfer students at the Seattle campus described earlier.

48. The University of Washington is now engaged in an effort to more comprehensively identify the distribution of its student body by family income, but for now nothing more than the Pell grant recipient percentage is available.

49. Where outside grants or fellowships pay the tuition bill, there is net revenue to the university. In the case of grant-funded research assistants at the University of Washington, the grant pays the resident portion of tuition while the nonresident portion is waived.

50. Resident tuition rates in these fields are still projected to be below peer norms, however.

51. University of Washington (2005c). Including nonfederal support, the total was more than $953 million.

52. The UW's basic indirect cost rate is a comparatively modest 51.6 percent of direct costs, although this will shortly be increasing.

53. The other public institutions in Washington, including the community colleges, have also increased their fund-raising efforts, but none has nearly the revenue potential of the UW.

54. University of Washington fiscal reports cited in Shanahan (2005, 6). The other data cited in this paragraph come from the same source.

CHAPTER 14

Consequences of a Legacy of State Disinvestment: Plunging State Support Reduces Access and Threatens Quality at University of Wisconsin System Institutions

David W. Olien

Wisconsin's public university system has struggled with serious financial problems since its creation in the early 1970s. Although before the merger of two systems into one in 1971, Wisconsin institutions enjoyed the same golden era of increased funding and enrollment growth as peers around the nation, an examination of the University of Wisconsin (UW) System financial situation reveals that since the merger, the pattern has been one of gradual downward trends in state support, interrupted by brief bursts of state investment followed by base budget funding reductions.

The boom and bust cycles of public investment that generally characterized public institution finance nationally were less pronounced on the boom side and more pronounced on the bust side in Wisconsin. Wisconsin institutions did not gain in public support in the 1990s when the economy was booming but rather faced two major budget reductions as state priorities shifted to K12 education, prisons, tax relief, and Medicaid. The reductions that occurred in the last decade left the UW System struggling to preserve quality while demands for access increased. Between 1993–1994 and 2003–2005, the system sustained actual net base reductions 5 of 12 years. The UW System's share of state tax dollar investments began declining in 1975 when it totaled 13.7 percent with occasional recovery until 1988 when the system share of the state budget began a steady decline from 12.1 percent of state tax expenditures to 8.27 percent in 2005. State spending on prisons, aid to local schools, and medical assistance increased substantially over the period.[1]

The latest reductions in state support coupled with substantial increases in tuition with no commensurate increase in state funded financial aid has reduced access to the system by students from lower income families while overall enrollment has increased. Furthermore, the latest reductions in state support, $250 million for the 2003–2005 biennium—the largest in the system's history—has put significant pressure on the institutions and is reflected in a dramatic loss of faculty positions and concern about eroding academic quality in the system. Although a 37.5 percent tuition increase for the biennium helped the institutions absorb the shock of the reduction, $100 million in reductions were not offset with tuition, causing what outgoing University of Wisconsin System President Katharine Lyall called a "serious reduction in services to UW undergraduates. In effect UW students were paying more for less," Lyall told the UW System Regents in her final remarks to the regents in August 2004 adding: "I'm worried about the future. Our constituents are telling us that cracks are appearing in the foundation."[2] Reflecting on what she called a 10-year trend, Lyall expressed concern that reductions in numbers of faculty had over a decade reduced faculty-student contact by 20 percent so that nearly 40 percent of UW System student credit hours are now delivered by adjunct faculty and graduate assistants.

Lyall expressed special concern about declines in the system's service to lower income students. "The rather large decline in low and moderate income students is not acceptable for a public university that takes its public purpose seriously."[3] UW-Madison Chancellor John Wiley in November 2003 writing in Madison magazine warned that: "More than a decade of state budget cuts and partially offsetting tuition increases have left the base operating budgets of Wisconsin's public higher education systems in the worst condition since the Great Depression. Access to, and affordability of, the university system are already endangered at precisely the time when the Wisconsin economy needs more high-paying jobs and a more highly educated workforce."[4]

UW System accountability measures released in March 2005 reveal slippage in system retention rates, concerns about funding for technology, and a continuing decline in service by system institutions to nontraditional students. The report notes: "State funding has been more volatile in recent years."[5] However, pointing to a serious long-term problem, the report states that, "When adjusted for inflation, State GPR (General Purpose Revenues) appropriations declined substantially from 1974 through the early 1980's."[6] From 1974 through 2005, the system's tax supported appropriation dropped from over half the budget to slightly more than a quarter, declining from 52 percent to 26 percent while tuition and fees increased from 13 percent to 21 percent and gifts and grants increased from 20 percent to 35 percent of the total system budget. Program revenues of the UW institutions rose from 15 percent to 18 percent of the total budget during the period. Tax support dropped two percentage points for the system budget in the FY 2005 fiscal year, the largest decline in the system's history.[7]

STATE SUPPORT PLUNGES

The UW proportion of the state budget dropped from being 13.7 percent of the state budget in the biennium ending in 1975 to 8.4 percent for the biennium ending in 2005.[8] Using the measure of state support per $1,000 of personal income in Wisconsin, state support over the period dropped by more than half from $14.25 per $1,000 of personal income to approximately $6.25 per $1,000 of personal income.[9]

A review of Wisconsin tax support per full-time equivalent (FTE) student for the UW System reveals that between 1994–1995 and 2004–2005, the annualized rate of change was 0.80 percent compared with tuition increases of 10 times that amount at 8.08 percent.[10] At the beginning of the period, the state support per FTE student was $6,800, a number that peaked at $8,111 in 2002–2003 before dropping to $7,361 in FY 2004–2005, a reduction in state support of 9.25 percent in the 2003–2005 period.[11] Demonstrating the instability of state funding over the decade, the support per student figure of $6,800 in 1994–1995 declined to $6,722 in 1995–1996 and to $6,670 the subsequent year before increasing in 1997–1998 to $6,907, with subsequent modest increases until the 2002–2003 peak of $8,111.[12]

The declining state support has been only partly offset by tuition increases. Instructional costs have grown less than inflation over the last 14 years, but the state contribution to instructional costs has declined from 69 percent to 53 percent while the student share rose sharply from 31 percent to 47 percent system-wide.

Adjusted for inflation, the state contribution for instructional costs has declined 34 percent for the period while UW System enrollments grew 7 percent.[13] The result is a widening gap between Wisconsin support per student and the national average, with Wisconsin now falling more than $1,000 below the national average.[14]

Although Wiley in his November 2003 comments was generally upbeat about the state of UW-Madison, stating that "By almost every measure, the UW-Madison is entering the 21st century in admirable condition," he warned that "A continued decline in state support could bring it all crashing down." Wiley noted that the UW-Madison portion of the budget had plunged as state support for the entire system eroded over three decades of state support for the campus has declined from 43 percent of the budget in 1973 to less than 21 percent in 2003. Wiley also said that between 1991 and 2003, the campus had experienced a net reduction of $33.4 million when adjusted for costs such as legislatively approved wage adjustments and increased utility costs.[15]

Wiley's concern was reflected in the 1999 UW-Madison accreditation review by the North Central Association of Colleges and Schools, which has accredited the institution since 1913. Although the report praised the campus, saying it "continues to rank among the nation's (and the world's) leading research universities," the team labeled UW-Madison "an institution at risk," similar to other public higher education institutions.[16] While spotlighting many positives including what it saw as "a substantial enhancement of the quality of the undergraduate experience", the team expressed alarm about what it called "Continuing stringently limited state funding support." The state funding limits came at a time when the accreditation team said great universities were facing new "sometimes unprecedented, demands and challenges."[17]

Commenting on its impressions gathered during the on-site team visit, the report said it "detected repeatedly with a variety of UW-Madison groups and individuals what might be characterized as a muted but widespread angst and uncertainty about whether the principles and practices that have made the University great can continue to keep it great in a changing local, state, and global competitive environment."[18] The report cites concerns over "continuing constriction of state funding" and a lack of administrative flexibility caused by "an uncommonly high level of state-policy-related regulation and bureaucratic constraints accompanied by a high and counter-productive degree of administrative inflexibility."[19]

In a section of the report intended as advisory, team members suggested a "redoubled" effort to improve the state funding of the campus, observing that "Wisconsin's leaders may not fully appreciate and understand that their university has made their state a luminous feature on the global map of academic excellence, that is to say, the state's premier asset in the new and very competitive global knowledge-based economy." Recognizing some constraints on the state's ability to increase its investment in the campus, the accreditation team stated that "other states have shown that 'where there's a will there's a way.'"[20]

DRAMATIC TUITION INCREASES

Like most other public institutions, UW System campuses have increased undergraduate tuition significantly during the last decade. With the drop in state tax support, students at all UW institutions are picking up a dramatically increased percentage share of instructional cost. For students from lower income families, the increases have been particularly dramatic as a percentage of family income. Average UW tuition has increased from 13 percent of family income in the lowest quartile to 33 percent between 1980 and 2003. By comparison, tuition represents only 3 percent of income for families in the highest quartile.[21]

UW-Madison began the decade charging $2,415 annual for tuition. Tuition increases over the decade ranged from a low of zero percent one year to a high of 18.2 percent in 2003–2004, an increase of 114 percent over the decade. The percentage of instructional cost being paid by UW-Madison undergraduates increased from 31.4 percent in 1994–1995 to 52.3 percent a decade later in 2004–2005, the first year UW-Madison undergraduates were paying more than half of the instructional cost.[22]

UW-Milwaukee undergraduates began the decade paying $2,359 and with similar changes over the decade as Madison tuition ended up paying $5,138 in 2004–2005, more than doubling undergraduate tuition. The share of instructional cost borne by UWM students increased from 33.3 percent in 1994–1995 to 58.5 percent in 2004–2005.[23]

Students attending the University of Wisconsin System's four-year comprehensive institutions experienced slightly less growth in the share of the instructional cost they picked up, with the percent increasing from 31.3 percent in 1994–1995 to nearly half at 49.5 percent for 2004–2005. Tuition at the comprehensive institutions increased from $1,916 in 1994–1995 to $4,000 in 2004–2005, an increase over the period again of more than 100 percent.[24]

The lowest tuition institutions, the two-year UW Colleges, saw their share of instructional cost nearly double from 30.3 percent to 57.3 percent. In 1994–1995, students paid 30.3 percent ($1,568 annually) of their instructional cost; in 2004–2005, they paid 57.3 percent ($3,700 annually). The tuition charged students attending the two-year campuses increased again by more than 100 percent.[25]

Even with sizable tuition increases during the last decade, Wisconsin undergraduate tuition remains below tuition at many peer institutions. For 2004–2005, UW-Madison undergraduate tuition ranked eighth among the nine public Big Ten institutions, $1,585 from the public Big Ten midpoint. The gap between Madison tuition and the most expensive Big Ten institution—The University of Michigan was nearly $3,000 annually. Madison tuition was $230 more than the next lowest institution and $880 less annually than the sixth most expensive Big Ten campus. Iowa undergraduate tuition was lowest in the Big Ten for the period at $464 below the Madison level.[26]

Students attending UW-Milwaukee pay tuition that ranks 11th among the 15 UWM peer institutions, $1,028 from the peer midpoint. UWM tuition was $3,271 below the peer leader, Temple University, and $76 less than the institution that compared to UWM had the next highest in-state tuition, SUNY-Buffalo.[27]

For students attending the UW comprehensive institutions, their average tuition was $902 below the midpoint of its 34 peer institutions, and $3,691 below the most expensive peer, the University of Minnesota-Duluth. UW comprehensive campus average tuition was $30 less than Indiana University-South Bend, which ranked immediately above them in the peer group.[28]

Dramatic tuition increases for out-of-state students have not brought to the UW institutions the resources state government believed would result when the governor and legislature increased out-of-state student tuition by a greater amount than system and campus officials believed was practical because the number of out-of-state students paying the higher tuition has declined at virtually all UW institutions. The number of undergraduates coming to UW System institutions from out-of-state dropped approximately 8 percent between 2001 and 2004 alone, leaving the campuses with significantly fewer resources than they were counting on from the difficult 2003 budget. The number of new entering freshmen coming from out-of-state system-wide has declined by 15 percent from the 2001–2002 academic year to 2003–2004, creating an additional shortfall that will continue moving through the pipeline and potentially growing if the trend continues.[29]

Out-of-state students among new freshmen enrolling at UW-Madison, for example, peaked at 1,511 in 2001–2002, dropping to 1,406 in 2003–2004. The percentage of students being admitted from in-state actually dropped from 64.4 to

63.3 percent as total UW-Madison undergraduate enrollment declined from 6,095 to 5,579 for the period. Although there were 105 fewer out-of-state undergraduates in 2003–2004, there were 415 fewer Wisconsin residents. Students admitted from states with reciprocal admission agreements were steadily increased from 637 to 641. For the decade, however, the percentage of Wisconsin residents admitted as new freshmen to UW-Madison changed relatively little, moving from 64 percent in 1994–1995 up to a high of 65.5 percent in 1997–1998 before declining to 63.3 percent in 2003–2004. Madison experienced its largest growth percentage wise from students from states with tuition reciprocity, but even that number dipped. In 1994–1995, 460 students enrolled under reciprocity, a number that grew to a high of 674 in 1999–2000 and then dipped in 2003–2004 to 641 students.[30] Given that out-of-state and reciprocity students pay tuition that is greater than cost of instruction, the loss meant UW-Madison had less revenue to support its in-state students. Also, because of a longtime state government budget practice, the difference between the costs paid by reciprocity students over and above the in-state rate does not accrue to the UW institutions but instead goes to the general state treasury.

System-wide, the lost revenue because of the loss of out-of-state students was also significant. Out-of-state student growth once represented an income stream, growing from 9,955 in 1994–1995 to 10,618 in 2001–2002, before the large tuition increases became effective and undergraduate headcount for the group declined to 9,800 in 2003–2004. System-wide the number of reciprocity students enrolled grew from 9,780 to 12,542 for the decade, but again the increased income went to the state treasury as opposed to the UW System.[31]

INSUFFICIENT STATE FINANCIAL AID PROGRAM

Wisconsin's state financial aid program was designed for a low-tuition environment, an environment that prevailed until the 1990s. As tuition increased, the failure of the state of Wisconsin to increase financial aid left a glaring disparity between the Wisconsin aid program and those of other Midwestern states. Wisconsin offers far less financial aid to lower income students than surrounding states. The maximum state grant award of $1,677 is less than a third of the other Midwestern states, which averages $5,400. The average state financial aid award for Wisconsin students who actually received grants was $1,244 in 2003–2004 compared with a Midwest average of $2,115.[32]

In addition to a significantly smaller grant, far fewer Wisconsin students received grants than in other Midwestern states, with only 24.8 percent of UW students receiving state financial aid compared with an average of 32.2 percent in the other states. A review of the 10-year change in funding for state aid grants in all states reveals Wisconsin's funding for grants increased only 44 percent of the average of the states.[33] UW System officials are continuing to seek an increase in financial aid grants to match proposed tuition increases. Concern over a decline in lower income students as a percentage of all UW system students led the system to seek funding for a new financial aid grant program for resident undergraduates with incomes below 150 percent of the poverty level, or the corresponding family contribution, to in effect hold harmless these students from proposed tuition increases.[34] The proposal was not funded in the Governor's FY 2005–2007 budget.

ACCESS TO SYSTEM REDUCED FOR LOWER INCOME STUDENTS

In Wisconsin, accessibility to potential students from all income levels has for decades been a widely shared and accepted state public policy goal. A 1995 Study of the UW System in the twenty-first century outlined goals of "Preserving and Enhancing Access to Quality and Keeping College Affordable." Noting the stresses of funding reductions, however, the UW Regents stated: "When faced with a choice between educational quality and access, the UW System must choose to maintain educational quality."[35] Six years later in 2001, regents, in a move that sparked political controversy, froze undergraduate admissions at all UW institutions in response to legislative consideration of a large base budget reduction. The tactic was successful, as the legislative proposal was withdrawn and the UW System institutions then proceeded with admitting students for fall.

Regents had addressed student cost issues in 1995 by stating: "The Board of Regents Affirms the current tuition policy: tuition increases should be moderate and predictable. State-funded financial aid should increase at a rate no less than the rate of tuition increases and should also reflect increases in the number of aid-eligible students."[36] In 2004, UW Regents in an additional study, "Charting a New Course for the UW System," echoed the findings of their colleagues a decade earlier emphasizing, "maintaining the high quality of a UW education. keeping UW education open and affordable."[37]

Among recommendations of the 2004 Regent study was that the state stabilize state support for higher education. After reviewing "all potential revenue streams," the Regent study noted that "Each potential revenue source has serious limitations and is not consistent with supporting undergraduate education." Regents called for an increase in student financial aid "to ensure access for students of all income levels" The regents spotlighted "a disturbing trend: fewer and fewer low-income students are enrolling in UW institutions. Specifically, 37 percent of new UW freshmen from the lowest two family income quartiles enrolled in 1992. Ten years later that measure was 30 percent."[38]

In 2003, in remarks to the system's regents, Joni Finney, of the National Center for Public Policy and Higher Education, noted: "Over the last few years Wisconsin has slipped in low-income participation declining by 15 percentage points—the fourth largest loss in the nation moving from 43 percent college participation rate in 1998 to 28 percent in 2001. The national average for the decline in participation rates by low-income students for the period was 3.5 percent."[39]

An additional study completed in November 2004 revealed a dramatic drop in access for students admitted as freshmen at UW institutions from the two lowest family income quintiles, from 36.4 percent of UW students to in 1992 to 30.3 percent in 2003, even while overall enrollment within the system surged from 125,097 to 135, 653 undergraduates in 2003–2003. Enrollments from students from families in the upper two family income quintiles grew from being 38.5 percent of students to 45 percent. Students from families in the middle family income quintile also dropped between 1992 and 2002, from 25.1 percent of enrollments to 24.7 percent.[40] The study also revealed a growing disparity between the median family income of students attending the various campuses compared with Madison students. Median family income for new Madison freshman in 2003 was $71,000, a figure $18,000 above their counterparts attending UW two-year institutions and significantly above family incomes of families attending the comprehensive four-year institutions as well.[41]

For UW-Madison, freshmen students from the lower two quintiles dropped from 24.5 percent of the student body in 1992 to 20.7 percent in 2003. Madison enrollments from the upper two income quintiles increased from 54.6 percent to 58.1 percent for the same period. Freshmen coming from the middle quintile showed an increase from 20.8 percent to 21.2 percent for the period.[42] Chancellor Wiley decried the change: "The median family income in Wisconsin is a little over $45,000 per year. For this year's new freshmen at UW-Madison, it is nearly $90,000 per year. Yet, the distribution of brains, talents, ambition, and creativity is independent of family income. We ignore that fact and freeze out the children of average- and low-income families at our great peril. No society is rich enough to waste any of these assets."[43]

UW-Milwaukee suffered the greatest loss of lower income quintile enrolling students, with the enrollment dropping from 38.8 percent in 1992 to 29.2 percent of new freshmen in 2003. UWM's share of the freshmen from the upper two quintiles rose from 36.8 percent to 47.7 percent for the time period while new freshmen from the middle quintile dropped from 24.4 percent to 23.1 percent. Median family income for entering freshmen at UWM in 2003 was $62,000. UW comprehensive institution campuses experienced similar declines in access to families from the lowest income quartiles with the exception of UW-Superior, which saw an increase in the percentage of freshman students coming from these quintiles from 42.7 percent to 44.8 percent for the time frame. Median family incomes for entering freshmen ranged from $67,000 at UW-La Crosse to $49,000 at UW-River Falls. For the lower cost two-year institutions, access to students from the lower two quintiles declined as well, demonstrating that the large tuition increases were also affecting these students. In 1992, 43 percent of new freshmen came from families in the lowest two income quintiles; in 2003, that figure dropped to 38.3 percent. Students in the middle quintile also declined while students in the upper two quintiles made up an increased share of new freshmen, growing from 28.1 percent to 33.8 percent. Median family income at the two-year institutions for new freshmen was $53,000 in 2003, lower than all but two of the comprehensive institutions.[44]

ACCESS TO UW SYSTEM REDUCED FOR NONTRADITIONAL STUDENTS

At a time when nationally an increasing percentage of college students are nontraditional, access to the UW System has dramatically reduced for these students. The lower numbers of nontraditional students are particularly startling in that they have occurred at all UW institutions. System-wide, in 1994–1995, 28,732 nontraditional undergraduate students were enrolled compared to 20,221 in 2004. At UW-Madison nontraditional undergraduate enrollment declined over the same period, from 4,361 to 2,264; overall undergraduate enrollment grew from 27,907 to 29,728. The largest decline came in the years between 1994 and 1998, when Madison nontraditional undergraduate numbers declined by more than 1,000 students. Other UW institutions experienced similar declines, with only one institution experiencing growth in the number of nontraditional students from 1994 to 2004. The numbers of nontraditional students declined for the period even at the UW two-year institutions, historically a relatively open access point for nontraditional students, where the numbers for the period dropped from 4,207 to 3,783 students. The decline came at a time when the two-year institutions actually increased overall enrollment from 9,821 students to 12,453. Although the system's enrollment management plan aims at increasing access for nontraditional students, enrollment of nontraditional students has been dropping each academic year since 2001–2002.[45]

Enrollments of nontraditional graduate students has also declined system-wide, from 12,161 in 1994 to 9,568 in 2004. At UW-Madison the decline has been from 4,794 nontraditional graduate students to 3,539 for the same period. Only 2 of the 13 system campuses offering graduate programs saw growth in the numbers of nontraditional students, but increases at both campuses were substantial.[46]

SOME INSTITUTION RETENTION NUMBERS SLIP

The UW System is seeing retention of students between the first and second years decline for the first time after a period of significant improvement. After a decade of consistent improvement where second-year retention rates increased from 76.6 percent in 1994 to 80.3 percent in 2002, the retention number dropped back to 79.7 percent in 2003.[47] The decline was not uniform across the system, however. At UW-Madison the number slipped marginally from 92.5 percent to 92.1 percent, which translates to 21 students.[48] The decline at UW-Madison is small enough that it is not possible to view the decline as statistically significant. Even with the decline, UW-Madison continues to retain at a level above its 92 percent target. Retention of students of color on the campus improved from 86.4 percent in 1999 to 90 percent for fall 2003.[49] Also, six of the four-year institutions saw continued improvement in retention rates, but the decline in the other seven was large enough to offset the increases when the system-wide statistics are examined.[50] Some decline in retention may well be caused by factors that the

UW institutions cannot influence. During the period, many Wisconsin reserves and national guard units have been called up for service in Iraq, and students at Madison and other institutions have been forced to interrupt their academic careers to fulfill military service obligations. UW campuses have exempted these students from the large tuition increases that have occurred while they have been in military service.

SIGNIFICANT REDUCTION IN FACULTY RANKS

System-wide, faculty contact with undergraduate students has dropped 20 percent in the last decade. Adjunct faculty and graduate assistants now teach nearly 40 percent of all student credit hours in the system, up from 30 percent a decade ago.[51] Since initiation of enrollment management system-wide in 1987–1988, the ratio of total FTE enrollment to total instructional FTE has remained at approximately 17 to 1 Hiring of non-tenure–track instructional staff has kept instructional workload relatively unchanged for the period 1996–2002. In 2003, there were more than 600 fewer UW faculty (6,072) compared with 1993 (6,673). By contrast, the numbers of instructional academic staff grew during the same time period, from 1,802 to 2,838. During this period, UW-Madison lost 144 faculty positions or 6.5 percent of the total even while enrollment grew. Between 1990 and 2003, adjusted for inflation, the state contribution to total UW System instructional costs has declined 34 percent while enrollment grew 7 percent (8,742 FTE).[52]

SYSTEM STRUGGLES TO OFFER COMPETITIVE SALARIES

Most UW institutions have lost significant ground against their peers in salaries in recent years. UW System salary data focus on four institutional peer groups, those for UW-Madison, UW-Milwaukee, the UW comprehensive institutions, and finally the UW's 13 two-year undergraduate institutions. Wisconsin institutions have been challenged for decades when it comes to offering competitive salaries comparable to peer institutions for faculty, academic staff, and administrative salaries. During the 1980s, concern over a "brain drain" of top faculty led to adoption by the governor and legislature of two pay plans in 1985–1987 and 1989–1991 to help the institutions "catch up" with peers. The disparity in 1985 was so wide that an adjustment of 15 percent in salaries was approved for UW-Madison and for the UW two-year campuses with a 10 percent amount for faculty at the UW four-year campuses.[53] Four years later, a smaller "catch-up" pay plan of half that amount was approved. The twin actions kept the institutions relatively competitive until the state budget of 1995, which began a trend of widening the gap between the UW System institutions and their public institution peers. That gap continued to grow until it was exacerbated when budgets in 2003–2004 provided no pay adjustments and 2004–2005 provided a modest 1 percent adjustment.[54]

The salary situation has become especially critical because of the aging of the UW faculty and staff, making retirement an attractive option for many individuals. In a report to the UW System Regents in the fall of 2004, System Associate Vice President George Brooks noted, "with 34 percent of our faculty retirement eligible, we have a situation where faculty can retire and receive larger post-retirement increases than their increases if they remain working for the UW System. The institutions are increasingly challenged to keep pace both in terms of matching outside offers and recruiting new faculty to replace those who leave or retire."[55]

UW-Madison, which carefully monitors its success at retaining faculty with outside offers, has seen its percentage of faculty with outside offers retained decline significantly. In 1999–2000, the campus successfully retained 73 percent of those faculty it attempted to keep by offering counter-offers. By 2003–2004, that figure had dropped to 51 percent. In addition, the numbers of UW-Madison faculty receiving offers from other institutions nearly doubled from 51 in 1999–2000 to 98 in 2003–2004.[56]

UW-Madison has suffered nearly a doubling of the gap with its public peers from FY2000–2001 when it trailed the public peers by an average of 2.45 percent to a 4.92 percent deficit in 2003–2004. In an effort to protect its competitive position, the campus has focused on keeping associate and assistant professor salaries more competitive to stay $3,400 and $1,300 ahead, respectively, of the peer group median. Madison salaries at the professor rank at the end of 2003–2004, however, trailed the peer median by $7,000. In fact UW-Madison full professor ranks salaries ranked 11th of the 12 public peer institutions the UW System uses to benchmark salary averages. Madison trails its Midwestern peers the University of Michigan, University of Illinois, and Ohio State University by $21,600, $10,800, and $7,300, respectively, at the full professor rank. UW System data reveal that Madison has fallen 7.28 percent behind the median of its public peers.[57] UW-Madison salaries at the associate professor level in 2003–2004 trail Michigan by $7,700 while slightly ahead of Illinois by $1,300 and Ohio State by $7,400. At the assistant professor rank Wisconsin trails Michigan by $3,100 and Illinois by $900, while leading Ohio State by $1,300.[58]

The UW System data survey is reflective of public peers only, but in reality UW-Madison competes to recruit new faculty and retain existing faculty of all ranks in a broader marketplace that includes private-independent and select church-related institutions. The Madison competitive situation in this marketplace is dire. Using AAUP data for 2003–2004, at the full professor rank UW-Madison trails private-independent doctoral institutions by an average of $25,958 and church-related doctoral institutions by $7,275. At the associate professor level Madison trails the private-independent institutions by $5,563 but leads the church-related doctoral institutions by approximately $1,068. At the assistant professor rank UW-Madison trails the private-independent institutions by $9,318 and the church-related doctoral campuses by $1,126.[59]

The system's other doctoral campus, UW-Milwaukee, is in a somewhat better position in terms of its peers than UW-Madison. The Milwaukee deficit measures against its public peers for all ranks of faculty has actually declined from 4.53 percent in 2000–2001 to 2.13 percent in 2003–2004. UWM trails the median of its public peer group at the full professor level by $4,300 at the associate professor level by $100 and leads the median at the assistant professor level by $3,100. At the full professor level UWM ranked 13th of the 14 public peer institutions used by UW System administration for comparative purposes, trailing its Chicago peer, the University of Illinois at Chicago, by $17,000; the University of Louisville by $4,300; and the University of Missouri-Kansas City by $4,100. At the associate professor level UWM ranks eighth among its 14 public peers, trailing Illinois-Chicago and Louisville by $6,700, and $100, respectively, while leading Missouri-Kansas City by $900. At the assistant professor rank UWM ranks seventh among its 14 public peers, trailing Illinois-Chicago by $4,200, while leading Louisville by $6,500 and Missouri-Kansas City by $4,900.[60]

Using AAUP data, UWM also generally trails in compensation comparisons with private institutions. Competing against the private-independent doctoral campuses, UWM trails by $38,758 at the full professor rank, $14,263 for associate professors, and $11,618 at the assistant professor rank. UWM also trails the nation's church-related doctoral campuses on average by $20,075 at the rank of full professor, by $7,632 for associate professors, and $3,426 at the assistant professor level.[61]

Larger gaps between system institutions and peers occur at the four-year comprehensive campuses. In 2000–2001, the gap between those institutions and their public peers was 5.3 percent, a number that grew to 9.18 percent in 2003–2004. Given the differing disciplines among the UW comprehensive institutions average salaries at all levels vary considerably. That said, the UW four-year campuses trail their peer medians at all faculty ranks with the exception of one of the institutions, which pays its assistant professors $1,000 above the peer median. The four-year institutions considered in a discrete cluster, however, trail at the professor rank by an average of $7,900 at the full professor rank, $5,600 for associate professors, and $2,100 at the assistant professor rank.[62]

Gaps between campus salaries and the four-year peer median cluster vary greatly from a deficit of $12,200 at UW-River Falls to $2,600 at UW-La Crosse. At the associate professor rank the gap varies from $8,600 at UW-Superior to $1,500 at UW-Parkside. Assistant professor salaries vary from $5,400 below peers to $1,000 above peers at UW-Superior. Considered as a cluster among 33 peer institutions, the UW comprehensives rank last, with a shortfall of $8,000 at the full professor rank; last at the associate professor rank, with a gap to the median of $5,900, and 24th among 33 four-year peers $2,000 below the peer median. The UW institutions fall fully $17,900 below the top Midwestern peer institution, Wright State University; $17,400 below Western Michigan University, which ranks second in the peer cluster; and $14,600 behind third place Michigan Technological University at the full professor rank. At the associate professor rank the gaps are $11,000 below the top Midwestern peer, the University of Minnesota-Duluth; $9,500 behind second place University of Michigan-Dearborn; and $8,900 behind third place Michigan Technological University. UW comprehensive salaries at the assistant professor rank trail Midwestern, leading peers Michigan-Dearborn by $11,000, Michigan Technological University by $9,700, and Oakland University by $7,700.[63]

Increasingly UW officials have also become concerned at the inability of the comprehensive institutions to also compete for faculty with comparable private-independent and church-related institutions. The gap at full professor between UW comprehensive campuses and those at private-independent campuses is $14,870; the gaps at the associate and assistant ranks are $8,434 and $12,330, respectively. The corresponding gaps at church-related institutions are $9,503 for full professors, $8,183 for associate professors, and $8,845 for assistant professors.[64]

The UW System two-year campuses also face wide gaps between salaries at all faculty ranks, falling $12,500 below their peers at the professor level, $9,000 at the associate professor level, and $10,000 behind peers at the assistant professor level.[65]

FOCUS ON INSTITUTIONAL EFFICIENCY

Resource limitations have been part of the motivation behind system-wide efforts to achieve both reductions in average credits-to-degree taken by UW System students while improving institutional retention and graduation rates. As far back as the 1996, Regent study on the system's future regents saw a link between reducing the number of credits students were taking as they progressed toward graduation and increasing access. A year earlier, regents had adopted a policy goal of decreasing attempted credits-to-degree from 145 to 140 by 2001.[66] Six of the 13 four-year campuses met the goal. In fact, system-wide, the average decreased from 145 to 137 by 2000–2001. Two institutions reduced the figure by 13 credits and one by 11. UW-Madison achieved one of the larger reductions at 9 credits.[67]

A second initiative aimed at cutting the time-to-degree stated: "The length of time bachelors degree recipients take to complete their degrees is one measure of student effectiveness. Getting students to graduate sooner, in addition to encouraging them to graduate with fewer credits, frees up resources and allows UW institutions to serve more students."[68] Between 1993–1994 and 2000–2001, the percentage of students finishing in four years rose from 21 to 33 percent. Similarly, system institutions showed dramatic improvements in the numbers of students graduating in six years. At UW-Madison the 1981 entering freshmen cohort statistics revealed that 64.5 percent had graduated from UW-Madison and 68.6 percent had received bachelors degrees when those students who transferred to and graduated from other UW institutions were included. The UW-Madison figures for the 1995 cohorts were 75.8 percent and 78.3 percent, a major improvement. System-wide, the figures increased from the 1981 cohort of 44.4 percent at the institution first attended and 51.4 percent, including those transferring to and graduating from other institutions in the system. The system-wide cohort for the entering class in 1995 had improved to 54.2 percent and 60.5 percent, a substantial improvement.[69]

CLASSROOM MODERNIZATION AND TECHNOLOGY CHALLENGES

UW System institutions have proceeded with a major classroom modernization program despite declining state support. Significant funds for technology improvements are coming from a special technology fee enacted for UW-Madison students in 1993 and students on the other campuses two years later, as well as from significant internal reallocations. The system's 2003–2004 accountability report, "Achieving Excellence," states that technological change has "dramatically altered traditional models of teaching and learning with electronic media playing an increasingly vital role in today's university curriculum."[70] Both the 2003–2004 and 2004–2005 reports warn that the internal reallocations are not meeting "expanding demands for the replacement and upgrade of equipment. State support is needed to ensure that the UW System maintains its role as a leader in providing quality education for the increasingly technologically sophisticated economy."[71] The reports note that even in the difficult budget environment of the last decade, the system has still made what it calls "substantial progress" in moving the system institution classrooms toward improved technology environments.[72] The picture for technology upgrades to facilities is somewhat more positive. The system has received $42.5 million in state support in the last decade to upgrade approximately 430 classrooms system-wide of the system's over 1,700 general assignment classrooms. The 2004 progress report states that 60 percent of the instructional space remains yet to be updated with new technology and 54 percent require remodeling.[73]

In addition to concerns about modernizing classrooms, the UW System has focused significant attention on spotlighting facilities maintenance needs. For the 2003–2005 biennium, the system maintenance backlog for tax-supported facilities was estimated at $650 million. The system anticipates receiving state funding in the upcoming two-year biennial state budget to address $90 million in backlog needs from a special state facilities maintenance program and an additional $12 in maintenance needs through state major construction projects. The system anticipates making major progress in the 2005–2007 biennium to further address the large maintenance backlog, but state funding for maintenance has met only half of what the system sees as its need since 2001, although the 2003–2005 state budget provided what the accountability report labeled a "record amount" for maintenance.[74]

BUDGET IMPACT ON GRADUATE AND RESEARCH FUNCTIONS

Both graduate education programs and the research function remained relatively healthy at UW System institutions between 1992 and 2004. Although some research is conducted on virtually all UW campuses, the lion's share occurs at UW-Madison. Federal and research funding from private sources increased 116 percent for the period, from $273 million to $589 million. External sources provided approximately $4.2 billion over the 1994–2004 period.[75] The difficult decade did not see a major departure of research faculty bringing in large grants. Indeed, UW-Madison saw major research breakthroughs, especially in the areas of medicine and the biological sciences. Teams on the Madison campus attracted international attention with breakthroughs in areas as varied as stem cell research, treating neurological disorders, vascular health and heart disease, insecticides, and nanotechnology. Although the federal research support was generally improving during the period, partly as a result of federal government decisions to increase funding for research for the National Institutes of Health and the National Science Foundation, the current proposed federal budget now before Congress halts the growth in federal funding that had been occurring in the last decade. Total research awards for UW-Madison increased from $362 million in 1997–1998 to more than $704 million in 2003–2004 with the average faculty research award growing from over $255,000 to more than $436,000 for the period.[76]

The UW System did not significantly reduce graduate enrollments system-wide for the period 1993–2003 as a result of the erosion of state support. That said, however, the enrollments did not reflect a steady-state over the decade. Graduate enrollments declined significantly at most institutions between 1993 and 1998 before beginning a recovery process. During the same period, most system campuses experienced large increases in undergraduate enrollments. An analysis of enrollments for the decade does not reveal any diminishment in undergraduate enrollment in attempt to preserve the institution's graduate programs. In fact, quite the opposite appears to have occurred. Between 1993 and 2003, system-wide the FTE count of professional/graduate students declined from 15,797 to 15,760 and undergraduate enrollment increased from 111,261 to 120,037 FTE.[77]

The UW 11 comprehensive institution graduate programs, which are all masters programs, began the decade with 3,117 enrollments, dipping to a low of 2,883 in 1999 before growing to 3,081 in 2003. Reviewing the enrollments on a campus-by-campus basis, campuses that recovered were either offering programs in the allied health area or through new on-line or other distance education avenues. The institutions that suffered net losses were those that primarily offered masters programs in education. Four-year campus undergraduate enrollment began 1993 with 65,248 declining to 64,826 in 1995 before hitting an enrollment peak of 69,314 in 2002 and then declining slightly in 2003 to 69,023. All of the four-year institutions finished the decade with more undergraduate FTE than they began it with. UW-Milwaukee actually increased its graduate enrollments over the period examined. Masters enrollments began the period in 1993 with 1,784 FTE and hit a low point of 1,643 FTE in 2000 before rebounding to finish with 1,863 in 2003. The institution's doctoral programs had 599 FTE in 1993 and finished the decade with 638 after hitting a low of 530 FTE in these programs in 2000. Milwaukee began 1993 with 13,545 FTE undergraduate enrollment, a figure that dipped to a low point of 12,674 in 2005 before beginning a period of steady growth, reaching 16,103 in 2003.[78]

The largest portion of the system's graduate enrollments occur at UW-Madison where graduate and professional FTE dropped slightly from 10,297 in 1993 to 10,178 in 2003. The low point in professional and graduate enrollments occurred in 1997, when they declined to 8,974. Madison's masters FTE enrollments declined from 3,427 in 1993 to a low of 2,612 in 1998 before growing to 2,722 in 2001 and then declining in 2003 to 2,652. Madison finished the decade with a higher doctoral FTE count at 5,175 than it had in 1993, when there were 5,035 FTE in doctoral programs on campus. Doctoral FTE declined to a low point of 4,376 in 1998 before recovering gradually until 2003. Professional program FTE enrollment in 1993 reached 10,297 and then declined to a low enrollment figure of 8,974 in 1998 before beginning a period of growth annually through 2003.[79]

REGENTS STUDY SYSTEM FUTURE

After the dramatic budget reductions adopted by the state in the spring of 2003 for the 2003–2005 biennium, the UW System Regents undertook a yearlong study in collaboration with students, faculty, staff, administrators, and private citizens and, in June 2004, released the study's findings "Charting a New Course for the UW System." Regent Guy Gottschalk, who served as the board president viewed the study as "essential to helping focus attention on the financial challenges of the system" when the study was launched.[80] The Regent study stated that nationally a confluence of forces was combining that "threaten the operation and effectiveness of many public colleges and universities across the United States." Acknowledging the historic boom and bust cycles that parallel the U.S. economic situation, the report noted: "But there is an ominous quality to the current situation that is causing a collective shiver from coast to coast."[81]

Among the trends spotlighted by the UW Regent study was the overall 20-year decline in some measures of state support for public higher education. Regents observed that public funding was declining while demand for higher education was growing, thanks to both demographic factors and the national economic downturn that began in the fall of 2000. Other challenges resulted from losses in endowments caused by the downturn in the stock market, growing pressure to improve information technology infrastructures, which the Regent study labeled "a new and costly necessity for delivering quality education."[82] Finally, the regents noted that the institutions were increasingly being asked to enhance local and regional economies by forming public/private industry partnerships and spinning off research results that could stimulate economic growth.[83] The study added that "In short, public universities across the country are struggling to educate more students and are grappling over fewer dollars while striving to preserve quality and meet greater public expectations. All this suggests a mounting crisis."[84]

Placing the Wisconsin challenge in the national context, the study noted that the UW system had lost $250 million in state assistance in 2003–2005 on top of a net $50 million cut the previous year. Meanwhile, the study noted that enrollment at UW institutions was strong, growing by more than 8,700 students to a total enrollment of nearly 161,000 students over the previous decade, while the numbers of faculty have been reduced by 670 during the same period.[85]

The yearlong study endorsed a series of recommendations designed to help address the System's fiscal challenges, ranging from a call for stabilization of state tax support and a review of further streamlining of administration to innovative approaches to increase revenues by focusing on new markets. The study recognized that while "there are no alternative revenue streams that can take the place of adequate, stable state support for the UW System's instructional mission," nonetheless at the campus level, there were opportunities for some of the institutions to refocus on a new vision of market opportunities.[86]

Regents were especially vocal about the need to stabilize state support. "The one overarching fact that emerges from this study is that there are no substitutes for adequate, stable state support for our instructional mission. Wisconsin will make a grave error if it does not reverse the trend of diminishing support for its university system as we enter the new global information economy."[87]

Besides a plea for stabilizing state support, Regents endorsed development of innovative pricing and marketing strategies to take advantage of niche opportunities where underused physical plants could be used to generate significant net additional income for a campus. An example of this approach is occurring at UW-Platteville, a comprehensive institution in southwestern Wisconsin with a special focus on engineering. Campus officials, working with UW System leaders, created a pilot program for the previously somewhat underused campus physical plant. The concept aims at protecting in-state access to the campus while increasing enrollments over four years by 2000 engineering students from Iowa and Illinois. UW-Platteville Chancellor David Markee projects the program using additional tuition revenue from the additional students will pay for expansion and modernization of the campus engineering physical plant, as well as expansion of student housing. "This program will help our campus provide Wisconsin with additional graduates our state's business need in areas ranging from engineering to technology, creating a real brain gain for Wisconsin because over 80 percent of our graduates remain in state after they complete their studies. Beyond that, this program gives our campus the opportunity to grow, and to help spur economic growth statewide. We estimate the addition of these students will inject over $25 million annually into the economy of our region—the equivalent of us landing a gigantic new industry."[88]

Other Regent study recommendations include further administrative streamlining, examining nonresident tuition to charge a more market-competitive price, examining additional resident tuition flexibility, expanding opportunities for high school students to earn college credits, and facilitating transfer of students between institutions and between the state's technical colleges and the UW campuses.[89]

UW LEADERS SEEK STATE GOVERNMENT EFFICIENCIES

Although the system has adopted operating efficiencies in areas ranging from areas as varied as the campus admissions operations to speeding time to degree and reducing the number of credits attempted by undergraduates, the study called for further reviews of both state government and campus operations. Wisconsin remains perhaps the most state-regulated public university system in the country. The study estimated streamlining the Wisconsin state building process could save the UW System $400 million over 20 years. Then-UW System President Lyall told regents the state government-controlled building program was inefficient, with state bureaucratic operations adding to the cost of UW buildings through avoidable significant delays in the construction timetables, as well as excessive Wisconsin Department of Administration (DOA) overhead charges levied on the campuses with dubious justification.[90]

The Wisconsin state construction process was labeled by the Regent study as being "overly burdensome and time-consuming."[91] Regents noted that the current state building process adds approximately three years to the project approval process during which significant project cost escalation occurs as a result of inflation. In addition, regents and campus officials noted the Wisconsin DOA operating as a fee-for-service agency had no incentive to save institutions money, but in fact was rewarded financially as construction costs rose and timetables slipped because the agency charged a project management and construction supervision fee of 4 percent. Regents asked that the fee be optional and that the system have the option of choosing between state services and other providers on a competitive basis. Finally, the regents stated that if they could issue revenue bonds for projects supported entirely by program revenue "savings in time and cost to complete construction would be significant. In addition, a burden on state bonding would be lifted."[92]

UW Regents are also seeking authority to operate a procurement process "directly in the marketplace" without participating in state DOA mandatory contracts, which they argued use student tuition dollars to subsidize state agencies including DOA with no benefit to the campuses. Regents noted that UW System peers participate in consortial buying arrangements that save significant dollars. Currently, DOA has prevented most UW institutions from benefiting from major savings in commodities such as office supplies through consortial purchases, driving up institutional costs and hence UW tuition, without any offsetting benefit of participating in mandatory state contracts.[93]

The study also urged a joint UW System-state government examination of risk management programs to reduce costs for such programs. An outside consultant hired by the system estimated that the system, if allowed to function as its peer institutions function, could reduce its expenditures on insurance by a minimum of 10 percent, yielding an estimated $14 million in savings over a decade. An examination of recent experience of system peers that have created so-called captives to manage some of their insurance programs has demonstrated savings far in excess of those estimated by the UW System consultant.[94]

For long-term observers of the UW System, the current financial travails appear to fit a condition baseball great Yogi Berra once labeled "deja-vu, all over again."[95] The Regent study noted that UW System President John Weaver 30 years earlier had observed that: "The immediate public policy issue becomes clear. If we are to fulfill our missions as historically defined, we need to be certain the state still supports those missions, and supports them with the full realization that they can not be fulfilled on the basis of static or declining resources. If we are to plan for long-term fiscal austerity and retrenchment, this needs to be directed with the complete understanding that this will require a most basic change in direction for the State of Wisconsin—a deliberate decision to constrain for fiscal reasons, the levels of access to educational opportunity that have historically been provided."[96]

Weaver concluded his remarks by saying: "We should give fair warning, and we must continue to warn that we cannot go on reducing faculty and staff, as well as support for instructional materials and equipment and simultaneously undertake the teaching of ever-increasing numbers of students. To attempt such is an inescapable prescription for irreversible mediocrity."[97]

NOTES

1. UW System Budget Office, *Analysis of Major State Program Expenditures*, June 18, 2004. Available from the UW System Budget Office.

2. Katharine C. Lyall, Remarks to UW System Board of Regents, Minutes of the UW System Board of Regents, August 19, 2004.

3. Ibid.

4. John D. Wiley, "Higher Education at the Crossroads," *Madison Magazine* 45, no. 11 (November 2003): 61.

5. UW System *Achieving Excellence: Accountability Report 2004–2005*. Annual report to the Board of Regents from the UW System. Available from the UW System Budget Office.

6. Ibid.

7. Ibid

8. UW System Budget Office.

9. UW System Budget office, U.S. Bureau of Economic Analysis.

10. UW System Budget Office.

11. Ibid.

12. Ibid.

13. Ibid.

14. Ibid.

15. Wiley, 58.

16. Report of a Visit to the University of Wisconsin-Madison for the Commission on Institutions of Higher Education of the North Central Associate of Colleges and Schools, July 1999. Available from the UW–Madison Office of the Chancellor or the North Central Association of Colleges and Schools.

17. Ibid.

18. Ibid.

19. Ibid.

20. Ibid.

21. UW System Budget Office.

22. UW System Office of Policy Analysis and Research.

23. UW System Budget Office.

24. Ibid.

25. Ibid.

26. Ibid.

27. Ibid.

28. Ibid.

29. UW System Office of Policy Analysis and Research, *The New Freshman Class: Fall 2003*. June 2004.

30. Ibid.

31. Ibid.

32. UW System Budget Office.

33. UW System Office of Policy Analysis and Research.

34. *UW System Budget Proposal*, August 2004.

35. University of Wisconsin System Board of Regents, *Study of the UW System in the 21st Century*. Available from the UW System Budget Office.

36. Ibid.

37. University of Wisconsin Board of Regents, *Charting a New Course for the UW System*, June 2004. Available from the UW System Budget Office.

38. Ibid.

39. Joni Finney, Vice President, National Center for Public Policy and Higher Education, Presentation to University of Wisconsin Board of Regents, December 4, 2003.

40. UW System Office of Policy Analysis and Research, *Access to Higher Education by Income in Wisconsin*, April 2004. Available from the UW System Budget Office.

41. Ibid.

42. Ibid.

43. Wiley.

44. UW System Office of Policy Analysis and Research, *Access to Higher Education by Income in Wisconsin*. Available from the UW System Budget Office.

45. UW System, *Achieving Excellence: Accountability Report 2004–2005*. *Achieving Excellence: Accountability Report 2003–2004*. Available from the UW System Budget Office.

46. UW System Office of Policy Analysis and Research.

47. UW System, *Achieving Excellence: Accountability Report 2004–2005*. Available from the UW System Budget Office.

48. *Achieving Excellence at UW-Madison*, March 2005. Available from the UW System Budget Office.

49. Ibid.

50. UW System Achieving Excellence: Accountability Report 2004–2005.

51. UW System Budget Office, UW System Office of Policy Analysis and Research.

52. UW System Budget Office, UW System Human Resources Office, UW System Office of Policy Analysis and Research.

53. UW System Office of Human Resources.

54. Ibid.

55. George Brooks, Report to the UW System Regents, September 9, 2004.

56. UW System Office of the President.

57. UW System Office of Human Resources October 2004.

58. Ibid.

59. Ibid.

60. Ibid.

61. Ibid.

62. Ibid.

63. Ibid.

64. Ibid.

65. Ibid.

66. University of Wisconsin System Office of Policy Analysis and Research, *Institutional Efficiency and Student Success: The Relationship Between Credits-to-Degree, Time-to-Degree and Graduation Rates*, May 2002.

67. Ibid.

68. Ibid.

69. Ibid.

70. University of Wisconsin System, *Achieving Excellence: Accountability Report 2004–2005*. Available from the UW System Budget Office.

71. Ibid.

72. Ibid.

73. Ibid.

74. Ibid.

75. University of Wisconsin System Budget Office.

76. *Achieving Excellence at UW-Madison*, March 2005.

77. UW System Office of Policy Analysis and Research.

78. Ibid.

79. Ibid.

80. University of Wisconsin Board of Regents, *Charting a New Course for the UW System*, June 2004. Available from the UW System Budget Office.

81. Ibid.

82. Ibid.

83. Ibid.

84. Ibid.

85. Ibid.

86. Ibid.

87. Ibid.

88. David Markee, UW System Board of Regents. "Charting a New Course for the UW System." Presentation to Revenue Committee, September 2003.

89. University of Wisconsin Board of Regents. "Charting a New Course for the UW System," June 2004.

90. University of Wisconsin Board of Regents. "Charting a New Course for the UW System," April 2004.

91. University of Wisconsin Board of Regents. "Charting a New Course for the UW System," June 2004.

92. Ibid.

93. David W. Olien, University of Wisconsin Board of Regents. "Charting a New Course for the UW System." Revenue Committee March 2003.

94. University of Wisconsin System, Division of Administrative Services.

95. Mr. Berra's quote was in reference to home runs hit in a game by New York Yankee sluggers Mickey Mantle and Roger Maris.

96. John C. Weaver, Report to the Board of Regents. Minutes of the University of Wisconsin System Regents, April 18, 1975.

97. Ibid.

PART III

Looking to the Future

CHAPTER 15

Why We Won't See Any Public Universities "Going Private"

John D. Wiley

All around the country the story is the same: States are reducing taxpayer support for public higher education, offsetting those reductions with higher tuition. Using Wisconsin as an example, Table 15.1 illustrates the changes over the last 25 years. In some states, the changes have been even more dramatic; in others, less so. But the trend is essentially universal. Furthermore, the impacts of these changes vary, even within one state. At UW-Madison (the flagship institution of the UW-System), for example, state appropriations constituted 43.1 percent and tuition 10.5 percent of our budget in 1975. Today, those numbers are 19.5 and 15.7 percent, respectively. To make matters worse, nearly one-third of our state revenue comes to us with constraints requiring us to return it to the state for specific costs such as our share of the state utility bills, debt service, and mandatory payments to state agencies. Even if we were able to economize or find superior alternatives in any of those areas, we would not be able to reallocate the savings for other purposes. As a result, the state is providing only 13.5 percent of our base operating budget—the budget for hiring faculty and staff, and covering infrastructure and operating costs beyond debt service and utility bills. For the first time in the history of the institution, our students are contributing more to this portion of our operating budget than are the state taxpayers.[1]

Viewing these trends, many faculty, alumni, newspaper editors, and even legislators have urged us to consider "going private." By that, they have in mind that we could agree to forego all state support in our base operating budget and rely on increased tuition, coupled with some unspecified amount of additional student

Table 15.1
The Changing Mix of State Funding and Tuition at the University of Wisconsin
(UW) System over the Last 25 Years

Year	1974–1975	2004–2005
State appropriations for UW-System per $1,000 of personal incom	$12.50	$5.50
State appropriations for UW-System as a share of total state spending	11.5%	3.9%
State appropriations for UW-System per FTE student (2004 dollars)	$10,600	$7,400
State appropriations for UW-System as a percent of UW-System budget	49.50%	26%
Tuition as a percent of UW-System budget	12%	21%

financial aid (what they assume to be "the private model" of high tuition and high financial aid) for ongoing operations. These views are often expressed in terms of a comparison: "You're way underpriced at a resident tuition of $6000/year. I'm paying three times that for my daughter's tuition at (a private school), and the education she's getting is certainly not three times better. Even if you simply doubled your tuition, you would still be a bargain, and you could replace nearly all state funds. What's the problem?" Quite aside from political considerations (unwillingness of states to "let go" of prior investments and ongoing oversight), the larger problem is that the "private model," properly understood, simply cannot be scaled up to the extent required. It's a matter of simple arithmetic, and the numbers just don't work! Before explaining this assertion, it is important to review the overall context and scope of American higher education at the start of the twenty-first century.

At the beginning of the twentieth century, formal education was a relative rarity. Many did not complete what would today be called elementary school, and it was not until about 1940 that the percentage of adults over age 25 who had completed high school exceeded 25 percent. By 1940, the percentage of adults over age 25 who had completed college was still less than 5 percent. Today, nearly 90 percent of adults over 25 have high school diplomas, and nearly 30 percent have college degrees.[2] The great expansion of formal education at all levels, and especially the growth of college attendance, occurred during a 30-year period after the end of World War II, spurred, in great part, by the GI Bill. It is fair to say that the GI Bill and the dramatic expansion of postsecondary education powered the U.S. economy for the entire second half of the twentieth century.

Although the growth rate slowed in about 1975, both high school and college graduation attainment rates have continued to increase. What has made this dramatic growth possible is the conscious, thoughtful, well-planned expansion of public higher education. By and large, these new and expanded institutions, subsidized by the state taxpayers, have provided the increased access to affordable higher education as a matter of public policy.

Table 15.2 summarizes the current system of higher education in the United States. Our system today consists of a large number of small private institutions and a smaller number of *much* larger public institutions. Public schools constitute only 41 percent of the total, but they enroll 77 percent of the students, and educate them at about half the cost per student. Economies of scale are even more striking if you isolate the four-year institutions: Here, only 25 percent of the institutions enroll 65 percent of the students. Of the 100 largest -postsecondary institutions in the country, 92 are public, and *all* of the 25 largest institutions are public, including most of the public flagship institutions of the upper Midwest (the Big Ten schools).

There are good and simple reasons why there are so few large private colleges and universities, and the reasons have entirely to do with base budget realities. The operational incomes of all colleges and universities derive from only a few sources:

1. Federal revenues—primarily research funds and student financial aid
2. Program revenues*—revenues from sales of things like athletic tickets, dormitory space, food, books, hospital revenues, fees for continuing adult education, contract research, etc.

Table 15.2
Statistical Overview of the U.S. System of Higher Education

Institution Type	Public	Private	% Public
# of four-year institutions	631	1,835	25.6
Enrollments	6,236,455	3,440,953	64.4
Average enrollment	9,883	1,875	—
# of two-year institutions	1,081	621	63.5
Enrollments	5,996,701	253,878	95.9
Average enrollment	5,547	409	—
Total # of institutions	1,712.00	2,456.00	41.1
Total enrollments	12,233,156	3,694,831	76.8
Total expenditures	$170,344,841,000	$85,048,123,000	66.7
Average Expenditure/student	$13,924.85	$23,018.14	—

3. Gifts and endowment income*—annual gifts that can be expended immediately, as well as annual earnings on long-term endowments

4. Tuition—actual revenue received from students and their families, exclusive of institutional assistance

5. State support—state appropriations paid directly to the institutions.

The first two categories, federal and program revenues, are not available to support the general operations of the institution. It is not possible, for example, to accept a federal grant for research in geology and then reallocate those funds to hire a new Spanish instructor. Similarly, no president can sell tickets to a football game and then cancel the game, using the proceeds instead to add new sections of calculus. Many gifts are similarly restricted, but it is possible, over a period of many years, to build endowments that can support faculty salaries, program operations, and other "base-budget" needs. Thus, the base operating budgets of private and public universities are made up entirely of the same three kinds of revenue: gifts and endowment income, tuition, and state support. Table 15.3 shows how these three revenue categories contribute to the budgets of public and private colleges and universities.

It is no surprise that private schools derive so little of their revenues from state governments, nor that public schools have so little endowment income. What most people do find surprising is that the contribution of tuition revenues is so similar between public and private institutions. After all, the average tuition at private schools is $16,287/year, and the average tuition at public schools is only $3,746/year.[3] So why isn't this large difference reflected in the budget percentages? The answer is found mostly in the gross revenue numbers. The 3,308,460 students enrolled in private colleges and universities generated $29,257,523,000 in tuition and fees, for an average of $8844 per student, which is only about half the theoretical or "sticker-price" amount.[4] This reflects the substantial tuition discounting that is necessary for institutions having very high sticker-price tuition. In contrast, the 6,055,398 students enrolled in public institutions generated $23,376,317,000, for an average of $3861/student—close to the average advertised tuition of $3746.[5]

Therein lies the first lesson for those urging public universities to go private: If public universities raised their tuition to private school levels, they would not realize anything like the apparent theoretical increase in tuition revenue, because they would find it necessary to engage in the same tuition discounting as the private institutions. After all, a student or family that is unwilling or unable to pay the sticker-price tuition at private schools is hardly likely to be willing or able to do so at public schools.

The second important point should be obvious from Table 15.3. As a percentage of their overall budgets, private schools realize as much revenue from gift and

---

*Depending on the details of the agreement, nonfederal research grants and contracts are typically accounted for in one or the other of these categories.

Table 15.3
Percentage of Total Institutional Operating Budgets from the Three Major Categories
of Base-Budget Sources for Public and Private 4–Year Institutions

Institution Type	Public Four-year (%)	Private Four-year (%)
Endowment income	0.9	31.5
State appropriation	30.9	0.3
Tuition income	18.1	24.4

endowment income as public schools obtain from state subsidies. Put differently, public funds at public schools play the same role as gift and endowment income at private schools. Thus, even if public schools were able to raise their tuition to private school levels, they would still need substantially increased private giving and endowment income to offset any loss of public funding.

The percentages in Table 15.3 are based on averages over hundreds of institutions, and do not apply to any one institution. To illustrate the challenge of moving a specific institution from the public to the private model, I use the University of Wisconsin-Madison as a concrete example. In 2004, its total budget of $1.9 billion included $369.7 million in state appropriations, $297 million in tuition, and about $120 million in endowment income and the equivalent in annual gifts. Thus, the budget percentages for these categories were 19.5, 15.7, and about 6.3 percent, respectively. In round numbers, undergraduate tuition for nonresidents is $19,000, and for residents $6,000. Actually, there are lots of different tuitions at various degree levels, but setting all tuitions at the nonresident undergraduate level of $19,000 is a reasonable proxy for taking the first step toward the "private model."

If all tuitions were set at $19,000, the university's roughly 40,000 students would theoretically generate $760 million/year. Assuming the university was forced to do the same level of tuition discounting as the private institutions, however, this would yield only 54.3 percent of that amount, or about $413 million—an increase of $116 million over current tuition revenues. But if the university were to give up all state support, it would still be short $369.7−$116 = $253.7 million. The only feasible source for making up that difference is charitable gifts and endowment income. As a rule of thumb, endowments generate only about 4 to 5 percent of the principal as expendable income annually. Any earnings in excess of that are typically reinvested to allow the endowment to grow as a compensation for inflation. To generate an additional $253.7 million in endowment income, we would need to increase our endowment by at least $5 billion, to a total of about $7 billion. More realistically, we would need at least $8 billion, with most of the new endowment money being unrestricted or restricted for things such as faculty salaries and fringe benefits (endowed chairs).

There are several ways to put a hypothetical UW-Madison endowment of $8 billion in perspective:

1. Currently, only five of the nation's 4,168 colleges and universities have endowments that large (Stanford, $8.6 billion; the entire University of Texas System, $8.7 billion; Princeton, $8.7 billion; Yale, $11 billion; and Harvard, $19 billion), and all of these except the UT-System are much smaller institutions than UW-Madison. The UT-System is, of course, still public and still receives state support.

2. In the 60-year history of the UW-Foundation (our charitable fund-raising foundation), it has raised a total of about $3 billion, including net income and gains on prior investments, and approximately $1 billion of that remains today as a permanent endowment. In addition, the university has access to another $1 billion or so in highly restricted endowments, for a total of approximately $2 billion. By the time an additional $6 billion is raised, it would no longer be sufficient because of ongoing inflation.

3. The university is currently in a six-year campaign to raise $1.5 billion. But a substantial fraction of that total will be (is) restricted for things that have nothing to do with the base operating budget.

4. The 30 best-endowed private universities have per-student endowments in the $500,000/student range, and the best-endowed public universities are endowed in the $40,000/student range.[6] Even at an endowment of $8 billion, UW-Madison would still have only $200,000/student—less than half the endowment resources per student of peer private institutions unless it were downsized to a student body of perhaps 15,000 to 20,000 students, so the estimate of a required $8 billion endowment is *very* conservative for a school this size. Therefore UW-Madison has essentially no chance of raising an endowment large enough to offset a total loss of state funding. Nor could any other state flagship institution achieve this goal, and most of the smaller public institutions have no present endowments at all, nor any significant fundraising potential.

On a national scale, it would require endowments totaling about $1.3 trillion to generate enough endowment income to replace all state funding of higher education. That is about six times larger than the total of all public and private university endowments today. It is also a nontrivial fraction of the $37 trillion total financial assets of all U.S. households,[7] especially considering that much of the $37 trillion is tied up in home equity. Nevertheless, the financial resources do exist, in principle, to create an aggregate "trillion-dollar-plus" higher education endowment from private gifts. In 2002, private philanthropy in the United States totaled $240.9 billion, of which $183.7 billion was from gifts by individuals.[8] Of the total giving, $84.3 billion (35 percent) went to religious organizations, $37.6 billion (16 percent) to health and human service causes, and $31.6 billion (13 percent) to education at all levels. There is no reason to believe the patterns or magnitudes of charitable giving can or will change quickly, so from every perspective, this is a fool's pursuit. Furthermore, it is a pursuit that has not been launched by any form of reasoned public policy debate.

No legislature or other public forum has concluded and recommended that this massive shift in the finances of higher education from the public to the private sector is good public policy for any state or for the nation. Rather, the shift is occurring incrementally in small, expedient budget decisions that manage to get the states through one more budget year. In effect, the message is this: Instead of supporting public higher education by taxing all 285 million citizens about $220 annually each, let's ask 10 percent of them voluntarily to provide $2,200 a year, or 1 percent of them to pony up $22,000 a year. If there are 285 billionaires out there who would be willing to contribute $220 million/year to save everyone else a $220 tax bill, they haven't stepped forward to do so. In the meantime, states continue to push their public colleges and universities toward this ultimately impossible goal.

This stark budget reality of our public universities is already diminishing the health of the U.S. system of higher education, and every citizen has a huge stake in this problem. Access and affordability are not just issues for a few potential students and their families: These are issues on which the entire economy will either thrive or decline. Simple arithmetic confirms it. Today, the public invests a little more than $392 billion annually—nearly $1400 per capita, or about $8,000 per pupil—to provide universal, tuition-free education through grade 12. Multiplying $8,000 times 13 years of K12 education shows that taxpayers invest about $100,000 to produce a high school graduate. A glance at Table 15.4 shows that the average person who enters the workforce with only a high school education is unlikely ever to repay in state and local taxes the cost of his or her diploma. It is only at the bachelor's degree level and above that the public can expect to regain their investment in K12 education from tax revenues. Let me quickly add that many high school graduates obtain apprenticeship training or other skills that enable them to beat these odds. Similarly, some college graduates will fall far short of the earnings detailed in Table 15.4. Still, the overall economy consists of the accumulation of those averages, so the conclusions presented here are important for the economy as a whole.

In the middle of the last century, taxpayers and lawmakers alike seemed to understand this simple math. They wisely invested in a massive expansion of public higher education and provided affordable access to millions of citizens through the GI Bill, low tuition, and abundant scholarship support to those who needed it. Those decisions created the engine that powered the state and national economies for the entire second half of the twentieth century. The vast majority of readers of this chapter benefited personally from that affordable access, as did society at large. Why, then, would we even consider withdrawing it from our children and their children? But that is just what we are doing. Federal scholarships have all but disappeared and have been replaced by loans. More than three-fourths of students now work for pay during the school year when they should be studying—and they are working more hours every year. More than half of all UW-Madison graduates now graduate with student loan debts ranging, on average, from $15,000 at the bachelor's level to more than $100,000 for veterinary, law, and medical school graduates. The prospect of starting a career with large debt is now driving students

Table 15.4
Mean Earnings and Expected Mean Lifetime Earnings in Constant 2002 Dollars by
Degree of Educational Attainment, Assuming Retirement at Age 65

Highest Degree	Mean Earnings ($)	Years in School	Years Working	Lifetime Earnings ($)
No HS Diploma	18,826	11	50	941,300
HS Diploma	27,280	13	48	1,309,440
Some College	29,725	14	47	1,397,075
Associate Degree	34,177	15	46	1,572,142
Bachelors Degree	51,194	17	44	2,252,536
Masters Degree	60,445	19	42	2,538,690
Doctoral Degree	89,734	22	39	3,499,626
Professional Degree	112,845	22	39	4,400,955

away from careers that have only "average" lifetime earning potential, including
teaching, nursing, family practice medicine, rural medical or law practice, and
large animal veterinary practice. Even more important, the distribution of brains,
talents, ambition, and creativity is independent of family income. We will ignore
that fact and freeze out the children of average and low-income families at our
great peril. No society is rich enough to waste any of these assets.

When setting out on a path that leads toward an impossible goal, only one thing
is certain: you won't get there. There is no realistic possibility of providing high-
quality postsecondary education for the vast majority of high school graduates with
a purely private financing model. It is not clear how to get off this path, but the
longer we stay on it, the greater the cost in lost talent, lost opportunities, and economic stagnation. What is needed is a serious public policy discussion, setting out
the public, as well as private, benefits of having a highly educated workforce, and
deciding what fraction of the costs of education should be borne by the recipients
of that education and what fraction should be borne by the public at large for the
benefits they, too, receive. Continuing to drive blindly in the direction of privatization is a path to ruin.

A CONCRETE PERSONAL EXAMPLE

John D. Wiley

In 1960, when I graduated from high school in Evansville, Indiana, my father
(a hospital pharmacist) was earning about $10,000/year, which provided total or
partial support for himself, my mother, five children, and a grandmother. Without even considering private schools, I applied to Indiana University—my state

university. The tuition for my freshman year was $125, and the total cost of attendance, including room, board, books, and other expenses, was about $1,000/year. Through newspaper route savings and summer jobs, I managed to pay for about one full year of the costs. Scholarships provided the equivalent of another year, and my family paid for the other two years. As a result, I graduated in four years, totally debt-free. During my senior year, I was joined at IU by one of my sisters. What my parents could foresee for the next 15 years was that they would always have at least one of us in college, and sometimes up to three at once. Nevertheless, it looked manageable with good planning. Tuition was only 1.25 percent of their gross income.

Using the consumer price index to inflate a 1960 salary of $10,000 to today results in a 2005 salary of about $65,000—somewhat above today's median family income of $45,000. In 2005, the resident undergraduate tuition at UW-Madison is about $6,000, or 9.2 percent of $65,000- and 13 percent of $45,000. In 2005, my family would have needed an annual income of $480,000 to be in a position comparable to the reality of 1960. Only 1.3 percent of households have incomes above $250,000/year, so there is no doubt whatsoever that public higher education has become dramatically less affordable for nearly everyone.

NOTES

1. Data pertaining to the UW-System and UW-Madison are from the UW-Madison Office of Budget Planning and Analysis.

2. National Center for Education Statistics, Digest of Education Statistics, 2003.

3. "Chronicle Almanac 2003–04," Chronicle of Higher Education, August 29, 2003.

4. Ibid.

5. Ibid.

6. Ibid.

7. New York Times, May 22, 2005.

8. U.S. Census Bureau, Statistical Abstract of the United States: 2004–05, 124th ed. (Washington, D.C: U.S. Census Bureau, 2004).

CHAPTER 16

Concluding Remarks

F. King Alexander

The *Economist* recently stated in a special edition on the expansion of worldwide higher education that "if more and more governments are embracing massification, few of them are willing to draw the appropriate conclusion from their enthusiasm: that they should either provide the requisite funds or allow universities (public) to charge realistic fees. Many governments have tried to square the circle through tighter management, but management cannot make up for the lack of resources."[1] Embedded within this statement resides the general concept that universally accessible and affordable public higher education systems have become an economic and social necessity for all advancing nations, states, and communities. Unfortunately, however, many policymakers have not demonstrated much interest in providing the requisite public funding needed to acquire the obvious benefits. This dilemma has placed public universities in a difficult quandary as demands of aspiring students swell enrollments and legislators insist greater performance and productivity of the institutions themselves. The dilemma hanging in the balance is just how public and open that these institutions can remain. What is apparent from these conditions is that public colleges and universities are in serious trouble and a crisis is looming between expectations and funding that further challenges both the expansion of educational opportunities and the diversity of the American higher education system.

Throughout this book, *What's Happening to Public Higher Education?*, many of these concerns are discussed while numerous consequences resulting from the fiscal realities are analyzed to better define the magnitude of ongoing developments. In most states public colleges and universities are increasingly facing hard decisions about student tuition, academic offerings, and admissions restrictions.

As indicated in various chapters throughout the book, state public university appropriation reductions have caused many consequences including a proliferation of merit-based scholarship state aid for middle- and upper-class students and a persistent reduction in the share of higher education funding that goes directly to public institutions. Of importance, the slide in public tax support has led to a cyclical effect where expenditures have increasingly been supported by tuition increases that have concomitantly further led to state funding cutbacks for public campuses. Rizzo elucidates this problem in the first chapter of this book.

In reviewing the situations in the individual states discussed throughout this book, several themes emerge. First, all of the states have been hit hard by funding reductions, leading to consistent declines in per-student state funding. In some cases, California and Texas, for example, per-student funding declines can be attributed to only marginal funding growth while enrollments have significantly increased. Second, most states have used tuition revenues to offset state appropriation reductions or stagnation. This has resulted in little change in per-student revenues among the public universities during the last two decades. Third, rapidly increasing student tuition rates have led to many undesirable consequences including state tuition caps and other limitations. These developments have forced public universities such as the University of North Carolina and the University of Wisconsin to increase the urgency of their pursuit over tuition-setting authority. In one notable instance, three public universities in Virginia were willing to forego state funding in exchange for greater autonomy in setting their own tuition levels. Fourth, public universities are increasingly becoming less accessible to those from lower socioeconomic levels because of tuition increases and admissions restrictions. As states continue to cut their relative funding to public higher education, institutions become less open to expansion of access and the commitment to widening avenues of educational opportunity. This has occurred in several states including Georgia, Pennsylvania, Washington, California, Wisconsin, and Illinois, particularly in cases involving flagship and land-grant public universities.

What is truly apparent by analyzing the multiple common challenges facing public higher education is that these issues are widespread and will continue to occur unless a new national debate on the future of public higher education is initiated. Unfortunately, this nation has not engaged in a substantive debate on the developmental needs of a rapidly expanding higher education system for nearly four decades.

In the late 1960s and early 1970s, the debate was prompted by a national concern to address problems relating to poverty and educational opportunity in a period when the social condition of individuals and the viability of some institutions of higher education were held in balance. The debate entailed more than abstract discussions about the mechanics of federal support. The dialogue arose from deeper concerns regarding how the burden of providing resources for higher education would be shared and how to make the system more responsive to increased societal demands for broadened accessibility. Two further themes also permeated the federal policy discourse during this controversial period. First, it was argued that the federal government's role in higher education must remain secondary to the primary responsibilities of states in providing affordable and accessible higher education opportunities. This meant that the emerging federal polices were to be designed to augment state higher education support instead of replacing it. Second, it was argued that the federal policies must assist in protecting the great diversity of the American higher education system by making available public funds to private colleges and universities before a continually widening tuition gap forced many financially marginal independent institutions into financial hardship or bankruptcy. During this period private colleges and universities with the help of the Carnegie Commission on Higher Education established a strong lobbying effort to persuade Congress that direct student aid policies, instead of direct institutional aid policies, would not only meet the national demands to increase educational opportunity through expanding student choice, but would also provide a life preserver of needed fiscal resources to private institutions.[2]

Today, 40 years after these important initial discussions, the federal government has become the principal revenue supplier of higher education and has bailed out many financially starved private schools by means of tuition-based grant, loan and tax assistance policies, while states have steadily reduced their financial commitments and become only secondary contributors to their own state public higher education systems. Current federal government policies provide more than $80 billion in direct student aid grant ($17 billion), loan ($56 billion), and tax ($7 billion) support while state's supply approximately $75 billion for higher education.[3] This signifies an important milestone in the history of American higher education. Today, for perhaps the first time in history, federal government supported aid to postsecondary education has surpassed state government support as the primary supporter of higher education.[4] This was never anticipated when the federal policies were developed four decades ago.

Also, the reluctance on the part of state governments to address the rising fiscal demands pursuant to expansion of accessibility threatens once again the diversity of the American higher education system. Unlike the mid-1960s and early 1970s when private-sector institutions faced financial difficulty, however, today the public sector universities face an emerging financial crisis. According to Kane and Orszag, these trends are further dramatized by analysis of state tax effort for public higher education. From 1977 to 2002, state appropriations per student have fallen from an average of roughly $8.50 per $1,000 in personal income to an average of $7 per $1,000 in personal income. Tuition increases have been exploited to offset this decline in order for institutions to maintain current levels of per-student expenditures. A corresponding effect has been that educational spending per full-time equivalent (FTE) in public institutions has declined relative to private institutions, from 70 percent, in 1977 to 57 percent in 2002.[5] More recently, state financial data indicate that these trends have been exacerbated during the period of 2001 to 2004, when the combined effects of inflation and enrollment growth reduced state and local appropriations to public institutions per FTE student by 16.8 percent from approximately $6,700 per student to $5,800 per student.[6]

These data clearly elucidate the detrimental direction of public higher education finance in the coming years and show that a new national debate is needed to address this important public policy issue. Additional evidence demands a more in-depth analysis into the future of public higher education. A recent OECD report, *Education at a Glance*, shows that the United States has fallen from first to seventh among economically advanced nations in collegiate education attainment levels during the last 40 years.[7] Any new debate, however, should primarily focus on the crisis in American public higher education and the increasing lack of commitment by state governments to respond to the growing societal and economic demands for universal access to higher education. Unlike the earlier debate 40 years ago regarding the role of the federal government in higher education when policies were developed to address lower income student accessibility while also attempting to enhance student "choice" by significantly aiding private institutions, this new debate must address the fiscal crisis facing public higher education and the declining trends in tax effort by states to support institutions. Many economists, historians, and policymakers have forgotten that an important focus of the earlier federal debates was alleged to be the protection of the great diversity of the American higher education system, and that the creation of the policies that aided private institutions through the student choice concept was necessary before private higher education in America vanished forever. At that time, it was feared that private higher education institutions were suffering from a diminution in their share of student enrollment as a result of the emerging threat to their student market by a new kind of public institution, the community college. Today, the diversity of the American higher education system is under threat once again, but this time it is because of the overriding strength of many private institutions supported by public dollars and the overwhelming draw of privatization on public institutions because of state disinvestment that causes them to become quasi-private in their admissions and tuition policies.

The time is ripe to consider a number of new federal policies in this national discourse before all public sector universities fall victim to the idea that becoming quasi-public or quasi-private institutions does not come without detrimental social consequences. Under the current system, federal student aid policies in the form of grant, loan, and tax programs, as well as rapidly increasing state student aid programs, have inadvertently created incentive structures that discourage states from maintaining or increasing common tax support and have at the same time encouraged the continued shift of the costs of public higher education to students and families. Indirectly or directly, these policies give virtually no incentives to states to maintain above average or high levels of tax support to public colleges and universities in exchange for maintaining low-tuition strategies.

During the last few years, the federal government has been revisiting the assumption and analyzing the foundational premises that supports the current federal funding system in anticipation of reauthorizing the Higher Education Act. Most intriguing about this undertaking has been the emerging realization that the present system of student financial aid is a paradox, having the contrary effects of seeking to expand access while indirectly, but materially, contributing to the escalation of costs at many institutions. The laudable goal of expanding the college-going rate while improving student choice is, to a substantial degree, thwarted by implicit government incentives that disproportionately reward some colleges and universities for systematically utilizing tuition and fee revenues more readily.

Congressional leaders have apparently been concerned about these issues. During the last decade many policymakers have expressed concerns that some colleges and universities, particularly higher tuition and for-profit institutions, have been able to use their tuition-setting prerogatives to establish ever rising "sticker prices" that draw inflated federal and state student aid subsidies. In some cases, artificially inflated pricing has resulted in ever larger numbers of students sinking into debt in order to attend college or refusing to enroll in college. Despite much controversy over this issue, it has become more obvious that the cost-pull inflation caused by rising sticker prices and correspondingly endless university expenditures increases of some lead institutions draws more and more federal dollars while doing little to improve the relative financial capabilities of aspiring students from middle- and lower-income families. More important, however, these policies do relatively little for the public colleges and universities that kept their tuition and fee rates comparatively low and for states that insist that higher education is a public good and should maintain strong public investments or tax effort. Thus, the nature of present federal student aid policy in its entirety results in a deceptively logical, but yet countervailing, force that in the name of greater access and choice for middle- and lower-income students does actually create fiscal barriers by inducing some institutions to artificially raise their tuition and fees or sticker prices. In responding, students are either excluded altogether or condemned to suffer debilitating debt burdens.

Even though the perversity of this federal policy and its relationship with many state higher education funding policies is only one of many purposes for the continued escalation of college costs on many campuses, it does permit higher tuition institutions to benefit to a far greater degree than those institutions that strive to maintain low-cost opportunities. This is clearly evidenced by data from the National Postsecondary Student Aid Study in three separate reports during the last decade, where student income levels were controlled, yet drastic fluctuations existed in the amount and ability to qualify for various forms of federal and state direct student aid. This was particularly noticeable with regard to federal subsidized and unsubsidized loans that create an endless source of guaranteed revenues for banks, private lending authorities, and some postsecondary education institutions that are free from public constraints. The exception to the rule to a lesser extent has been Pell grants, which are less sensitive to cost of attendance variations but still demonstrate fluctuations in awards. Moreover, the federal policy gives fiscal incentive for public and private low-tuition institutions to join the race toward full privatization by raising tuition or inflating "sticker prices." This also gives an indirect incentive to states to further cut state appropriations to public higher education institutions and shift the costs from state taxpayers to students and the nation's taxpayers as a whole. This is in direct contrast with Title I elementary and secondary education policy, where states are not allowed to supplant federal funds for state educational funding, and Medicaid, where states are provided with federal matching funds to expand their Medicaid funding.

Under current policies private and public institutions with the greatest amount of autonomy and flexibility to raise prices fare far better than many public sector institutions that are regulated and restrained with cost controls imposed by state law and do not have complete pricing autonomy. States, of course, vary in their ability to maximize federal revenues through grant, loan, and tuition tax credit programs. However, those states that have in fact shifted the financial burden of financing higher education to students by substantially increasing tuition and fees, and therefore, have low tax effort, such as Colorado, Ohio, New York, and Vermont, are able to draw relatively greater federal direct student aid subsidies. On the other hand, states that struggle to keep tuition low by exercising higher tax effort, such as Kentucky, Iowa, Mississippi, California, New Mexico, and North Carolina, find themselves disproportionately disadvantaged in receipt of federal student aid grant and loan dollars.

Thus a difficult dilemma rises to face federal officials. How can the federal government restrain unnecessary and inefficient increases in college costs and at the same time enhance the ideals of universal educational need and expanded access? The inefficiency of the present system is manifest: at present $80 billion annually in tuition-based federal grants, loan subsidies, loans, and tax credits are expended while students incur substantial debt and the disparity in quality (expenditures) among private and public institutions continues to increase. The existing federal policy has been slowly evolving for nearly four decades, while no new macro-funding mechanisms have been seriously explored or even debated during this period.

An obvious omission in considerations of reform is interdependence of the federal mechanisms and the state funding policies. Under current practice the federal fiscal power pulls and somewhat distorts state funding provisions for most lower cost states and public institutions. Moreover, the federal policies tend to constitute inducement for institutions to engage in behavioral patterns that are contrary to their more sober and considerable purposes of expansion of educational opportunity. State governments, as the principal agents for the funding of higher education, have by-in-large exercised that responsibility with considerable commitment and dedication. This high degree of reliance on state governments, however, places state universities in a precarious fiscal environment that is variously impacted by the vagaries of economic cycles and by political caprice. Insofar as states are the primary source of revenue for the vast majority of public institutions, enrolling approximately 77 percent of all higher education students, it is surprising that relatively little attention has been given at the federal level to the considerable differences in state expenditures and tax effort among states for supporting higher education.

Therefore three logical alternatives to the present federal funding scheme would seem to more effectively ensure low-cost access for students to attend higher education institutions. First, mandate that all institutions both public and private use the "net tuition" or average "net cost" of attendance instead of the stated "sticker price" in all federal grant and loan programs to determine who qualifies for student aid awards and how much they should be awarded. Sticker prices do not reflect the actual cost of higher education and too frequently distort information to students and parents as consumers. Also, using sticker prices as the official institutional "cost of attendance" misrepresents the actual average cost of attendance in most federal and state student aid program formulas. If the federal government is to help improve the efficiency of the marketplace of higher education, it can contribute materially by using more accurate information as the viable basis for its allocation of federal subsidies. This would substantially level the playing field for lower cost institutions that do not have the luxury to substantially manipulate their sticker prices.

Second, design and fund a federal program that would impose disincentives on states that provide inadequate or declining tax effort. Such a federal policy would help stabilize the highly volatile state budgetary picture that public higher education must endure annually. Such a modification in federal policy would help ensure that student tuition and fees do not rise disproportionately creating greater barriers for access to higher education. A policy that addresses these issues should also include a feature to guarantee that federal funds do not directly or indirectly supplant state appropriations. The precedent for a supplanting policy resides in similar provisions in federal programs for elementary and secondary education. Such an initiative would simplify federal policies while not penalizing states that continue to adequately finance higher education institutions while keeping their actual costs low.

Third, a comparable policy could be implemented where the federal government provides incentives to states to stabilize their financing of public colleges and universities much like Medicaid and Title I federal directives in elementary and secondary education. This policy also would provide matching resources to states that maintained above-average support of their higher education systems. Policymakers could operationalize this program by establishing an adequate threshold of state tax effort for public higher education and per-student state support. The precedent for this kind of federal directive for states is found in a similar initiative adopted in the Higher Education Amendments in 1972, when the State Student Incentive Grant (SSIG) program, currently known as LEAP, was developed to encourage states to implement and finance direct student aid programs. This program was so successful that numerous attempts have been made by the U.S. Congress to eliminate LEAP because it has successfully completed its original purpose.

The challenges facing public colleges and universities today was the impetus for this unique gathering of public university administrators, economists, and higher education finance experts at Cornell University. For a number of years scholars and public university administrators have struggled to bring adequate attention to the fact that public higher education is increasingly in jeopardy because of instability and disinvestment on the part of most state governments. The consequences of this detrimental trend have varied in individual states from limiting student access to substantial increases in student tuition and fees on many public university campuses. In some cases many public flagship universities have simply selected to privatize many of their operations while reducing their commitment to increasing public needs. This is perhaps an attractive option for a small number of public universities seeking to be quasi-public institutions such as the University of Virginia, University of Michigan, and UCLA. The vast majority of public campuses enrolling the majority of America's students, however, do not have this option or luxury as Chancellor Wiley correctly points out earlier in this book. Increasingly, it appears that public colleges and universities are faced with a number of difficult decisions that will all impact society in multiple ways. Currently, there is not a great deal of optimism in public higher education as evidenced from nearly two decades of financial trends discussed throughout this book. Perhaps this is a good indication that the environment is ready for a new national dialogue about the essential role of the states and the federal government in financing universal access to postsecondary education.

NOTES

1. "A Survey of Higher Education." *The Economist* September 10, 2005: 4–5
2. See David Breneman and Chester Finn, *Public Policy and Private Higher Education*, (Washington, D.C.: The Brookings Institute, 1978). Also see L.E. Gladieux and T.R. Wolanin, *Colleges and the Congress: The National Politics of Higher Education* (Lexington, Mass.: Lexington Books, 1976). Carnegie Commission on Higher Education, *Institutional Aid: Federal Support to Colleges and Universities* (New York: McGraw Hill, 1972). Carnegie Council on Policy Studies in Higher Education, *The Federal Role in Postsecondary Education: Unfinished Business, 1975–1980* (San Francisco: Jossey-Bass). Carnegie Council on Policy Studies, *The States and Private Higher Education* (San Francisco: Jossey-Bass, 1977).
3. College Board, *Trends in Student Aid 2004*. Washington, D.C.
4. Federal research related support is not included.
5. Thomas Kane, Peter Orszag, "Funding Restrictions at Public Universities: Effects and Policy Implications" (September, 2003).
6. State Higher Education Finance, FY 2004, (SHEEO, 2005).
7. Organization for Economic Cooperation and Development, *Education at a Glance: OECD Indicators 2005* (Paris, France: OECD Publishing, March, 2005).

REFERENCES

ACT Institutional file. 2005. National Collegiate Dropout and Graduation Rates. Available from http://www.act.org.path/postsec.pfd/2003.pdf. Accessed July 18, 2005.

Adelman, C. 1999. *Answers in the Tool Box*. Washington, D.C.: U.S. Department of Education.

Advisory Committee on Student Financial Assistance. 2001. *Access Denied: Restoring the Nation's Commitment to Equal Educational Opportunity*. Washington, D.C.: U.S. Department of Education.

Advisory Committee on Student Financial Assistance. 2002. *Empty Promises: The Myth of College Access in America*. Washington, D.C.: U.S. Department of Education.

Alexander, F. King. 2001. Disparities in state tax effort for financing higher education. Paper presented at Conference, Financing Higher Education Institutions in the 21st Century. Cornell Higher Education Research Institute Higher Education Policy Research Conference, May 22–23, 2001.

Alexander, F. King. 2001. "The Silent Crisis: The Relative Fiscal Capacity of Public Universities to Compete for Faculty." *The Review of Higher Education* 24: 113–29.

Alexander, F. King. 2002. "Comparative Study of State Tax Effort and the Role of Federal Government Policy in Shaping Revenue Reliance Patterns." In *Maximizing Revenues in Higher Education*, eds. F. Alexander and Ronald G. Ehrenberg. San Francisco: Jossey-Bass.

Anderson, Eugene L. 2002. *The New Professoriate: Characteristics, Contributions and Compensation*. Washington, D.C.: American Council on Education.

Anonymous. 1988. "Michigan Sets Penalties for Discriminatory Acts." *The Chronicle of Higher Education* (March 30, 1988): A3.

Arellano, M. and S. Bond. 1991. "Some Tests of Specification for Panel Data: Monte Carlo Evidence and an Application to Employment Equations." *The Review of Economic Studies* 58 (2): 277–97.

Astin, A. W. 1992. *What Matters in College: Four Critical Years Revisited*. San Francisco: Jossey-Bass.

Atkinson, Robert D. 2002. *The 2002 New Economy Index*. Washington, D.C.: Progressive Policy Institute.

Avery, C., M. Glickman, C. Hoxby, and A. Metrick. 2004. A Revealed Preference Ranking of US Colleges and Universities. National Bureau of Economic Research working paper no. 10803, Cambridge, Mass.

Balch, Pamela. 1999. "Part-Time Faculty Are Here to Stay." *Planning for Higher Education* 27(3): 32–41.

Baldwin, Roger G. and Jay L. Chronister. 2001. *Teaching Without Tenure: Policies and Practices for a New Era*. Baltimore: Johns Hopkins Press.

Ballard, C. and M. Johnson. 2005."Gender, Expectations and Grades in Introductory Macro Economics at a U.S. University." *Feminist Economics*11(1): 95–122.

Barron's Educational Series. 1997. *Barron's Profiles of American Colleges*, 21st ed. Hauppauge, N.Y.: Barron's Educational Series.

Baumgartner, F. R., and B. D. Jones. 1993. *Agendas and Instability in American Politics*. Chicago: University of Chicago Press.

Bean, J. 1980. "Dropouts and Turnover: The Synthesis and Test of a Casual Model of Student Attrition." *Research in Higher Education* 12: 155–87.

Belsley, D. A., E. Kuh, and R. E. Welsch. 1980. *Regression Diagnostics*. New York: John Wiley.

Berger, J. B., and S. Lyons. in press. "Past to Present: A Historical Look at Retention." In *College Student Retention: Formula for Student Success*, ed. A. Seidman. Westport, Conn.: Praeger Press.

Bettinger, Eric and Bridget Terry Long. 2004. Do College Instructors Matter: The Effects of Adjuncts and Graduate Assistants on Students' Interests and Success. National Bureau of Economic Research working paper no. W10370, March 2004. Cambridge, Massachusetts.

Bettinger, Eric and Bridget Terry Long. 2005. "Help or Hinder? Effects of Adjunct Professors on Student Dropout Rates." Case Western Reserve University Mimeo., Cleveland, Ohio.

Betts, J. R. 2000. *The Changing Role of Education in the California Labor Market*. San Francisco: Public Policy Institute of California.

Biggs, Michael L. and Jayasri Dutta. 1999. "The Distributional Effects of Education Expenditures." *National Institute Economic Review* 169: 68–77.

Bolge, Robert D. 1995. "Examination of Student Learning as a Function of Instructor Status (Full-time vs. Part-time) at Mercer Community College. Unpublished paper, Mercer Community College, available from ERIC (ED382241).

Borge, Lars-Erik and Jorn Rattso. 1995. "Demographic Shift, Relative Costs and the Allocation of Local Public Consumption in Norway." *Regional Science and Urban Economics* 25(6): 705–26.

Borjas, George. 2000. Foreign-Born Teaching Assistants and the Academic Performance of Undergraduates. National Bureau of Economic Research working paper no. 7635. Cambridge, Massachusetts.

Bound, John, Jeffrey Groen, Gabor Kezdi, and Sarah Turner. 2004. "Trade in University Training: Cross-State Variation in the Production and Use of College-Educated Labor." *Journal of Econometrics* 121(1–2):143–73.

Bracco, K. R. 1997. *State Structures for the Governance of Higher Education: Michigan Case Study Summary*. The California Higher Education Policy Center. Available from www.capolicycenter.org.

Braxton, J. M. and A. S. Hirschy. in press. "Theoretical Developments in the Study of College Student Departure." In *College Student Retention: Formula for Student Success*, ed. A. Seidman. Westport, Conn.: Praeger Press.

Breneman, David W. 2004. Are the States and Public Higher Education Striking a New Bargain? AGB Public Policy Paper Series, no. 04-02. Washington, D.C.: Association of Governing Boards.

Breneman, D. W. and C. E. Finn. 1978. *Public Policy and Private Higher Education*. Washington, D.C.: Brookings Institution.

Breneman, D. and J. Finney. 1997. "The Changing Landscape: Higher Education Finance in the 1990s." In *Public and Private Financing of Higher Education: Shaping Public Policy for the Future*, eds. Callan and Finney.

Brewer, Dominic, Eric Eide, and Ronald Ehrenberg. 1999. "Does it Pay to Attend an Elite Private College? Cross-Cohort Evidence on the Effects of College Type on Earnings." *Journal of Human Resources* 34: 104–23.

Bucks, B. 2004. Affirmative Access versus Affirmative Action: How Have Texas' Race-Blind Policies Affected College Outcomes. Ph.D. diss., University of Wisconsin–Madison, Madison, Wisconsin.

Bureau of Labor Statistics. 2004. *Statistics on Employment and Unemployment*. Available from http://www.bls.gov/bls/employment.htm.

Bureau of Labor Statistics. 2005. *Consumer Price Index—All Urban Consumers*. U.S. Department of Commerce. Available from http://www.bls.gov/cpi/home.htm.

Burgan, M., R. Weisbuch, and S. Lowry. 1999. A Profession in Difficult Times: The Future of Faculty. *Liberal Education* 85(4): 6–15.

Card, D. and A. Krueger. 2004. Would the Elimination of Affirmative Action Affect Highly Qualified Minority Applicants? Evidence from California and Texas. National Bureau of Economic Research working paper no. 10366, Cambridge, Massachusetts.

Cardak, Buly A. 1999. "Heterogeneous Preferences, Education Expenditures and Income Distribution." *Economic Record* 75(228): 63–76.

Carnegie Foundation for the Advancement of Teaching. 1994. *A Classification of Institutions of Higher Education*. Princeton, N.J.: Carnegie Foundation for the Advancement of Teaching.

Carnevale, Anthony P. and Richard A. Fry. 2000. *Crossing the Great Divide: Can We Achieve Equity When Generation Y Goes to College?* Princeton, N.J.: Educational Testing Service.

Case, Anne C., Harvey S. Rosen, and James R. Hines, Jr. 1993. "Budget Spillovers and Fiscal Policy Interdependence: Evidence from the States." *Journal of Public Economics* 52(3): 285–307.

Cavalier Daily. 2000. "Thawing Tuition." Available from http://cavalierdaily.com/lead.asp?pid=636.

Cavalier Daily. 2003. "A Prudent Tuition Hike." Available from http://www.cavalierdaily.com/CVArticle.asp?ID=15845&pid=1003.

Center for the Study of Education Policy. various years. *Appropriations of State Tax Funds for Operating Expenses of Higher Education*. Normal: Illinois State University.

Center for the Study of Education Policy. 2004. *Appropriations of State Tax Funds for Operating Expenses of Higher Education*: Normal: Illinois State University.

Chapa, J. and V. A. Lazaro. 1998. "*Hopwood* in Texas: The Untimely End of Affirmative Action." In *Chilling Admissions: The Affirmative Action Crisis and the Search for Alternatives*, ed. G. Orfield and E. Miller, 51–70. Cambridge: Harvard Civil Rights Project.

Chronicle of Higher Education. 2004, August 27. Almanac Issue 2004–2005, 51(1).

Colbeck, Carol L. 2001. *Crucial Issues in Pennsylvania Higher Education: Financing Higher Education.* University Park, Pa.: Center for the Study of Higher Education, The Pennsylvania State University.

Coleman, M. S. (2005). *The Public Purpose of Higher Education: A Priority at Risk.* Midwest Forum of the College Board. Available from http://www.umich.edu/pres/speeches/050228finaid.html.

College Board. various years. *Annual Survey of Colleges.* Washington, D.C.: College Board.

College Board. 1988. *Student Financial Aid 1980–88.* New York: College Board.

College Board. 2004. *Trends in Student Aid, 2004.* Washington, D.C.: College Board.

"College Participation Rates for Students From Low-Income Families by State 1992–2002." 2004. *Postsecondary Higher Education Opportunity* 150: 1–8.

College and University Professional Association for Human Resources. 2001. *National Faculty Salary Survey.* Knoxville, Tenn.: College and University Professional Association for Human Resources.

Commission on the Growth and Support of Graduate Education. 2001. "Innovation and Prosperity at Risk: Investing in Graduate Education to Sustain California's Future." University of California, Oakland. Available from http://www.ucop.edu/services/gradeduc.html.

Committee on Affordability. 2003, October. "The Distribution of Student Financial Aid in Illinois." Illinois Board of Higher Education and the Illinois Student Assistance Commission. Available from http://www.ibhe.org/Affordability/default.htm.

Conley, Valerie, David Leslie, and Lind Zimbler. 2002. *Part-Time Instructional Faculty and Staff: Who They Are, What They Do, and What They Think.* Washington, D.C.: U.S. Department of Education.

Cornwell, Christopher M. and David B. Mustard. 2002. "Race and the Effects of Georgia's HOPE Scholarship." In *Who Should We Help? The Negative Social Consequences of Merit Scholarships,* eds. Donald E. Heller and Patricia Marin. Cambridge, Mass.: The Civil Rights Project, Harvard University.

Cornwell, Christopher M. and David B. Mustard. 2003. "Georgia's HOPE Scholarship Program: Enrollment Gains and Lottery Finance." *Insights on Southern Poverty* 1(3): 5–8.

Cornwell, Christopher M. and David B. Mustard (2005). "Merit Aid and Sorting: The Effects of HOPE-Style Scholarships on college Ability Stratification. "University of Georgia Department of Economics working paper, Athens, GA.

Cornwell, Christopher M., Kyung Hee Lee, and David B. Mustard. 2005. "Student Responses to Merit Scholarship Retention Rules." *Journal of Human Resources* 40: 895–917.

Cornwell, Christopher M., Mark Leidner, and David B. Mustard. 2005. "Rules, Incentives and Policy Implications of Large-Scale Merit-Based Financial Aid." University of Georgia working paper, Athens, Georgia.

Cornwell, Christopher M., David B. Mustard, and Deepa Sridhar. forthcoming. "The Enrollment Effects of Merit-Based Financial Aid: Evidence from Georgia's HOPE Scholarship." Journal of Labor Economics.

Curris, Constantine. 2005. "Public Higher Education: Is the Public Lost?" Unpublished David Dodds Henry Lecture. University of Illinois at Urbana-Champaign.

Curtis, J. W. 2005. "Inequities Persist for Women and Non-Tenure-Track Faculty: The Annual Report on the Economic Status of the Profession, 2004–2005." *Academe* 91(2): 38, 88.

Davis, G. 2001. Speech presented at the 75th Annual Sacramento Host Breakfast, Sacramento California, September 2001.

De Give, M. L., and S. Olswang. 1999. "Coalition Building to Build a Branch Campus System." *The Review of Higher Education* 22(3): 287–313.

DesJardins, S. L., D. Kim, and C. S. Rzonca. 2002–2003. "A Nested Analysis of Factors Affecting Bachelor's Degree Completion." *Journal of College Student Retention: Research, Theory & Practice* 4(4): 407–36.

Dickson, L. 2006. "Does Ending Affirmative Action in College Admissions Lower the Percent of Minority Students Applying to College?" *Economics of Education Review* 25: 109–19.

Do, C. 2004. "The Effects of Local Colleges on the Quality of College Attended." *Economics of Education Review* 23: 249–57.

Drucker, P. F. 1959. *Landmarks of Tomorrow*. New York: HarperCollins Publishers.

Dynarski, S. 2005. "Finishing College: The Role of Schooling Costs in Degree Attainment." Harvard University working paper, April 2005.

Dynes, R. C. 2005. "Testimony before the Senate Budget and Fiscal Review Subcommittee on Education." Available at http://budget.ucop.edu/pres/200506/dynes-senate22805.pdf.

Ehrenberg, Ronald. 2000. *Tuition Rising: Why College Costs So Much*. Cambridge, Mass.: Harvard University Press.

Ehrenberg, Ronald G. 2004. "Don't Blame Faculty for High Tuition: The Annual Report on the Economic Status of the Profession, 2003–04." *Academe* 90 (March/April): 20–46

Ehrenberg, R. G. 2004. Key Issues Currently Facing American Higher Education. Paper presented at the NACUBO annual meeting, Milwaukee Wisconsin, July 2004.

Ehrenberg, R. and D. Brewer. 1994. "Do School and Teacher Characteristics Matter? Evidence from the High School and Beyond." *Economics of Education Review* 13(1): 1–17.

Ehrenberg, Ronald, and Liang Zhang, 2004. The Changing Nature of Faculty Employment, Cornell Higher Education Research Institute working oaper no. 44. Ithaca N.Y.: Cornell Higher Education Research Institute. Available at www.ilr.cornell.edu/cheri.

Ehrenberg, Ronald G. and Liang Zhang. 2005. "Do Tenure and Tenure-Track Faculty Matter?" *Journal of Human Resources* 40: 647–59.

Ehrenberg, Ronald and Michael J. Rizzo. 2004. "Financial Forces and the Future of American Higher Education." *Academe* 90: 28–31.

Ehrenberg, R. and D. Sherman. 1984. "Optimal Financial Aid Policies for a Selective University." *The Journal of Human Resources* 19(2): 202–30.

Ehrenberg, R. G. and C. L Smith. 2003. "The Sources and Uses of Annual Giving at Selective Private Research Universities and Liberal Arts Colleges." *Economics of Education Review* 22, no. 3 (June 2003): 223–35.

Ferguson, Niall. 2001. *The Cash Nexus: Money and Power in the Modern World, 1700–2000*. New York: Basic Books.

Ferris State University. 2003. *Michigan Higher Education System. A Guide for State Policymakers*. Lansing, Mich.: Presidents Council, State Universities of Michigan.

Figlio, David and Kim Rueben. 2001. "Tax Limits and the Qualifications of New Teachers." *Journal of Public Economics* 80(1): 49–71.

350 References

"Financial Aid Agency Proposes Boosting College Grant Awards." 2005, April 5. Associated Press State and Local Wire.

Financial Aid Grant Awards for 2005–06 School Year Increased. 2005, April 22. Associated Press State and Local Wire.

Fulton, R. 2000. "The Plight of Part-Timers in Higher Education." *Change* 32(3): 38–43.

Gappa, Judith M. 2000. "The New Faculty Majority: Somewhat Satisfied but not Eligible for Tenure." *New Directions for Institutional Research* 27(1): 77–86.

Georgia Department of Education. 2002. "2002 Report Cards." Atlanta, Ga.: Georgia Student Finance Commission.

Georgia Student Finance Commission. 2004, June 1. "HOPE Scholarship and Grant Program Highlights: A Summary of Changes and Requirements." Available from http://www.gsfc.org/main/publishing/pdf/2004/hope_highlights.pdf. Accessed September 30, 2004.

Goldin, Claudia and Lawrence Katz. 1999. "The Shaping of Higher Education: The Formative Years in the United States, 1890–1940." *The Journal of Economic Perspectives* 13(1): 37–62.

Greene, William H. 2000. *Econometric Analysis*, 4th ed. Upper Saddle River, N.J.: Prentice Hall.

Greenwood, M.R.C. 2005. "Master Plan Partnerships: Undergraduate Student Financial Aid and Campus-Based Fees." University of California, Oakland. Available from http://www.ucop.edu/acadaff/financialaid.pdf.

Griswold, Anna. 2005. Informational Report on Student Financial Aid. University Park, Pa.: University Faculty Senate; Committee on Admissions, Records, Scheduling, and Student Aid.

Groen, Jeffrey A. 2004. "The Effect of College Location on Migration of College-Educated Labor." *Journal of Econometrics* 121(1–2): 125–42.

Gutman, A. 1987. *Democratic Education*. Princeton, N.J.: Princeton University Press.

Habley, W.R. and R. McClanahan. 2004. "What Works in Student Retention? Four Year Public Colleges, ACT." Available from http://www.act.org.path/postsec.pfd/droptebles/pdf/fouryearpublic/pdf. Accessed July 18, 2005.

Haeger, John D. 1998. "Part-Time Faculty, Quality Programs, and Economic Realities." *New Directions for Higher Education* 26(4): 81–88.

Hamermesh, D.S. 1993. "Treading Water: The Annual Report on the Economic Status of the Profession, 1992–1993." *Academe* 79(2): 24, 78.

Hansen, W.L. and B.A. Weisbrod. 1969a. *Benefits, Costs, and Finance of Public Higher Education*. Chicago: Markham Publishing.

Hansen, W. Lee and Burton Weisbrod. 1969b. "The Distribution of Costs and Direct Benefits of Public Higher Education: The Case of California." *The Journal of Human Resources* 4(2): 176–91.

Hanushek, E. 1986. "The Economics of Schooling: Production and Efficiency in Public Schools." *Journal of Economic Literature* 24(3): 1141–78.

Harrington, Charles and Timothy Schibik. 1969. "The Distribution of Costs and Direct Benefits of Public Higher Education: The Case of California." *Journal of Human Resources* 4(2): 176–91.

Harrington, Charles and Timothy Schibik. 2001. Caveat Emptor: Is There a Relationship Between Part-Time Faculty Unionization and Student Learning Outcomes and Retention. Paper presented at the 41st Annual Meeting of the Association for Institutional Research. Long Beach, California, June 2001.

Hechtkopf, K. 2001. "University Works to Limit Impact of Reduced State Funding: Deans of Three Schools Freeze Hirings; Department Heads Cope with Less Government Support." *The Cavalier Daily* (November 28). Available from http://www.cavalierdaily.com/CVArticle.asp?ID=10481&pid=799.

Heller, Donald E. 1997. "Student Price Response in Higher Education: An Update to Leslie and Brinkman." *Journal of Higher Education* 68(6):624–59.

Heller, Donald E. 1999. "The Effects of Tuition and State Financial Aid on Public College Enrollment." *The Review of Higher Education* 23(1): 65–89.

Heller, Donald E. 2000. *Tuition Pricing and Higher Education Participation in Colorado*. Denver: Colorado Commission on Higher Education.

Heller, Donald E. 2004. State Funding for Higher Education: The Impact on College Access. Paper read at the Symposium on Financing Higher Education, April 2004, at Illinois State University, Normal.

Heller, Donald E. in press. "The Changing Nature of Public Support for Higher Education in the United States." In *Cost-sharing and Accessibility in Higher Education*, eds. P. Teixeira, B. Jongloed, and H. Vossensteyn. Dordrecht. Netherlands: Kluwer Academic Publishers.

Heller, Donald E., ed. 2002. *Condition of Access: Higher Education for Lower Income Students*. Westport, Conn.: Praeger Publishers.

Heller, Donald E., ed. 2001. *The States and Public Higher Education Policy Affordability, Access and Accountability*. Baltimore: The John Hopkins University Press.

Heller, Donald E., and Patricia Marin, eds. 2002. *Who Should We Help? The Negative Social Consequences of Merit Scholarships*. Cambridge, Mass.: The Civil Rights Project at Harvard University.

Heller, Donald E. and Patricia Marin, eds. 2004. *State Merit Scholarship Programs and Racial Inequality*. Cambridge, Mass.: The Civil Rights Project at Harvard University.

Heller, D. and C. Rasmussen. 2001. *Merit Scholarships and College Access: Evidence from Two States*. Cambridge, Mass.: The Civil Rights Project, Harvard University.

Hendry, D. F., E. E. Leamer, and D. J. Poirier. 1990. "The ET Dialogue." *Econometric Theory* 6: 171–261.

Henry, Gary T., Ross Rubenstein, and Daniel T. Bugler. 2004. "Is HOPE Enough? Impact of Receiving and Losing Merit-Based Financial Aid." *Educational Policy* (November): 686–709.

Higher Education Coordinating Board. 1987. *Building a System: The Washington State Master Plan for Higher Education*. Olympia, Wash.: Higher Education Coordinating Board.

Higher Education Coordinating Board. 1988. *Review of Branch Campus Proposals*. Olympia, Wash.: Higher Education Coordinating Board.

Higher Education Coordinating Board. 2005. "Key Facts about Higher Education in Washington." Higher Education Coordinating Board, State of Washington. Available from http://www.hecb.wa.gov/news/newsfacts/2005KeyFactsaboutHigherEducationinWashington.asp.

Hight, Joseph E. and Richard Pollock. 1973. "Income Distribution Effects of Higher Education Expenditures in California, Florida and Hawaii." *Journal of Human Resources* 8(3): 318–30.

Hill, Catherine, Gordon Winston, and Stephanie Boyd. 2004. Affordability: Family Incomes and Net Prices at Highly Selective Private Colleges and Universities. Williams Project on the Economics of Higher Education, discussion paper no. 66r.

Hofstadter, R. 1962. *Anti-Intellectualism in American Life*. New York: Vintage Books.

Holbrook, Thomas M. and Emily Van Dunk. 1993. "Electoral Competition in the American States." *The American Political Science Review* 87(4): 955–62.

HOPE Scholarship Joint Study Commission. 2004. Available from http://www.cviog.uga.edu/hope/. Accessed September 30, 2004.

Hovey, Harold A. 1999. *State Spending for Higher Education in the Next Decade: The Battle to Sustain Current Support*. San Jose, Calif.: National Center for Public Policy and Higher Education.

Hoxby, Caroline. 1997. How the Changing Market Structure of U.S. Higher Education Explains College Tuition. National Bureau of Economic Research working paper no. 6323.

Hoxby, Caroline. 2002. Would School Choice Change the Teaching Profession? National Bureau of Economic Research working paper no. 7866. Cambridge, Massachusetts.

Illinois Board of Higher Education. 2002, June 4. "Assessing the Affordability of Illinois Higher Education." Meeting Agenda Item no. 11. Springfield, Ill.: Illinois Board of Higher Education. Available from http://www.ibhe.org/Board/Agendas/2002/June/June2002.htm.

Illinois Board of Higher Education. 2004, October 5. "Setting a Context for Fiscal Year 2006 Budget Development." Meeting Agenda Item no. 14. Springfield, Ill.: Illinois Board of Higher Education. Available from http://www.ibhe.org/Board/Agendas/2004/October/Default.htm.

Illinois Board of Higher Education. various years. "Salaries and Fringe Benefits at Illinois Colleges and Universities." Springfield, Ill.: Illinois Board of Higher Education Annual reports available at http://www.ibhe.org/Fiscal%20Affairs/faculty.htm.

IPEDS (Integrated Post Secondary Education Data System). FY 2000–01. *Financial Statistics Survey*. Available from http://nces.ed.gov/ipeds.

IPEDS (Integrated Post Secondary Education Data System). Fall 2000. *Fall Enrollment Survey*. Available from http://nces.ed.gov/ipeds.

IPEDS (Integrated Post Secondary Education Data System). AY 2000–01. *Completions Survey*. Available from http://nces.ed.gov/ipeds.

IPEDS (Integrated Post Secondary Education Data System). AY 2003. *Graduation Rate Survey*. Available from http://nces.ed.gov/ipeds.

Jackson, Gregory A., and George B. Weathersby. 1975. "Individual Demand For Higher Education." *Journal of Higher Education* 46(6): 623–52.

Jackson, Maureen. 1999. *Study of the Employment Status of Faculty at Maryland Public Campuses*. Annapolis, Md.: Maryland Higher Education Commission.

Jen, K. I. 2004. *Fiscal Focus: Net Tuition Costs After Financial Aid at State Universities*. Lansing: Michigan House Fiscal Agency.

Johnson, W. R. 2003, March 9. "Lawn of Averages." *The Washington Post*.

Kahlenberg, Richard D. 2004. *America's Untapped Resource: Low-Income Students in Higher Education*. Washington, D.C.: Century Foundation Press.

Kane, Thomas. 1995. *Rising Public College Tuition and College Entry: How Well Do Public Subsidies Promote Access to College?* Cambridge, Mass.: National Bureau of Economic Research.

Kane, Thomas. 1999. *The Price of Admission: Rethinking How Americans Pay for College*. Washington, D.C.: Brookings Institution Press.

Kane, Thomas and P. R. Orszag. 2003. "Higher Education Spending: The Role of Medicaid and the Business Cycle." Brookings Institution Policy Brief No. 124. Washington D.C.: Brookings Institution.

Kane, Thomas J., and Peter R. Orszag. 2004. "Financing Public Higher Education: Short-Term and Long-Term Challenges." Brookings Institute working paper.

Keith, A. 2005. "Crowded Out of Class." *The Cavalier Daily* (January 31). Available from http://www.cavalierdaily.com/CVArticle.asp?ID=22022&pid=1244.

Kingdon, J. W. 1995. *Agendas, Alternatives, and Public Policies.* 2nd ed. New York: Harper Collins.

Kirp, D. L. 2003. *Shakespeare, Einstein, and the Bottom Line: The Marketing of Higher Education.* Cambridge, Mass.: Harvard University.

Kokkelenberg, E. C., M. Dillon, and S. M. Christy. 2006. "The Effects of Class Size on Student Grades at a Public University." Mimeo., Binghampton University, Binghampton, New York.

Krueger, C. 2001. *Merit Scholarships.* Denver, Col.: Education Commission of the States.

Kuh, G. D. 2002. *The College Student Report.* 4th ed. Bloomington, Ind.: National Survey of Student Engagement, Center for Postsecondary Research and Planning, Indiana University.

Ladd, Helen F. and Sheila E. Murray. 2001. "Intergenerational Conflict Reconsidered: County Demographic Structure and the Demand for Public Education." *Economics of Education Review* 20(4): 343–57.

Lamesa, A. 2003. "Is a Faculty Famine Plaguing Popular Departments? Politics and Economics Professors Say Their Departments Cannot Meet Student Demand." *Cavalier Daily* (November 12). Available from http://www.cavalierdaily.com/CVArticle.asp?ID=17725&pid=1079.

Lawrence, Michael. 2005. "Public Universities Need Dynamic Leadership." *The State Journal-Register* (Springfield, Ill.), April 26, p. 12.

Ledbetter, Jim and Jason Seligman. 2003. "Changing Eligibility Requirements: HSGPA and SAT." Carl Vinson Institute of Government (October 22). Available from http://www.cviog.uga.edu/hope/031022requirements.pdf. Accessed September 30, 2004.

Lee, Seong Soo, Rati Ram, and Charles W. Smith. 1999. "Distributive Effect of State Subsidy to Undergraduate Education: The Case of Illinois." *Economics of Education Review* 18(2): 213–21.

Legislative Evaluation and Accountability Program. 2005. "Capital Budget," Legislative Evaluation and Accountability Program, State of Washington. Available from http://leap.leg.wa.gov/leap/analysis/HistEnroExpwithConstant$2005Rev1.xls.

Leslie, David W. 1998a. "The Growing Use of Part-Time Faculty: Understanding Causes and Effects." *New Directions for Higher Education* 26(4): 1–7.

Leslie, David W. 1998b. "Part-Time, Adjunct, and Temporary Faculty: The New Majority? Sloan Conference on Part-Time and Adjunct Faculty." Conference Report from the Conference on Part-Time and Adjunct Faculty. December 3, 1997, Arlington, Virginia.

Leslie, David W. and Judith M. Gappa. 1995. "The Part-Time Faculty Advantage." *Metropolitan Universities: An International Forum* 6(2): 91–102.

Leslie, Larry L. and Paul T. Brinkman. 1988. *The Economic Value of Higher Education.* New York: American Council on Education/Macmillan Publishing.

Lingenfelter, Paul. 2004, April 20. The National Higher Education Scene. Presentation at Symposium on Financing Higher Education: Putting Illinois in the National Context, Center for the Study of Education Policy, Illinois State University, Bloomington.

Long, Bridget Terry. 2004. "How Do Financial Aid Policies Affect Colleges? The Institutional Impact of the Georgia HOPE Scholarship." *Journal of Human Resources* 39(4): 1045–66.

Long, M.C. 2004. "Race and College Admissions: An Alternative to Affirmative Action." *Review of Economics and Statistics* 86(4): 1022–33.

Lowry, Robert C. 2001. "The Effects of State Political Interests and Campus Outputs on Public University Revenues." *Economics of Education Review* 20(2): 105–19.

Marklein, Mary. 2004. "The Wealth Gap on Campus: Low-income Students Scarce at Elite Colleges." *USA Today* (September 20): 1A.

McGuinness Jr., A.C. 1997. "The Changing Structure of State Higher Education Leadership." In *Public Policy and Higher Education*, eds. L. Goodchild et al. Needham Heights, Mass. Pearson Custom Publishing.

McIntyre, R.S. et al. 2003. *Who Pays? A Distributional Analysis of the Tax Systems in All 50 States*, 2nd ed. Washington, D.C.: Institute on Taxation and Economic Policy.

McMillion, R., J. Ramirez, and J. Webster. 2005. State of Student Aid and Higher Education in Texas. Texas Grant Student Loan Corporation. Available from http://www.tgslc.org/pdf/sosa.pdf#search = 'State%20of%20student%20aid%20in%20Texas'. Accessed September 2005.

McNeely, J.H. 1937. *College Student Mortality*. U.S. Office of Education Bulletin 1937,11. Washington, D.C.: U.S. Government Printing Office.

McPherson, Michael S. and Morton Owen Schapiro. 1991. *Keeping College Affordable: Government and Educational Opportunity*. Washington, D.C.: The Brookings Institution.

McPherson, M. and M. Schapiro. 1998. *The Student Aid Game*. Princeton, N.J.: Princeton University Press.

McPherson, M.S., M.O. Schapiro, and G.C. Winston. 1989. "Recent Trends in US Higher Education Costs and Prices: The Role of Government Funding." *AEA Papers and Proceedings* 79(2): 253–57.

Measuring Up. 2002. *The National Report Card on Higher Education*. San Jose, Calif.: The National Center for Public Policy and Higher Education.

Measuring Up. 2004. *The National Report Card on Higher Education*. San Jose, Calif.: The National Center for Public Policy and Higher Education.

Metzger, K. 2004. "Michigan in 2004: Who We Are?" Presentation to the Governor's Policy Retreat, September 23, Mackinac Island, Michigan.

Michigan Community College Association. 2002. *Community Colleges: A Multi-Faceted Resource*. Lansing, Mich.: Michigan Community College Association.

Michigan Information Center, State of Michigan. 2004. *Higher Education Institutional Data Inventory (HEIDI)*. Data file available from https://mcgiweb1.mcgi.state.mi.us/heidi/index.htm.

Michigan League for Human Services. 2004. *Proposal A, School Aid, and the Structural Deficit*. Lansing, Mich.: Michigan League for Human Services.

Middaugh, M.F. 2001. *Understanding Faculty Productivity*. San Francisco: Jossey-Bass. Also available from http://www.udel.edu/IR/cost/.

Modern Language Association. 2002. "Ensuring the Quality of Undergraduate Programs in English and Foreign Languages: MLA Recommendation on Staffing." Available from http://www.mla.org. Accessed June 12, 2003.

Modern Language Association. 2004. "Ensuring the Quality of Undergraduate Programs in English and Foreign Languages: MLA Recommendation on Staffing." Available from http://www.mla.org/ensuring_the_quality. Accessed July 15, 2005.

Moe, Terry. 1990. "The Politics of Structural Choice." In *Organization Theory: From Chester Barnard to the Present and beyond*, ed.Oliver Williamson. New York: Oxford University Press.

Moore, Melanie and Richard Trahan. 1998. "Tenure Status and Grading Practices." *Sociological Perspectives* 41(4): 775–82.

Moore, V., and I. Lefberg. 2005, February 1. Initiative 601: Experience and Context. Presentation to the House Finance Committee, Washington State Legislature, Olympia, Washington.

Moretti, Enrico. 2004. "Human Capital Externalities in Cities." In V. Henderson and J.F. Thisse, eds., *Handbook of Regional and Urban Economics*. Vol. 4, pt. I. North Holland-Elsevier.

Mortenson, T. 2003. "Interstate Migration and Geographic Mobility of College Graduates, 1972 to 2002." *Opportunity Issues*, no. 130 (April). Available from www.postsecondary.org.

Mortensen, T. 2004. "College Participation Rates for Students From Low-Income Families by State 1992–2002." *Postsecondary Higher Education Opportunity* 150: 1–8.

Mortensen, T. 2005. "State Tax Fund Appropriations for Higher Education FY 1961–FY 2005." *Postsecondary Higher Education Opportunity* 151: 1–7.

Mumper, Michael. 1996. *Removing College Price Barriers: What Government Has Done and Why It Hasn't Worked*. Albany: State University of New York Press.

Mumper, M. 2001. "The Paradox of College Prices: Five Stories with No Clear Lesson." In *The States and Public Higher Education Policy Affordability, Access and Accountability*, ed. D.E. Heller, 39–63. Baltimore, Md.: The John Hopkins University Press.

Murray, Sheila E., William N. Evans, and Robert M. Schwab. 1998. "Education-Finance Reform and the Distribution of Education Resources." *American Economic Review* 88(4): 789–812.

Nagowski, M. 2004. Associate Professor Turnover at America's Public and Private Institution of Higher Education. Cornell Higher Education Research Institute working paper no. 33.

National Association of State Scholarship and Grant Programs. various years. *Annual Survey Reports*. Academic years 1988–1989 to 2002–2003. Available from http://www.nassgap.org/researchsurveys/. Accessed September 30, 2004.

National Association of State Student Grant and Aid Programs. 2004. *34th Survey Report on State-Sponsored Student Financial Aid, 2002–03 Academic Year*. Washington, D.C.: National Association of State Student Grant and Aid Programs.

National Association of State Student Grant and Aid Programs. 2004. *NASSGAP 34th Annual Survey Report on State-Sponsored Student Financial Aid 2002–2003 Academic Year*. Springfield: Illinois Student Assistance Commission.

National Association of State Universities and Land-Grant Colleges (NASULGC). 2001. *Shaping the Future: The Economic Impact of Public Universities*. Washington, D.C.: NASULGC Office of Public Affairs.

National Center for Education Statistics. 1997. *Instructional Faculty and Staff in Higher Education Institutions: Fall 1987 and Fall 1992*. National Center for Education Statistics working paper no. 97–470, Washington, D.C.

National Center for Education Statistics. 2001. Institutional Policies and Practices: Results from the 1999 National Study of Postsecondary Faculty, Institutional Survey. National Center for Education Statistics working paper no. 2001–201. Washington, D.C.

National Center for Education Statistics. 2003. *Projection of Education Statistics to 2013.* By Debra Gerald and William Hussar. Washington, D.C.: U.S. Department of Education.

National Center for Education Statistics. 2003. *Digest of Education Statistics, 2002.* Washington, D.C.: U.S. Department of Education.

National Center for Education Statistics. 2004. *Paying for College: Changes between 1990 and 2000 for Full-Time Dependent Undergraduates.* Washington, D.C.: National Center for Education Statistics. Available from http://nces.ed.gov/pubs2004/2004075.pdf.

National Center for Education Statistics. 2005. *Common Core of Data.* Washington, D.C.: U.S. Department of Education. Available from http://nces.ed.gov/ccd/.

National Center for Education Statistics. 2005. *IPEDS Peer Analysis System.* Washington, D.C.: U.S. Department of Education. Online data file available from http://nces.ed.gov/ipedspas.

National Center for Education Statistics. *Integrated Postsecondary Education Data System (IPEDS).* Washington D.C.: U.S. Department of Education.

National Center For Public Policy and Higher Education. 2004. *Measuring Up 2004: The State Report Card on Higher Education—Pennsylvania.* San Jose, Calif.: National Center For Public Policy and Higher Education.

National Institute of Education. 1984. *Involvement in learning: Realizing the Potential of American Higher Education.* Washington, D.C.: U.S. Department of Education.

Niskanen, William A. 1968. "Nonmarket Decision Making: The Peculiar Economics of Bureaucracy." *American Economic Review* 58(1): 293–305.

Norris, Timothy. 1991. "Nonnative English-speaking Teaching Assistants and Student Performance." *Research in Higher Education* 32(4): 433–46.

North Carolina State Education Assistance Authority. "Measures of College Affordability in North Carolina." November 2003.

Office of Financial Management. 2004. "2004 Total Population Estimates by Age, Gender and Race: Washington and Its Counties." Office of Financial Management, State of Washington. Available from http://www.ofm.wa.gov/pop/race/2004%20race_estimates.xls.

Office of Financial Management. 2005a. "Participation Rates by Age Public Four-Year Institution." Office of Financial Management, State of Washington. Available from http://www.ofm.wa.gov/databook/education/et121.htm.

Office of Financial Management. 2005b. "Participation Rates of U.S. Average, State at 70 Percent, and Washington State and Washington State Ranking by Type of College and Division, Fall 1990 to 1998." Office of Financial Management, State of Washington. Available from http://www.ofm.wa.gov/hied/partrate/partraterank.pdf.

Office of Planning and Institutional Assessment. 2005. *Strategic Indicators: Measuring and Improving University Performance.* University Park: The Pennsylvania State University.

Ogren, C. A. 2005. *The American State Normal School: "An Instrument of Great Good."* New York: Palgrave-Macmillan.

Orszag, Peter R. and Thomas Kane. 2003. *Funding Restrictions at Public Universities: Effects and Policy Implications.* Brookings Institution. September 2003.

Palmer, James. 1998. Enhancing Faculty Productivity: A State Perspective. Education Commission of the States Policy Paper, Denver, Colorado.

Palmer, James. 2004. "Grapevine." Illinois State University, *Opportunity*, no. 151 (January 2005): 1–6.

Pascarella, E. T., and P. T. Terenzini. 1991. *How College Affects Students: Findings and Insights from Twenty Years of Research.* San Francisco: Jossey-Bass.

"A Pass-Fail Test for Charter Colleges." 2004. *The Virginian-Pilot* (December 26, Commentary).

Pennsylvania Department of Education. 2005. *PA Higher/Adult ed.: PDE Role in Higher Education 2005.* Available from http://www.pdehighered.state.pa.us/higher/cwp/view.asp?a = 133&Q = 41002.

The Pennsylvania State University Department of Public Information. 2005a. *Faculty Salaries Are Top Priority Despite Tight Budget Year.* The Pennsylvania State University 2000. Available from http://www.psu.edu/ur/archives/intercom_2000/May4/salaries.html.

The Pennsylvania State University Department of Public Information. 2005b. *Budget Shortfall Spurs Tuition Rate Increase; Differential Tuition Plan Approved for 2003–2004.* The Pennsylvania State University 2002. Available from http://www.psu.edu/ur/2002/12jul02bottuition.html.

Peterson, M. W., and M. K. McLendon. 1998. "Achieving Independence Through Conflict and Compromise: Michigan." In *Seeking Excellence Through Independence: Liberating Colleges and Universities from Excessive Regulation,* ed. MacTaggart, T. J. San Francisco: Jossey-Bass.

Pisani, Anoush M., and Nathan Stott. 1998. "An Investigation of Part-Time Faculty Commitment to Developmental Advising." *Research in Higher Education* 39(2): 121–42.

Porter, S. R. 2003–2004. "Understanding Retention Outcomes: Using Multiple Data Sources to Distinguish Between Dropouts, Stopouts, and Transfer-Outs." *Journal of College Student Retention: Research, Theory & Practice* 5(1): 53–70.

Poterba, James. 1994. "State Responses to Fiscal Crises: The Effects of Budgetary Institutions and Politics." *Journal of Political Economy* 102(4): 799–821.

Poterba, James M. 1997. "Demographic Structure and the Political Economy of Public Education." *Journal of Public Policy and Management* 16: 48–66.

Poterba, James. 2001. *Profiles of American Colleges,* 24th ed. Hauppauge, N.Y.: Barron's Educational Series, Inc.

Poterba, James M. and Kim S. Rueben. 1995. "The Effect of Property-Tax Limits on Wages and Employment in the Local Public Sector." *American Economic Review* 85(3): 384–89.

Presidents Council State Universities of Michigan. 2005. TITLE. Lansing.

Prince, Hank. 2003. *The Long View: State University Enrollments, Revenues, and Expenditures FY 1977 through FY 2002.* Lansing, Mich.: House Fiscal Agency Report.

Public Sector Consultants. 2003. *Michigan in Brief: 2002–03.* Lansing, Mich.: Nonprofit Association and the Council of Michigan Foundations.

Quantum Research Corporation. 2005. *WebCASPAR database system.* Bethesda, Md.: Quantum Research Corporation. Available from http://caspar.nsf.gov/.

Research Associates of Washington. 1998. *Inflation Measures for Schools, Colleges and Libraries: 1998 Update.* Washington, D.C.: Research Associates of Washington.

Richardson, R. C., K. R. Bracco, P. M. Callan, and J. E. Finney. 1999. *"Illinois",* in *Designing State Higher Education Systems for a New Century.* Phoenix, Ariz.: Oryx Press.

Rizzo, Michael J. 2004. "A (Less Than) Zero Sum Game? State Funding for Public Education: How Public Higher Education Institutions Have Lost." Ph.D. diss., Cornell University.

Rizzo, Michael J., and Ronald G. Ehrenberg. 2004. "Resident and Nonresident Tuition and Enrollment at Flagship State Universities." In *College Choices: The Economics of Which College, When College, and How to Pay For It*, ed. Caroline M. Hoxby. Cambridge: The University of Chicago Press.

Rockoff, Jonah E. 2004. "The Impact of Individual Teachers on Student Achievement: Evidence from Panel Data." *American Economic Review* 94(2): 247–52.

Ryan, John F. 2004. "The Relationship Between Institutional Expenditures and Degrees Attainment at Baccalaureate Colleges." *Research in Higher Education* 45: 97–114.

Seligman, Jason. 2003. "Georgia's HOPE: Costing out Policy Recommendations." Presented at the November 13, 2003 meeting of the HOPE Scholarship Joint Study Commission, Carl Vinson Institute of Government, Athens, Georgia.

Seligman, Jason, Richard Milford, John O'Looney, and Jim Ledbetter. 2004. *HOPE Scholarship Joint Study Commission Report*. Athens, Ga.: Carl Vinson Institute of Government. Available from http://www.cviog.uga.edu/hope/report.pdf.

Selingo, Jeffrey. 2001. "Grant Program Angers Pennsylvania Colleges." *The Chronicle of Higher Education*, August 17, A22.

Shanahan, S. Y. 2005, May. "An Analysis of How Development Is Funded at the University of Washington." Master's Degree Project, Daniel J. Evans School of Public Affairs, University of Washington, Seattle.

Shannon, B. 2003. "House Tinkers with Initiative 601." *The Olympian*, April 3, 2003.

Sheppach, R., 2003. "What Ails the States?" Washington D.C.: National Governors Association. Available from http://www.nga.org/nga/legislativeUpdate/1,1169, C_ISSUE_BRIEF^D_4804,000.html.

Singell, Larry D. Jr., Glen R. Waddell, and Bradley R. Curs. forthcoming. "Hope for the Pell? The Impact of Merit-Aid on Needy Students." Southern Economic Journal.

Smallwood, Scott. 2003. "Non-Tenure-Track Faculty Members Vote to Unionize at U. of Michigan." *Chronicle of Higher Education* 49(May 9): A15.

Spady, W. 1971. "Dropouts from Higher Education: An Interdisciplinary Review and Synthesis." *Interchange* 1: 64–85.

SRI International. 2002. *The Economic Impact of Michigan's Public Universities*. SRI Project no. PDH 02–019.

State Council of Higher Education for Virginia. 2003. "Condition of Higher Education Funding in Virginia: A SCHEV Report." Richmond, Va.: State Council of Higher Education for Virginia.

State Higher Education Executive Officers (SHEEO). 2004. *State Higher Education Finance: FY 2003*. Denver, Col.: SHEEO.

State Higher Education Executive Officers (SHEEO). 2005. "State Higher Education Finance FY 2004." Denver, Col.: SHEEO.

"State Tax Fund Appropriations for Higher Education FY 1961–FY 2005." *Postsecondary Higher Education Opportunity* 151 (January 2005).

Stinebrickner, Ralph and Todd R. Stinebrickner. 2003. "Understanding Educational Outcomes of Students from Low-Income Families: Evidence from a Liberal Arts College with a Full Tuition Subsidy Program." *Journal of Human Resources* 38: 591–617.

Subcommittee on Higher Education. 1998. *Costs of Postsecondary Education*. Harrisburg: Pennsylvania House of Representatives.

Switkes, E. 1999. "University of California Peer Review System and Post-Tenure Evaluation." *Innovative Higher Education* 24: 39–48.

Switkes, E. 2001. "The University of California Voluntary Early Retirement Incentive Programs." In *To Retire or Not? Retirement Policy and Practice in Higher Education*, ed. Robert C. Clark and P. Brett Hammond. University Park: University of Pennsylvania Press.

Task Force on Higher Education Funding of the Pennsylvania House of Representatives. 1994. Report. Harrisburg: Pennsylvania House of Representatives.

Tebbs, Jeffrey M. 2005. "Redefining 'Access': A Preliminary Evaluation of the University of Virginia's New Financial Aid Initiative." Senior Thesis, University of Virginia, Charolettesville.

Texas Education Agency. 2005. "Pocket Editions Texas Public School Statistics." Texas Education Agency. Available from http://www.tea.state.tx.us/perfreport/pocked/index.html.

Texas Higher Education Coordinating Board. 1996. "High School Graduates Enrolled in Higher Education." Texas Higher Education Coordinating Board. Available from http://www.thecb.state.tx.us/reports/PDF/0960.PDF.

Texas Higher Education Coordinating Board. 2002. "Average Faculty Salary in Public Universities in Texas and the Ten Most Populous States for Fiscal Year 2002." Texas Higher Education Coordinating Board. Available from http://www.txhighereddata.org/Reports/PDF/0452.PDF

Texas Higher Education Coordinating Board. 2002, June. "Data and Performance Report." Texas Higher Education Coordinating Board. Available from http://www.txhighereddata.org/Reports/PDF/0464.pdf

Texas Higher Education Coordinating Board. 2003, May. "Data and Performance Report." Texas Higher Education Coordinating Board. Available from http://www.txhighereddata.org/Reports/PDF/0611.pdf.

Texas Higher Education Coordinating Board. "Financing Higher Education: The Appropriate Balance among Appropriations, Tuition and Fees, and Financial Aid to Achieve the Goals of Closing the Gaps." Texas Higher Education Coordinating Board. Available from http://www.thecb.state.tx.us/reports/pdf/0513.pdf.

Texas Higher Education Coordinating Board. "First-Time Undergraduate Applicant, Acceptance, and Enrollment Information." Texas Higher Education Coordinating Board. Available from http://www.txhighereddata.org/Interactive/AppAccEnr.cfm.

Texas Higher Education Coordinating Board. "Per-Student Revenue Available to Texas Public Universities Fiscal Year 1990 to Fiscal Year 2001." Texas Higher Education Coordinating Board. Available from http://www.thecb.state.tx.us/reports/pdf/0521.pdf.

Texas Higher Education Coordinating Board. "Prep Query Tool." Texas Higher Education Coordinating Board. Available from http://www.thecb.state.tx.us/InteractiveTools/PREP/menu.htm.

Texas Higher Education Coordinating Board. "Statistical Reports." Texas Higher Education Coordinating Board. Available from http://www.txhighereddata.org/Reports/HTM/0777.HTM.

Tienda, M., and K. Lloyd. UT's Longhorn Opportunity Scholars (LOS) and A&M's Century Scholars Programs. Texas Higher Education Opportunity Project. Available from http://texastop10.princeton.edu/reports/misc/longhorn_century.pdf.

Tienda, M., Cortes, K., and S. Niu. 2003. College Attendance and the Texas Top 10 Percent Law: Permanent Contagion or Transitory Promise. Texas Higher Education Opportunity Project working paper.

Tienda, M., Leicht, K., Sullivan, T., Maltese, M., and K. Lloyd. 2003. Closing the Gap?: Admissions and Enrollments at the Texas Public Flagships before and after Affirmative Action. Texas Higher Education Opportunity Project working paper.

Timberg, Craig. 1998, December 22. "Va. Makes Colleges a Priority; Cutting Tuition to Be a Focus of Assembly Session." *Washington Post*, Metro Section: D01.

Tinto, V. 1975. Dropout from Higher Education: A Theoretical Synthesis of Recent Research." *Review of Educational Research* 45: 89–125.

Tinto, V. 1993. *Leaving College: Rethinking the Causes and Cures of Student Attrition*. Chicago: The University of Chicago Press.

UNESCO. 2003. *Financing Education—Investments and Returns*. Paris: UNESCO Publishing.

U.S. Census Bureau. 2000. 2000 U.S. Census. Summary File 3 Sample Data. Available from http://www.census.gov/Press-Release/www/2002/sumfile3.html.

U.S. Census Bureau. 2002. Population Projections. Available from http://www.census.gov.

U.S. Census Bureau. 2004. Population Estimates. Available from http://www.census.gov/.

U.S. Census Bureau. 2004. "Table 5. Population Estimates by Sex, Race and Hispanic or Latino Origin: April 1, 2000 to July 1, 2002." Available from http://www.census.gov/popest/archives/2000s/vintage_2002/ST-EST2002-ASRO-05.html.

U.S. Census Bureau. 2005. *Median Income for 4-Person Families, by State*. Washington, D.C.: U.S. Census Bureau. Available from http://www.census.gov/hhes/www/income/4person.html.

U.S. Census Bureau. 2005. *Statistical Abstract of the United States: 2004–2005*. Washington, D.C.: U.S. Census Bureau.

U.S. Department of Education, National Center for Education Statistics. 2001. *Background Characteristics, Work Activities, and Compensation of Faculty and Instructional Staff in Postsecondary Institutions: Fall 1998*, NCES 2001–2152, ed. Linda J. Zimbler. Washington, D.C. (NSOPF:99).

U.S. News and World Report. 2002. "The Top 50 Public National Universities." In *America's Best Colleges*.

U.S. News and World Report. 2004. "Best Universities—Master's (By Region)." In *America's Best Colleges 2004*.

U.S. News and World Report. "National Universities." Available from http://www.usnews.com/usnews/edu/college/rankings/ranknatudoc_brief.php.

University of California. 2002. "Long-Range Planning: Maintaining Excellence in a Period of Exceptional Growth." Available from http://www.ucop.edu/planning/lrp/lrp.html.

University of California. 2003. "Long-Range Planning Regents' Update: Maintaining Excellence in a Period of Exceptional Growth." Available from http://budget.ucop.edu/pres/200304/lrpsept2003updatefinal.ppt.

University of Georgia Fact Book Annual editions. 2005. Edited by University of Georgia Institutional Research and Planning, Athens, Georgia. Available from http://www.oir.uga.edu/factbks.htm.

University Investment Commission. 2003. "Final Report." Public Sector Consultants. Available from http://www.pscinc.com/Documents/uic/UIC_index.htm.

University of Virginia, Board of Visitors, Finance Committee. 2005, February 3. "Minutes of the Meeting of the Finance Committee." Available from http://www.virginia.edu/bov/meetings/05feb/%2705%20Feb%20Finance%20Comm%20Book.pdf.

University of Washington. 2005a. "Accountability Program and Performance." Available from http://www.washington.edu/admin/factbook/Accountability.

University of Washington. 2005b. "Graduation, Retention and Student Attrition (Undergraduates)." Available from http://www.washington.edu/admin/factbook/OisAcrobat/OisPDF.html#anchor19.

University of Washington. 2005c. "University of Washington Awards and Expenditures, FY 04." Available from http://www.washington.edu/research/annualreport/2004/fig01_04.pdf.

University of Washington. 2005d. "Washington by the Numbers." Available from http://depts.washington.edu/beahusky/numbers/facts.shtml.

University of Washington. 1988. Plan to Expand Upper Division and Graduate Programs in Puget Sound Region. Report to Higher Education Coordinating Board. Seattle: University of Washington.

Verry, D. and B. Davies, eds. 1976. *University Costs and Outputs*. Amsterdam: Elsevier Scientific Publishing Company.

Washington Higher Education Coordinating Board. 2005. *2004–05 Tuition and Fee Rates: A National Comparison*. Olympia: Washington Higher Education Coordinating Board.

Weill, A. et al. 2003. *Social Program Spending and State Fiscal Crisis*. Assessing the New Federalism Project. Washington D.C.: The Urban Institute.

Western Interstate Commission for Higher Education. 2003. Knocking at the College Door: Projections of High School Graduates by State, Income, and Race/Ethnicity 1988–2018. Boulder, Col.: Western Interstate Commission for Higher Education.

White, M. 2004. "Comment." In *College Choices: The Economics of Where to Go, When to Go, and How to Pay for It*, ed. C.M. Hoxby, 349–53. Chicago: The University of Chicago Press.

Windham, Douglas M. 1972. "Equity Implications of State Tuition Policy and Student Loans: Comment." *Journal of Political Economy* 80(3): S172–74.

Winston, Gordon. 1999. "Subsidies, Hierarchy and Peers: The Awkward Economics of Higher Education." *Journal of Economic Perspectives* 13(1): 13–36.

Wooldridge, Jeffrey M. 2002. *Econometric Analysis of Cross-Section and Panel Data*. Cambridge, Mass.: The MIT Press.

Zumeta, W. 1996. "A Case Study: Where Can We Put All the Students?" *Thought & Action* 12(2): 7–44.

Zumeta, W. 2001. "Public Policy and Accountability in Higher Education: Lessons from the Past and Present for the New Millennium." In *The States and Public Higher Education Policy: Affordability, Access, and Accountability*, ed. D.E. Heller, 155–97. Baltimore: Johns Hopkins University Press.

INDEX

116; grant aid compared with U.S., 119–20; grant aid per FTE, 119; Pell Grants, 127; private four-year schools, 111; public postsecondary institutions, 110; rank among all states, 119; recession 2001 aftermath, 107; student aid programs, 7; student migration to public institutions, 111; technical schools, 110; tuition and fees, 113, 118; tuition/fees compared with SREB states, 118; tuition/fees compared with institutions nationwide, 118; two-year colleges, 110. *See also* Georgia (state); Georgia, University System of; HOPE program

Georgia, University System of (USG), 110–34; administration of technical schools, 110; enrollment changes, 110; enrollment totals, 110; Georgia Institute of Technology, 110; Georgia Tech and Pell recipients, 127; Georgia tech and selectivity, 127; public HBCUs, 111; regional universities, 110–11; research universities, 110–11; state colleges and universities, 110–11; two-year colleges, 111; University of Georgia, 110. *See also* Georgia, public higher education; HOPE program

Georgia's HOPE scholarship program. *See* HOPE program

GI Bill, 333; impact on postsecondary education, 328; impact on US economy, 328

Gifts and endowment income, explained, 330

Governing mechanisms, in public institutions, 107, 110–13

Governors, 24; and substantial appropriative power, 24–25

GPA. *See* Grade-point average

Grade-based retention requirements, and HOPE program, 131

Grade-point average (GPA): in North Carolina, 197; and UGA freshmen, 131

Graduate student education, 56; assistantships for, 295; fees at UC, 102; and financially viable programs at UW, 296; recruitment at UC, 101; trends at UW,

295–96; trends at WSU, 295–96; and tuition hikes at UW, 295

Graduate teaching assistants (GTAs): effectiveness of, 55; international GTAs, 198; teaching first-semester students, 67; total at UNC, 198; training program at UNC, 198; at UNC-CH, 198; at UNCG, 198; use of at UW system, 312

Graduation rates, 39–40, 71, 75, 329; and access, 77; and BA degree, 48; consequences of falling, 78; and contingent faculty, 37; effects of funding on, 76; and enrollment for full-time study, 77; equations, 42; factors affecting, 72; five-year, 38, 72, 76, 101; four-year, 38, 76–77, 101; and freshmen at UC, 101; in Georgia, 133; impact of funding cuts on, 71–82; increasing accuracy of evaluating, 79; and in-state students, 40–42; and institution's reputation, 78; and institutional funding expenditures per student, 72–73; and length of time to degree, 76; males compared with females, 77, 80; as a measure of institutional quality, 71; at Michigan four-year colleges, 179; and out-of-state tuition, 76; and Pell Grants, 40; and percentage of full-time faculty, 39; predicted by modeling, 75; and retention rates in Georgia, 129; and SAT scores, 40, 76; and six-year graduation, 38, 71, 76, 246–47; at UC, 101; at UGA, 131; and undergraduate students, 38; at UNC, 195; and an unprepared workforce, 78; at USG, 125; at UW-Madison, 315

Grants. *See* Federal loans; Financial aid; Pell Grants

Grapevine Project at Illinois State University, 211

Gratz v. Bollinger, 169

Greenspan, Alan, and optimism about research universities, 106

Gross revenue: of private colleges and universities, 330; of public educational institutions, 330

Grutter v. Bollinger, 169

Harvard University, endowments, 332
HECB. *See* Higher Education Coordinating Board
Helping Outstanding Pupils Educationally (HOPE). *See* HOPE program
Hendry, and seeking a parsimonious model, 76
HEPI. *See* Higher Education Price Index
Higher education: alternatives to present federal funding scheme, 343; budget expenditures, 8, 219; declining appropriations, 28; expansion after World War II, 328; funding, fluctuating levels of, 4; history of, 328; percent of U.S. population with college degrees, 328; political factors and the education budget, 23; statistical overview, 329; worldwide, 337
Higher Education Act, 29, 340
Higher Education Amendments, 343
Higher Education Cooperation Act, 146
Higher Education Coordinating Board (HECB), 278; limited powers of, 278
Higher Education Price Index (HEPI), 91, 172; authors of, 244; compared with Consumer Price Index, 244; purpose of, 244
High-tuition/high-aid policy, 328; as affecting composition of entering classes, 269; concerns about, 270; and demand adjustment, 269; in Pennsylvania, 207, 215–16; states aggressively pursuing, 217; as a stopgap response to crises, 267; in Virginia, 252, 266–70; versus low-tuition policy, 266–67
Hiring faculty. *See* Recruiting faculty
Hispanic students: and need-based financial aid in Texas, 239; in Texas institutions, 230–32
Historically Black Colleges and Universities (HBCUs), in Georgia, 107
HOPE program, 7, 110, 121, 125; amount of aid in dollars, 114; awards by institution type, 114; compared with U.S. grant aid, 120; connection to tuition, 119; disbursements per undergraduate FTE, 116; effects on enrollment,

130; effects on persistence, 130; and enrollment of Pell-eligible students, 121; ensuring financial stability of, 115; and faculty hiring, 132; freshman enrollment and, 127–28; and grade-based retention requirements, 131; and graduation, 133; and grant-aid share of college expenses, 120; and higher-achieving students, 133; and homeschool students, 114; imitation by other states, 132; impact of, 120; importance to Georgia education, 132; as incentive for achievement, 133; as inducing course withdrawals, 133; as influence on enrollment, 128; as influence on SAT scores, 128; and limiting tuition increases, 132; long-term financial stability of, 133; and Georgia lottery revenues, 113, 119; and minimizing tuition increases, 119; and motivation for studying, 130; and nontraditional students, 114; number of awards, 114; origins, 113; pre-K programs, 115; and private schools, 114; program overview, 113; qualifications for a scholarship, 113; requirements after acceptance, 113; and retention rates, 129–30, 133; retroactive awards, 114; and SAT scores, 128; and state appropriations to students, 115; and stratification in Georgia, 127; strong political support for, 133; and student quality, 133; and summer school credits, 131; and taking easier courses, 130; and technical schools, 113; and time-to-degree, 131; as transforming Georgia's grant aid, 119; and tuition policies, 132; and types of financial aid, 113; value of the award, 113; wide political support for, 120
HOPE Teacher Scholarship, 114
Hopwood v. University of Texas, 230

IBHE. Illinois Board of Higher Education, 140
Illinois (state): diverse population, 137; education funds per capita, 141; fiscal

223; at USG, 117; in Washington state, 294

New Professoriate: Characteristics, Contributions, and Compensation, The (Anderson), 37

New York (state): decline in state appropriations, 7; percentage of education and higher education shares of the general fund, 13

Non-means-tested aid, as not altruistically motivated, 28

Non-merit-based grants, in HOPE program, 113

Non-need-based aid program expansion, popularity of, 3

Nonresidents, 38; in Wisconsin, 307–8

Non-tenure-track faculty. *See* Adjuncts

Nontraditional students: and access in UW system, 311; and HOPE program, 114

North Carolina higher education, 183–206. *See also* University of North Carolina

Occupations: categories by Bureau of Labor Statistics, 86–87; fasting growing, 86; professional and managerial jobs, 86

Ohio, higher education: adjuncts as instructors, 61; Board of Regents, 52; characteristics of students, 60; graduate-student instructors, 61; public colleges, 59

Out-migration, 10; defined, 15; as predictor of higher education health, 19

Out-of-state students, 38; in Wisconsin, 307–8

Output measures, 107; assessing, at USG, 125. *See also* Enrollment; Graduation rates; Retention rates

Part-time faculty. *See* Adjuncts

Part-Time Instructional Faculty and Staff: Who They Are, What They Do, and What They Think (Conley, Lesley, and Zimbler), 37

Patashnik, Eric, and contracts with the state, 268

Pell Grants, 27, 29, 341; in Georgia, 126–27; and graduation rates, 40–41; and HOPE program, 114, 121; and leading universities, 103; and recipients, 42; and shrinking availability of funds, 20; at UC, 102; variables, 20; at Washington state, 294. *See also* Financial aid; Need-based aid

Penn State, 208–28; cost-cutting efforts, 225; differentiated missions, 215; enrollments, 210; erosion of state support, 225; faculty salaries, 225; expense compared with University of Vermont, 215; increasing volume of private loans, 218; state appropriations to, 211; tuition increases, 215, 225. *See also* Pennsylvania higher education

Pennsylvania (state): appropriations to education, 219–20; college-age population, 224; high school graduates, 224; recession, 211

Pennsylvania higher education, 207–28; adjuncts, 42–43; autonomous governance, 208–9; community colleges, 208–11; doctoral-granting institutions, 208; enrollment, 209–11, 217–18; instructors, 207; migration patterns, 211; private college lobby, 226; student population, 207; tripartite structure, 208. *See also* Penn State

Pennsylvania higher education (accessibility), 222–24; borrowing in private loan programs, 225; financial need, 217; financial gaps between students, 225; high-tuition/high-aid policy, 215–16; income needed to pay for education, 224; low-income students, 225; maximum grants, 223; measures of affordability, 223; median incomes, 217; merit-aid programs, 223; need-based aid, 216–18, 223–24; Pell Grants, 226; tuition and fees, 208, 218, 221

Pennsylvania higher education (financing), 211–15; decline in state appropriations, 7; dependence on private institutions, 223; funding for community colleges, 212; funding trends, 208, 218–24; future funding, 224; growth

ABOUT THE
EDITOR AND THE
CONTRIBUTORS

THE EDITOR

Ronald G. Ehrenberg is Irving M. Ives Professor of Industrial and Labor Relations and Economics, Cornell University and director of the Cornell Higher Education Research Institute. He is also chair of the American Association of University Professors Committee on the Economic Status for the Faculty. Dr. Ehrenberg holds a Ph.D. in economics from Northwestern University and is the author or co-author of 16 books and more than 110 papers.

THE CONTRIBUTORS

F. King Alexander is the President of California State University, Long Beach.

Allison Bell is a graduate research assistant at the Center for the Study of Higher and Postsecondary Education at the University of Michigan.

Eric P. Bettinger is an assistant professor of economics at Case Western Reserve University and a faculty research fellow at the National Bureau of Economic Research.

Gary L. Blose is the assistant provost for institutional research at the State University of New York (SUNY) system administration.

Betsy E. Brown is the associate vice president for faculty support and international programs in the office of the president of the University of North Carolina system.

Robert L. Clark is a professor of economics and a professor of business management at North Carolina State University.

Christopher Cornwell is a professor of economics at the University of Georgia and a senior fellow at the Institute of Higher Education at the University of Georgia.

Stephen L. DesJardins is an associate professor at the Center for the Study of Higher and Postsecondary Education at the University of Michigan.

Lisa M. Dickson is an assistant professor of economics at Xavier University (Ohio).

Donald E. Heller is an associate professor of education and a senior research associate at the Center for the Study of Higher Education at the Pennsylvania State University.

Gerald R. Kissler is the assistant vice president for budgetary planning and fiscal analysis in the Office of the President of the University of California system.

Edward C. Kokkelenberg is a professor of economics at Binghamton University and a faculty associate at the Cornell Higher Education Research Institute.

Daniel Layzell is assistant Vice President for Strategic Planning and Budgetary Analysis, University of Illinois.

Bridget Terry Long is an associate professor of education and economics at Harvard University and a faculty research fellow at the National Bureau of Economic Research.

David B. Mustard is an associate professor of economics and fellow at the Institute of Higher Education at the University of Georgia, and a research fellow at the Institute for the Study of Labor.

David W. Olien is a Regent Professor at the University of Wisconsin and former Senior Vice President for Administration at the University of Wisconsin system.

John D. Porter is an associate provost at the State University of New York (SUNY) system administration.

Iria Puyosa is a graduate research assistant at the Center for the Study of Higher and Postsecondary Education at the University of Michigan.

Michael J. Rizzo is an assistant professor of economics at Centre College (Kentucky) and a faculty associate at the Cornell Higher Research Education Institute.

Ellen Switkes is the assistant vice president for academic advancement in the Office of the President of the University of California system.

Sarah Turner is an associate professor of education and economics at the University of Virginia and a faculty research associate at the National Bureau of Economic Research.

John D. Wiley is the Chancellor of the University of Wisconsin—Madison.

Liang Zhang is an assistant professor of higher education at the University of Minnesota and a research associate at the Cornell Higher Education Research Institute.

William Zumeta is a professor at the Daniel J. Evans School of Public Affairs and the College of Education at the University of Washington.